The Price of Silence

Muslim-Buddhist War of Bangladesh and Myanmar
A Social Darwinist's Analysis

Shwe Lu Maung *alias* **Shahnawaz Khan**

DewDrop Arts and Technology
Columbia, Missouri, USA

1

Published by DewDrop Arts & Technology
Columbia, Missouri, USA.
http://www.shwelumaung.org/DewDrop

Editors: Sabiha Khan and Ellen E. Abbott
Computer software and technology: Shahthureen Khan
Text and cover image design: Shahnawaz Khan and Shahthureen Khan
Cover photo: Poverty in Arakan, courtesy of Narinjara News
Cover design: Arakan (Kingdom of Rakkhapura) in poverty is presented here as a victim of
Muslim-Buddhist war, being sandwiched between the Islamic Bangladesh and Buddhist Myan-
mar. Islamic Bangladesh is symbolized by her flag crowned with the Islamic Crescent Moon and
Star, while Myanmar by her flag topped with the pentacolor international Buddhist flag.

Library of Congress Control Number: 2005906134

ISBN-13: 978-1-928840-03-9

ISBN:10: 1-928840-03-5

Printed in the United States of America

Contents	Page

Chapters

Contents

To my childhood friends:-
Mae Tha Aung,
Maung Tha Noe,
Maung Pu,
Aung Tun Oo,
Nyo Chay, Phru Chay,
Kyaw Mra Aung,
Mabain Shedog, etc., and etc.

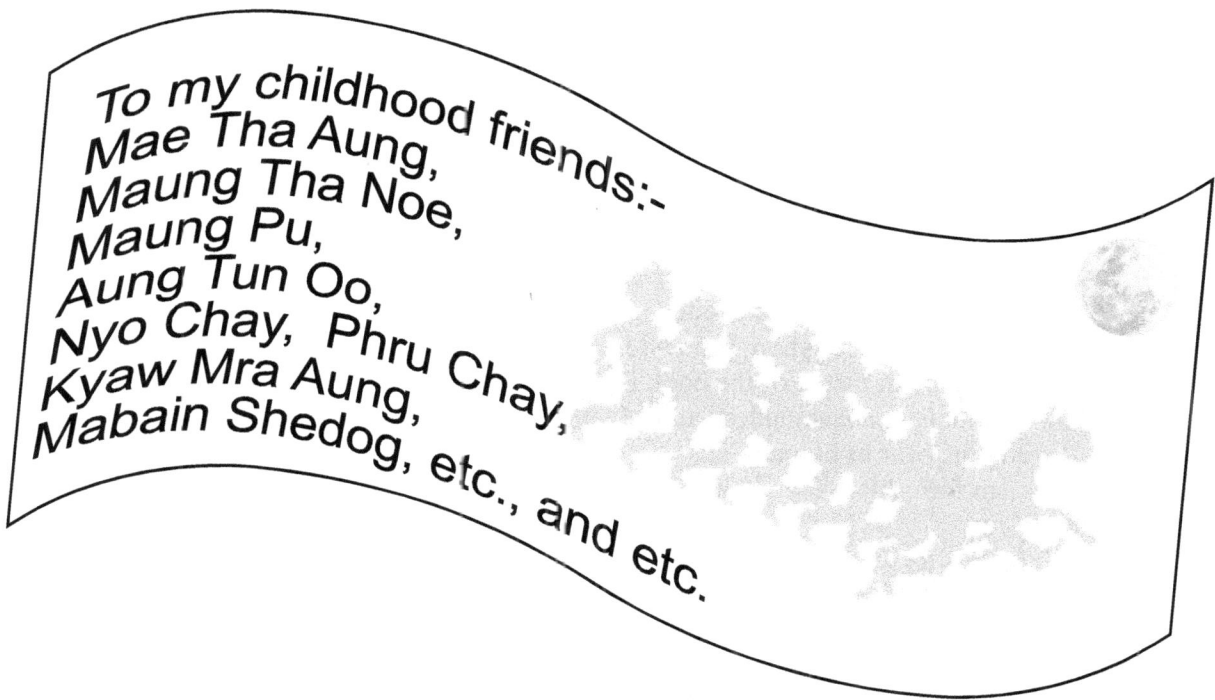

PLEASE SEE PAGE 18

Before you read

I would like to tell you that:

* I am uniquely qualified to present this book to you, *The Price of Silence,* as I was a Burmese Buddhist, later a Bangladeshi Muslim, and I am now a powerful person in the capacity of an American citizen.
* This book is designed in such a way that a high school student (in American, British, or equivalent education system) can understand.
* The style of presentation is narrative with illustrations, based on my own experiences.
* The main text is in American English, but most of the quotes are in British or Asian English.
* The quotes are as they are without any change.
* A Glossary-cum-Index is given to make it easy to find the names, synonyms, and meanings.
* The main theme of the book is the cultural conflict of Islam and Buddhism in Bangladesh and Myanmar as a representative religious war of humankind.
* Racism forms the second theme of the cultural conflict presented here.
* Such factors as science, technology, population explosion, and economy, which ferment the cultural conflict, are also considered and featured as relevant.
* Nature of the conflict is analyzed with the view of a Social Darwinist.
* From reading this book you will learn about Pan-Islam, Jihad, and Myanmar ultranationalism in both historical and contemporary contexts.
* Hopefully, you will be able to devise a means to stop the conflict, solve its root-causes and bring about peace and harmony in the given region and set an example for the world.

Thank you for reading my book.

SLM(SK)

Acknowledgement

First of all, my thanks go to the anonymous Indian diplomat who suggested I write a book on the Bangladesh-Myanmar conflict in 1989, see Preface, page 9. I started preparing for this book at that time.

I would like to express my utmost thanks to Sabiha A. Khan, a MCA of Sears Roebuck and Co., Columbia, Missouri, and Substitute Teacher of the Columbia Public Schools, for her tireless effort of reading 400 pages of the first manuscript of this book. As a graduate of psychology, she analyzed the manuscript with superb rationale, made critical comments and put forward logical suggestions. She also edited the English composition as well as the grammar. Her analysis and editing produced a second draft of 350 pages. I must also thank her for her enthusiastic editing and polishing of the second draft of Chapters 4, 5, 6, 7, and Epilogue to produce the final draft.

My sincere thanks go to Ellen E. Abbott, Administrative Assistant, Department of Veterinary Pathobiolgy, College of Veterinary Medicine, University of Missouri, Columbia, for her editing and polishing Preface, Prologue, and Chapters 1, 2, and 3 of the second draft. Her professional experience helps me produce better tables and figures in Chapter 1, which is filled with statistical data.

I owe a debt of gratitude to Shahthureen F.A. Khan, now a Junior (i.e. third year student), majoring in Computer Science at Columbia College, for his skillful help with Adobe Photoshop, Adobe Acrobat, Microsoft Excel, Mircosoft Publisher, general computer applications, and digital camera. He also helped me with the images as well as the text from the beginning in 2000 to the end of this acknowledgement in 2005. Without his help I would not have produced the images and pictures, which beautify this book. In addition, he put in untiring effort copyediting the manuscript.

I also thank Gary S. Johnson, Ph.D., D.V.M., Associate Professor of Veterinary Pathobiology, for his encouragement and reading part of the pre-press proof.

I must also mention my heartfelt thanks to my comrades from Arakan for giving me necessary information and materials making this book a success. Among them I would like to mention Dr. Khin Maung (President of National United Party of Arakan), Br. Nurul Islam (President of Arakan Rohingya National Organization), Khaing Mrat Kyaw (Editor-Publisher of Narinjara News and Arakanpost), the unknown editors of Kaladan Press, Br. Mohd. Mohiuddin (founding Coordinator of Arakan Democratic Forces), Br. San Tun Maung (Coordinator of Arakan Democratic Forces), Br. Mohammad Islam (Joint-Coodinator of Arakan Democratic Forces), Br. Arif Hussain (President of National Democratic Party for Human Rights (in exile), U Kyaw Hla (President of Muslim Liberation Organization of Burma), U Maung Tin (former General Secretary of Arakanese Muslim Association), and members of Arakan People Unity Forum who discussed sensitive matters openly and candidly.

The acknowledgement cannot be complete unless I warmly express my thanks to Professor Sirajul Islam, Ph.D., D. Litt., (a Professor of Philosophy and Islamic philosopher), Kamal Mama (an acetic Muslim), Dr. M. Ibrahim, F.R.C.P., (a National

Professor), Abdul Hakim Khan (a retired Justice), Abdur Razzek Khan (an education-ist) and many other colleagues, relatives and friends in Bangladesh, for teaching me Islam, making me understand Bengali culture, and accepting me as a fellow Bangladeshi, friend and clan member. I must also thank Sultannuz Zaman Khan (a former Secretary of Bangladesh Government Secretariat and retired Chief of the Agricultural Division of UNESCAP) and Enyetullah Khan (a former Cabinet Minister and Editor of Holiday Weekly and New Age Daily) for their help with my Bangladeshi citizenship, and appreciation of my earlier book. My sincere thanks also go to numerous political activists and students from various political parties for taking me to their parties' headquarters and explaining their party programs. Among them were a good number of freedom fighters and I learned firsthand account of Bangladesh freedom struggle from them. I voted for Awami League in 1986 election and for BNP in 1991.

Above all, I must thank my wife, Shaima Khan, Ph.D., who took early retirement from her professorship at Dhaka University to follow me to the United States. She stood warmly and firmly by me in my critical days.

Lastly, I would like to express my warmest thanks to Bernard Cloutier for his permission to use his excellent photographs of Burmese pagodas and temples (p135, 284) and to Sara for her kindness to let me use her wonderful photograph, *Amazing the boat is still afloat,* p21. Her photograph explains all I write in many pages. My thanks are also due to various web authors and websites, without their permissions, copyleft, and contributions this book would be impossible.

Thank you all.

SLM(SK)

Preface

Lions of Sarnath
Asoka
(ca 322-185 BC)

What will India do?

Singh   Sonia

What will India do?

"What will India do if a war breaks out between Bangladesh and Burma?"

"I .....really do not know. Why don't you write another book on it?"

It was I who asked the question whereas the answer came from the Indian diplomat at whom the question was targeted. We were sitting in a cozy restaurant in the beautiful city of Chiang Mai, northern Thailand. The lunch was being hosted by a prominent Burmese dissident leader.

The diplomat went through my recent book- *Burma: Nationalism and Ideology*[1] that I presented to him. With the speed of a skillful diplomat he read the book and without any comment simply suggested, "Why don't you write another book on that question?"

"Well, I shall", I replied to him.

The Burmese dissident leader changed the topic of conversation and started briefing the diplomat on the most current political development at the Thai-Burma border.

This uneventful meeting took place sometime in late 1989. Since then, *Burma: Nationalism and Ideology* has reached many libraries and the desks of policy makers across the world. The greater the failure of the opposition forces, the more valuable my book has become. The book presents an analysis of society, culture and politics, pointing out and emphasizing major fundamental deficiencies that cripples the building of a healthy democratic nation.

The present book '*The Price of Silence*' is a microscopic presentation of the religious perspective, which incapacitates Burma (Myanmar). Historically, the southeastern region of the Indian subcontinent, part of which today stands as Bangladesh, had played a great role in determining Myanmar's political fate. Presently, she holds the key to the door of Myanmar's future.

"*Each and every religion preaches peace, love and brotherhood among mankind, and each and every religion fights with every other. In Burma there is no exception*[2]". My previous

Notes.
1. Shwe Lu Maung, *Burma: Nationalism and Ideology*, the University Press Ltd., Dhaka, Bangladesh, 1989.
2. See Chapter 6.4, Ibid.

statement was a mild expression with a precaution of not annoying the parties concerned. Today, however, I have taken a bold step in presenting "the war of religions" in detail before the eyes of the planetary citizens. Some will welcome and others will denounce. I may make few friends, but more adversaries.

Nevertheless, I hope this book will help research the basic causes of the Muslim-Buddhist wars across the world, leading to a lasting solution for peace among the *Homo sapiens*.

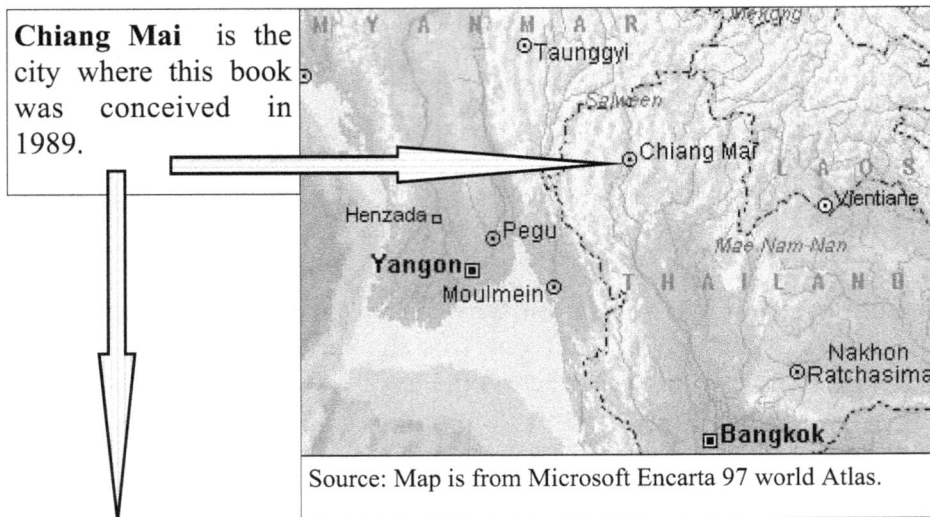

Chiang Mai is the city where this book was conceived in 1989.

Source: Map is from Microsoft Encarta 97 world Atlas.

Popularly known as the Rose of the North, **Chiang Mai**[1] is blessed with stunning natural beauty and unique indigenous cultural identity. Founded by King Mengrai the Great as the capital of the Lanna Thai kingdom by merging the various city-states in the region in 1296. Today Chiang Mai is the economic, communications, cultural and tourism centre of Northern Thailand.

About 700 kilometres from Bangkok, Chiang Mai is situated on the Mae Ping River basin some 310 metres above sea level. Surrounded by high mountain ranges, it covers an area of approximately 20,107 square kilometres.

Notes.
1. http://www.tourismthailand.org/Top Destinations.

Prologue

The Price of a Voice. Socrates (470-399 BCE) was executed for questioning the Athenian state religion and society's wisdom. Democratic Athenian juries found Socrates guilty of denying the official gods of the state, introducing new gods and corrupting the young. He was sentenced to death by poisoning with a drink of hemlock. His pupil Plato told us that in this prison cell, in the presence of friends and students, he defiantly sipped the poison as he cheerfully kept talking of his philosophy. With irony, he died at the age of 70 and a voice was

This was the price of a voice. What will be the price of silence?

The view shown here is a centerpiece of the 1787 famous painting by French artist David, Jacques-Louis (1748-1825). It is a masterpiece of *Homo sapiens* creation in oil on canvas, 129.5 x 196.2 cm, and is proudly displayed by its owner, The Metropolitan Museum of Art, New York, USA. If you happen to be in New York City, please do not forget to go and see the full canvas in beautiful color.

The Death of Socrates

"I am not an Athenian or Greek, but a citizen of the world".
(Famous words of Socrates[1]).

"Crito, I owe a cock to Asclepius. Will you remember to pay the debt?"
(The last words of Socrates[2])

Socrates (470?-399? BC), Greek philosopher, who profoundly affected Western philosophy through his influence on Plato.....In the Peloponnesian War with Sparta he served as an infantryman with conspicuous bravery at the battles of Potidaea in 432-430 BC, Delium in 424 BC, and Amphipolis in 422 BC......Socrates's contribution to philosophy was essentially ethical in character. Belief in a purely objective understanding of such concepts as justice, love, and virtue, and the self-knowledge......Plato's *Apology* gives the substance of the defense made by Socrates at his trial; it was a bold vindication of his whole life. He was condemned to die,.....Socrates' friends planned his escape from prison, but he preferred to comply with the law and die for his cause. His last day was spent with his friends and admirers, and in the evening he calmly fulfilled his sentence by drinking a cup of hemlock according to a customary procedure of execution. Plato described the trial and death of Socrates in the *Apology,* the *Crito,* and the *Phaedo.*
(Excerpt from "Socrates," *Microsoft® Encarta® 97 Encyclopedia CD.*)

silent in the democratic Athens. Today, even after some 2,500 years he remains the martyr for the freedom of expression. But, how many of us are ready to die like him?

Religions and Humans. Today the Muslim-Buddhist War has opened a new chapter as Pan-Islam and Buddhist Fundamentalism confront each other at Bangladesh-Myanmar border.

The Muslim-Buddhist war is not new. It started when the Muslims crushed the Buddhists in Afghanistan and Lahore in the 10th century of Christian Era (CE) which nowadays is referred

---

Notes.
1. http://www.age-of-the-sage.org/socrates_greek_philosopher.html#Socrates_Greek_philosopher.
2. http://www.geocities.com/Athens/Acropolis/6537/real-q.htm

to as the Common Era (CE). The Buddhists lost Bihar and Bengal in the 12th and 16th centuries respectively. In recent decades, the Renaissance of Pan-Islam in Bangladesh since 1987 has renewed Pan-Islam and its expansionism. In a parallel occurrence Buddhist Fundamentalism has been rising in a neighboring country known as Burma (Myanmar). The rise in religious fundamentalism took the stage in 1962 when the military generals seized power from her parliamentary government, abolished the democratic constitution, and introduced a form of Buddhist-socialism in the name of Burmese Way to Socialism. Please see Chapter 6.2 of my book *Burma: Nationalism and Ideology*[1]. In other words, as the Muslim-Buddhist rivalry makes a new twist, Pan-Islam makes a move to Islamize the remaining infidel nations of Southeast Asia. The Southeast Asian Buddhists prepare their last stand along the Bangladesh-Myanmar border. The resulting war will be dirty and nasty. Rivers of blood will flow into Bay of Bengal. The apocalypse is eminent as early as 2015 or by 2025, if late.

As a Social Darwinist I view every move of mankind as a *'struggle for existence'*. The *'nature'* will *'select'* and the *'fittest will survive'*. Accordingly, this presentation constitutes a Social Darwinist's view of the Muslim-Buddhist War, explaining everything within the frame of 'Struggle for Existence', 'Natural Selection', and 'Survival of the Fittest". In 1963, I read Charles Darwin's "THE ORIGIN OF SPECIES[2]" and became a Zoology Honours student at Rangoon University. I used to walk along the Chancellor Road carrying the book and declaring, "I am a *Homo sapiens,* we're all *Homo sapiens"*.

 Skulls such as these serve as the surviving physical evidence and suggest that the transition from **Homo erectus,** the earliest forms of our own species, to the most recent **Homo sapiens**, occurred approximately 300,000 to 400,000 years ago. Early artifacts, such as wooden tools and weapons, give evidence of a hunting life-style. The skull shown at far left, approximately 300,000 years old, was found near Petralona in north-eastern Greece and is the most complete find of early (or archaic) **Homo sapiens**. Classification of this skull initially proved difficult, however, because it exhibits features of late **Homo erectus**. The same skull is shown in profile in the center image[2].

Struggle For Existence
(*Origin of Species*[3], page 90)

"Struggle for life most severe between individuals and varieties of the same species:
As the species of the same genus usually, though by no means invariably, much similar in habits and constitution, and always in structure, the struggle will generally be more severe between them, if they come into competition with each other..."

Charles Darwin
British Naturalist,
1809 -1882

Notes.
1. Shwe Lu Maung, *Burma: Nationalism and Ideology*, the University Press Ltd., Dhaka, Bangladesh, 1989.
2. http://www.wsu.edu:8001/vwsu/gened/learn-modules/top_longfor/timeline/h-sapiens/h-sapiens-a.html
3. Charles Darwin, *Origin of Species*. The Harvard University Classics , PF Collier & Son, New York, 1909.

Some glimpses
of Rangoon University that seeds my becoming of a Social Darwinist
and later a rebel

Chancellor Road
This is the gate of Chancellor Road that leads to and ends at the Convocation Hall shown at the left. The gate opens to the University Avenue Road. Student dead bodies piled up here on the night of 7th July 1962. In 1963, I read Charles Darwin's "THE ORIGIN OF SPECIES" and became a Zoology Honours student at Rangoon University. I used to walk along the Chancellor Road carrying the book and declaring, "I am a *Homo sapiens,* we're all *Homo*

Rangoon University Convocation Hall. Degree awarding ceremonies known as Convocations are held here. University Vice-Chancellor, known as Rector in Burma, officiates here. The University Chancellor is the Prime Minister of the country as per constitution. As a Fresher (i.e. a freshman) I met Prime Minister U Nu as my Chancellor on the 1960 Freshers Day, June the First.

University Students Union Building (USUB) stood at your right as you enter the Chancellor Road. Opposite, across the road, is Mandalay Hall (see below).

The ruins of USUB
Across the ruins Mandalay Hall can be seen.

The USUB was dynamited on the night of 7th July 1962 by the military junta. On 2nd March 1962 the junta seized power, abolished the National Union Constitution, Nation's Parliament and Parliamentary Government led by my hero, Prime Minister U Nu. That night we had two student assemblies in the conference hall of the USUB. We reached the unanimous decision to oppose the military government. Consequently, the students put up a strong protest. The junta crushed them killing more than 100 and dynamited USUB. Mandalay Hall across the Chancellor Road can be seen at the top left corner of the picture.

Acknowledgement: The pictures are from http://www.geocities.com/abfsu2003/7july.html, the web site of All Burma Federation of Students Unions (*Bhakatha*). Legends are mine. I was a member of *Bhakatha* and *Rakatha* (Rangoon University Students Union) from 1960 to 1964.

Natural Selection

"Owing to this struggle, variations, however slight and from whatever cause proceeding, if they be in any degree of profitable to the individuals of a species, in their indefinitely complex relations to other organic beings and to their physical conditions of life, will tend to the preservation of such individuals, and will generally be inherited by the offspring. The offspring, also, will thus have a better chance of surviving, for, of the many individuals of any species which are periodically born, but a small number can survive. I have called this principle, by which each slight variation, if useful, is preserved, by the term Natural Selection, in order to mark its relation to man's power of selection. But the expression often used by Mr. Herbert Spencer of the Survival of the Fittest is more accurate, and is sometimes equally convenient........But Natural Selection, as we shall hereafter see, is a power incessantly ready for action, and is as immeasurably superior to man's feeble efforts, as the works of Nature are to those of Art." (*Origin of Species*[1], p77)

Survival of the Fittest

"When we reflect on this struggle, we may console ourselves with full relief, that the war of nature is not incessant, that no fear is felt, that death is generally prompted, and that the vigorous, the healthy, and the happy survive and multiply." (*Origin of Species*[1], p92)

Survival and Civilization. Civilization exists when man is clothed, sheltered and fed. When the clothes get torn, the shelter disappears, and the hunger sets in, civilization fades into the thin air of bare existence. Then, like a pack of hungry wolves, men kill men. The 'dog-eat-dog' phenomenon prevails.

Nevertheless, man just does not fight for sheer existence. He fights for love, faith and glory. He fights for his family. He fights for his nation. He fights for his religion. He fights for his pride. The highest glory is vested in the fight for God and Nation as *"the faith"* and *"the Patriotism"* are provoked, requisitioned and summoned. Therefore, very soon, Bangladesh-Myanmar's struggle for existence will take place in the name of God and Nation.

It will be a cruel and dirty confrontation of fundamentalist versus fundamentalist. Human nature is complex and sophisticated. Still, basically human beings are nothing but animals.

Notes.
1. Charles Darwin, *Origin of Species*. The Harvard University Classics edited by Charles W. Eliott LL.D., PF Collier & Son, New York, 1909.

Imagine. History, in all its stupidity, will once again prove that John Lennon (1940-1980) is just another drifting dreamer. After all, there always must be something to kill and die for as much as to live for. Without a kill or a death living is meaningless. The following website is hosted by John Lennon's fans. His song *'Imagine'* is the pure gold of a dreamer. I myself am a dreamer. After all *'nothing happens unless first a dream'* as per quotation of Carl Sandburg in his sunset poster D-R-E-A-M.

John Lennon (1940-1980):
A dreamer or a revolutionary?
Find out in the world wide web!
Go to http://www.john-lennon.com/

The heartbeat of Homo Sapiens is music
John was the greatest singer songwriter and
the most influential political artist of our time

Imagine honoring John's 65th birthday
Sunday October 9, 2005
And every October 9th with an International holiday
Celebrating Peace and Love on Earth

Please sign our online petition in order to gather
the 10 million signatures needed to accomplish this

Nothing Happens Unless First A Dream (Carl Sandburg)

Carl Sandburg (1878-1967) was a modern American poet and author, a native of Galesburg, Illinois . You can learn more about him online. A good number of websites such as http://www.sandburg.org and http://carl-sandburg.com/index.htm etc. are dedicated to this remarkable *Homo sapiens*. A beautiful *'Nothing happens unless first a dream'* hangs in my house lobby.

As a dreamer I signed the online **'petition'**. Please see next page and please also visit the website. At the same time, I keep hearing the words of Brother Dil Muhmud, a Burmese Rohingya Muslim refugee in Saudi Arabia. In 1985, he said in sadness but with a ray of hope, "What is wrong if we Muslims will go to our Mosques and the Buddhists can go to their Monasteries? We can all live together peacefully. We are all humans".

Please go to http://www.john-lennon.com/petition.htm and

Sign the John Lennon Day For Peace And Love On Earth Petition

This could turn out to be the best investment for peace. I have signed it.

JOHN LENNON DAY
Peace And Love On Earth

View Current Signatures - Sign the Petition

To: Humanity

Imagine
John Lennon Day
Peace And Love On Earth

"Imagine there's no heaven, it's easy if you try, no hell below us, above us only sky, Imagine all the people, living for today. Imagine there's no countries, it isn't hard to do, nothing to kill or die for, and no religion too, Imagine all the people, living life in peace. You may say I'm a dreamer, but I'm not the only one, I hope someday you'll join us, and the world will be as one.

Imagine no possessions, I wonder if you can, no need for greed or hunger, a brotherhood of man, Imagine all the people, sharing all the world. You may say I'm a dreamer, but I'm not the only one, I hope someday you'll join us, and the world will live as one."

We endorse the John Lennon Day For Peace And Love On Earth Petition to Humanity.

Read the John Lennon Day For Peace And Love On Earth Petition

Use the Reload button in your web browser to see new signatures

Name

35849.   Shahnawaz Khan, Ph.D.

$W = (ps)^n$?. Obviously, $W = (ps)^n$ is an adaptation of Albert Einstein's $E = mc^2$. In Einstein's formula, 'E' represents energy, 'm' designates mass, and 'c^2' is the square of the speed of light. Although he did not participate in its development, his equation was instrumental in the development of the atomic bomb. He, however, did sign the letter, dated August 2nd 1939, to the US President, Franklin Delano Roosevelt, urging him to build the atomic bomb.

In my equation, $W = (ps)^n$, 'W' stands for war, 'p' for population, 's' for the struggle for existence, and the exponential factor 'n' is the population growth rate. I hypothesize that 'war' is an exponential increase of the product 'the population' and its 'struggle for existence, and the exponential factor is conditioned by the population growth rate. Of course, we do not have a unit of measurement for war or struggle for existence. Can we assign a unit of measurement to the WWI, WWII, Vietnam War, Indo-Pakistan Wars, Bangladesh Liberation War, Gulf War or recent US-Iraq War? The same question exists for the struggle of existence. Can we measure qualitatively or quantitatively the struggle for the existence, say, of the South Saharan people and the American people? The speed of light, 299,792,458 m/s (meters per second), that we usually refer is the speed in vacuum. It travels with different speeds in different medium such as air, water, ice and glass. Similarly, the struggle for existence varies in different societies and culture. Can we quantize[1] the variable values of human nature? Will it be possible for us to predict a war by studying only two factors, namely the population and the struggle for existence, in the way I am describing here? Indeed, the struggle for existence covers all human activities. I have assumed that the struggle for existence increases or decreases in an exponential factor in the same way the population does. (Remember Lily Pond Parable! Please see page 65).

> "Here, then, is the problem which we present to you, stark and dreadful and inescapable: Shall we put an end to the human race or shall mankind renounce war? People will not face this alternative because it is so difficult to abolish war." Albert Einstein (1879-1955), source: http://www.aip.org/history/einstein/nuclear2.htm#indexp, as of August 29, 2004.)

In this book, I am presenting a looming Bangladesh-Myanmar war in the light of my understanding of the struggle for existence of the people in the two countries.

My theory is very simple and based upon Charles Darwin's theory that species struggles for existence and the fittest will survive under the natural selection. Application of these scientific principles in the study of the human society is known as Social Darwinism. Under this theory, the communal wars, clan wars, tribal wars, feudal wars, national wars, etc. are nothing but the struggles for existence. The human species, that is now known as the *Homo sapiens*, has come a long way in its struggle for existence, some five million years now. It is the most successful species on this planet, but it also is the most destructive species that practices well-organized aggression with weapons of mass destruction. Its success depends on its power of destruction.

The nature of humans is extremely sophisticated. Human nature encompasses the entire universe and beyond. Definition of human existence is very broad, deep, and multidimensional.

Notes.
1. Quantize means to subdivide (as energy) into small but measurable increments or to calculate or express in terms of quantum mechanics. Please see Merriam-Webster Online Dictionary or Webster's College Dictionary, Random House, New York, 1991. It is a word derived from the scientific term quantum.

It exists in a form of an object (e.g. body) as well as in a form of an abstract (e.g. soul). It exists beyond the realm of food, shelter, and reproduction. It exists in its intellectuality. It struggles not only for the existence in this life but also in next life. It struggles for eternal existence. Subsequently, religion becomes a major part of its nature, with its eternal abode known as heaven. Buddhistic Nibban (Nivirna) is also a form of eternal existence, in spite of the fact that Buddha discards such metaphysical nature in his explanation to the wanderer Vacchagotta, in Majjhima Nikaya 72 Aggi-Vacchagotta Sutta, and to Malunkya in Majjhima Nikaya 63 Cula-Malunkyovada Sutta.

As can be seen, the human struggles for eternal existence, and its struggle is very strong and crafty. It struggles not only individually but also in groups and in communities, eliminating the oppositions and the obstacles that may compromise its existence of here and next. It exploits the natural resources available on this planet and beyond. It has developed sophisticated and mass destructive weapons and recruited God or Buddha as its eternal leader. War is nothing but a manifestation of the struggle for existence.

Therefore, I formularize that war is the exponential product of the population and its struggle for existence or $W = (ps)^n$. Peace (P_e) is the goal of a civilized human, and it is inversely

$$P_e = \frac{1}{W}$$

proportional to war. That means, more wars less peace, fewer wars more peace, and no war total peace. It can be expressed in a formula as below:

In other words, we may postulate that $P_e W = 1$ or 'K', a constant, that can be defined as the balance of power, a situation where probability of war is checked by a no-win situation, e.g. between USSR and USA. This is a condition of peaceful coexistence.

I must admit that I am not a social scientist who studies conflicts and wars. My formulas may simply be a load of rubbish. Nevertheless, it surely will provoke your intellect. I am ignorant of the solutions of the conflicts, which the social scientists may have put forward. On the other hand, I strongly believe that the more we understand the nature of the conflict the better solution we may formulate. With this belief, I present this account of conflict, a Muslim-Buddhist War that is looming over Bangladesh and Myanmar, from a Social Darwinist's angle.

When I was young I used to play with my friends in the moonlit nights, sometimes, about 20 of us, boys and girls. We used to race with the moon. As we ran we saw the moon running along with us, probably at the same speed. When we stopped the moon also stopped! We used to laugh with fun and ask each other for the explanation of this strange phenomenon. I did not know that we were experimenting with the laws of relativity or time and space. Those were the days when I was between 7 and 12 or in the years 1952 and 1957. When I studied at the Rangoon University I came to learn about Albert Einstein and his theories. Physics was the only subject I ever scored cent per cent[1] in a semester examination. Nevertheless, I chose to become a biologist after reading Charles Darwin's *Origin of the Species*, as mentioned earlier. My childhood friends, who used to play with me racing the moon, did not even finish Middle School. They left

---

Note.
1. *Cent per cent* is a very common expression for hundred out of hundred in British and Asian English.

school to help their parents in the farms and paddy fields. Today, their grandchildren may be playing the same kind of game, racing with the moon in the summer nights, amidst the poverty and atrocities of the 42-year misrule of the military generals. Their future seems darker when I see a greater conflict is looming in their horizon. Perhaps, the world might give a moment to look at them if I could present the situation before the concerned audience. With these thoughts, I present the readers with this critical analysis.

I was born in the conflict during WWII when the Allied Forces were waging war against the Japanese in Burma. I grew up in the conflict; the civil war was burning in independent Burma. I got into the conflict; I counted myself in a guerrilla organization, raging as a member of the warring faction. War is the severest form of a conflict. With this bitter experience I present to you this account of conflict- *The Price of Silence* - in an effort to break the silence, and encourage the adversaries to come to a round table.

Chapter-1. Money and People

Now let me present you the facts, nothing but facts, in support of my analytical report. Without bump and fair, let us quietly sneak into the world of struggle for existence in Bangladesh and Myanmar *aka* Burma. Keep your mind open, but still be on a look out since a tricky journey lies ahead of us.

Please take time to view the details of the tables and figures in the coming pages. The sources of the information are given and the International System of Units[1] (SI) are used in the interest of global readers.

> Today focus is on Bangladesh and Myanmar, the two time-bombs, which are rapidly approaching the zero hour. The base maps are from Uncle Sam's CIA web site[2]. The pasted maps are not to the original scale.

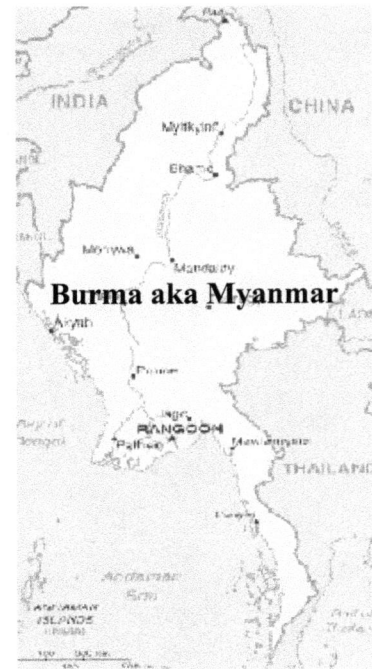

Facts and Figures. I will present the facts of Bangladesh and Myanmar in tables and figures with relevant legends. The main objective is to show how overpopulated and poor Bangladesh is in contrast to Myanmar, which is equally poor but not yet overpopulated. Seven other countries namely, Thailand, India, China, Australia, Japan, Mexico, and USA are included as the comparative references.

Notes.
1. Brownridge SI Material from http://lamr.colostate.edu/~hillger/brownridge.html.
2. http://www.odci.gov/cia/publications/factbook/index.html.

Some readers may find it hard to grasp, heavy, and boring. I include these statistics and the professional information so that the reader may use them as references when he comes across a confusion in my report. At the same time it will help the reader make educated judgement of my conclusions. The main philosophy behind these facts and figures is to educate ourselves with the demographic and economical indicators so that we can understand the demographic and economic growth and implications. We are not trying to become a demographer or an economist.

1.1. Instance of a Ferryboat. What happens when a ferryboat is over loaded with passengers? It can capsize; it can sink. Right? Well? (1) It depends on how much overcrowded it is in the given size and condition of the boat. (2) It will also depend on the weather and the sea condition. (3) It will also depend on the skill of her crew and captain. (4) It will as well depend upon the discipline of the passengers. These four factors determine the condition. Please keep these in mind for I will be discussing their pros and cons. I see Bangladesh as an overcrowded ferryboat that is sailing in a stormy ocean of poverty and Islamic fundamentalism. I say overcrowded because it is overpopulated. When I surfed the world wide web in search of Bangladesh, I came across a photo that exactly illustrates the picture in my mind. Please see it below. What will happen when the ferryboat sinks?

"amazing the boat is still afloat"

Photo by Sarah.
Thank you Sarah for the photo.
It is great!

This photo of Sarah depicts the *state* of Bangladesh.
The caption *'amazing the boat is still afloat'* is hers. The photo and caption (http://www.joesvideos.com/sarah/album10, as of May 18, 2003) are reproduced here with her kind permission.

1.2. How big are Bangladesh and Myanmar? First of all, let us remember that the world is 510.072 million sq km is size, having a small land area, 148.94 million sq km, that is surrounded by 361.132 million sq km of water territory[1]. With 6.44 billion passengers aboard, our planet earth is cruising at a velocity of 106,000 km/hr or 66,000 mph, along its orbit around the sun, which itself is travelling at a speed of 72,360 km/hr or 45,000 mph toward the constellation of Hercules[2]. The following table and pie-graphs in the coming pages present how big Bangladesh and Myanmar are. Sources of the information used in Table1 are:

1. The World Fact Book 2001, at http://www.odci.gov/cia/publications/factbook, for the countries profiles.
2. Microsoft Encarta 97 Encyclopedia for the area of the states of USA.
3. http://geography.about.com/library/maps/blindex.htm

Pie-graphs are also given for those who prefer figurative visualization rather than reading the numerals.

Standard International units or SI units are used. Definition and conversion of the SI units to the traditional units are given in Table1.2, next page.

Table 1.1
How Big is Bangladesh and Myanmar? This table presents a comparison with neighbors and some other countries.

Country	Area in 1000 square kilometers (i.e. x1000km^2)					
	Total Area (TA)	Land Area (LA)	Water Area (WA)	% (TA) of USA	% (LA) of USA	% (WA) of USA
Bangladesh	144.00	133.91	10.09	1.00	1.00	2.00
Myanmar	678.50	657.74	20.76	7.00	7.00	4.00
Thailand	514.77	511.77	2.23	5.35	5.59	0.47
India	3,287.59	2,973.19	314.40	34.14	32.46	66.87
China	9,596.96	9,326.41	270.55	99.67	101.83	57.55
Australia	7,686.85	7,617.93	68.92	79.83	83.17	14.66
Japan	377.84	374.74	3.09	3.92	4.09	0.66
Mexico	1,972.55	1,923.04	49.51	20.49	21.00	10.53
USA	9,629.09	9,158.96	470.13	100.00	100	100

Table1.1-Additional information:
1. Bangladesh is slightly smaller than the USA's state Wisconsin that is 169.64 x 1000 km^2.
2. Myanmar is slightly smaller than the USA's state Texas that is 692.24 x 1000 km^2.
3. Thailand is slightly bigger than twice the size of USA's state Wyoming that is 253.35 x 1000 km^2.
4. India is slightly bigger than one-third of the USA.
5. China and Australia are slightly smaller than the USA as a whole.
6. Japan is slightly smaller than the USA's state California that is 411.47 x 1000 km^2.
7. Mexico is slightly less than three times the size of the USA's state Texas that is 692.25 x 1000 km^2.

Notes.
1. CIA World Fact Book 2004, http://www.odci.gov/cia/publications/factbook/fields/2147.html.
2. Earth, Microsoft Encarta 97 Encyclopedia, contributed by Earl Cook.

Now, please take a close look at Table1.1. These are in numerals. In the next pages I will convert these numerals into figures because numerals and figures have a different kind of impact on our senses, hence in perception, cognition, and awareness. In these figures I will use the size of the USA as the standard reference in order to produce a uniform visual comparison. The USA is used as the standard since she is the most well known country across the globe. Millions of people love her along with a large number of people who hate her.

Table1.2.
Explanation of the SI units used in Table1.1

Sq. km or km^2	=	square kilometers
1 km or 1 kilometer	=	1,000 meters or 1,000 m
Therefore, 1 sq. km	=	1,000 x 1 000 square meters, or 1,000,000 sq. m or 10^6 m^2
Traditional 1 square mile	=	2.59 km^2
1 yard	=	0.9144 m
Commonly used 1 hectare or square hectometer	=	10^4 m^2 or 10,000 m^2 or 0.01 sq. km

For more information please see Brownridge SI Material at http:// lamar.colostate.edu/~hillger/brownridge.html and the metric conversion factors at http://www.wsdot.wa.gov/Metrics/factors.htm or any relevant reference.

Please see these figures with reference to table1.1. Please note that figures 1.1f and 1.1h create visual illusion as if China is about 50% and Australia is about 45% of USA in the pie graphs. They appear so because they are almost the same size. Please compare the data in numeral given in the figures and table 1.1.

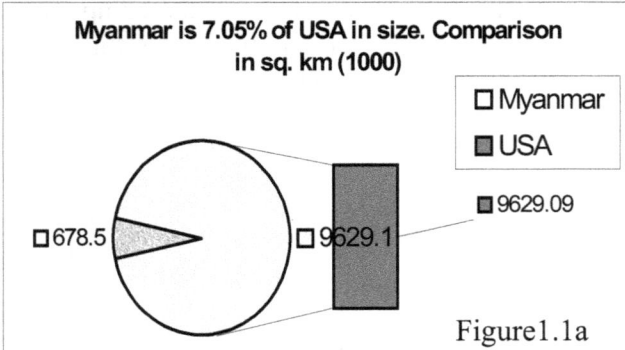

Myanmar is 7.05% of USA in size. Comparison in sq. km (1000)

□ Myanmar
■ USA

■ 9629.09

□ 678.5   □ 9629.1

Figure1.1a

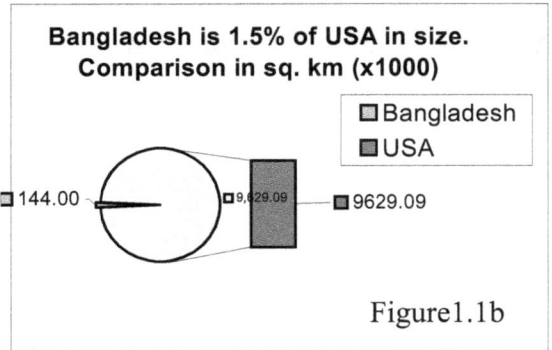

Bangladesh is 1.5% of USA in size. Comparison in sq. km (x1000)

□ Bangladesh
■ USA

□ 144.00   □ 9,629.09   ■ 9629.09

Figure1.1b

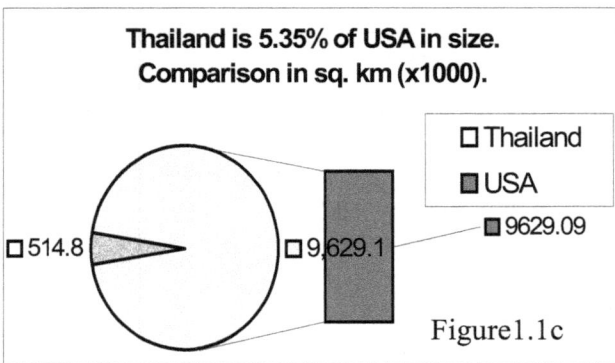

Thailand is 5.35% of USA in size. Comparison in sq. km (x1000).

□ Thailand
■ USA

■ 9629.09

□ 514.8   □ 9,629.1

Figure1.1c

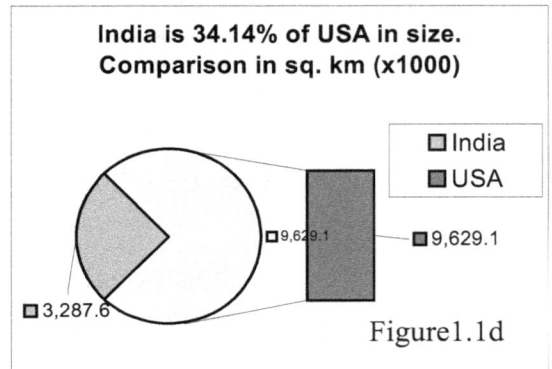

India is 34.14% of USA in size. Comparison in sq. km (x1000)

□ India
■ USA

■ 9,629.1   ■ 9,629.1

□ 3,287.6

Figure1.1d

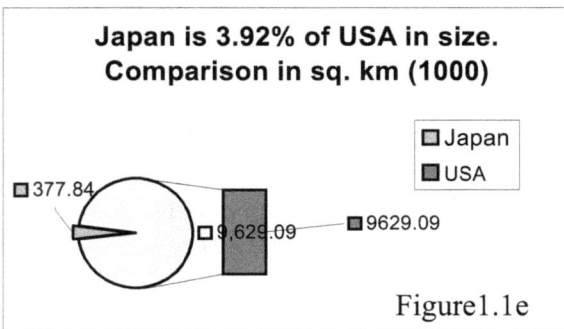

Japan is 3.92% of USA in size. Comparison in sq. km (1000)

□ Japan
■ USA

□ 377.84

□ 9,629.09   ■ 9629.09

Figure1.1e

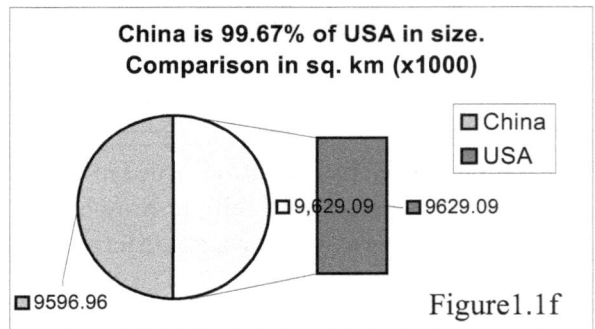

China is 99.67% of USA in size. Comparison in sq. km (x1000)

□ China
■ USA

□ 9,629.09   ■ 9629.09

□ 9596.96

Figure1.1f

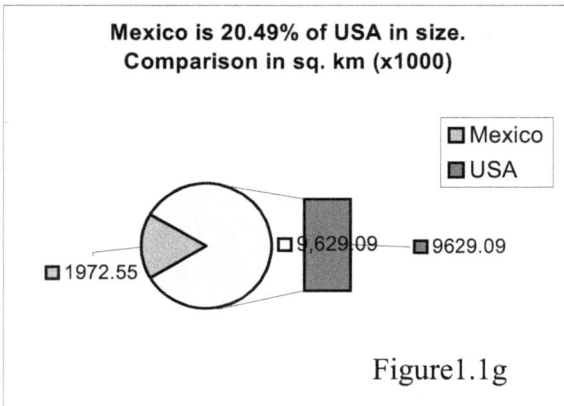

Mexico is 20.49% of USA in size. Comparison in sq. km (x1000)

□ Mexico
■ USA

□ 9,629.09   ■ 9629.09

□ 1972.55

Figure1.1g

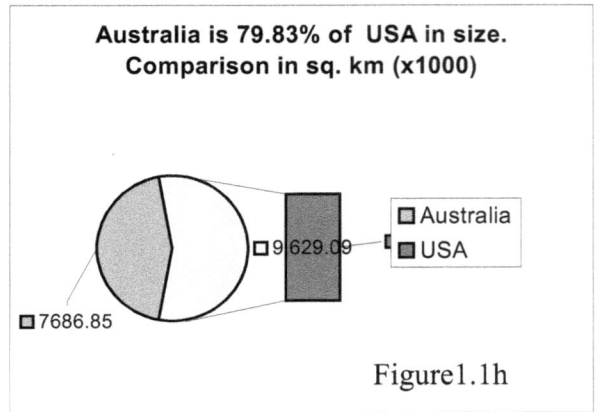

Australia is 79.83% of USA in size. Comparison in sq. km (x1000)

□ Australia
■ USA

□ 9629.09

□ 7686.85

Figure1.1h

So far I have shown that Bangladesh is a small country. A comparative account of her total area, land and water area with eight other countries has been presented to give a clear picture. In the coming pages I will present her population. The focal point will be: "Is Bangladesh big enough to support her population?". Now, you have seen the size of Bangladesh and Myanmar in numerals as well as figures. Next, we shall see their population.

1.3. Population of Bangladesh and Myanmar. I will present to you the present and future population projections of Bangladesh and Myanmar, along with the population density. Please remember to focus your attention in the year 2015 when I predict the turmoil could begin if early and at 2025 if late.

The population prospects of the continents, and the countries of interest are presented in alphabetical order after those of the world. Please spend adequate time to grasp a good picture of these tables. Also please get acquainted with the definitions of the fertility variants. We shall discuss their significance after a few more pages.

The population statistics are taken from the United Nations Population Information Network[1,2], of 2002. In order to get a broad overview I will present to you a comparison of 8 countries, 5 continents, and the world. Then, I shall focus on Bangladesh and Myanmar. Please pay close attention to these figures and numerals so that you will gain an in-depth view of the problem and feel the weight of the concern I am projecting.

Before doing so I am presenting the definition of the variants that are used in the population statistics. You may like to have some understanding of what these variants represent or indicate.

Again, both numerals and graphs are given for the choice of individual preference. Population projections are complicated. The key factor is the population growth rate, which varies depending on various factors such as birth rate, infant mortality rate, expected life span, famine, wars, and natural disasters. Therefore, the projections are made using four variants, namely: constant, low, medium and high variants. Definition of these variants used by the United Nations is presented here for your reference.

Definition of the variants mentioned in the population statistics

ASSUMPTIONS UNDERLYING THE RESULTS OF THE
2000 REVISION OF WORLD POPULATION PROSPECTS

The preparation of each new revision of the official estimates and projections of the United Nations involves two distinct processes: (a) the incorporation of all new and relevant information regarding past demographic dynamics of the population of each country or area of the world; and (b) the formulation of detailed assumptions about future paths of fertility, mortality and international migration.

Notes.
1. http://www.UN.org/popin.
2. Population Division of the Department of Economic and Social Affairs of the United Nations Secretariat, World Population Prospects: The 2000 Revision and World Urbanization Prospects: The 2001 Revision, http://esa.un.org/unpp, 24 July 2002; 10:56:01 AM.

Definition of the variants mentioned in the population statistics (continued)
Source: http://esa.un.org/unpp/assumptions.html

The database that can be queried through this site presents past estimates of population trends covering the period 1950-2000 and the results of four projection variants for the period 2001-2050. The four variants are known as the low, medium, high and constant-fertility variants. These variants differ among themselves only with respect to the assumptions made about future fertility trends. The assumptions underlying them are described briefly below.

FERTILITY ASSUMPTIONS

Fertility assumptions are described in terms of the following groups of countries:

- High-fertility countries: Countries that until 2000 have had no fertility reduction or only an incipient decline;
- Medium-fertility countries: Countries where fertility has been declining but whose level is still above replacement level (2.1 children per woman);
- Low-fertility countries: Those countries with fertility at or below replacement level (2.1 children per woman) plus a few with levels very close to replacement levels that are expected to fall below replacement level in the near future.

Fertility assumptions underlying the medium variant:

- Fertility in high-fertility countries is generally assumed to decline at an average pace of nearly one child per decade starting in 2005 or later. Consequently, some of these countries do not reach replacement level by 2050.
- Fertility in medium-fertility countries is assumed to reach replacement level before 2050.
- Fertility in low-fertility countries is generally assumed to remain below replacement level during most of the projection period, reaching by 2045-2050 the fertility of the cohort of women born in the early 1960s or, if that information is lacking, reaching 1.7 children per woman if current fertility is below 1.5 children per woman or 1.9 children per woman if current fertility is equal to or higher than 1.5 children per woman.

Fertility assumptions underlying the high variant:

- Fertility in high-fertility and medium-fertility countries remains above the fertility in the medium-fertility assumption and eventually reaches a value 0.5 children above that reached by the medium-fertility assumption in 2045-2050.
- For low-fertility countries, the value eventually reached is 0.4 children per woman above that reached by the medium-fertility assumption in 2045-2050.

Fertility assumptions underlying the low variant:

- Fertility in high-fertility and medium-fertility countries remains below the fertility in the medium-fertility assumption and eventually reaches a value 0.5 children below that reached by the medium-fertility assumption in 2045-2050.
- For low-fertility countries, the value eventually reached is 0.4 children per woman below that reached by the medium-fertility assumption in 2045-2050.

Definition of the variants mentioned in the population statistics (continued)
Source: http://esa.un.org/unpp/assumptions.html

Fertility assumptions underlying the constant-fertility variant:

♦ For each country, fertility remains constant at the level estimated for 1995-2000.

MORTALITY ASSUMPTIONS

Mortality is projected on the basis of the models of increases of life expectancy produced by the United Nations. In countries highly affected by the HIV/AIDS epidemic, estimates of the impact of the disease are made explicitly through assumptions about the future course of the epidemic, that is, by projecting the yearly incidence of HIV infection.

INTERNATIONAL MIGRATION ASSUMPTIONS

The future path of international migration is set on the basis of past international migration estimates and an assessment of the policy stance of countries with regard to future international migration flows.

Table 1.3. Population forecast in millions (1 000 000)

Table 1.3a. Entire World

Year	Constant-fertility variant	Low variant	Medium variant	High variant
2000	6,056.72	6,056.72	6,056.72	6,056.72
2005	6,484.93	6,396.53	6,441.00	6,483.79
2010	6,958.61	6,702.33	6,825.74	6,938.38
2015	7,479.80	6,983.14	7,207.36	7,415.02
2020	8,040.87	7,241.11	7,579.28	7,901.12
2025	8,647.50	7,469.79	7,936.74	8,391.17

Table 1.3b. Africa (Continent)

Year	Constant-fertility variant	Low variant	Medium variant	High variant
2000	793.63	793.63	793.63	793.63
2005	899.97	882.87	891.69	898.19
2010	1,026.07	974.58	996.96	1,014.25
2015	1,177.31	1,071.32	1,110.01	1,142.99
2020	1,357.77	1,172.50	1,230.98	1,282.97
2025	1,573.82	1,274.65	1,358.12	1,434.29

Table 1.3. Population forecast in millions (1,000,000), continued.
The countries are presented in alphabetical order

Table 1.3c. Asia

Year	Constant-fertility variant	Low variant	Medium variant	High variant
2000	3,672.34	3,672.34	3,672.34	3,672.34
2005	3,938.88	3,882.55	3,910.66	3,938.85
2010	4,229.58	4,065.16	4,144.94	4,217.21
2015	4,543.06	4,224.05	4,370.63	4,503.48
2020	4,869.12	4,360.73	4,581.58	4,788.69
2025	5,207.33	4,474.37	4,776.60	5,068.00

Table 1.3d. Europe

Year	Constant-fertility variant	Low variant	Medium variant	High variant
2000	727.30	727.30	727.30	727.30
2005	722.67	720.08	720.90	721.71
2010	716.88	709.99	713.21	716.38
2015	708.84	697.95	704.51	710.98
2020	697.94	684.62	694.88	704.97
2025	684.22	669.25	683.53	697.59

Table 1.3e. Latin America (subregion)

Year	Constant-fertility variant	Low variant	Medium variant	High variant
2000	518.81	518.81	518.81	518.81
2005	561.52	551.90	557.08	562.10
2010	606.94	580.21	594.31	608.21
2015	653.88	605.26	630.11	654.73
2020	701.61	626.65	663.69	700.51
2025	750.51	643.88	694.76	745.99

Table 1.3. Population forecast in millions (1,000,000), continued.
The countries are presented in alphabetical order

Table 1.3f. Australia

Year	Constant-fertility variant	Low variant	Medium variant	High variant
2000	19.14	19.14	19.14	19.14
2005	20.12	20.08	20.11	20.15
2010	21.06	20.95	21.03	21.15
2015	21.93	21.76	21.91	22.14
2020	22.73	22.49	22.75	23.12
2025	23.45	23.12	23.52	24.07

Note: Australia is a continent as well as country.

Table 1.3g. Bangladesh

Year	Constant-fertility variant	Low variant	Medium variant	High variant
2000	137.44	137.44	137.44	137.44
2005	153.92	150.33	152.55	154.72
2010	173.07	162.86	167.93	173.02
2015	194.61	174.39	183.16	191.95
2020	218.46	184.18	197.64	211.17
2025	244.97	191.48	210.82	230.73

Table 1.3h. China

Year	Constant-fertility variant	Low variant	Medium variant	High variant
2000	1,275.13	1,275.13	1,275.13	1,275.13
2005	1,321.37	1,312.42	1,321.36	1,330.31
2010	1,362.80	1,340.21	1,366.22	1,385.38
2015	1,401.84	1,364.40	1,410.22	1,443.25
2020	1,432.94	1,381.15	1,446.09	1,498.30
2025	1,453.07	1,386.54	1,470.79	1,543.05

Table 1.3. Population forecast in millions (1,000,000), continued.
The countries are presented in alphabetical order

Table 1.3i. India

Year	Constant-fertility variant	Low variant	Medium variant	High variant
2000	1,008.94	1,008.94	1,008.94	1,008.94
2005	1,101.41	1,082.82	1,088.58	1,094.38
2010	1,205.04	1,145.76	1,164.02	1,182.28
2015	1,317.66	1,192.08	1,230.48	1,268.93
2020	1,436.37	1,228.34	1,291.29	1,354.37
2025	1,562.20	1,262.43	1,351.80	1,442.16

Table 1.3j. Japan

Year	Constant-fertility variant	Low variant	Medium variant	High variant
2000	127.10	127.10	127.10	127.10
2005	127.69	127.69	127.98	128.33
2010	127.49	127.49	128.22	129.06
2015	126.26	126.26	127.52	128.93
2020	124.08	124.08	125.96	128.01
2025	121.21	121.21	123.80	126.59

Table 1.3k. Mexico

Year	Constant-fertility variant	Low variant	Medium variant	High variant
2000	98.87	98.87	98.87	98.87
2005	107.27	105.18	106.14	107.09
2010	115.97	110.23	112.88	115.52
2015	124.74	114.40	119.18	123.92
2020	133.48	117.86	124.98	132.07
2025	142.26	120.45	130.19	140.05

Table 1.3. Population forecast in millions (1,000000), continued.
The countries are presented in alphabetical order

Table 1.3l. Myanmar

Year	Constant-fertility variant	Low variant	Medium variant	High variant
2000	47.75	47.75	47.75	47.75
2005	51.47	50.09	50.60	51.11
2010	55.69	51.64	52.99	54.34
2015	60.39	52.86	55.26	57.66
2020	65.46	54.25	57.76	61.27
2025	70.80	55.54	60.24	65.01

Table 1.3m. Thailand

Year	Constant-fertility variant	Low variant	Medium variant	High variant
2000	62.81	62 81	62.81	62.81
2005	66.78	65 94	66.50	67.06
2010	70.51	68 29	69.68	71.11
2015	74.00	70 00	72.49	74.95
2020	77.29	71 50	75.10	78.65
2025	80.36	72.63	77.48	82.31

Table 1.3n. USA

Year	Constant-fertility variant	Low variant	Medium variant	High variant
2000	283.23	283.23	283.23	283.23
2005	297.17	294.80	296.06	298.02
2010	311.12	305.27	308.56	313.83
2015	325.31	314.78	321.23	330.71
2020	339.63	324.33	334.20	348.16
2025	353.45	333.13	346.82	365.75

In the previous pages, I have presented the comparative accounts of five continents and eight countries. The comparisons will serve as the reference frame for Bangladesh and Myanmar. Now, let us focus on Bangladesh and Myanmar, the two main characters in the coming drama.

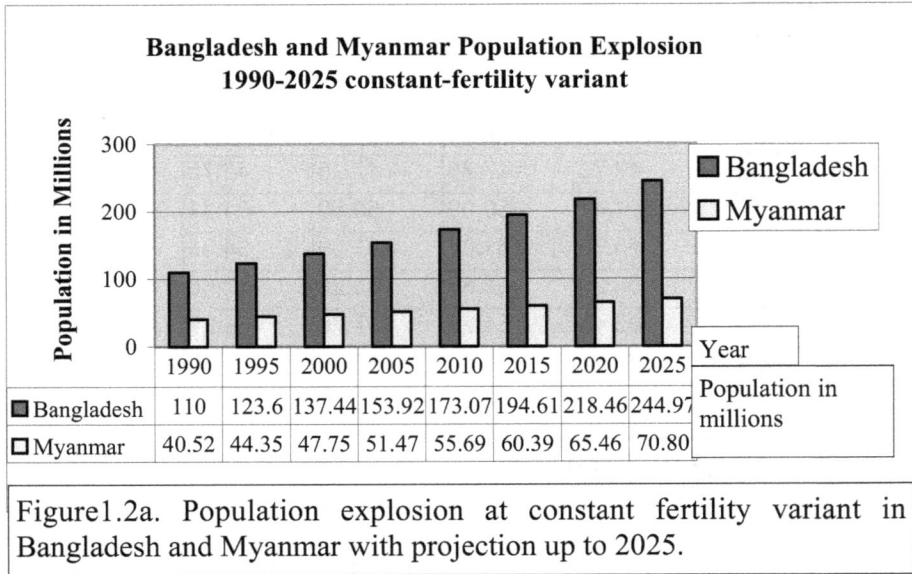

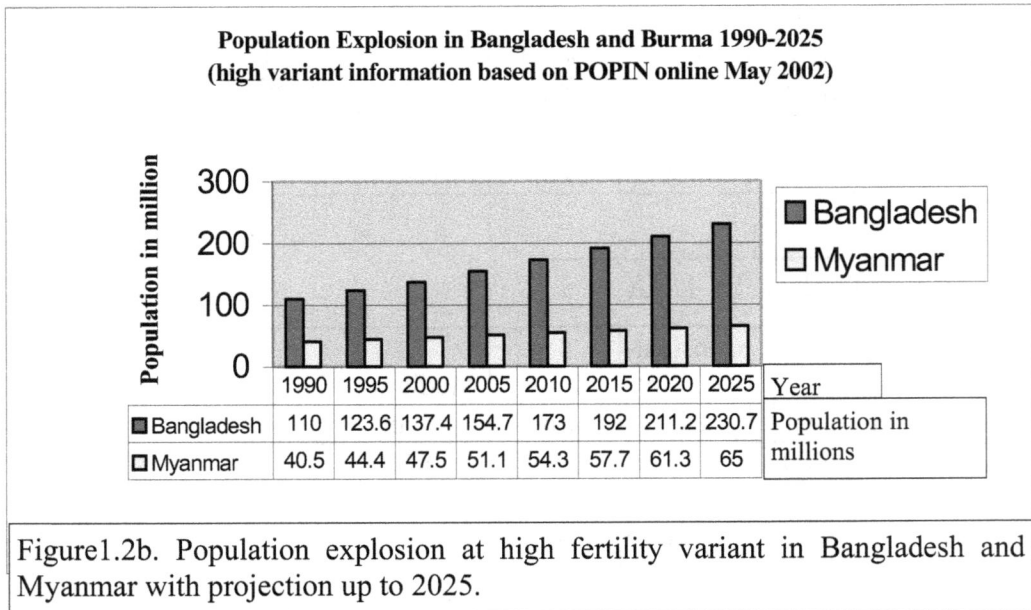

Bangladesh and Myanmar Population Explosion
1990-2025 constant-fertility variant

	1990	1995	2000	2005	2010	2015	2020	2025	Year
Bangladesh	110	123.6	137.44	153.92	173.07	194.61	218.46	244.97	Population in millions
Myanmar	40.52	44.35	47.75	51.47	55.69	60.39	65.46	70.80	

Figure1.2a. Population explosion at constant fertility variant in Bangladesh and Myanmar with projection up to 2025.

Population Explosion in Bangladesh and Burma 1990-2025
(high variant information based on POPIN online May 2002)

	1990	1995	2000	2005	2010	2015	2020	2025	Year
Bangladesh	110	123.6	137.4	154.7	173	192	211.2	230.7	Population in millions
Myanmar	40.5	44.4	47.5	51.1	54.3	57.7	61.3	65	

Figure1.2b. Population explosion at high fertility variant in Bangladesh and Myanmar with projection up to 2025.

Population Explosion in Bangladesh and Burma 1990-2025
(medium variant information based on POPIN online May 2002)

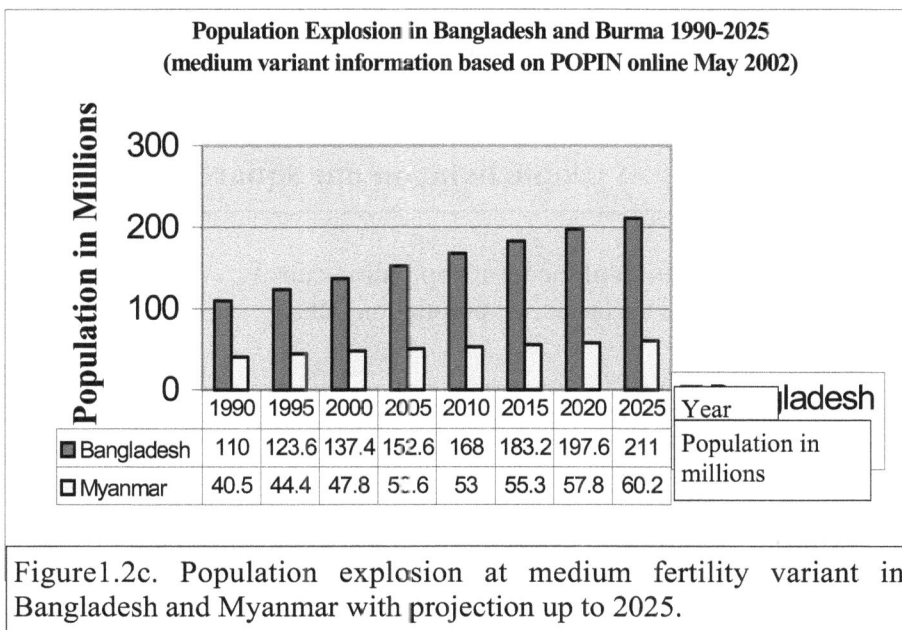

Year	1990	1995	2000	2005	2010	2015	2020	2025
Bangladesh	110	123.6	137.4	152.6	168	183.2	197.6	211
Myanmar	40.5	44.4	47.8	51.6	53	55.3	57.8	60.2

Figure1.2c. Population explosion at medium fertility variant in Bangladesh and Myanmar with projection up to 2025.

Population Explosion in Bangladesh and Burma 1990-2025
(low variant information based on POPIN online May 2002)

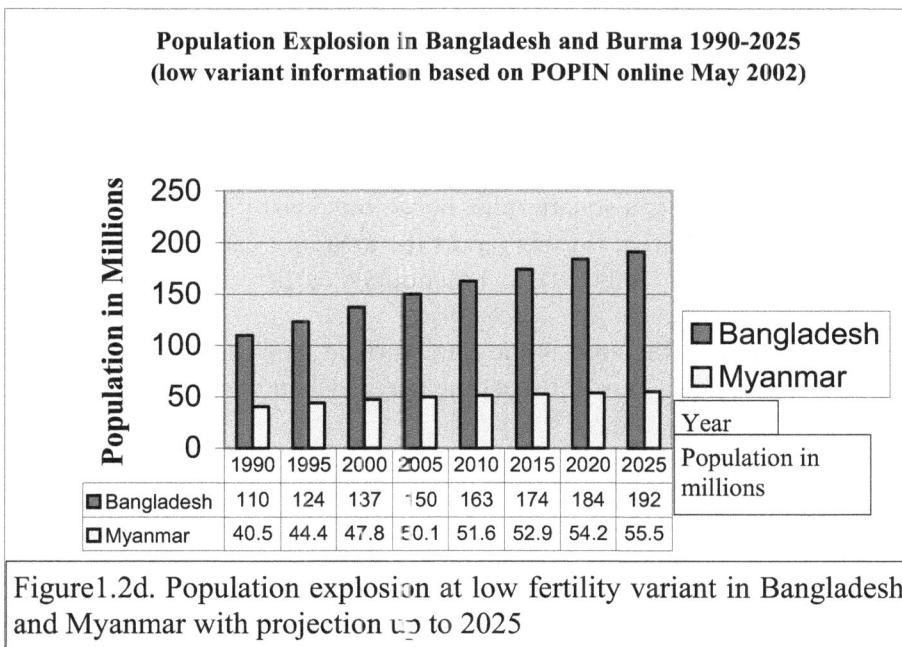

Year	1990	1995	2000	2005	2010	2015	2020	2025
Bangladesh	110	124	137	150	163	174	184	192
Myanmar	40.5	44.4	47.8	50.1	51.6	52.9	54.2	55.5

Figure1.2d. Population explosion at low fertility variant in Bangladesh and Myanmar with projection up to 2025

1.4. Population Density. This is the time to make an initial analysis of the population in relation to the size of the given country before we go to other parameters that determine viability of a country. It is commonly analyzed in terms of the population density.

Q. What Is Population Density?

A. Number of people living in one square kilometer.

This is a simple explanation of the term population density. When the total population of a country is divided by her total surface area, population density is obtained.

Example: Bangladesh in the year 2005 (high variant)
Total population
(rounded figure) = 154 720 000
Total surface area
(rounded figure)= 144 000 square kilometers

Therefore,
population density = 154 720 000 ÷ 144 000 = 1074.44
(see Figure1.3b).

**Population density demonstrates how crowded a country is.
The bigger the number the more crowded.**

Traditionally, area unit is a square mile, hence the density is expressed as the number of persons in one square mile of area. In this report the area unit used is square kilometers in par with the International Standard Units (SI), as I mentioned earlier. Please refer back to Table1.2, on page 13.

It is good to note that the area is the total surface area including land and water, both inhabitable and un-inhabitable. This will become useful when we scrutinize the seriousness of overcrowding.

Population Density of Bangladesh and Myanmar
(people per square kilometer surface area,
constant-fertility variant)

	1990	1995	2000	2005	2010	2015	2020	2025
Bangladesh	764	858	954	1069	1202	1351	1517	1710
Myanmar	60	66	71	76	82	89	97	105

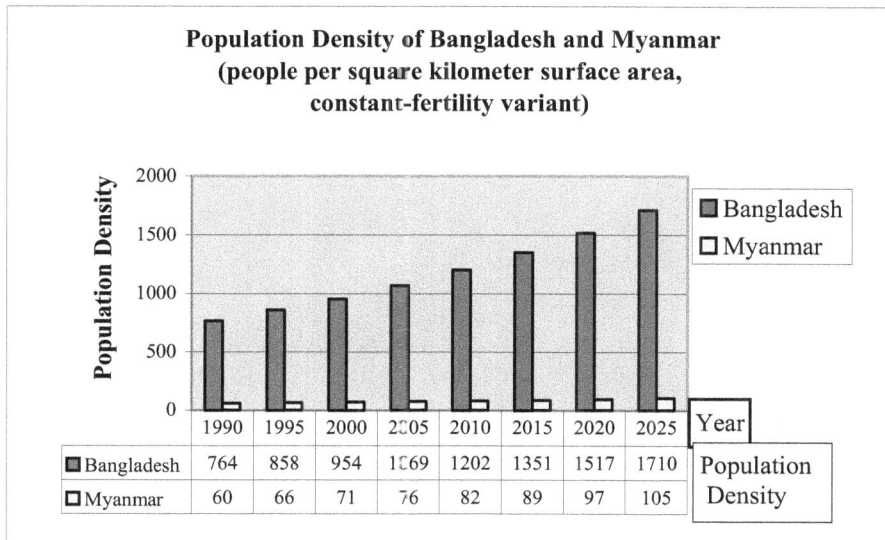

Figure 1.3a. Population density at constant-fertility variant of Bangladesh and Myanmar showing from 1990-2000 and the projected figure up to the year 2025.

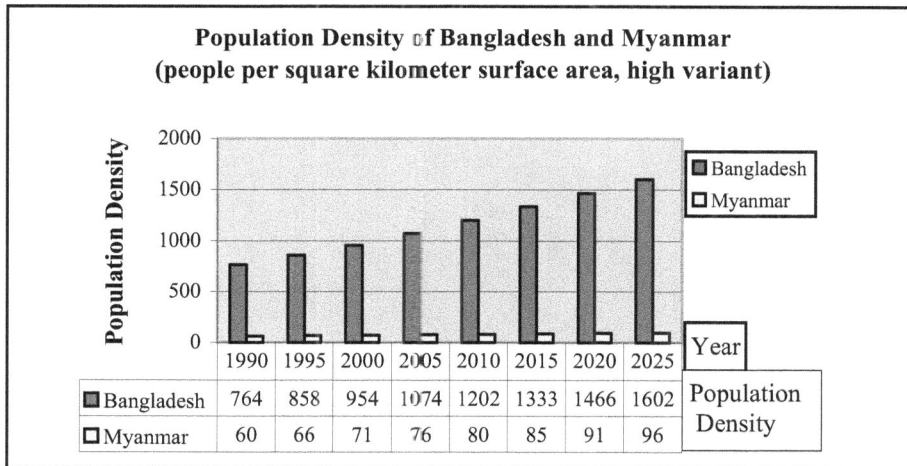

Population Density of Bangladesh and Myanmar
(people per square kilometer surface area, high variant)

	1990	1995	2000	2005	2010	2015	2020	2025
Bangladesh	764	858	954	1074	1202	1333	1466	1602
Myanmar	60	66	71	76	80	85	91	96

Figure 1.3b. Population density at high variant of Bangladesh and Myanmar showing from 1990-2000 and the projected figure up to the year 2025.

Population Density of Bangladesh and Myanmar
(people per square kilometer surface area, medium variant)

Year	1990	1995	2000	2005	2010	2015	2020	2025
Bangladesh	764	858	954	1059	1166	1272	1373	1464
Myanmar	60	66	71	75	78	82	85	89

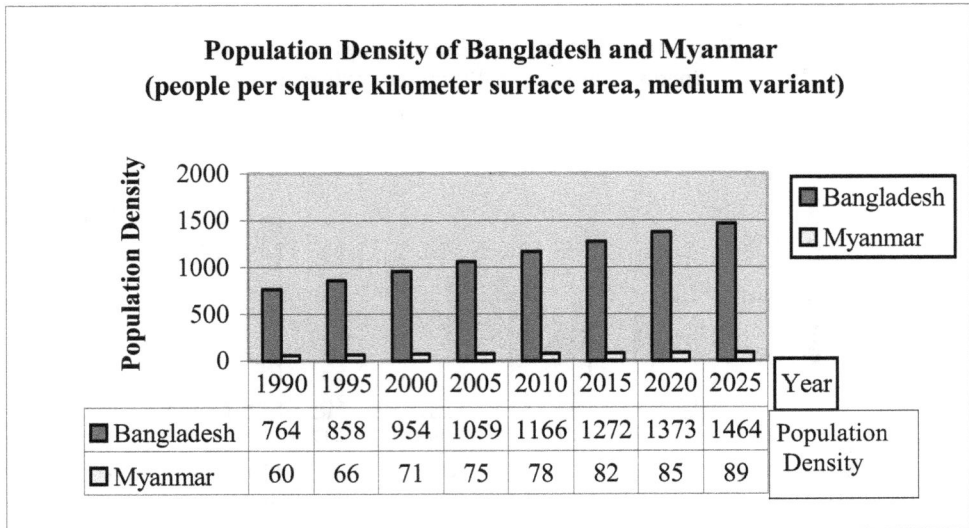

Figure1.3c. Population density at medium variant of Bangladesh and Myanmar showing from 1990-2000 and the projected figure up to the year 2025.

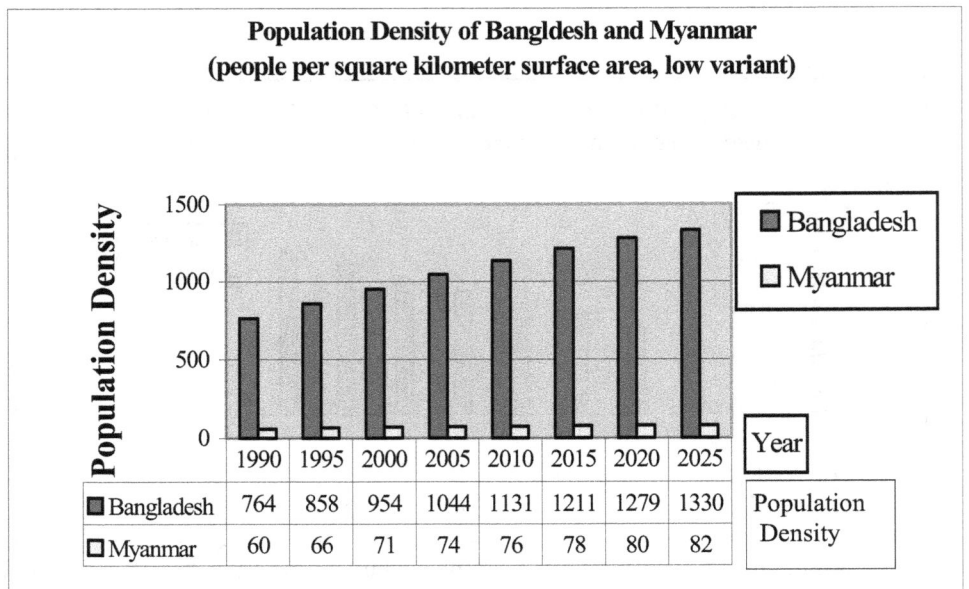

Population Density of Bangldesh and Myanmar
(people per square kilometer surface area, low variant)

Year	1990	1995	2000	2005	2010	2015	2020	2025
Bangladesh	764	858	954	1044	1131	1211	1279	1330
Myanmar	60	66	71	74	76	78	80	82

Figure1.3d. Population density at low variant of Bangladesh and Myanmar showing from 1990-2000 and the projected figure up to the year 2025.

Let us focus on the population figures of the years 2015 and 2025 at low variant. Why? Because, in Bangladesh, even with low variant increase, the chaos will set in at a population density of 1,211 in the year 2015; whereas at a population density of 1,330 in the year 2025 it will boil over. How will this affect Myanmar? I will try to paint a clear picture.

First, I will present the worsening situation of the population densities in Bangladesh by comparing with the population densities of some selected countries across the world. Then, I shall give the economic conditions of Bangladesh and Myanmar. In terms of the population density, Myanmar is not in danger like Bangladesh, but economically, both countries are at the brink of collapse. The data are presented in the coming tables.

Table 1.4. Population density as a dependent of fertility variant

Table1.4a. If the population variant remains constant without any change this is the predicted population density

Sl. No.	Countries and Continents	Population Density (per sq. km.) Constant Fertility Variant In Given Year						Comment
		2000	2005	2010	2015	2020	2025	
1	Australia	2	3	3	3	3	3	
2	Bangladesh	954	1,069	1,202	1,351	1,517	1,701	
3	China	133	138	142	146	149	151	
4	India	307	335	367	401	437	475	
5	Japan	336	340	341	339	334	327	decrease
6	Mexico	50	55	59	64	68	73	
7	Myanmar	71	76	82	89	97	105	
8	Thailand	122	130	137	144	151	157	
9	USA	30	32	33	35	36	38	
10	Africa	26	30	34	39	45	52	
11	Asia	116	124	133	143	153	164	
12	Europe	32	31	31	31	30	30	decrease
13	Latin America	25	27	30	32	34	37	
14	World	45	48	51	55	59	64	

Sl. No.	Countries and Continents	Population Density (per sq. km.) Low Variant In Given Year						Comment
		2000	2005	2010	2015	2020	2025	
1	Australia	2	3	3	3	3	3	
2	Bangladesh	954	1,044	1,131	1,211	1,279	1,333	
3	China	133	137	140	142	144	144	
4	India	307	329	349	363	374	384	
5	Japan	336	338	337	334	328	321	decrease
6	Mexico	50	54	56	58	60	62	
7	Myanmar	71	74	76	78	80	82	
8	Thailand	122	129	133	136	139	142	
9	USA	30	31	33	34	35	36	
10	Africa	26	29	32	35	39	42	
11	Asia	116	122	128	133	137	141	
12	Europe	32	31	31	30	30	29	decrease
13	Latin America	25	27	28	29	31	31	
14	World	45	47	49	51	53	55	

Table 1.4b. If the population variant remains low this is the predicted population density

Table 1.4c. If the population variant remains medium this is the predicted population density

Sl. No.	Countries and Continents	Population Density (per sq. km.) Medium Variant In Given Year						Comment
		2000	2005	2010	2015	2020	2025	
1	Australia	2	3	3	3	3	3	
2	Bangladesh	954	1,059	1,166	1,272	1,373	1, 464	
3	China	133	138	142	147	151	153	
4	India	307	331	354	374	393	411	
5	Japan	336	339	339	338	333	328	decrease
6	Mexico	50	54	58	61	64	66	
7	Myanmar	71	75	78	82	85	89	
8	Thailand	122	130	136	141	146	151	
9	USA	30	32	33	34	36	37	
10	Africa	26	29	33	37	41	45	
11	Asia	116	123	130	138	144	150	
12	Europe	32	31	31	31	30	30	decrease
13	Latin America	25	27	29	31	32	34	
14	World	45	47	50	53	56	59	

Sl. No.	Countries and Continents	Population Density (per sq. km.) High Variant In Given Year						Comment
		2000	2005	2010	2015	2020	2025	
1	Australia	2	3	3	3	3	3	
2	Bangladesh	954	1074	1202	1333	1466	1602	
3	China	133	139	144	150	156	161	
4	India	307	333	360	386	412	439	
5	Japan	336	340	342	341	339	335	decrease
6	Mexico	50	55	59	63	67	72	
7	Myanmar	71	76	80	85	91	96	
8	Thailand	122	131	139	146	153	160	
9	USA	30	32	34	35	37	39	
10	Africa	26	30	33	38	42	47	
11	Asia	116	124	133	142	151	160	
12	Europe	32	31	31	31	31	30	decrease
13	Latin America	25	27	30	32	34	36	
14	World	45	48	51	55	58	62	

Table 1.4d. If the population variant remains high this is the predicted population density

Let us now highlight the ratio of the total surface area and the population in terms of the population density which is here considered as the Causative Factor-1 of National Well-Being. I am presenting here those of Bangladesh and Myanmar with reference to those of the USA and Thailand. The USA is an advanced nation in the World Bank group of high income nations and Thailand is an emerging economy in the World Bank lower middle income group, hence they will serve as the immediate references. The other countries can be referred back to the previous tables whenever relevant. It is focused at the values of the years 2015 and 2025 for I predict upheavals would take place as early as the year 2015, or if late by the year 2025. The value at medium variant is highlighted for it is reasonable to assume that the medium variant is the most achievable demographic goal.

Remember

I have identified the population density as the Causative Factor-1 of National Well-Being. The higher population density the worse is the situation. Bangladesh has the highest population density in the world!

(Note: Microstates such as Monaco, Grenada, etc. are not considered here because these states have very high population density due to their small size. For example, in 2000 Monaco's population density was 16,923 whereas her total population was 33,000 in a total   area of 1.95 square kilometers).

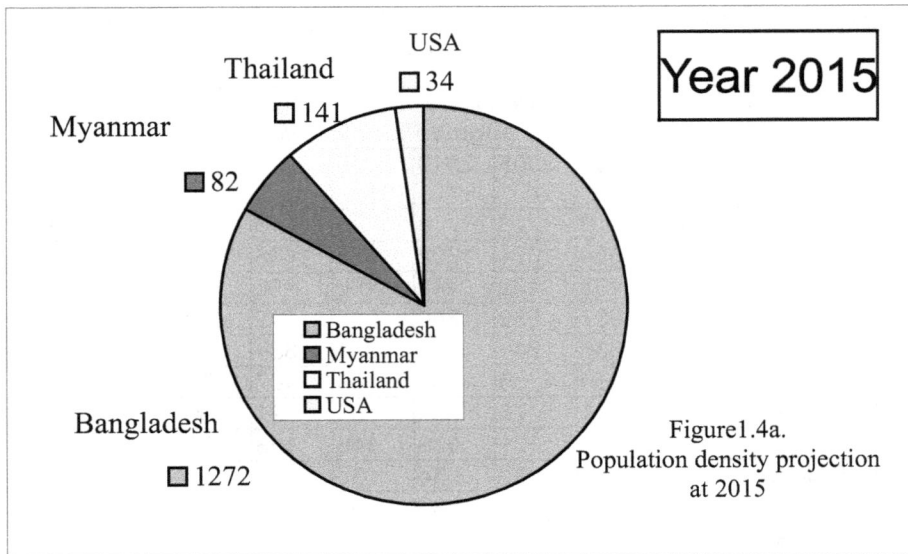

Year 2015

Thailand
USA

Myanmar

Bangladesh

Figure1.4a.
Population density projection
at 2015

- Bangladesh
- Myanmar
- Thailand
- USA

USA ☐ 34
Thailand ☐ 141
Myanmar ■ 82
Bangladesh ☐ 1272

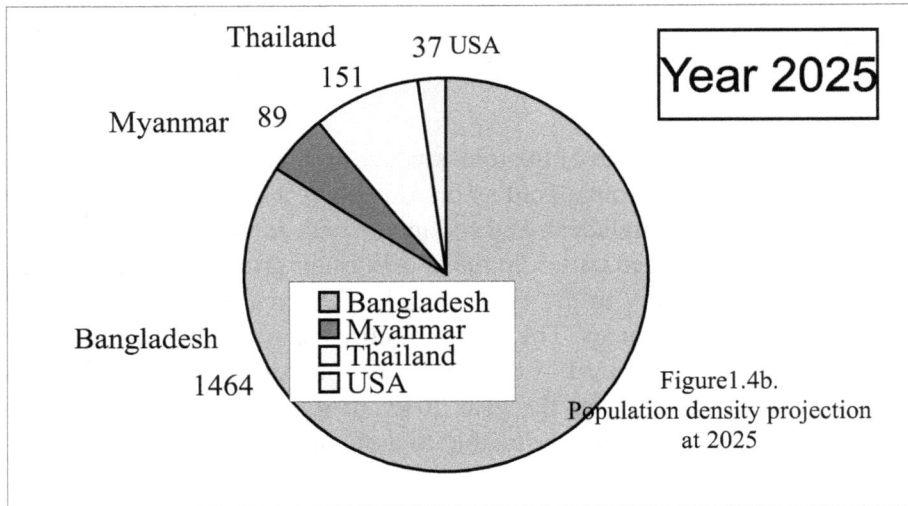

Year 2025

Thailand 151
Myanmar 89
37 USA

Bangladesh 1464

- Bangladesh
- Myanmar
- Thailand
- USA

Figure1.4b.
Population density projection
at 2025

Figure 1.4. Population Density of Bangladesh and Myanmar in comparison with the USA and Thailand in the years 2015 and 2025 at medium variant. Please note the proportion of the circle area taken up by Bangladesh population density.

Why do we have to worry about the total population or the population density? We should be concerned because both Bangladesh and Myanmar are not capable of supporting their peoples.

http://www.un.org/esa/population/publications/longrange2/LR_EXEC_SUM_TABLES_FIGS.xls

Figure 1.5. World population according to different scenarios, 2000-2300

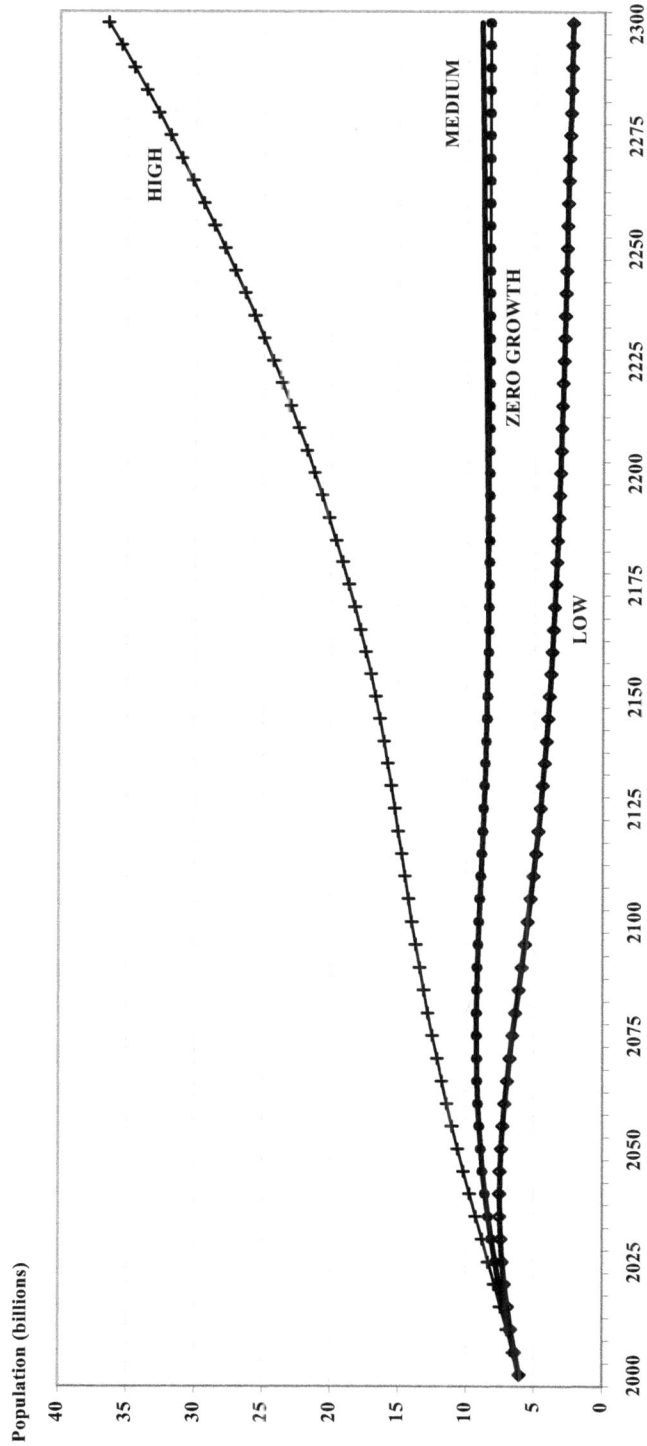

If you go to http://www.ibiblio.org/lunarbin/worldpop/index.html you will find a population meter increasing every second. It hit 6,505,332,363 at 06:10:00 pm US Central Standard Time on March 13, 2005. According to Joseph A. McFalls Jr.,258 babies are born every minute around the world (source: Joseph A. McFalls Jr., Population: A Lively Introduction, http://www.prb.org/).

1.5. Poverty of Bangladesh and Myanmar. My plan is to convince you that:
1. They have **no** sufficient income to support their people.
2. They have **no** sufficient food to feed their people.
3. They have **no** sufficient natural and/or technological resources to overcome the above-mentioned deficiencies.

It is generally agreed that the advancements of science and technology are the key to the well-being of a nation. In addition, I believe that the population to land ratio also plays an equally important role in keeping a nation wealthy and healthy. I have shown earlier that Bangladesh's area is too small to support her growing population. Today, Bangladesh's predicaments are compounded by underdevelopment and large population. The same is true for Myanmar though her population pressure is not as bad as Bangladesh.

Question#1. Do they have sufficient income to support their peoples?
Answer#1. No, they do not.

As a matter of fact, poverty exists in its extreme form in both Bangladesh and Myanmar. According to the classification of the United Nations they are the Least Developed Countries (LDCs) along with 47 others in the family of 191 UNCTAD (United Nations Conference On Trade And Development) members.

Before we go deeply into the subject of poverty let us get acquainted with UNCTAD. This is to let you know that I am citing a publication of a respectable global body, not an anti-establishment organization. The following information of UNCTAD is from "http://www.unctad.org/en/aboutorg/index.htm" as of August 15, 2002.

UNCTAD IN BRIEF

Established in 1964 as a permanent intergovernmental body, UNCTAD is the principal organ of the United Nations General Assembly dealing with trade, investment and development issues.

MAIN GOALS: Maximize the trade, investment and development opportunities of developing countries and assist them in their efforts to integrate into the world economy on an equitable basis.

MEMBERSHIP: 191 member States

HEADQUARTERS: Palais des Nations, E-Building, Geneva, Switzerland

SECRETARIAT: Secretary-General: Mr. Rubens Ricupero (Brazil),
Deputy Secretary-General: Mr. Carlos Fortin (Chile),
400 staff members

BUDGET: US$ 45 million a year from the United Nations regular budget and US$ 24 million from extra budgetary resources.

The least developed countries (LDCs) are defined and grouped by the United Nations. Under the UN classification there are 49 LDCs. They are Afghanistan, Angola, **Bangladesh**, Benin, Bhutan, Burkina Faso, Burundi, Cambodia, Cape Verde, the Central African Republic, Chad, the Comoros, the Democratic Republic of the Congo, Djibouti, Equatorial Guinea, Eritrea, Ethiopia, Gambia, Guinea, Guinea-Bissau, Haiti, Kiribati, the Lao People's Democratic Republic, Lesotho, Liberia, Madagascar, Malawi, Maldives, Mali, Mauritania, Mozambique, **Myanmar**, Nepal, Niger, Rwanda, Samoa, Sao Tome and Principe, Senegal, Sierra Leone, Solomon Islands, Somalia, Sudan, Togo, Tuvalu, Uganda, the United Republic of Tanzania, Vanuatu, Yemen and Zambia. This information is taken from *Least Developed Countries Report 2002*, United Nations Conference On Trade And Development. Statistical Annex. http://www.unctad.org/en/docs/ldc02annex.en.pdf, downloaded on August 15, 2002 and it is still true as of June 04, 2004 as per *World Statistics Pocketbook Least Developed Countries* (containing data available as of 31 May 2003), Department of Economic and Social Affairs Statistics Division, UN-ECOSOC; http://www.un.org/esa/coordination/ecosoc/LDCpocket-book.pdf.

The following excerpt tells us the classification criteria of a least developed country.

WHAT ARE THE LEAST DEVELOPED COUNTRIES?

Forty-nine countries are currently designated by the United Nations as "least developed countries" (LDCs). The list is reviewed every three years by the Economic and Social Council (ECOSOC).

The criteria underlying the current list of LDCs are:

a low income, as measured by the gross domestic product (GDP) per capita;

weak human resources, as measured by a composite index (Augmented Physical Quality of Life Index) based on indicators of life expectancy at birth, per capita calorie intake, combined primary and secondary school enrollment, and adult literacy;

a low level of economic diversification, as measured by a composite index (Economic Diversification Index), the share of the labour force in industry, annual per capita commercial energy consumption, and UNCTAD's merchandise export concentration index.

Different thresholds are used for inclusion in, and graduation from the list. A country qualifies to be added to the list of LDCs if it meets inclusion thresholds on all three criteria. A country qualifies for graduation from the list if it meets graduation thresholds on two of the three criteria. For the low-income criterion, the threshold on which inclusion in the current list is based has been a GDP per capita of $800, and the threshold for graduation has been a GDP per capita of

GDP Definition. The United Nations Economic and Social Council defines the Gross Domestic Product (GDP) as follows. (Source: http://www.un.org/esa/coordination/ecosoc/LDCpocketbook.pdf).

"Gross domestic product total and per capita estimates (GDP) in United States dollars are

Statistics Division estimates from the National Accounts Database of the Division. These estimates should be considered as measures of the total and per capita production of goods and services of the countries represented in economic terms, not as measures of the standard of living of their inhabitants. In order to have comparable coverage for as many countries as possible, these US dollar estimates are based on official GDP national currency data, supplemented by national currency estimates prepared by the Statistics Division using additional data from national and international sources. The estimates given here are in most cases those accepted by the United Nations General Assembly Committee on Contributions for determining United Nations members' contributions to the United Nations regular budget."

Table 1.5. Per capita GDP comparison	
Country	Per Capita GDP
Australia	19,056
Bangladesh	345
China	918
India	467
Japan	32,809
Mexico	6,144
Mozambique	189
Myanmar	717
Switzerland	34,274
Thailand	1,865
United States	34,788

Table1.5 at the right gives us the estimates of Per Capita Gross Domestic Product in US dollars for Bangladesh and Myanmar. Comparative figures of nine other countries are included here. Information is collected from the United Nations statistics data at http://un-stats.un.org/unsd/snaama/results-GDP.asp?Series=5&CCode=36,50,156,356,392,484,508,104,756,764,840&Year=2001&SLevel=0&Selection=Series; last data update was April 2003. This information is as of May 31, 2004.

Please note that India is not classified as a LDC despite its low Per Capita GDP of $467. China is barely above the LDC graduation level of $900. It is not that a country automatically becomes a LDC just because she falls into the UN category of least developed countries. The country has to apply for the classification. Once she is recognized as a LDC, she has certain privileges such as writing of certain international debts, gaining access to special loan and development programs from UN, World Bank (WB), and International Monetary Fund (IMF), etc. It is similar to bankruptcy filing of a business, in gross comparison.

The United Nations Conference On Trade And Development (UNCTAD) characterizes the 'Least Developed Countries' as follows. The following excerpt is from its report "Least Developed Countries Report 2002", Escaping the Poverty Trap, June 2002. (Source: http://www.unctad.org/en/pub/ps1ldc02.en.htm, as of August 15, 2002. For the full text please visit the website).

"THE LEAST DEVELOPED COUNTRIES REPORT 2002
Escaping the Poverty Trap
June 2002

The least developed countries (LDCs) are a group of 49 countries that have been identified by the UN as "least developed" in terms of their low GDP per capita, their weak human assets and their high degree of economic vulnerability........
.............extreme poverty is pervasive and persistent in most LDCs, and that the incidence of extreme poverty is highest in those LDCs that are dependent on primary commodity exports. The incidence of poverty is so high because most of the LDCs are caught in an international

poverty trap. Pervasive poverty within LDCs has effects at the national level that cause poverty to persist and even to increase, and international trade and finance relationships are reinforcing the cycle of economic stagnation and poverty. The Report argues that the current form of globalization is tightening the poverty trap.

....It also shows that effective poverty reduction in the LDCs needs a more supportive international environment. This should include increased and more effective aid and debt relief, a review and recasting of international commodity policy, and policies which recognize the interdependence between the socio-economic marginalization of the poorest countries and the increasing polarization of the global economy......."

1.6. Poverty Measurement by GNP or GNI. As seen in the previous page a Least Developed Country is low income, as measured by the gross domestic product (GDP) per capita. However, a country earns more than it produces at home. These are the foreign earnings remitted by her citizens who work abroad plus the profits and the interest from the investment abroad by the citizens. For example, many countries such as Bangladesh, India, and Philippine, etc. export labor, doctors, and engineers to the middle eastern countries. They are known as *the wageearners.* Bangladesh earned above 300 million dollars annually under the wageearner programs in the 1980s. Their remittance is not included in the definition of the gross domestic product (GDP). When the wageearner's remittance and other income generated abroad are added to the gross domestic product it is called the gross national product (GNP).

Now, the term gross national product (GNP) has been replaced by Gross National Income (GNI), for better clarity of expression and meaning. This is what happened. "In 1993 the Commission of the European Communities, the International Monetary Fund, the Organization for Economic Cooperation and Development, the United Nations, and the World Bank revised the System of National Accounts. One of the changes from A System of National Accounts 1968 to its successor System of National Accounts 1993, was the replacement of the term GNP (Gross National Product) with GNI". (Source: Estimation of Internationally Comparable Per Capita Income Numbers for Operational Purposes. World Bank).

However, World Bank and UNCTAD reports used the term gross national product (GNP), rather than the gross national income (GNI) in their online publications in 2002. As such, knowing GNP is the same as knowing GNI. Accordingly, I am presenting here the definition and meanings of the term GNP, which is the old synonym of GNI. Only in 2004, I found these international bodies updated to GNI. The following is a part of teaching material

---

Source: 'http://www.un.org/esa/agenda21/natlinfo/indicato/econ.htm', Gross national product (GNP) per capita, this will take you to 'http://wbln0018.worldbank.org/psd/compete.nsf/ 7349593d593389e88525648f00641829?OpenView', as of August 15, 2002.

Gross National Product (GNP) per Capita
GNP per capita figures are calculated according to the World Bank Atlas method (see 1997 World Development Indicators for a description of the Atlas methodology). The resulting estimate of GNP is then divided by the midyear population to obtain the per capita figures. GNP measures the total domestic and foreign value added claimed by residents. It comprises Gross Domestic Product (GDP) plus net factor income from abroad which is the income residents receive from abroad for factor services (labor and capital) less similar payments made to nonresidents who contributed to the domestic economy.

Source: 1999 Global Development Finance & World Development Indicators Central, available online from the World Bank Statistical Information Management and Analysis.
Unit: US$
Coverage: 1996, 1997.
Ranking: Highest to lowest. Available for 155 countries.
Private investment covers outlays by the private sector (including private nonprofit agencies) on additions to its fixed domestic assets. Gross domestic fixed investment includes similar outlays by the public sector.

1.7. What does GNP or GNI per capita indicate? We need to know what GNP or GNI indicates. What does it show? The following information is taken from the World Bank website 'http://www.worldbank.org/depweb/english/modules/economic/gnp/index.htm', GNP per Capita Learning Module, as of August 15, 2002. Again, this teaching module is written using the old term GNP. Please remember it has been replaced with the new term GNI from 2003 onwards. I visited http://www.worldbank.org again on June 06, 2004 to find that it has not yet updated its *Learning Modules* materials as per web page at http://www.worldbank.org/depweb/ english/modules/economic/gnp/index.html. As such I am giving it here as it is with the old vocabulary. It is a good website where one can learn various aspects of world development programs and economic situations.

GNP per Capita

Gross national product (GNP) per capita is the dollar value of a country's final output of goods and services in a year, divided by its population. It reflects the average income of a country's citizens. Countries with a GNP per capita in 1998 of $9,361 or more are described as high income, between $761 and $9,360 as middle income, and $760 or less as low income.

What GNP per capita shows

GNP per capita shows what part of a country's GNP each person would have if this GNP were divided equally. Knowing a country's GNP per capita is a good first step toward understanding the country's economic strengths and needs, as well as the general standard of living enjoyed by the average citizen. A country's GNP per capita tends to be closely linked with other indicators that measure the social, economic, and environmental well-being of the country and its people. For example, generally people living in countries with higher GNP per capita tend to have longer life expectancies, higher literacy rates, better access to safe water, and lower infant mortality rates.

Economic productivity and growth

Low- and middle-income countries produce about 20 percent of the world's goods and services, but have more than 80 percent of the world's population. As Chart 1 *(please see next page)* illustrates, this trend results in people in low- and middle income countries having a smaller share of the world's goods and services than people in high-income countries.

A general objective of nations is to increase the size of their economies and hence their GNP per capita. Economic growth depends on people—both men and women—having better health, education, and work skills. It also depends on improving transportation, communication, and energy systems; having better tools and technology; having access to raw materials and capital; getting fair wages and prices for goods and services; encouraging savings and investment; increasing the value and variety of exports; and having better access to world markets to sell these exports.

Effects of population growth rate on GNP per capita

Between 1980 and 1998, GNP grew moderately in many low-income countries, although in some cases—most notably China—growth was substantial. However, in many developing countries, economic growth is often counteracted by rapid population growth. As Chart 2 *(please see next page)* illustrates, between 1980–1998, GNP per capita has tended to grow at a slower rate in low- and middle-income countries than in high-income countries.

Many countries are trying to slow their population growth in order to raise standards of living. In general, countries that have managed to increase their GNP per capita have tended to contain population growth while following sensible economic policies that can encourage stability and increases in both human and physical capital.

The following graphs show the relationship between poverty and per capita GNP (GNI). It is good to know since a program called *globalization* has been initiated by the developed countries, and the underdeveloped or developing countries are against it. I present this information to highlight the effect of population on economic development. Please note that China is trying to reduce her population, but Bangladesh and Myanmar are not.

Chart 1. GNP, Population, and GNP per Capita, 1998

☐ Low- and Middle-income economies
■ High-income economies

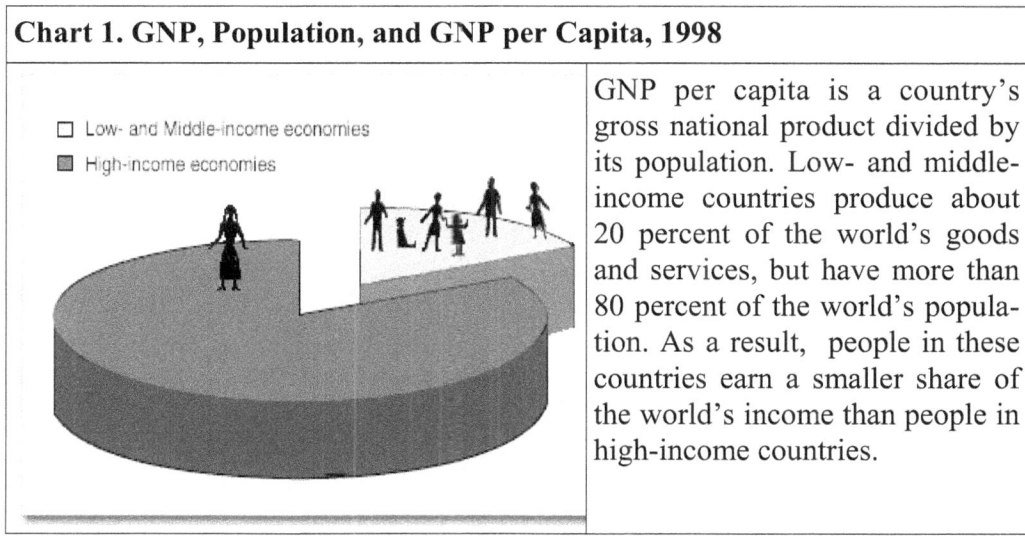

GNP per capita is a country's gross national product divided by its population. Low- and middle-income countries produce about 20 percent of the world's goods and services, but have more than 80 percent of the world's population. As a result, people in these countries earn a smaller share of the world's income than people in high-income countries.

Chart 2. Growth of GNP, Population, and GNP per Capita, 1980–1998 (with and without China & India)

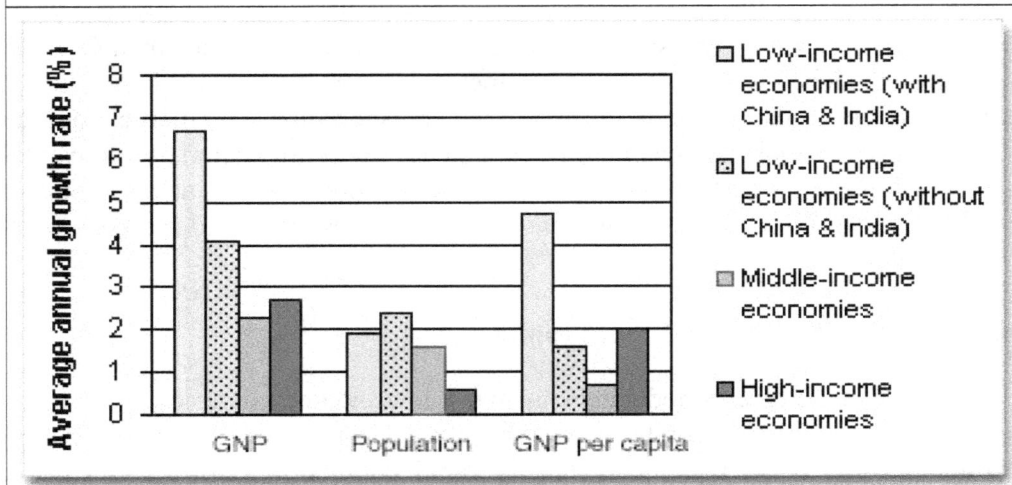

In many developing countries, moderate GNP growth is counteracted by rapid population growth. As a result, between 1980 and 1998, the average annual GNP per capita growth rate for middle- and low-income countries (excluding China and India) was less than high-income countries.

Excerpt continued from 'http://www.worldbank.org/depweb/english/modules/economic/gnp/index.htm', GNP per Capita Learning Module, as of August 15, 2002.

What GNP per capita does not show

GNP per capita helps measure the material output of a country, but it does not show what kinds of goods and services the country produces, whether all people share equally in the wealth of a country, or whether these people lead fulfilling lives. †*(Income disparity of rich and poor is not essential point of interest in my presentation. Therefore, I will not go further than this).*

......

......

GNP does not always capture activity in the informal economy, such as unreported cash payments for goods and services, bartering, or blackmarket trading. The informal sector can generate a lot of income that never shows up in standard economic indicators. Many countries are encouraging programs that help people in the informal sector get loans and business training, with the goal that they eventually become part of the formal economy.

Author's Note: In the informal economy, blackmarket trading constitutes a significant contribution to the economy of Bangladesh and Myanmar, with significant income from the international drug trade. While Myanmar is a large producer of the drugs, from her Chittagong and Khulna ports, Bangladesh serves as a major distributor. Bay of Bengal high sea is a well-known transit station.

†Information in italics inside the parenthesis is mine.

Now, I must introduce you to *purchasing power parity* (PPP), one more term that the economists use to analyze a nation's economy. For example, one US dollar in Bangladesh will buy a person a dinner at a local Bangladeshi restaurant, but it will not in USA. Thus, purchasing power is different. As of June 05, 2004, one US dollar will get Bangladesh Taka 60.2649 at prevailing inter-bank exchange rate as per Bangladesh Bank data at http://www.bangladesh-bank.org/econdata/exchrate.html. In USA, a small business will have to pay its manager minimum $3000.00 a month whereas the maximum pay in Bangladesh will be $1000.00 for the same job. One can hire labor at a rate of one dollar per hour in Bangladesh while the minimum wage per hour in USA is $5.15. Therefore, an indicator known as *purchasing power parity* (PPP) is used to standardize the purchasing power of the given income in each country in order to reflect the actual money value in terms of the commodity it can purchase. In short PPP is the international standard system that indicates the cost-of-living of a country. The following excerpt from the World Bank Learning Module gives the official explanation of PPP.

Excerpt from 'http://www.worldbank.org/depweb/english/modules/economic/gnp/index.htm', GNP per Capita Learning Module, as of August 15, 2002. *Italics* are mine.

Some more issues...

Going beyond GNP per capita helps reveal other important development issues. For example, GNP per capita is given in dollars, but a dollar may buy more in one country than in another. To compare the actual purchasing power of per capita incomes across countries, you can look at purchasing power parity (PPP). Another issue is that GNP per capita does not recognize the cost of depleting natural resources and damaging the environment. The concept of natural resource accounting, although still being developed, strives to measure and allow for these costs.

Author's Note: I will not be discussing the concept of natural resource accounting here in order to avoid complications.

---

10 Taka note with Sheikh Mujibur Rahman, the Father of Nation

50 Taka note with National Martyr's Monument

1 Dollar bill with George Washington, the Father of Nation

Tk10 + Tk50 = $1.00 This is the official rate. In the streets, just outside the bank, $1 gets two Taka more. Taka value is much more stable than Myanmar currency. Please see in the coming pages.

1.8. GNI of Bangladesh and Myanmar. Now we have educated ourselves with the basic economic parameter which measures the wealth of a country. Let us then have a look at the actual figures of the gross national income (GNI) of Bangladesh and Myanmar. We shall also compare their GNI with some other developed and developing countries. The GNI information is obtained from the World Bank website http://devdata.worldbank.org. The reader may also visit 'http://www.bangladesh-bank.org for more information on Bangladesh. No such information is available for Myanmar.

Table1.6. Gross National Income (GNI) Per Capita and Purchasing Power Parity (PPP)of Bangladesh and Myanmar in comparison with selected countries of the world as of 2002. The highest GNI, ranking world number 1, is Bermuda, but no figure is given by the World Bank. Therefore I include Luxembourg that ranks #2, whose GNI figure is available. It ranks #1 in PPP. The lowest GNI, $100.00, is reported for Burundi, Ethiopia,and Democratic Republic of Congo; their ranking number is 206. Myanmar cannot be ranked as no data is available. She is estimated to be low income, $735.00 or less. GNI is as per Atlas methodology. Purchasing Power Parity (PPP) is defined as the international dollars. Source: World Development Indicators database, World Bank, 2004 (http://devdata.worldbank.org/data-query/).

	Countries	GNI per capita US$	GNI per capita rank in the world	Purchasing Power Parity (PPP)	PPP rank in the world
1	Australia	19,530.00	29	27,440.00	19
2	Bangladesh	380.00	171	1,770.00	165
3	China	960.00	136	4,520.00	125
4	India	470.00	161	2,650.00	146
5	Japan	34,010.00	7	27,380.00	20
6	Mexico	5,920.00	66	8,800.00	80
7	Mozambique	200.00	195	990.00	189
8	Myanmar	not available	not available	not available	not available
9	Luxembourg	39,470	2	53,290.00	1
10	Thailand	2,000.00	104	6,890.00	88
11	United States	35,400.00	6	36,110.00	4

1.9. Poverty in Myanmar. It is disappointing to note that World Bank cannot give any figure of GNI per capita and PPP for Myanmar, in spite of the fact that she is a member of the United Nations and UNCTAD. As a result, her poverty has to be judged on the basis of her LDC status and GDP $717, see Table1.5, page 38. The figure given by the United Nations statistics data is based upon the official currency exchange rate which is K6.42 for one US dollar on June 11, 2004 (source:http://finance.yahoo.com/currency?u). Myanmar currency is called Kyat and the official rate is set stable by the government. However, the actual street value or gray market value is around K900.00 for one US dollar. In past three years the street exchange rate has been fluctuating between K700 and K1200 as per reports of Narinjara News (http:// narinjara.com). Today it hovers around K900.00. Please note that I describe it as gray market, but not black market, because it is allowed by the government. Tourists and foreign official visitors can buy Foreign Exchange Certificates (FECs) at the official exchange rates, that can be openly sold at street market values without any problem. As such I prefer to call it gray market being created by the government itself.

Now, if we convert Myanmar per capita GDP $717.00 into Myanmar currency in the official rate K6.42 we get a value of K4603.14. When we re-convert this value back to US dollars at the street rate K900.00 we get an appalling value of only $5.1146, which represents the genuine market value. Yes, it is just above five dollars. I do not know of any other nation having a GDP of only five dollars. Accordingly, I would like to conclude that Myanmar is the poorest country in the world. On the other hand it must be noted that Myanmar poverty is not due to lack of natural resources. She has oil, gas, coal, rice, teak, timber, bamboo, gold, silver, tin, lead, wolframite (an important source of tungsten), rubies, jades, emerald, fish, seafood etc., just to name some. Her poverty is entirely due to mismanagement and political chaos.

1.10. Let us Refresh Our Mind. In the beginning of this section, I said:
1. They have **no** sufficient income to support their peoples.
2. They have **no** sufficient food to feed their peoples.
3. They have **no** sufficient natural and/or technological resources to feed, clothe, and shelter their peoples.

With the information presented above I have substantiated my answer #1 with a good amount of data. So far I have shown that:

1. Bangladesh and Myanmar do not have sufficient money or income to feed their populace. Please note here that I use the word 'populace' because there exists a class of high income privileged people in both countries. For them money is not a problem. These classes of rich and poor, haves and have-nots, privileged and underprivileged are in confrontation with each other, getting aggravated as the economy worsens.

2. Bangladesh's total surface area including agricultural land has diminished greatly with high population density whereas Myanmar still has a good amount of land area available for development.

Now, let us open an investigation into the question of food availability.

K1000 note with Myanmar Lion	1 Dollar bill with George Washington, the Father of Nation

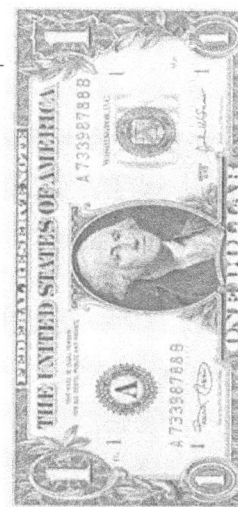

K1000 = $1.00
This is the street value, which fluctuates between K700 and K1200 in past three years. Officially, it is rhetorically set at K6.42. At Bangladesh-Myanmar border one has to pay up to K120 for one Bangladesh Taka.

1.11. Rice: the Staple Food. We all understand that 'food' is something to eat or drink to quench our hunger, and give nourishment and energy to our body and mind. In other words 'food' is the basic requirement for our survival! Each country has her own food-culture and established staple food. In Bangladesh and Myanmar it is rice. Bangladesh also has wheat, but it accounts for only 10.24% of the average total 1713.04 daily calories that a person consumes. In Myanmar, the wheat consumption constitutes only about 1.5% of 2000 calories a day. These calculated results are the average values of 10 years from 1992 to 2001, based upon the data available at the FAO website as of June 2004. Potato, another source of carbohydrate, is taken in very small quantity as vegetables in both countries. Therefore, I shall focus on rice production in these countries. Please pay attention to the following factors.

1. Total rice area in hectares harvested.
2. Rice yield in metric tons per hectare.
3. Total rice production in metric tons.
4. Total rice import and export, in terms of quantity as well as in dollar value.
5. Rice availability, which also means consumption.

The information on these factors are obtained from FAO website. Since FAO database is somewhat complicated I am presenting here the directory path I have followed in acquiring the data I use here.

Step-1. http://apps.fao.org/default.jsp

Step-2. Go to 'ALL DATABASES'

Step-3. Under the domain 'Agricultural Production' go to 'Crops Primary'

Address: http://apps.fao.org/default.jsp

- AGRICULTURE
- NUTRITION
- FISHERIES
- FORESTRY
- FOOD QUALITY CONTROL
- ALL DATABASES

Notes	Domain	Data Collection		
		(Provisional 2003 Production and Production Indi		
	Agricultural Production	Crops Primary	Crops Processed	Live Animals

Step-4. Select 'Country', 'Item', 'Element' and 'Year' and 'Submit To Database'.

Address: http://apps.fao.org/faostat/form?collection=Production.Crops.Primary&Domain=Production&servlet=1&hasbulk=0&version=ext&lan

Select Country , Item , Element and Year to define your query   Help

Australia	Raspberries	Area Harv	2003
Austria	Rice, Paddy	Yield	2002
Azerbaijan, Republic of	ROOTS AND TUBERS,TOTAL+	Production	2001
Bahamas	ROOTS AND TUBERS,TOTAL>	Seed	2000
Bahrain	Roots and Tubers nes		1999
Bangladesh	Rye		1998
Barbados	Safflower Seed		1997
Belarus	Seed Cotton		1996

Submit To Database   Reset   © FAO 2004

Output : Table   **Table :** X-axis Years   **Y-axis** Countries

52

Table1.7. Rice Production of Bangladesh and Myanmar in comparison with selected countries. The data is collected from http://www.riceweb.org/riceprodasia.htm, and http://apps.fao.org/default.htm. The figures are rounded to the last digit or decimal point.
Note: 1 metric ton (Mt) = 1000 kilograms (kg)

Table1.7a. Rice area harvested

Countries	Rice Area Harvested in million Hectares from 1994 to 2003										
	1994	1995	1996	1997	1998	1999	2000	2001	2002	2003	Average of 10 years
Australia	0.12	0.12	0.14	0.16	0.14	0.15	0.13	0.19	0.15	0.04	0.13
Bangladesh	9.92	9.95	10.20	10.26	10.12	10.71	10.80	10.66	11.06	11.10	10.48
China	30.54	31.11	31.75	32.13	31.57	31.64	30.30	29.14	28.51	27.40	30.41
India	42.81	42.80	43.40	43.47	44.80	41.56	44.71	44.62	40.10	44.00	43.23
Japan	2.21	2.12	1.98	1.95	1.80	1.79	1.77	1.71	1.69	1.67	1.87
Mexico	0.09	0.08	0.09	0.11	0.10	0.08	0.08	0.05	0.05	0.05	0.08
Myanmar	5.74	6.03	5.77	5.41	5.46	6.21	6.30	6.41	6.20	6.65	6.02
Thailand	8.98	9.11	9.27	9.91	9.51	9.97	9.89	10.13	9.99	11.00	9.78
United States	1.34	1.25	1.13	1.26	1.32	1.42	1.23	1.34	1.30	1.21	1.28

Table1.7b. Rice yield

Countries	Yield Rice Paddy Mt/Ha from 1994 to 2003										
	1994	1995	1996	1997	1998	1999	2000	2001	2002	2003	Average of 10 years
Australia	8.36	8.54	7.07	7.65	9.43	9.16	8.24	9.46	8.61	10.29	8.68
Bangladesh	2.53	2.65	2.76	2.74	2.94	3.21	3.48	3.40	3.42	3.43	3.06
China	5.83	6.02	6.21	6.31	6.35	6.33	6.26	6.15	6.19	6.07	6.17
India	2.86	2.70	2.82	2.85	2.88	3.24	2.85	3.14	2.68	3	2.90
Japan	6.77	6.34	6.54	6.42	6.22	6.41	6.70	6.64	6.58	5.85	6.45
Mexico	4.26	4.68	4.54	4.14	4.51	4.78	4.18	4.26	4.50	3.79	4.36
Myanmar	3.17	2.98	3.06	3.08	3.13	3.24	3.38	3.42	3.67	3.71	3.28
Thailand	2.35	2.42	2.41	2.38	2.47	2.42	2.61	2.62	2.61	2.45	2.47
United States	6.69	6.30	6.86	6.61	6.35	6.57	7.04	7.28	7.37	7.45	6.85

Table1.7c. Rice production

Countries	Rice Production in million Metric Tons (Mt) from 1994 to 2003										
	1994	1995	1996	1997	1998	1999	2000	2001	2002	2003	Average of 10 years
Australia	1.04	1.02	0.97	1.26	1.33	1.39	1.10	1.76	1.29	0.39	1.15
Bangladesh	25.12	26.40	28.18	28.15	29.71	34.43	37.63	36.27	37.85	38.06	32.18
China	177.99	187.30	197.03	202.77	200.57	200.40	189.81	179.31	176.34	166.42	187.80
India	122.64	115.44	122.50	123.70	129.06	134.50	127.47	140.01	107.60	132.01	125.49
Japan	14.98	13.44	12.93	12.53	11.20	11.47	11.86	11.32	11.11	9.74	12.06
Mexico	0.37	0.37	0.39	0.47	0.46	0.39	0.35	0.23	0.23	0.19	0.35
Myanmar	18.20	17.96	17.68	16.65	17.08	20.13	21.32	21.91	22.78	24.64	19.83
Thailand	21.11	22.02	22.33	23.58	23.45	24.17	25.84	26.52	26.06	27.00	24.21
United States	8.97	7.89	7.78	8.30	8.36	9.34	8.66	9.76	9.57	9.03	8.77

The harvested rice, rice yield, and rice production mentioned in the previous tables are in paddy form. The paddy has to be milled to get the rice that we eat. Please see the illustrated photos. When we mill the paddy we get (1) the husks which are a good source of making activated charcoal for industrial use, (2) the bran and endosperm flour which are rich in vitamins and mainly used as the animal feed, (3) some broken grains that are ground into flour and used for animal feed as well as for making rice cake and crackers, etc., and (4) the whole grain rice that is marketed for human consumption. Please see the photos and word diagram below.

http://www.imaginatorium.org/sano/tanbo.htm

Ripen paddy field.

Photo clips from http://imaginatorium.org/sano/tanbo.htm. The website is created by and belongs to Brian Chandler (i.e. copyright © Brian Chandler 1999-2002). However, it is *copylefted* by him. Please visit his website for more information. Thank you Mr. Brian Chandler for your copyleft permission to use. The legends are mine.

Paddy plant ➡

Golden Paddy. The Burmese call these 'the fruits of gold' ➡

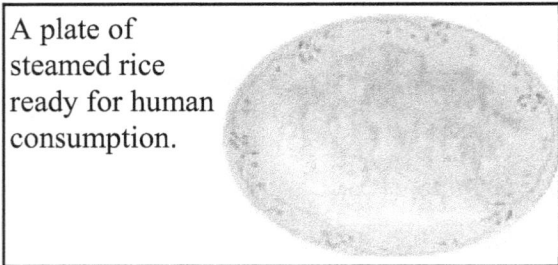

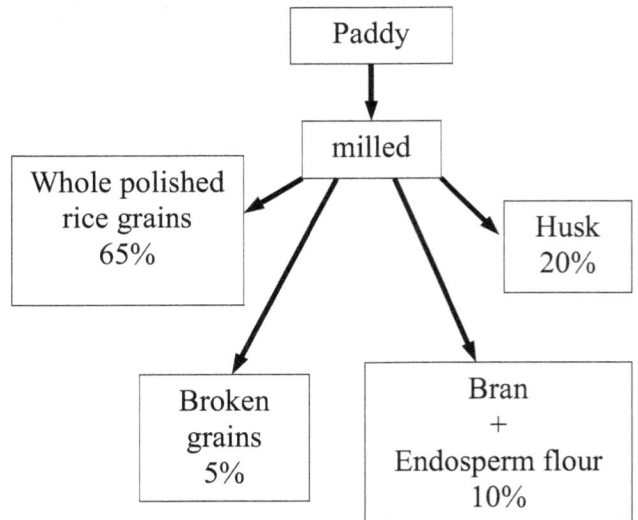

A bowl of milled and polished rice. Shown in the photo is the popular fragrant long grain Thai Jasmine rice.

A plate of steamed rice ready for human consumption.

Paddy

milled

Whole polished rice grains
65%

Husk
20%

Broken grains
5%

Bran
+
Endosperm flour
10%

The rice yield at the end of milling is 70% at best, according to FAO experts. The yield could be as low as 60% depending on the machinery and technology (http://www.fao.org/docrep/x5427e/x5427e0h.htm). Accordingly, it is reasonable to reconsider 65% yield of milled rice from the paddy. Therefore, we have to keep in mind that the available rice for human consumption is about 65% of the paddy produced.

Since domestic rice production is not sufficient for the nation both Bangladesh and Myanmar have to import rice. Rice import/export data was obtained from the FAO database following the direction illustrated below, and data are presented in the tables.

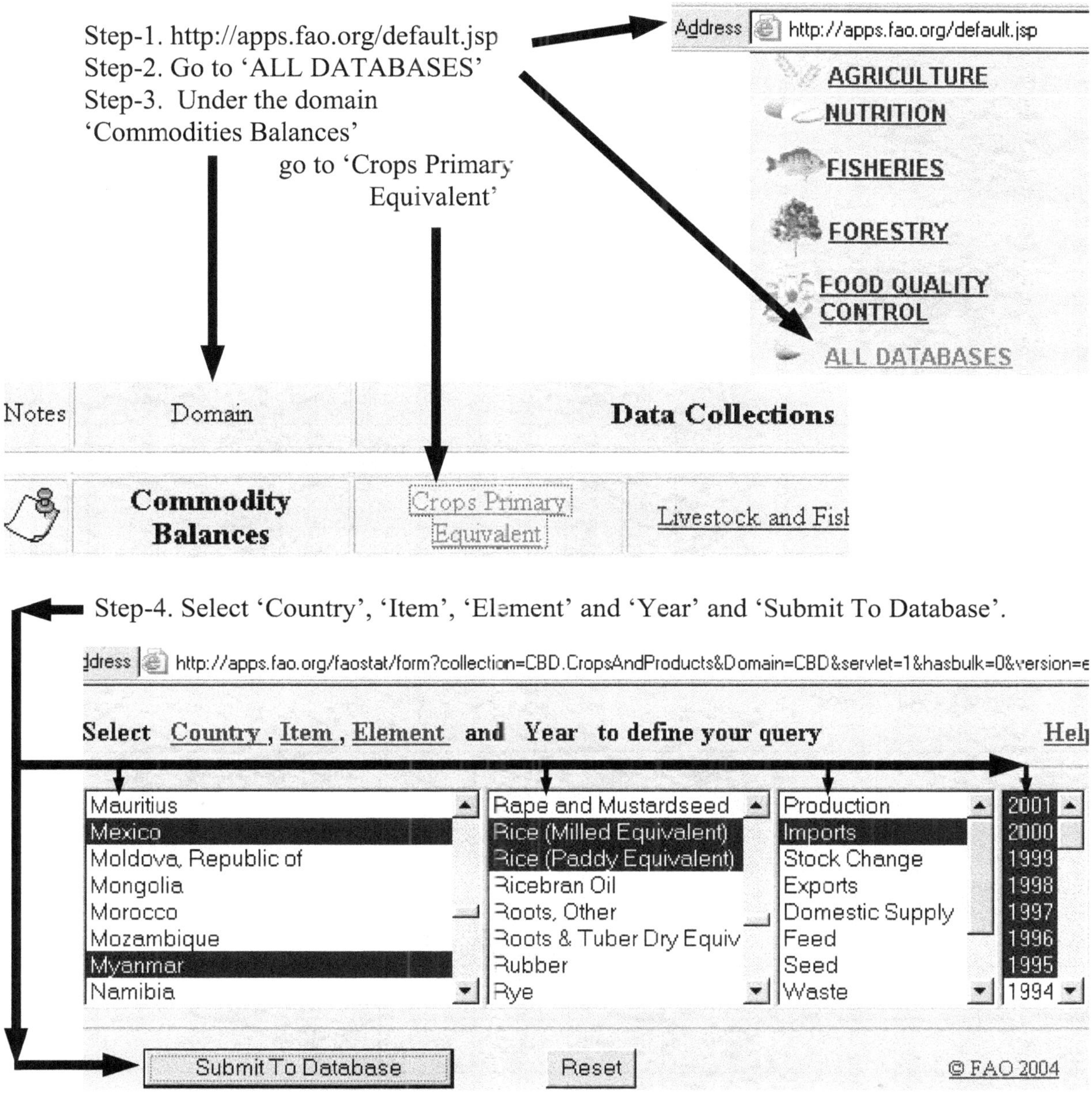

Step-1. http://apps.fao.org/default.jsp
Step-2. Go to 'ALL DATABASES'
Step-3. Under the domain 'Commodities Balances'
　　　　　go to 'Crops Primary Equivalent'

Address [🔲] http://apps.fao.org/default.jsp

🌾 **AGRICULTURE**

🐟 **NUTRITION**

🐟 **FISHERIES**

🌳 **FORESTRY**

🌿 **FOOD QUALITY CONTROL**

　 ALL DATABASES

Notes	Domain	Data Collections	
📄	**Commodity Balances**	Crops Primary Equivalent	Livestock and Fish

Step-4. Select 'Country', 'Item', 'Element' and 'Year' and 'Submit To Database'.

Address [🔲] http://apps.fao.org/faostat/form?collection=CBD.CropsAndProducts&Domain=CBD&servlet=1&hasbulk=0&version=e

Select Country , Item , Element and Year to define your query　　　　Help

Country	Item	Element	Year
Mauritius	Rape and Mustardseed	Production	2001
Mexico	Rice (Milled Equivalent)	Imports	2000
Moldova, Republic of	Rice (Paddy Equivalent)	Stock Change	1999
Mongolia	Ricebran Oil	Exports	1998
Morocco	Roots, Other	Domestic Supply	1997
Mozambique	Roots & Tuber Dry Equiv	Feed	1996
Myanmar	Rubber	Seed	1995
Namibia	Rye	Waste	1994

Submit To Database　　　　Reset　　　　© FAO 2004

Table1.8. Tables showing rice import/export of Bangladesh and Myanmar in a course of 8 years from 1995 to 2002

Table1.8a. Rice imports in metric tons (Mt)

Rice Imports - Qty (Mt)	Year							
	1995	1996	1997	1998	1999	2000	2001	2002
Australia	31,000	39,518	42,822	37,156	49,914	52,316	58,919	62,401
Bangladesh	995,946	1,038,199	179,444	1,127,208	2,215,322	260,029	152,130	943,433
China	1,645,837	765,132	330,393	246,892	172,106	244,735	274,589	339,695
India	52	2	54	6,635	34,498	13,193	63	872
Japan	28,971	444,992	568,729	499,383	664,227	655,760	645,675	650,805
Mexico	246,432	324,281	310,489	291,775	405,023	426,120	462,165	477,675
Myanmar	0	457	1,633	952	6,662	10,143	13,000	6,556
Thailand	68	188	325	836	1,406	524	265	898
United States of America	224,338	275,394	361,654	278,592	353,644	304,505	405,801	409,856

Table1.8b. Rice imports in dollar value

Rice Imports - Val (1000$)	Year							
	1995	1996	1997	1998	1999	2000	2001	2002
Australia	15,426	21,599	25,790	23,124	28,343	29,427	26,925	27,454
Bangladesh	218,256	253,581	40,264	234,819	540,918	64,069	22,420	146,030
China	435,273	288,090	141,821	121,184	79,477	114,890	100,815	110,007
India	15	5	17	1,298	6,956	3,959	15	225
Japan	22,346	267,196	331,243	272,565	309,328	265,405	197,410	213,641
Mexico	79,638	123,298	129,127	111,486	125,052	101,463	104,833	89,907
Myanmar	0	245	560	295	1,720	2,680	2,000	795
Thailand	51	132	252	562	819	232	139	389
United States of America	141,220	178,488	235,976	203,045	217,029	209,913	198,613	162,339

Table1.8c. Rice export in metric tons (Mt)

Rice Exports - Qty (Mt)	Year							
	1995	1996	1997	1998	1999	2000	2001	2002
Australia	541,848	566,508	654,603	551,775	668,591	621,666	615,223	330,941
Bangladesh	58	0	56	105	170	700	1,500	561
China	235,934	356,854	1,009,916	3,791,615	2,819,010	3,070,644	2,011,320	2,067,839
India	4,913,156	2,511,974	2,388,788	4,962,941	1,895,250	1,532,598	2,193,736	5,053,242
Japan	12,568	43	35,851	358,178	143,953	42,148	560,586	23,903
Mexico	630	1,887	1,921	7,471	8,726	323	1,150	742
Myanmar	353,800	92,330	28,300	120,400	54,319	251,400	939,100	730,300
Thailand	6,197,990	5,454,350	5,567,519	6,537,492	6,838,900	6,141,356	7,685,051	7,337,561
United States of America	3,083,609	2,640,356	2,296,002	3,112,693	2,668,066	2,736,462	2,622,087	3,266,872

Table1.8d. Rice Export in dollar value

Rice Exports - Val (1000$)	Year							
	1995	1996	1997	1998	1999	2000	2001	2002
Australia	215,470	243,816	281,623	225,783	268,122	229,424	184,893	86,276
Bangladesh	37	0	25	69	130	500	400	242
China	56,486	137,047	277,892	936,071	674,592	578,271	351,517	392,271
India	1,416,104	888,260	910,169	1,507,380	726,056	655,458	706,828	1,212,481
Japan	2,830	344	9,503	143,307	65,840	13,610	933,412	5,808
Mexico	309	1,075	1,194	2,047	2,261	292	554	407
Myanmar	77,370	20,879	6,032	26,354	10,319	31,970	111,607	107,390
Thailand	1,951,828	1,999,922	2,157,457	2,097,924	1,950,411	1,638,431	1,578,213	1,531,963
United States of America	996,530	1,031,043	932,432	1,208,368	945,483	835,996	717,457	775,301

In Table 1.9, the data of total rice availability represent the quantity of rice that is available for national consumption. It is the net value of total production plus imports (including the donors' aid), then minus exports and seed-feed-wastage. Interestingly, it is expressed in terms of kilogram per capita. This is the most important data that we should be concerned with. I have presented a 10-year data and worked out the mean and its standard variation, which is the indicator of variation in the given course of time. As the standard deviation is less than 4 in Bangladesh, and less than 6 in Myanmar in a course of 10 years it is reasonable to accept that the rice availability is scrupulously maintained almost constant in terms of per capita consumption in both countries. Therefore, I will be using this figure as the basis for calculating the future need of rice in these two countries. Bangladesh rice availability can also be found in the Bangladesh Bureau of Statistics website, http://www.bangladesh.gov.bd/mof/availability.html. Myanmar government has no statistics website.

Table1.9. Table showing total rice availability											
	Rice (Milled Equivalent) Availability Supply/Cap/Yr (Kg)										
Countries	Year										
	1992	1993	1994	1995	1996	1997	1998	1999	2000	2001	Mean($\pm$SD)
Australia	5.6	6.2	6.7	7.2	8.1	8.2	8	8.2	9	9.5	7.67($\pm$1.23)
Bangladesh	156.3	151.3	155.3	146.1	152.8	156.3	158.6	154.6	156.5	155.2	154.3($\pm$3.52)
China	94.3	93.2	90.9	91.3	92.1	91.6	90.7	90	89.2	86.4	90.97($\pm$2.18)
India	78.8	73.1	75.3	81.2	75.8	78.8	74	75.4	75.7	76.3	76.44($\pm$2.46)
Japan	64.2	63.7	61	62.5	61.9	61.4	60	59.9	59.4	58.5	61.25($\pm$1.86)
Mexico	4.5	4.8	5.2	4.6	5.5	5.6	5.3	5.6	5.7	5.4	5.22($\pm$0.44)
Myanmar	213.6	214.3	215	213.3	214	212.1	214.6	207.3	206.1	197	210.73($\pm$5.73)
Thailand	109.8	106.2	107.7	108.1	106.8	106.2	108.1	108.5	109	108.9	107.93($\pm$1.21)
United States	7.4	7	7.7	8.3	7.9	8.3	8.5	9	9.2	9.2	8.25($\pm$0.76)

Now let us do some calculation to project the need for paddy and rice in 2015 and 2025, the years in which I predict an apocalypse could occur.

On the basis of the average (i.e. Mean) rice consumption calculated in the above table, it is reasonable to conclude that Bangladesh needs 154 Kg, or 0.154 Mt, of rice (i.e. milled rice) per person per year.

In the year **2015** with 183.2 million expected population, the rice demand in Bangladesh will be:

183.2M x 0.154 Mt = 28,212,800 Mt.

Please remember that I have mentioned 65% yield of rice when we mill the paddy a few pages earlier. Therefore, the need of paddy production in Bangladesh will be:

(28,212,800 Mt ÷ 65) x 100 = 43,404,307.69 Mt.

Similarly, in **2025** with 211 million expected population, the projected figures will be:

211 M x 0.154 Mt = 32,494,000 Mt. for the rice, and

(32,494,000 Mt ÷ 65) x 100 = 49,990,769.23 Mt for the paddy.

Figure 1.2c, showing the projected population at medium fertility variant in Bangladesh and Myanmar, is reproduced in the next page for the sake of convenient of reference.

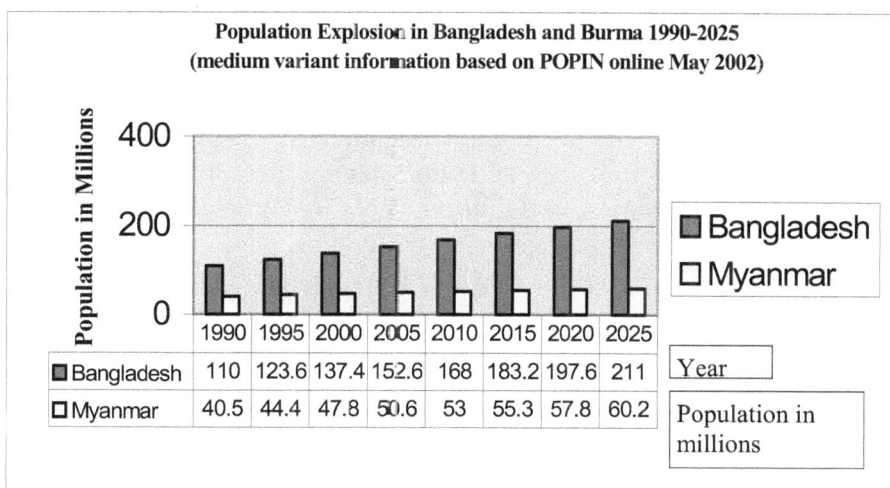

Figure1.2c. Population explosion at medium fertility variant in Bangladesh and Myanmar with projection up to 2025

1.12. Will Bangladesh be able to produce the needed rice in 2015 and 2025?

From Tables 1.7a,b, and c we can see that the increase in 2003 total rice production is a combined result of an increase in harvested area (i.e. 11.90% up from the 1994 value) augmented by the increase in yield (i.e. 35.57% up from the 1994 value). Please note harvested area is different from cultivated area. All cultivated area may not reach harvesting stage due to damage caused by flood or draught. If Bangladesh can technologically and financially come up to the standard yield of average 6 Mt/ha like China and Japan we can expect a total production at 66,600,000 Mt per year, provided that the harvested area remains the same as 2003.

i.e. harvested area 11.1 Million hectares x yield 6 Mt/ha

= 66,600,000 Mt total production.

If this is so, we do not have to worry about the shortage of food. Only two concerns namely (1) poverty, including the cost of rice production, and (2) overcrowding, including the shrinkage of agricultural land, have to be addressed. The big question, however, is:

"Can Bangladesh achieve this goal?"

"No, Bangladesh cannot achieve this goal". This is my answer because Bangladesh, in order to achieve this goal, will need three factors:

1. Technological innovation such as invention of higher yield rice variety, mechanization of farming, and fertilizer-pesticide application with due environmental values.

2. Chinese political will such as one-family-one-child, and

3. Japanese techno-economical discipline. For example the Japanese scientific output is coming ahead of the traditional scientific power houses such as Russia, France, and Germany, though still behind the United States and United Kingdom. The Japanese industries put 64% of their money into R&D whereas the US industries invest only 32% (Arthur J. Alexander, "Basic research and science in Japanese economy", Japan Economic Institute Report No. 11, March 21, 1997, http://www.jei.org/Archive/JEIR97/9711f.html#comparative). Japanese industries are free of production disruption due to labor problems or political instability in the known industrial history.

Based on the experience of the past 50 years, I do not believe that Bangladesh will acquire these impetuses in the next 50 years. Could it then be possible to overcome this technological and economical weakness by means of extending the area of the farm land? In other words, if the yield per hectare per se cannot be increased, will it be possible to increase the cultivated area, hence the harvested area, and thus total production?

My answer to this question is a definitive "no". In Bangladesh, nearly 70% of the land area of the country has been brought under crop cultivation. More than two-thirds of the land is double- or triple-cropped. The harvested rice area is about 105% of the arable land.
Let us look into this matter more closely. Bangladesh has a:
1. Total area of 144,000 square kilometers,
2. Land area of 133,910 square kilometers, and
3. Water area of 10,090 square kilometers, with 250 rivers.

A crop land 70% of the total land area means 93,737 square kilometers, leaving behind a residential land area of 41,073 square kilometers. Squeezed in this residential area of 41,073 square kilometers will be a population of 183.16 million in the year 2015 and 210.82 million in the year 2025, provided that population increases at the medium fertility variant. Please refer back to Figures 1.2s and 1.3s. When we consider only the residential land area we get a population density (i.e. persons per square kilometer) of 4,459 in the year 2015 and 5,133 in the year 2025. Now please compare these figures with those 1,272 for the year 2015 and 1,464 for the year 2025 of Figure1.3c. In the light of this microscopic analysis, you can vividly figure out how grave the situation will be in coming years. **The main concern is that we may be losing up to 40% of total land area that would include 15% of coastal land area and 25% of inland flood plains due to the greenhouse effect or global warming. There virtually is no chance of increasing the crop land area.** Now, let us study the prospective fate of Bangladesh in the scope of global warming, which is being augmented by global dimming.

In the website of the United Nations-Food and Agricultural Organization (UN-FAO) , there posted in March 1998 an interesting article on the *"Potential Impacts of Sea-Level Rise on Populations and Agriculture"* by FAO officials R. Gommes, J. du Guerny, F. Nachtergaele and R. Brinkman, at http://www.fao.org/sd/eidirect/eire0047.htm. The following map clipped from the article shows the possible loss of the coastal area along the Indian Ocean. It appears that the sea will drown the entire country of Bangladesh. Some environmental scientists have warned that the entire country of Bangladesh could become boat-people floating in the Bay of Bengal looking for a dry spot to land. The FAO scholars wrote global warming will "seriously affect the major deltas, such as the Ganges-Brahmaputra, Mekong and Nile. In both the cases of deltas and

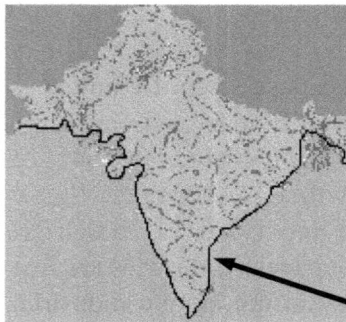

small islands, a likely scenario could be out migration when disasters due to sea-level rise reach levels or frequencies considered unacceptable. It is at such thresholds that maximum damage and loss of life could be expected". You can get this article from the Food and Agriculture Organization of the United Nations (FAO),   Viale delle Terme di Caracalla, 00100   Rome, Italy, or from the FAO website cited here.

The black line along the India Subcontinent on the map shows predicted lost of the coastal area along the Indian Ocean with the sea level rise.

The rise of sea level is not the only concern. Heavy monsoons, melting of Himalayan ice caps, overflowing of the river basins, erosion, and the subsequent loss of land mass also constitute grave concern for Bangladesh. While I am writing this chapter Bangladesh is inundated with severe flood. In the map from the Bangladesh government website shown below, it can be easily seen that more than 30% of the country is inundated.

This map is as of August 03, 2004 showing the flood situation in Bangladesh. (Source: Government of Bangladesh, Ministry of Water Resources, Flood Forecasting and Warning Center, http://www.ffwc.net). The legends are mine.

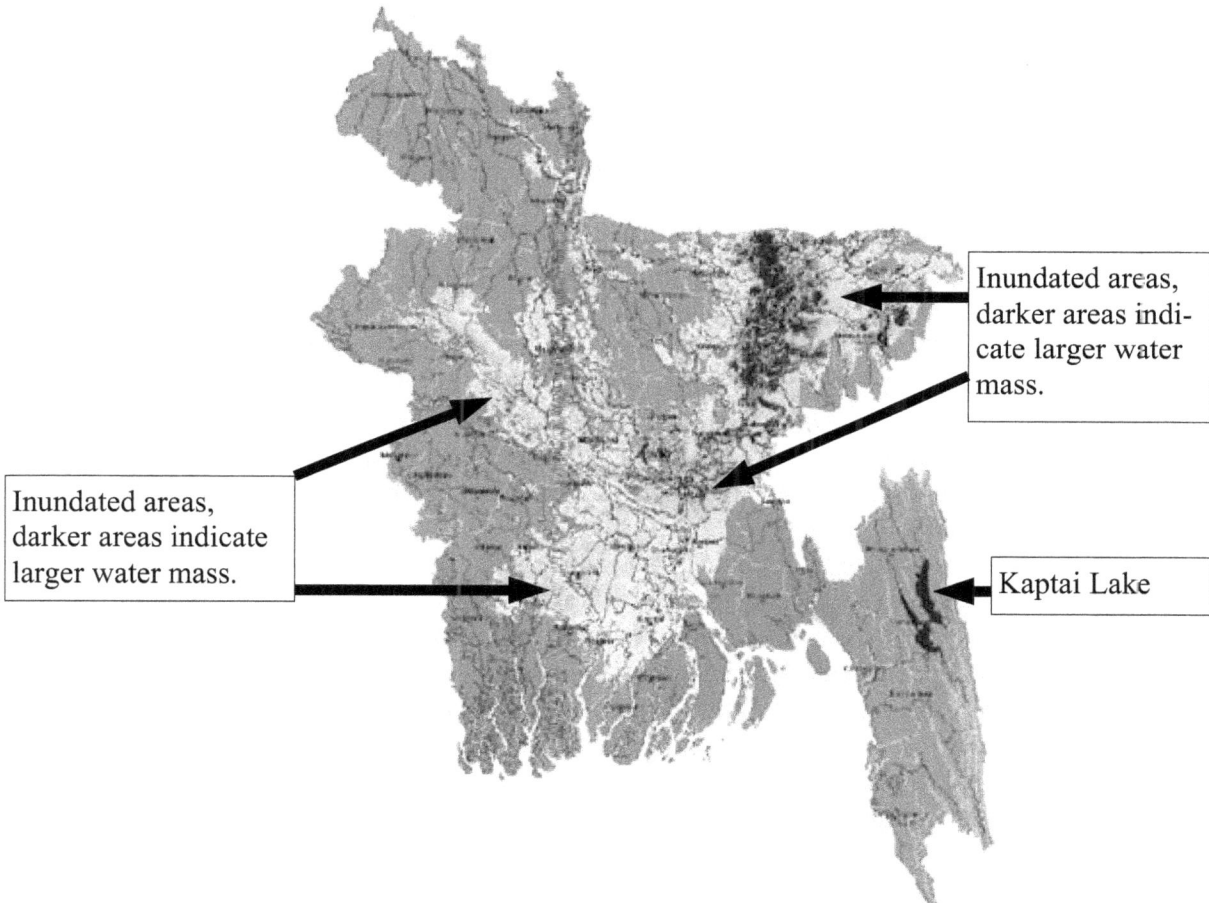

Inundated areas, darker areas indicate larger water mass.

Inundated areas, darker areas indicate larger water mass.

Kaptai Lake

The 2004 flood is characterized by the following disasters.

1. As many as 30 million people in Bangladesh, hit by the worst floods in six years, will need food aid for the next five months, according to a report of the Minister for Food and Disaster Management, Chowdhury Kamal Ibne Yousuf. {Dhaka (AFP) Aug. 03, 2004, http://www.terradaily.com/2004/040803094924.dwe5xh8u.html}. AFP stands for Agence France-Presse.

2. Health Directorate officials said that a total of 1,10,599 people have contacted diarrhoea and 58 of them died as of July 12. The number of the affected people is rising everyday. {The Bangladesh Observer, August 09, 2004, http://www.bangladeshobserveronline.com/new/2004/08/09/front.htm#head2}.

3. The U.N. World Food Programme has assessed the damage bill to farms, factories and infrastructure from the floods, at $7 billion with more than 10 million Bangladeshis homeless.{Dhaka, Aug 6 (Reuters), 2004, http://www.reliefweb.int/w/rwb.nsf}.

4. The floods submerged more than 24,000 square kilometers in 40 out of 64 administrative districts. About three million homes were destroyed, 49,000 kilometers of roads broken, 2,500 kilometers of river embankments damaged, and 4,300 small bridges and culverts washed away by the flood waters. One million hectares of rice, the country's staple food, was also lost in the floods.{Dhaka (dpa), August 05, 2004, http://www.reliefweb.int/w/rwb.nsf}. DPA stands for Deutsche Presse Agentur.

Now, let us analyze two main concerns of these characteristics in the context of the years 2015 and 2025.

1. As many as 30 million people are affected. As of July 2004 total Bangladesh population is estimated to be around 141.3 million (source: CIA Factbook, http://www.cia.gov/cia/publications/factbook/geos/bg.html). Therefore, about 21.2% of the total population is affected by the flood. At this affected percentage, some 32 million people will be affected in the year 2015, when the population will be 152.6 million. The figure will be 44 million in 2025 when her population will hit the 211 million mark. These numbers are as big as the entire national population of several countries including Algeria, Canada, Kenya, Iraq, Malaysia, Saudi Arabia, Spain, Venezuela, and many times larger than the populations of Australia, Central American nations and Scandinavian countries. It is not a small number to ignore.

2. The severe floods submerge 24,000 square kilometers or 16.7% of the total Bangladesh area of 144,000 square kilometers for more than two months, from June to August. This is the peak season for the paddy growing. Furthermore, the frequency of severe flood is increasing with narrower intervals. In recent decades, severe floods have occurred in 1988, 1998, and now 2004.

The size of the affected population and inundated area could be doubled with the 15% loss of the coastal area in the second and third decades of this century. If this comes true the disaster will be beyond our imagination. It will be an apocalypse. It is even likely that Bangladesh might happen to join the myth of Atlantis and her people evolve into mermaids and mermen. Hopefully this may not happen till next century, when the sea level is expected to rise more than one meter.

3. In national economy, an estimated damage of $7 billion incurred in about 3 months is a fatal blow for Bangladesh whose gross national income is only about $54 billion, in contrast to $10.4 trillion of USA. Please note a Bangladeshi earns only $1.00 whenever an American earns $192.00, in an approximate comparison. If we ponder how much investment in terms of resources such as money, technology, labor, and time will be needed to fix the damage, we may end up with a nightmare.

I may happen to exaggerate the situation, but I would like to present to you some more information, just for your consideration.

"Sea level is rising more rapidly along the U.S. coast than worldwide. Studies by EPA and others have estimated that along the Gulf and Atlantic coasts, a one foot (30 cm) rise in sea level is likely by 2050 and could occur as soon as 2025. In the next century, a two foot rise is most likely, but a four foot rise is possible; and sea level will probably continue to rise for several centuries, even if global temperatures were to stop rising a few decades hence (see Sea Level in the Climate System section)". This concern is brought up by the US Environmental

Protection Agency, a conservative industrialist organization , at its website http://yosemite.epa.gov/OAR/globalwarming.nsf/content/ImpactsCoastalZones.html, as of March 2004. Please contrast a *conservative industrialist* from *a progressive conservationist*.

"The United Nations Secretary General, Kofi Annan, has warned that a rise in sea level could lead to the disappearance of much of the world's largest delta, Bangladesh. Mr. Annan said a recent report by the United Nations Panel on Climate Change, predicted more extreme droughts, floods and storms and the inundation of low-lying islands and coastal areas could lead to the displacement of hundreds of millions of people". This quotation is from http://www.un.org/News/ossg/sg/index.shtml, as of October 12, 2003.

Mr. Annan may have a point in his concern. The following information substantiates Mr. Annan's concern. The excerpt is from Bangladesh Environment Network, http://www.ben-center.org/flood_essay.htm, as of August 08, 2004.

"Bangladesh is a Delta"

"The fundamental physical fact regarding Bangladesh is that, together with West Bengal, it constitutes a delta. While most other deltas are creation of single river, (like the deltas of the Nile, Mississippi, Yangtze, etc.), the Bengal delta is the creation of three mighty rivers, namely the Ganges, the Brahmaputra, and the Meghna. This makes the dimensions of Bengal delta simply enormous. To have some comparative perspective, we may note the following facts:
* The combined catchment basin of the Ganges, the Brahmaputra, and the Meghna measures 1,758,000 square kilometers, which is more than 12 times the size of Bangladesh.
* The amount of rainfall in the catchment basin of the Bengal rivers is more than four times the rainfall in the Mississippi basin, although in terms of area the former is less than half of the latter.
* The amount of sediment carried annually by the rivers of the Bengal delta is about two billion tons. This is far more than any other river system anywhere in the world.
* Under average conditions, from June to September, 775 billion cubic meters of water flow into Bangladesh through the main rivers and an additional 184 billion cubic meters of streamflow is generated by rainfall in Bangladesh. This may be compared with the annual flow of only 12 billion cubic meters of the Colorado River at Yuma, Arizona, US.
* The combined channel of the Ganges, Brahmaputra, and Meghna is about three times the size of the Mississippi.

These numbers clearly show what a massive hydraulic system is at work in the Bengal delta. It is this gigantic scale of delta formation process that one has to take into account before thinking of any intervention into this system."

We cannot ignore the fact that global warming is a sabotage to the Bengal delta formation that might result in the disappearance of Bangladesh. Recently, the effect of the global dimming has emerged. We are just beginning to learn the syngergistic action of the global dimming on the global envirnmental changes. If desire to learn more, the reader may visit http://news.bbc.co.uk/2/hi/science/nature/4171591.stm and http://www.globalissues.org/EnvIssues/GlobalWarming/globaldimming.asp. Beyond doubt, the situation in Bangladesh poses the greatest challenge to mankind in terms of humanitarianism as well as science and technology.

1.13. Chapter One Overview

I have presented more emphasis on Bangladesh than Myanmar. This is because Bangladesh faces more serious concerns of population explosion and environmental disasters than Myanmar. Her political, cultural, educational, scientific and technological institutions, systems, and management stand on foundation of reasonable strength, and carry promises. On the other hand, Myanmar has a manageable population size, great deal of natural resources, and favorable environmental conditions. However, her political, cultural, educational, scientific and technological institutions, systems, and management are poor in foundation and show great deterioration. I have highlighted these points in my earlier book *Burma: Nationalism and Ideology*, University Press Ltd., Dhaka, 1989. The situation in Myanmar has not improved, but is getting worse in recent years, as presented in this chapter. Therefore, I can comfortably conclude that Bangladesh and Myanmar have (1) no sufficient income to support their peoples, (2) no sufficient food to feed their peoples, and that (3) the weakness of Bangladesh is due to her lack of sufficient natural and technological resources whereas, in the case of Myanmar, it is mainly due to mismanagement. As a result, both countries fail to overcome the political and economical disasters which are bringing them down. Eventually, the oncoming natural calamities will draw them into the whirlpool of an apocalypse.

The earlier scholars of India's history and anthropology suggest that there was an Aryan invasion some time around 1500 years before Jesus Christ was born. This view is being refuted by a number of modern scholars. According to the scholars of Burma's history the Mongolian tribes invaded Irrawady plains in ancient days of unknown date. I believe these southward invasions of the northern peoples, if at all true, took place during the last glacial period, some 10,000 years ago. European invasions of America and Australia in the form of massive migration is very recent. It is therefore very realistic to conclude that there will be a massive migration of the Bangladeshi people in their struggle for existence. You may call it migration, immigration, resettlement, exodus, refuge or pilgrimage. In the bottom line, whatever it may be termed, it is a form of invasion because it is always accompanied by violence and war.

The question now is:
1. Where will they invade?
2. How will they invade?

I believe you have heard of the communal riots between the Bengalis and the locals in Assam, India. Have you heard of the news that the Indian government is erecting a barbed-wire fence along the India-Bangladesh border to deter illegal immigration from her neighbor? You have heard the news that Myanmar military government has been driving out the people known as the Rohingyas accusing them of being illegal Bengali immigrants!

This gives us a clear idea of the invasion target. Nevertheless, more exciting question is:
What will be the strategies and tactics of invasion?
Let us examine these questions in the coming chapters.

Similarly, in every move, big or small, there is a form of organization and an underlying strategy with planned tactics. Due to the uncontrolled population explosion, economic disaster, and natural calamities there will be an out migration of Bangladeshis. This prediction is advancing towards higher probability year after year. As a matter of fact, this topic has become a common discussion both in Bangladesh and Myanmar among concerned authorities as well as the commoners. The consensus in Bangladesh is that the people will just go where the land and the hope is; there is no way the government will be able to control or prevent it. This does sound like a universal truth. In such an out migration of the Bangladeshi people, majority of which are Muslims, it is quite natural that they will be guided by their religion, Islam. Accordingly, Islam will be the basis of their strategies and tactics. It is most likely that an Islamic Commune will emerge in the style of the 1871 Paris Commune.

On the side of Myanmarese, a national solidarity and defense system has been strengthening under renewed Myanmarism.

I will be presenting the features and characteristics of Bangladeshi Islam and Myanmarism in the coming chapters.

Lily Pond Parable (Magic Lily)

In my school days, following the common practice of the mathematics teachers, Sara U Shwe Mra introduced the Lily Pond Parable in our class of Standard 7, before the beginning of the algebra lessons in 1957. It is a parable, but it is asked as a mental question in the school as follows.

There was a large pond, but one single lily plant with one flower was there. The King saw it and told his Minister that the large pond looked very empty with only one lily. We have a saying that *a pond's beauty is its Lilies.* Consequently, the Minister asked the Pond Caretaker to populate the pond with more lilies. Next morning, the Pond Caretaker went to the pond and gave a shake at the lily, asking, "Why are you not multiplying?" To his surprise the lily doubled up. Now there were two lilies. With amazement he shook it again, but nothing happen. Next day, he came to the pond and shook the lilies and they again double up. Now there were four lilies. These are the magic lilies that double up with each shake, but only one multiplication per day. In that manner, after fifteen days, half of the pond became filled with lilies. The question is how many days more the Pond Caretaker has to shake to fill up the entire pond with lilies? The answer is given at the end of the parable.*

With the question, the parable ends in a classroom. However, in our Rakhaing tradition the parable continues as below.

Next day, the King came for the inspection of the pond without any prior notice and the Pond Caretaker was glad that he was at the pond. The King was amazed to see one half of the pond filled with lilies.

"What happened?" He asked the Pond Caretaker with an air of disbelief. The Pond Caretaker answered him that it was a magic lily and each day he just had to shake it to multiply in double. With curiosity the king asked him to shake it in his presence. The Pond Caretaker followed His Majesty's order and lo - with one shake, the whole lake was filled with water lilies.

As the king's party looked at the pond and lilies with awe and fear the King said, "Now, my water pond is useless with all these lilies. Get rid of them."

Eventually, the lilies were cleaned up except for a few to beautify the pond. The parable ends here with the following sayings.

"Lily destroys the pond whereas pleasure destroys the wisdom." This saying is a balance of "Lily beautifies the pond whereas wisdom beautifies a person."

ကန်၏ ကြက်သဆေ မှာ ကြာ၊ လူ၏ ကြက်သဆေ မှာ အလိမ္မာ
ကန် ကိုဖျက် ကြာ၊ အလိမ္မာ ကိုဖျက် တဏှာ

We were told by our parents and elders that this parable was a part of the royal syllabus in teaching the young princes and princesses to check the beauty and pleasure that are bound to destroy their worthiness. In the World Wide Web I found the lily pond parable in a variant form of the magic lily parable that I learned in my native land, Rakhaingpray. Interestingly, it is used in population study because of its exponential function. You may visit the websites:

http://www.mnforsustain.org/erickson_d_pond_lilly_parable.htm,
http://www.ecofuture.org/pop/facts/exponential70.html,
http://www.susps.org/why/lily.html. etc.

* **One day**. (Remember the lily responds to the shake only once a day).

بِسْمِ اللَّهِ الرَّحْمَٰنِ الرَّحِيمِ

بِسْمِ اللَّهِ الرَّحْمَٰنِ الرَّحِيمِ ۝ الْحَمْدُ لِلَّهِ رَبِّ الْعَالَمِينَ ۝ الرَّحْمَٰنِ الرَّحِيمِ ۝ مَالِكِ يَوْمِ الدِّينِ ۝ إِيَّاكَ نَعْبُدُ وَإِيَّاكَ نَسْتَعِينُ ۝ اهْدِنَا الصِّرَاطَ الْمُسْتَقِيمَ ۝ صِرَاطَ الَّذِينَ أَنْعَمْتَ عَلَيْهِمْ غَيْرِ الْمَغْضُوبِ عَلَيْهِمْ وَلَا الضَّالِّينَ ۝

THE EXORDIUM[1]

IN THE NAME OF ALLAH
THE COMPASSIONATE
THE MERCIFUL
Praise be to Allah, Lord of Creation,
The compassionate, the Merciful,
King of Judgement-day!
You alone we worship, and to you alone we pray for help,
Guide us to the straight path,
The path of those whom you have favoured,
Not of those who have incurred Your wrath,

Chapter 2. Pan-Islam and Islamic Expansionism

Allah created humans. Mankind is one nation. Those who have gone astray divided mankind into different nations. It is the duty of the Faithfuls to reunite them as one nation under Allah. The religion of Allah is Islam. The Faithfuls are called the Muslims meaning those who have submitted to the call of Allah through his last Prophet Mohammed, reciting the oath of allegiance 'There is only one God, Allah and Mohammed is His Messenger' (*La illaha illalahu, Mohammed ur Rasulu'Allah).* This is the theological philosophy that forms the foundation of Pan-Islam since the time it was born some 1,400 years ago.

As you can see it is a very simple philosophy, nothing extraordinary or different from other religious ambitions of the Christians or the Buddhists. Interestingly, the Hindus do not have the ambition of converting the world to their religion.

With this strength of plain Pan-Islamic philosophy, the Faithfuls have been expanding Islam since the time their Prophet summoned them to the call of Allah in circa 610 CE. The spread of Islam is dramatic and dynamic. Rather than giving the past history I present a summary

---

Notes.
1. The Arabic version of Al-Fatiha or the Exordium, which is the opening verse (1:7) of Qur'an is taken from http://www.islamicity.com/mosque/arabicscript/1/1.htm. The English version of Qur'anic verses 1:1 and 1:7 are from *The Koran*, by N.J. Dawood, Penguin Books, 1974. You may may compare Dawood's translation with that of Yusuf Ali, which is considered the standard English version by most Muslims.

of the Islamic expansion in the map below. We shall better focus on the events of recent past and recent days. Please note that the westward expansion of Islam was stopped by the Crusades in the 12th century and its expansion in Asia was paused by the arrival of the western powers that weakened the Mogul Muslim Empire. The Moguls seized Chittagong of Arakan Empire in circa 1666 CE and failed to make any further advancement beyond that point.

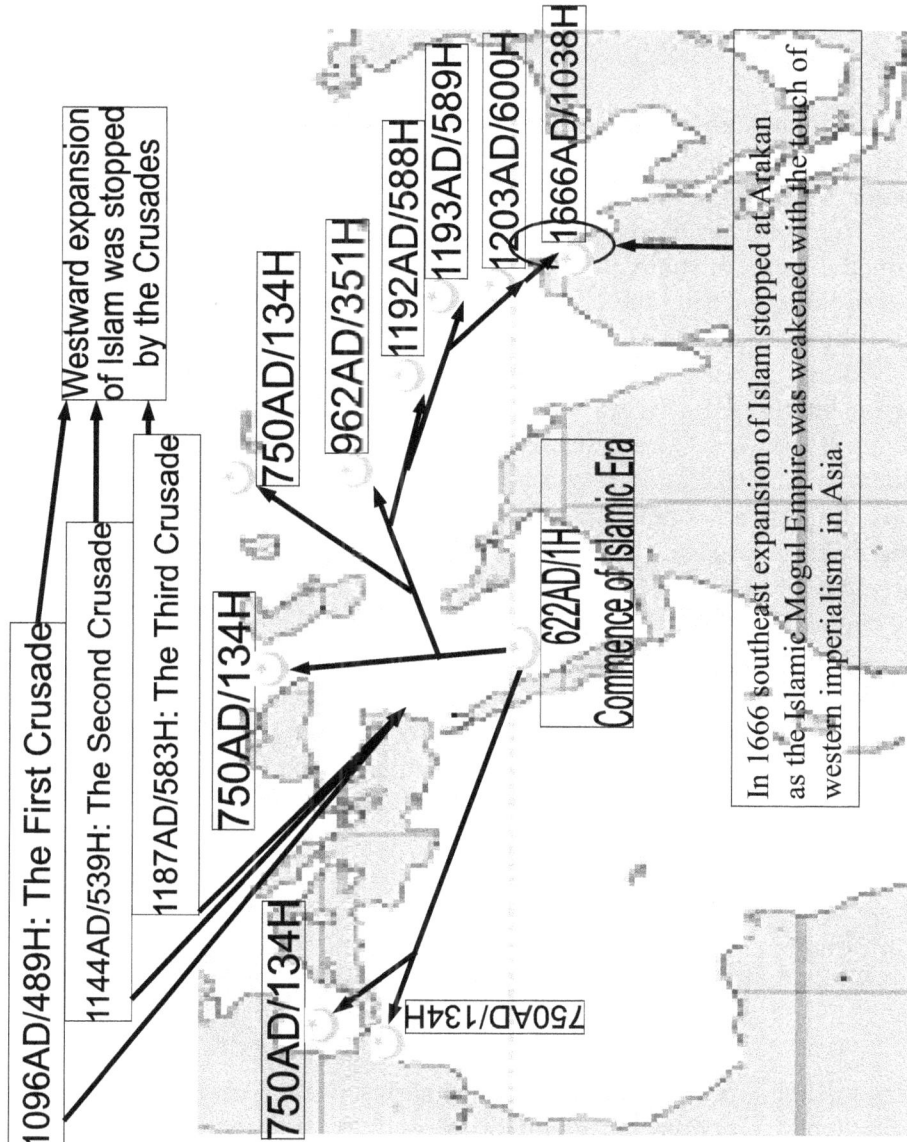

The advancement of Islamic Expansionism

- 1096AD/489H: The First Crusade
- 1144AD/539H: The Second Crusade
- 1187AD/583H: The Third Crusade

Westward expansion of Islam was stopped by the Crusades

750AD/134H
962AD/351H
1192AD/588H
1193AD/589H
1203AD/600H
1666AD/1038H

750AD/134H
750AD/134H
750AD/134H
750AD/134H

622AD/1H: Commence of Islamic Era

In 1666 southeast expansion of Islam stopped at Arakan as the Islamic Mogul Empire was weakened with the touch of western imperialism in Asia.

2.1. Jihad. *Jihad* is the force behind the Islamic expansionism, whereas Pan-Islam is the governing philosophy. When Jihad is compounded to the simple governing philosophy Pan-Islam becomes a sophisticated doctrine. Therefore we must know what Jihad is to its fullest meaning. We will begin with a simple, then advance to a complex definition.

In recent days there have been many definitions of Jihad. I shall try to present them to the best of my understanding through my experience. The numbers given in parenthesis, e.g. (2:256), represent Qur'anic verse number.

Let us begin with Information 1 that is an excerpt from http://www.unn.ac.uk/societies/islamic/jargon/keycon1.htm#JIHAD. The authors are Muslims, probably British Muslims.

Information 1

" JIHAD"

"It is an Arabic word the root of which is Jahada, which means to strive for a better way of life. The nouns are Juhd, Mujahid, Jihad, and Ijtihad. The other meanings are: endeavor, strain, exertion, effort, diligence, fighting to defend one's life, land, and religion.

This word has been in frequent use in the Western press over the past several years, explained directly or subtly, to mean holy war. As a matter of fact the term "holy war" was coined in Europe during the Crusades, meaning the war against Muslims. It does not have a direct counterpart in the Islamic glossary, and Jihad is certainly not its translation.

Jihad is not a war to force faith on others, as many people think...... It should never be interpreted as a way of compulsion of the belief on others, since there is an explicit verse in the Qur'an that says: "There is no compulsion in religion" Al-Qur'an: Al-Baqarah (2:256).

Jihad is not a defensive war only, but a war against any unjust regime. If such a regime exists, a war is to be waged against the leaders, but not against the people of that country. People should be freed from the unjust regimes and influences so that they can freely choose to believe in Allah.

Not only in peace but also in war Islam prohibits terrorism, kidnapping, and hijacking, when carried against civilians. Whoever commits such violations is considered a murderer in Islam, and is to be punished by the Islamic state. During wars, Islam prohibits Muslim soldiers from harming civilians, women, children, elderly, and religious men, like priests and rabbis. It also prohibits cutting down trees and destroying civilian constructions.

The term may be used for/by Muslims as well as non-Muslims".

Information 2 below is from www.unn.ac.uk/societies/islamic/jargon/jihad1.htm. The authors are the Muslims, probably the British Muslims.

Information 2

"The word Jihad means striving. In its primary sense it is an inner thing, within self, to rid it from debased actions or inclinations, and exercise constancy and perseverance in achieving a higher moral standard. Since Islam is not confined to the boundaries of the individual but extends to the welfare of society and humanity in general, an individual cannot keep improving himself/herself in isolation from what happens in their community or in the world at large, hence the Quranic injunction to the Islamic nation to take as a duty "to enjoin good and forbid evil." (3:104) It is a duty which is not exclusive to Muslims but applies to the human race who are, according to the Qur'an, God's vicegerent on earth. Muslims, however, cannot shirk it even if others do. The means to fulfil it are varied, and in our modern world encompass all legal, diplomatic, arbitrative, economic, and political instruments. But Islam does not exclude the use of force to curb evil, if there is no other workable alternative. A forerunner of the collective security principle and collective intervention to stop aggression, at least in theory, as manifested in the United Nations Charter, is the Quranic reference "..make peace between them (the two fighting groups), but if one of the two persists in aggression against the other, fight the aggressors until they revert to God's commandment." (49:9) ......"

I also present here Information 3 from *"Jihad in the Qur'an and Sunnah"* by Sheikh Abdullah bin Muhammad bin Humaid, published by Maktaba Dar-us-Salam, Publishers and Distributors, P.0. Box 21441, Riyadh 11475, Tel.4033962-Fax:4021659, Kingdom of Saudi Arabia. This is a big article, very elaborate and covers all Qu'ranic and Sunna scripture. Essential excerpts from the online version at http://www.islamworld.netjiad.html are presented to readers here.

Information 3

"In this article, Sheikh Abdullah bin Muhammad bin Humaid, ex-Chief Justice of Saudi Arabia, has presented Jihad in the light of Qur'an and Sunna. Never before such an article was seen, describing Jihad in its true colours-so heart evoking and encouraging! May Allah bless him with all His Blessings for all times.
Dr. Muhammad Muhsin Khan, the translator of the Noble Qur'an and the Sahih Al-Bukhari, has translated this article from Arabic to the English language with all its fervor and feelings. May Allah reward him with the best of His Rewards.
We are publishing this article and recommend every Muslim not only read it himself but offer every other Muslim brother within his read.
May Allah shower His Blessings on everyone of us- Ameen !"

"JIHAD IN THE QUR'AN AND SUNNA"

"Praise be to Allah (swt) Who has ordained Al-Jihad (the holy fighting in Allah's Cause):
1. With the heart (intentions or feelings),
2. With the hand (weapons, etc.),
3. With the tongue (speeches, etc., in the Cause of Allah)
Allah has rewarded the one who performs it with lofty dwellings in the Gardens (of Paradise)"......

........"The (pagan) Arabs and Jews had formed a united front against them (Muhammad pbuh and his followers) and had put up all their efforts of enmity, standing and fighting against them... and (in fact) they shouted against them from every corner. Then, at that time Allah permitted them (Muhammad pbuh and his followers) the (Jihad) fighting but He did not make it obligatory. He said: "Permission to fight is given to those (i.e. believers against disbelievers) who are fighting them (and) because they (disbelievers) have been wronged, and surely Allah is able to give them (believers) victory. Those who have been expelled from their homes unjustly only because they said:"Our Lord is Allah." (V.22:39,40). ...."

(Note: This describes Allah's granting of Jihad to the believers).

.... "Allah wants from His worshippers obedience with all their efforts. **As in His Statement:**

"So when you meet (in fight... Jihad in Allah's Cause) those who disbelieve smite at their necks till when you have killed and wounded many of them, then bind a bond firmly (on them, i.e. take them as captives). Thereafter (is the time) either for generosity (i.e. free them without ransom) or ransom (according to what benefits Islam), until the war lays down its burden. Thus you are ordered by Allah to continue in carrying out Jihad against the disbelievers till they embrace Islam (i.e. are saved from the punishment in the Hellfire) or at least come under your protection] but if it had been Allah's Will, He Himself could certainly have punished them (without you). But (He lets you fight) in order to test you, some with others. But those who are killed in the Way of Allah, He will never let their deeds be lost. He will guide them and set right their state. And admit them to Paradise which He has made known to them (i.e. they will know their places in Paradise more than they used to know their houses in this world)." (V.47:4, 5,6)." ....

(Note: This describes the ethics of Jihad).

.... "Then after that He made (Jihad) "fighting" obligatory against all those who fight you (Muslims); not against those who didn't fight you. So Allah ordered: "And fight in the way of Allah those who fight you..." (V.2:190).

Then Allah (swt) revealed in Sarah Tauba (Bara 'a) (Repentance, IX) the order to discard (all) the obligations (covenants, etc.) and commanded the Muslims to fight against all the Mushrikun as well as against the people of the Scriptures (Jews and Christians) if they do not embrace Islam, till they pay the Jizya (a tax levied on the non-Muslims who do not embrace Islam and are under the protection of an Islamic government) with willing submission and feel themselves subdued (as it is revealed in the Verse 9:29). So they (Muslims) were not permitted to abandon "the fighting" against them (Pagans, Jews and Christians) and to reconcile with them and to suspend hostilities against them for an unlimited period while they are strong and are able to fight against them (non Muslims)."....

(Note: This describes the ordinance of Jihad as an obligatory covenant of Islam).

...... "Allah (swt) made "the fighting' (Jihad) obligatory for the Muslims and gave importance to the subject-matter of Jihad in all the Sarah (Chapters of the Qur'an) which were revealed (at Al-Madina) as in Allah's Statement: "March forth whether you are light

(being healthy, young and wealthy) or heavy (being ill, old and poor), strive hard with your wealth and your lives in the Cause of Allah. This is better for you if you but knew." (V.9:41).
And He (Allah) said: "Jihad (holy fighting in Allah's Cause) is ordained for you (Muslims) though you dislike it, and it may be that you dislike a thing which is good for you and that you like a thing which is bad for you. Allah knows but you do not know." (V.2:216) ....."
(Note: This describes the ordinance of Jihad as an obligatory covenant of Islam).

..... "Allah (swt) made "the fighting' (Jihad) obligatory for the Muslims and gave importance to the subject-matter of Jihad in all the Sarah (Chapters of the Qur'an) which were revealed (at Al-Madina) as in Allah's Statement: "March forth whether you are light (being healthy, young and wealthy) or heavy (being ill, old and poor), strive hard with your wealth and your lives in the Cause of Allah. This is better for you if you but knew." (V.9:41).
And He (Allah) said: "Jihad (holy fighting in Allah's Cause) is ordained for you (Muslims) though you dislike it, and it may be that you dislike a thing which is good for you and that you like a thing which is bad for you. Allah knows but you do not know." (V.2:216)....."
(Note: This describes the order of Allah to march and his ordinance of Jihad upon the believers).

It is also worthwhile to note the stand of Pakistan-born leading British Muslim IMAM Dr Abduljalil Sajid on Jihad. He is the IMAM of Brighton Islamic Mission and is an Executive Committee member of the World Congress of Faiths (WCF). His definition of Jihad is given below under Information 4. The information is an excerpt from a report of Warsaw freelance reporter Jonathan Luxmoore, which appeared in the National Catholic Reporter, October 5, 2001, http://www.natcath.com/NCR_Online/archives/100501/100501g.htm.

Information 4

..... " numerous verses in the Quran urging Muslims to fight and accept martyrdom -- such as Verse 73 of Sura (Chapter) 9, which calls on Muslims to "make war on the unbelievers" -- dated from the War of the Ditch in 627 A.D., and were intended to encourage Muslims loyal to Muhammad in Medina to sacrifice their lives during a Meccan campaign.
....Islamic teaching forbade the use out of context of Quranic concepts such as jihad, which was not intended to have "military connotations."
In reality, jihad means the struggle to remain a faithful Muslim by resisting the world's temptations....Islam preaches salam, or peace, and resolutely opposes violence. Taking action for glory and possessions rather than for God is against the spirit of jihad.
Verse 151 of the Quran's Sura 6 states: "You shall not kill -- for that is forbidden by God -- except for a just cause."
Meanwhile, Verse 191 of Sura 2 says: "Fight for the sake of God those that fight against you, but do not attack them first. God does not love aggressors."
Another text, Verse 32 of Sura 5 recalls God's injunction to the Israelites that "whoever killed a human being, except as punishment for murder or other villainy in the land, shall be regarded as having killed all mankind; and that whoever saved a human life

shall be regarded as having saved all mankind."

.....the verses indicated war must be waged solely in self-defense, and never against ordinary civilians who had inflicted no harm".......

I believe this much information is sufficient enough to draw a reasonable conclusion with adequate rationale. To summarize the information I have presented here it is reasonable to understand that Jihad means a 'struggle for Allah's cause'. In the religious essence, it is a strive to follow *the straight path* that is revealed in the Qur'an. The Arabic word Jihad also has a number of other meanings such as endeavor, strain, exertion, effort, diligence, fighting to defend one's life, land and religion as per information presented by the British Muslims.

The wars of Prophet Muhammad in defense of Islam and Muslims were known as Jihad. His Muslim soldiers were called Mujahids or Mujahideens. Because of this, when it is translated to English, Jihad conveniently becomes Holy War and the Mujahideens the Holy Warriors. It is romantic, and makes the blood boil to the delight of a soldier. This is politic. Here we encounter a very diffused demarcation line between religion and politics. Not only in the feudal societies of the past but also in many societies of today, there never exists a clear and solid demarcation line between religion and politics. Indeed, when religious rights are challenged it becomes politic because religion is a part and parcel of patriotism. Even in the United States of America, where *state* and *religion* are constitutionally separated, no one will ever become president unless he or she knows how to say, "God bless America." This is the area where we face the dilemma in the definition of Jihad. As long as this area remains gray the religio-political controversy of Jihad will prevail.

For those readers who have interest in the subject of the Muslims and democracy I would like to recommend to read the writings of scholars like Professor Lord Bhikhu Parekh (http://imm-live.wmin.ac.uk/sshl/page-148-smhp=1   and   http://jmm.aaa.net.au/articles/ 1690.htm), others like Abdelwahab El-Affendi, Ehsan Massod, Merryl Wyn Davies, and M. Iqbal Asaria who write articles in the journal *New Internationalist* (http://www.newint.org/ issue345/democracy.htm).

2.2. Modern Pan-Islam. During the western domination of the world Muslims struggled for freedom. Modern Pan-Islam was born at that time, in early 19th century. Jamaluddin Afgani (1839-1897?) is considered the father of Modern Pan-Islam. Who is he? Is he the originator of the Pan-Islam? When does Pan-Islam come into existence? How big is Pan-Islam today? What is Pan-Islam doing today? How is Pan-Islam doing its job? There are many questions.

Obviously this is a very big subject. Numerous books can be found under the subject old Pan-Islamism in university and college libraries. The reader is advised to go for them for more indepth information. You should also compare Pan-Islamism and Pan-Arabianism. Here I will give an adequate account of Pan-Islam to substantiate my presentation. The reader may also read Jacob M. Landau's The Politics of Pan-Islam Ideology and Organization, Clarendon Press, Oxford, 1990. His book gives a good account of Afgani's philosophy.

There is only one form of Pan-Islam whose goal is to establish **one** Muslim Nation under **one** Caliph or **one** government that answers only to one God, Allah. The Pan-Islamic Muslims (the Pan-Islamist or simply Islamist) whom I met define the stages of Pan-Islam as follow.

Stage-1. *To establish Harmony among the Muslims.*

Stage-2. *To establish Islamic States within the given political boundary. That is to transform their residential country into an Islamic State.*

Stage-3. *To establish a Commonwealth (Confederation) of the Islamic States.*

Stage-4. *To finally establish a planetary Muslim Nation (a federation or a united states) under one Caliph or under one government under the Qur'anic Laws.*

These stages of operation are based upon the Pan-Islamic philosophy that states, ***"Muslims are one nation"***. The present geopolitical boundaries are artificial and immaterial. All Muslims across the world are governed by the Qur'anic Laws and bound by the Qur'anic culture and obliged to the Qur'anic Authority. As such they are one nation under the Qur'anic laws.

Pan-Islam is this simple.

Although today scholars and academicians attribute Pan-Islamism to Jamaluddin Afghani it actually was originated by Prophet Mohammad himself. Jamaluddin Afghani was just one of many advo-

said jamaluddin afghani (1837-97)
father of pan Islamic movement
and Islamic modernization, photo1888.

I strongly recommend that you study Pan-Islam. Please do not leave it in the hands of a fistful of university/college professors because it could mean your freedom. You must also study Khilafat (i.e. the line of succession to the Prophet Muhammad). Please start with S.R. Bakshi's *Gandhi and Khilafat*, Gitanjali Publishing House, New Delhi, 1985. Professor Bahshi gives a very good account useful for beginners. This book also presents the events and treaties that make Jamāl al-Dîn al-Afghāni a hero of modern Pan-Islam. He is just one of many. Most importantly read Qur'an with your own eyes and mind, to meet Allah yourself.

jamaluddin0.jpg., posted by Dildar Dasto Khel, on 2/5/2001, 58KB.
Source: http://groups.msn.com/Pashtanaloyepashtana.msnw?action=ShowPhoto&PhotoID=50.
This is the as-it-is photo and the legend from the web site. Please note the spelling variation.

cates of Pan-Islam. The Prophet Mohammad sent his emissaries to every king and his missions to every land, demanding and asking to accept the Revelation of Allah and embrace Islam and join the Muslim Nation. These emissaries and missionaries are the Mujahids.

Let us look at the Prophet himself. Prophet Mohammad was the son of Abdullah bin Abdul-Muttalib and Amina b. Wahb. He was born in AD 570 (source: N. J. Dawood's *The Koran*, Penguin Books, 1974). His father died just before he was born and his mother followed his father in 576. Dr. Zahoor and Dr. Haq give a good biography of the Prophet. A biographical excerpt is given below from http://cyberistan.org/islamic/muhammad.html. Please note the spelling variation of Mohammad and Muhammad. Both forms are accepted.

..... "Prophet Muhammad (s) was born in 570 CE in Makkah (Bakka, Baca, Mecca). His father, Abdullah, died several weeks before his birth in Yathrib (Medinah) where he went to visit his father's maternal relatives. His mother died while on the return journey from Medinah at a place called 'Abwa' when he was six years old. He was raised by his paternal grandfather 'Abd al Muttalib (Shaybah) until the age of eight, and after his grandfather's death by Abu Talib, his paternal uncle. 'Abd al Muttalib's mother, Salma, was a native of Medinah and he was born and raised as a young boy in Medinah before his uncle Muttalib brought him to Makkah to succeed him. Many years before Muhammad's birth, 'Abd al Muttalib had established himself as an influential leader of the Arab tribe 'Quraish' in Makkah and took care of the Holy sanctuary 'Ka'bah'. Makkah was a city state well connected to the caravan routes to Syria and Egypt in the north and northwest and Yemen in the south. Muhammad was a descendant of Prophet Ismail through the lineage of his second son Kedar".

Dawood in the introduction of his book, pp9-10, described the revelation as below.

"It was his habit to retire to a cave in the mountains in order to give himself up to solitary prayer and meditation. According to Muslim tradition, one night in Ramadhan about the year 610, as he was asleep or in trance, the Angel Gabriel came to him and said 'Recite!' He replied: 'What shall I recite?' the order was repeated three times, until the angel himself said:

'Recite in the name of your Lord who created, created man from clots of blood.'

'Recite! Your Lord is the most Bountiful One, who by the pen taught man what he did not know.'

When he awoke, these words, we are told, seemed to be 'inscribed in his heart'."

According to Zahoor and Haq, "Muhammad (s) was forty when, during one of his many retreats to Mount Hira for meditation during the month of Ramadan, he received the *first revelation from the Archangel Jibril (Gabriel). On this first appearance, Gabriel (as) **said to** Muhammad: "Iqraa," meaning Read or Recite. Muhammad replied, "I cannot read," as he had not received any formal education and did not know how to read or write. The Angel Gabriel then embraced him until he reached the limit of his endurance and after releasing said: "Iqraa." Muhammad's answer was the same as before. Gabriel repeated the embrace for the third time, asked him to repeat after him and said:

"Recite in the name of your Lord who created! He created man from that which clings. Recite; and thy Lord is most Bountiful, He who has taught by the pen, taught man what he knew not."

These revelations are the first five verses of Sura 96 of the Qur'an. Thus it was in the year 610 CE the revelation began.

Muhammad (s) was terrified by the whole experience of the revelation and fled the cave of Mt. Hira [Qur'an 81:19-29]. When he reached his home, tired and frightened, he asked his wife: 'cover me, cover me,' in a blanket. After his awe had somewhat abated, his wife Khadijah asked him about the reason of his great anxiety and fear. She then assured him by saying: "Allah (The One God) will not let you down because you are kind to relatives, you speak only the truth, you help the poor, the orphan and the needy, and you are an honest man. Khadijah then consulted with her cousin Waraqa who was an old, saintly man possessing knowledge of previous revelations and scriptures. Waraqa confirmed to her that the visitor was none other than the Angel Gabriel who had come to Moses. He then added that Muhammad is the expected Prophet. Khadijah accepted the revelation as truth and was the first person to accept Islam She supported her husband in every hardship, most notably during the three-year'boycott' of the Prophet's clan by the pagan Quraish. She died at the age of sixty-five in the month of Ramadan soon after the lifting of the boycott in 620 CE." (Excerpts from Zahoor and Haq end here).

If we analyze the Islamic chronology we can see the origin of Jihad and Pan-Islam. Let us have a go at it. The following chronology is mainly based on Dawood's presentation.
1. Circa 622: The Hijra (Flight or Migration) of Mohammad and his followers to Medina, and beginning of Muslim Era.
2. Circa 624: Battle of Badr: The Quraysh defeated by the Muslims.
3. Circa 625: Battle of Uhud: The Muslims defeated.
4. Circa 626: The Jewish tribe of al-Nadhir crushed and expelled.
5. Circa 627: 'The War of the Ditch' - the Meccans' expedition against the Muslims in Medina. Attackers driven off.
6. Circa 627: The Jewish tribe of Qurayza raided by Mohammad; some 800 men beheaded (only one Jew abjuring his religion to save his life) and all the women and children sold as slaves.
7. Circa 628. The Treaty of Hudaybiyya: truce with the Quraysh, who recognize Mohammed's right to proselytize without hindrance.
8. Circa 629. The Jews of Khaybar put to sword.
9. Mohammed sends letters and messengers to the Kings of Persia, Yemen, and Ethiopia and the Emperor Heraclius, inviting them to accept Islam.
10. Circa 630. Truce broken by Quraysh. Mecca taken by Mohammed - the entire population converted, and the Ka'ba established as the religious centre of Islam.
11. Circa 631. 'The Year of Embassies' - Islam accepted by the Arabian Tribes
12. Circa 632. Mohammed's Farewell Pilgrimage to Mecca.
13. Circa 632, 8 June. Death of Mohammed, three months after his return to Medina.

This historical evidence shows that from the year 624 to 630 Prophet Muhammad was at war building a strong base for Islam. **This was Jihad**. Therefore, we have Jihad today. In the year 631, Prophet sent out his emissaries and embassies to all nooks and corners of the world. This was the beginning of Pan-Islam. **As such we have Pan-Islam today**.

In the light of the article *"Jihad in the Qur'an and Sunnah"* by Sheikh Abdullah bin Muhammad bin Humaid that I presented earlier, it is clear that Pan-Islam is a part and parcel of Jihad. At this point I believe I have presented a sufficient amount of information on Jihad and Pan-Islam. However, the question is:

How can a Muslim say no to Jihad or Pan-Islam without compromising his faith?

The above question will remain burning in the hearts and minds of the Muslims for many, many centuries to come.

The Prophet's swords shown below constitute Jihad and the Prophet's letters command Pan-Islam. Prophet is still in Charge and he is still the Commander-in-Chief.

http://www.islamicsupremecouncil.com/tabarruk/tabarrukat.htm

Mazar-e-Mubarak (Grave) of Allah's Last Messenger, Muhammad (Peace be upon him)

These are the swords of Prophet Muhammad (Peace be upon him), Topkapy museum

Gunbad-e-Khadhra (Green Tomb) in Masjid Al Nabawi Sharif in Madinah tul Munawwarah

Prophet Muhammad's (Peace be upon him) letter to Musailma bin Kazzab (Topkapy Museum, Turkey)

For Your Information (FYI)
In 1985, during my Al-Haj, I visited the Mujahids graveyard of the 627 'War of the Ditch' that is mentioned on the page 69. It is customary that every pilgrim finds time to visit these fallen Mujahids and pray for their departed souls.

2.3. Twentieth Century Pan-Islam. Establishment of the Islamic Republic of Pakistan in 1947 was the crown of Pan-Islamists achievement in the 20th century. It was dramatic and violent in par with the birth of Islam itself, some fourteen hundred years ago. It marked the end of the Christian rule across the world freeing many enslaved Muslim countries.

In its best, Pakistan is an attempt to synthesize a new Islamic political doctrine based on the foundation of a 7th century revelation with ornamented decoration of modern democracy and socialism. In one sense it is very similar to today's Myanmar Road to Democracy, which is being framed on the foundation of Buddhism.

In the coming pages I summarize the nature of the Islamic Republic of Pakistan. These are the images and information I collected from the official Pakistan government website. These are the open windows that show awakening of Pan-Islam, amidst the popularity of modern democracy and socialism. Islamic political doctrine can be easily understood from the study of the Pakistan constitution. I am presenting some relevant constitutional excerpts. The reader may visit http://www.pakistani.org/pakistan/constitution/preamble.html to read full text.

It is also interesting to know that the Muslim League that struggled for a sovereign Muslim state was formed in 1906 as the All-India Muslim League by Aga Khan III (1877-1957). One of its leaders, Muhammad Iqbal (1877–1938), was the first person to advocate a separate Muslim State with the Indian Federation. Aga Khan III was pro-British during WWII.

**Pakistan shall be a Federal Republic
to be known as
the Islamic Republic of Pakistan,
hereinafter referred to as Pakistan.
(Constitution of Pakistan, Part 1, Introductory 1.(1),**
http://www.pakistani.org/pakistan/constitution/part1.html

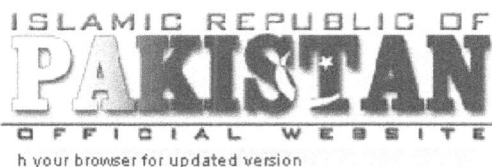

ISLAMIC REPUBLIC OF
PAKISTAN
OFFICIAL WEBSITE
h your browser for updated version

News Flash

- Govt believes in discussion and dialogue: PM [More]
- Pakistan to work for making ECO a dynamic entity: PM [More]
- Kasuri calls on ECO members to show commitment for desired objectives [More]
- Govt. believes in free media: Sheikh Rashid [More]

Photos & Cartoons

News in Brief   **Kashmir News**   **News Archive**

ELECTIONS 2002

White paper (1999-2002) - [PDF]

Father of the Nation
Quaid-i-Azam
Muhammad Ali Jinnah

President of Pakistan
General Pervez Musharraf

This web clip is from the Pakistan government official website as of November 28, 2002. For more information please visit http://www.pakistan.gov.pk/.

Constitution of Pakistan
as of 12th April, 1973

Preamble Whereas sovereignty over the entire Universe belongs to Almighty Allah alone, and the authority to be exercised by the people of Pakistan within the limits prescribed by Him is a sacred trust;

And whereas it is the will of the people of Pakistan to establish an order :-

Wherein the State shall exercise its powers and authority through the chosen representatives of the people;

Wherein the principles of democracy, freedom, equality, tolerance and social justice, as enunciated by Islam, shall be fully observed;

Wherein the Muslims shall be enabled to order their lives in the individual and collective spheres in accordance with the teachings and requirements of Islam as set out in the Holy Quran and Sunnah;

Wherein adequate provision shall be made for the minorities freely to profess and practise their religions and develop their cultures;

Wherein the territories now included in or in accession with Pakistan and such other territories as may hereafter be included in or accede to Pakistan shall form a Federation wherein the units will be autonomous with such boundaries and limitations on their powers and authority as may be prescribed;

Therein shall be guaranteed fundamental rights, including equality of status, of opportunity and before law, social, economic and political justice, and freedom of thought, expression, belief, faith, worship and association, subject to law and public morality;

Wherein adequate provision shall be made to safeguard the legitimate interests of minorities and backward and depressed classes;

Wherein the independence of the judiciary shall be fully secured;

Wherein the integrity of the territories of the Federation, its independence and all its rights, including its sovereign rights on land, sea and air, shall be safeguarded;

So that the people of Pakistan may prosper and attain their rightful and honoured place amongst the nations of the World and make their full contribution towards international peace and progress and happiness of humanity:

Now, therefore, we, the people of Pakistan,

Cognisant of our responsibility before Almighty Allah and men;

Cognisant of the sacrifices made by the people in the cause of Pakistan;

Faithful to the declaration made by the Founder of Pakistan, Quaid-i-Azam Mohammad Ali Jinnah, that Pakistan would be a democratic State based on Islamic Principles of social justice;

Dedicated to the preservation of democracy achieved by the unremitting struggle of the people against oppression and tyranny;

inspired by the resolve to protect our national and political unity and solidarity by creating an egalitarian society through a new order;

Do hereby, through our representatives in the National Assembly, adopt, enact and give to ourselves, this Constitution.

As can be seen the Pakistan constitution begins with the Arabic word "Bismillah" which means "in the name of God". Please compare this notion with the British "God save the King/Queen" and the US "this nation under God" or "in God we trust". Further, the Pakistan Constitution ,Part 1, Introductory 2, states "Islam Shall be the State religion of Pakistan". With such Islamic glory, Pakistan is the first Islamic nation to be born in modern days. She now stands strong as the only Islamic nuclear power.

The Pakistan government official document, http://www.infopak.gov.pk/Quaid/quaid_index.htm, calls the rise of the Muslims "the new awakening". It describes the process of the new awakening as follows.

"The New Awakening"

"As a result of Jinnah's ceaseless efforts, the Muslims awakened from what Professor Baker calls(their) "unreflective silence" (in which they had so complacently basked for long decades), and to "the spiritual essence of nationality" that had existed among them for a pretty long time. Roused by the impact of successive Congress hammerings, the Muslims, as Ambedkar (principal author of independent India's Constitution) says, "searched their social consciousness in a desperate attempt to find coherent and meaningful articulation to their cherished yearnings. To their great relief, they discovered that their sentiments of nationality had flamed into nationalism". In addition, not only had they developed" the will to live as a "nation", had also endowed them with a territory which they could occupy and make a State as well as a cultural home for the newly discovered nation. These two prerequisites, as laid down by Renan, provided the Muslims with the intellectual justification for claiming a distinct nationalism (apart from Indian or Hindu nationalism) for themselves. So that when, after their long pause, the Muslims gave expression to their innermost yearnings, these turned out to be in favour of a separate Muslim nationhood and of a separate Muslim state"

Further the official document states "...... 'We are a nation', they claimed in the ever eloquent words of the Quaid-i-Azam- 'We are a nation with our own distinctive culture and civilization, language and literature, art and architecture, names and nomenclature, sense of values and proportion, legal laws and moral code, customs and calendar, history and tradition, aptitudes and ambitions; in short, we have our own distinctive outlook on life and of life. By all canons of international law, we are a nation' .....".

With such awakening and demand the Islamic Republic of Pakistan was born on the 14th day of August 1947 as a sovereign Islamic state, free from the colonial yoke of the British Empire and Hindu hegemony. Today, she stands tall with her 159 million citizens as an Islamic nuclear power in this world.

The Islamic Republic of Pakistan was comprised of two wings, West Pakistan and East Pakistan, which were geographically separated 1,000 miles apart by the Hindu land of India, but firmly bound in the name of Almighty Allah. Praise be to Allah. Pan-Islam was the nationalism, and the Muslims were one nation. The birth of the Islamic Republic of Pakistan was a logical action of the British Indian Muslims in their struggle for existence. However, the Pan-Islam which they chose to adapt was found lacking essential ingredients to hold two cultures together as a nation. It is not the fittest ideology. Pan-Islamic nationalism was weakened by a crack as early as 1952, after only five years of independence. The crack was a result of the challenge posed by the East Pakistani people's love for their mother tongue, Bengali.

**Born in 1947, the Islamic Republic of Pakistan was a twin-nation,
the twins being separated miles apart.**

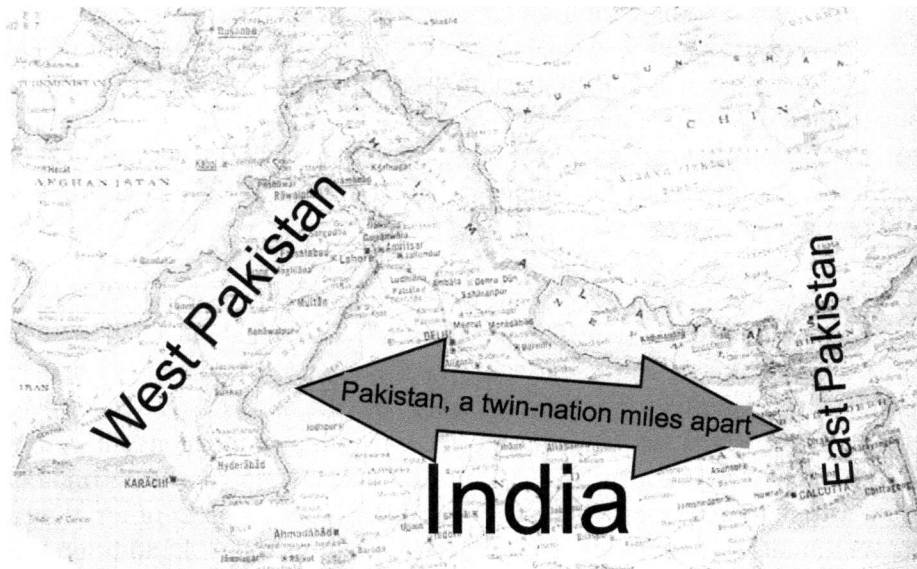

2.4. Ekhushe and The Birth of Bangladesh. Popularly known as *Ekhushe* or *the 21st* is a mighty force that crumbles Pan-Islam . It was 1952 February 21, to be exact. It was a very simple love for mother tongue that challenged mighty Pan-Islam. Mighty Pakistani Pan-Islam was humbled by *Sona Bangla*.

In 1948, when the Jinnah government adopted a major West Pakistani dialect, Urdu, as the State Language of Pakistan, protest immediately broke out in East Pakistan. The East Pakistani are Bengali in terms of ethnic classification. The land, culture, civilization, and language of Bengal and Bengali people are among the oldest on this planet. In the name of Muslim unity under the doctrine of Pan-Islam, the Muslim League of Pakistan tried to undo this beautiful piece of world cultural heritage.

{By the way, just by the way, have you read Rabindranath Tagore's poems such as *Gardeners, Crescent Moon, Gitanjali,* etc.? If not, please read them. Rabindranath Togore (1861-1941) was a Bengali Hindu, but he is loved, honored and cherished by the Bengali Muslims simply for the love of language. He was the one who put *Sona Bangla* on the top of the world with his poems. He translated his poems into English by himself and lo! won the 1913 Nobel literature prize for *Gitanjali* that was published in 1910. The Bangla word *Sona* means gold and is used to call someone who is very close to one's heart. For example a Bengali mother will call her child *'Amar Sona'* , meaning *my gold* in direct literal translation. They call their language *Amar Sona Bangla,* meaning their language is their heart}.

Subjugation of the language was only one of the many exploitations and oppressions that Jinnah Islamic government imposed upon its Muslim subjects of East Pakistan. For example, development projects in West Pakistan using the foreign currency that was earned by the Bengal *gold fiber* Jute whilst keeping East Pakistan in poverty angered almost all Bengalis. Worst of all, although Bengali people constitute 56% of the Pakistan population, their share of representation in the legislature and government was compromised by the West Pakistanis, creating a minority rule. Unsatisfied with such injustice of West Pakistan subordination in the name of Pan-Islamic

80

International Mother Language Day

The 21st February was adopted as the International Mother Language Day by the unanimous votes of the 30th General Conference of the UNESCO held in Paris, on November

---

Yahya Khan and Ayub Khan

General Yahya Khan was credited for holding the first free direct general election of Pakistan in 1970, after 23 years of independence. Before him, Pakistan was ruled by the autocracy of Field Marshal Ayub Khan, who called his military dictatorship *'Basic Democracy'*. Ayub Khan came into power in 1960 under his *'Basic Democracy'* and transferred his power to Yahya Khan in 1969. Yahya Khan was also discredited for his genocide of East Pakistan Bengali people in 1971. Bangladesh claimed that three million people perished during that 9-month brutal war.

Please compare Field Marshal Ayub Khan's *'Basic Democracy'* and today's Myanmar military ruler's 'Road Map to Democracy'.

Muslims unity, East Pakistan's Branch of Muslim League became *Awami Muslim League* in 1949, just two years after the emergence of Pakistan. The leader was *Maulana Abdul Hamid Khan Bhashani,* a towering figure in the Indian subcontinent. *Sheik Mujibur Rahman,* who today is honored as the Father of Nation, was one of his lieutenants as an Assistant General Secretary. In 1952 *Ekhushe,* or the Language Movement, occurred. The climax took place on February 21. Its significance and its role in the emergence of sovereign Bangladesh, and later language movements across the world, is a noble subject that is beyond the scope of this book. The reader is advised to look for more authoritative books in *Ekhushe.* While it ignited Bangladesh freedom it also gave the world International Mother Language Day in 1999. It has such a globalization impact even 47 years after its occurrence in 1952.

In 1953, Awami Muslim League dropped the word Muslim and boldly assumed secular nature, *Awami League (i.e. National League),* resulting in Pakistani military dictatorship with a series of oppressions and atrocities. In the 1970 election, which was the first ever held direct election, Awami League won a majority of seats, bagging 167 of the 313 in the National Assembly. President General Yahya Khan failed to hand over power to the majority leader. Instead, the Pakistani Army began its infliction of atrocities in East Pakistan by March 1971.

In April 1971 the Bengalis revolted against the atrocities resulting in a spontaneous revolution across East Pakistan. It was an apocalypse. Out of sympathy to human suffering, India interfered in November with a helping hand to the Bengali revolutionaries and they together seized Dhaka in December, accepting the surrender of the Pakistan army in East Pakistan.

East Pakistan became the People's Republic of Bangladesh, a secular sovereign state abandoning the Islamic Republic of Pakistan and her Pan-Islam. This was a historic event in the course of human civilization.

In the coming pages I give a diagram showing the course of history that leads to the birth of Bangladesh and a number of albums in her honor.

**A diagram showing the birth of Bangladesh
through major political landmarks**
(Note: Burma , not shown in the diagram, was separated from India in 1936).

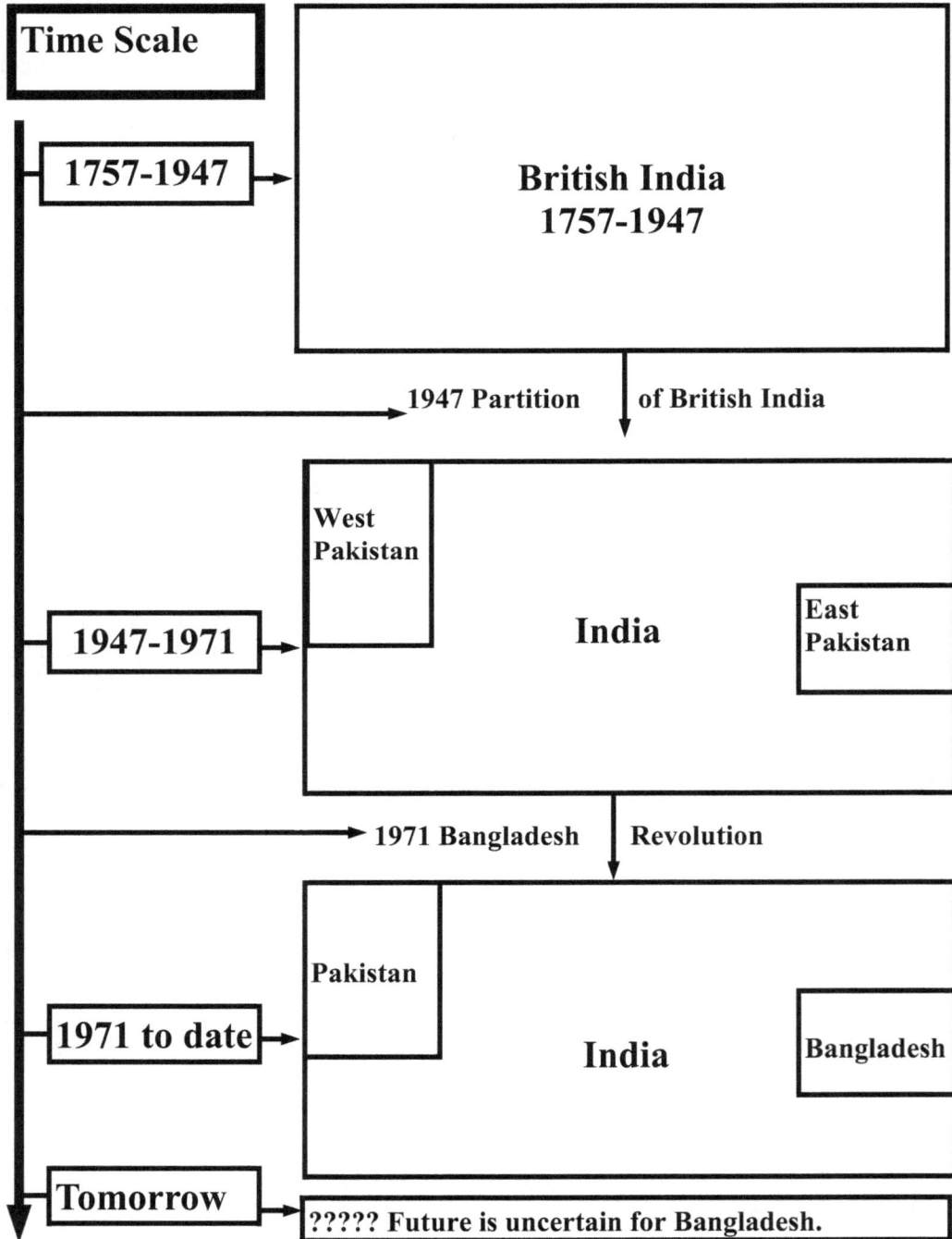

Time Scale	
1757-1947	**British India 1757-1947**

1947 Partition   of British India

| **1947-1971** | West Pakistan · **India** · East Pakistan |

1971 Bangladesh   Revolution

| **1971 to date** | Pakistan · **India** · Bangladesh |

| **Tomorrow** | **????? Future is uncertain for Bangladesh.** |

March 26 is observed as the Independence Day of Bangladesh. On the 25th March, Sheik Mujibur Rahman was arrested at Dhaka, and jetted away to West Pakistan where he was imprisoned. On the 26th March Pakistan's indulgence in genocide and Bengali revolution bursted out simultaneously. Bangladeshi people love Sheik Mujibur Rahman so much that they affectionately call him Bangabandhu or *Friend of Bengali*.

"Our struggle this time is for freedom. Our struggle this time is for independence."
Sheikh Mujibur Rahman (1920-1975) declared in response to the demand of two million Bengalis who rallied at Suhrawardy Uddyan, Dhaka on March 7, 1971. This is the most popular photo and can be found in many websites such as
http://www.virtualbangladesh.com/biography/mujib.html and http://www.ferdous.org/ohongkar.htm). This action must have been captured by a number of photographers.

Bangabandhu Sheikh Mujibur Rahman : Father of the Nation
By Jawadul Karim
(Excerpts from http://www.bangladeshgov.org/pmo/cevents/cevent15.htm, as of November 16, 2003. Bold emphasis in the text is mine).

The supreme test came on March 7, 1971. Sheikh Mujib spoke in a thundering voice to nearly two million freedomloving people in Dhaka using masterful, restrained language. His historic declaration in the meeting was : **"Our struggle this time is for freedom. Our struggle this time is for independence."**

The crackdown, however, came on March 25, when the junta arrested Sheikh Mujib for the last time and whisked him away to confinement in West Pakistan for the duration of the Liberation War. In the name of suppressing a rebellion, the Pakistani military violently confronted unarmed civilians throughout Bangladesh and perpetrated genocide, killing no less than three million men, women and children, raping women by the hundreds of thousands and destroying property worth billions of taka. Before their ignominious defeat and surrender they, with the help of their local collaborators, also killed a large number of intellectuals. In pursuing a scorched-earth policy they virtually destroyed the whole of the country's infrastructure. But they could not destroy the indomitable spirit of the freedom fighters, nor could they silence the thundering voice of the leader. Tape recordings of Bangabandhu Sheikh Mujib's March 7th speech inspired his followers throughout the war, and victory was achieved on December 16, 1971.

The birth of Bangladesh affirmatively re-asserts that a nation is not a religion or a religious institution. In coming pages I present a few faces of sovereign Bangladesh. You can read a very credible account of Bangladesh history and culture online. Simply search for Bangladesh in the World Wide Web. Many will pop up. Here are a few of them I present as examples.

The following is a clip from http://www.dhaka-bd.com/categories/History_Culture.htm, as of November, 28, 2002. At that time this website was full of historical photographs and information. When I revisited in August 2004 the links were no longer available.

http://www.dhaka-bd.com/categories/History_Culture.htm **as of November 28, 2002.**

History & Culture

- Genocide 1971 (Rare Photographs)
- Rare Photographs from 1952 to 1971

Year wise liberation movement

1947 - The Indian Subcontinent was partitioned
1948 - Sheikh Mujibur Rahman, a law student of Dhaka University, forms the East Pakistan Student League ......
1949 - Maulana Abdul Hamid Khan Bhashani, a prominent Bengali leader, founded the Awami Muslim league at Narayanganj (Dacca). Sheikh Mujibur Rahman became one of its three assistant General Secretaries .....
1951 - Mr. Liaquat Ali khan was assassinated while addressing a public meeting in Rawalpindi. Khwaja Nazim-ud-Din stepped down to take his place as the Prime Minister.......
1952 - **21st February the International Mother Landuage Day:**

- Declaration of Feb. 21st as the International Mother Language Day by UNESCO
- Pathway of Bengali language movement (1947 to 1952)
- Why language movement
- Reminding the day 21 February, 1952
- Martyrs of Bengali language (Bhasa Shahids)

After the independence, the martyrs of the Language Movement were honored in the Shahid Minar (Martyrs Monument). At dawn of every 21st February the Bangladeshi people rally at Dhaka and march barefoot across the city to the monument which is decorated with the Bengali alphabet. They lay the flower wreaths and honor the martyrs with all heart and soul. Today, UNESCO has adopted February 21st as the International Mother Language Day of the world.

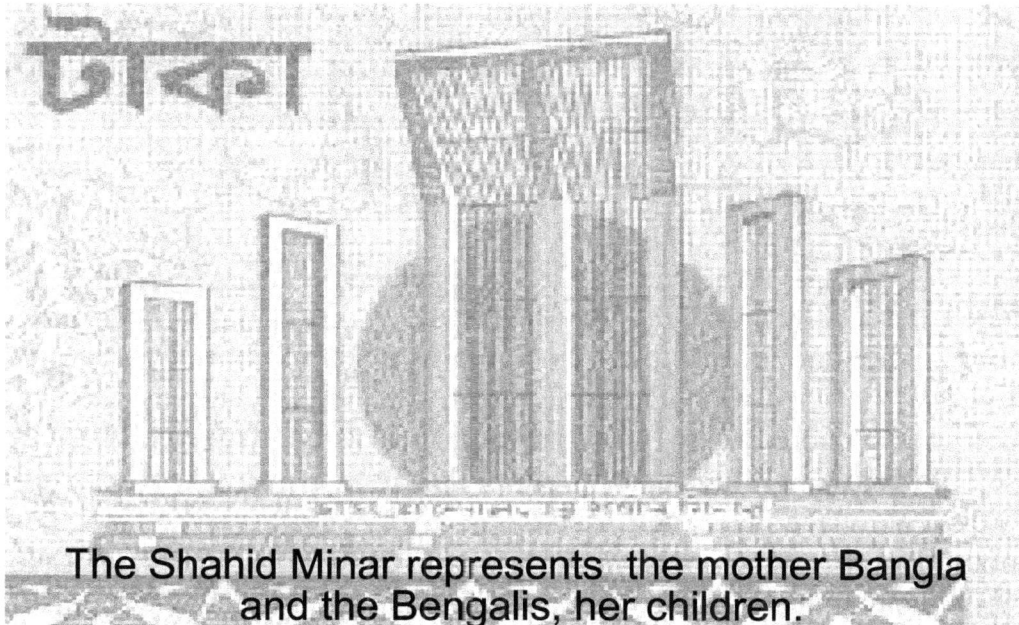

The Shahid Minar represents the mother Bangla and the Bengalis, her children.

enlarged

The spirit of Ekhushe Shahid Minar is circulated across the nation in 2-Taka bill. Its presence is felt every moment, every day.

It was my family culture to visit Sahid Minar every year when I was in Dhaka. The following piece of information was taken in October 2003 from Bangladesh government website - http://www.bangladeshgov.org/pmo/21february/shahid_minar.htm.

The Central Martyr's Monument in Dhaka was erected in memory of those who laid down their lives for establishing the dignity and rightful place of Bangla on February 21, 1952. The monument, designed by noted artist Hamidur Rahman assisted by the well-known sculptor Novera Ahmed, symbolises the mother protecting her children. Language has been visualised as the mother who provides nourishment to the people, her offsprings. On this day every year, the people pay homage to the language martyrs and throng the monument barefoot by the thousands. The celebration starts at zero hour and continues the whole day. The monument is bedecked with flowers and wreaths. The whole country joins in the celebration.
(http://www.bangladeshgov.org/pmo/21february/shahid_minar.htm)

A postcard (Azad Products, Dhaka) depicts a lady's homage to the martyrs of Ekhushe.

Those three million who died so that Bangladesh could be free are remembered, honored, and immortalized with the **National Martyr's Monument** (*Srito Shodho*) by the sovereign Bangladesh. It is circulated on the Tk50 bill reaching everyone's pocket in every nook and corner of the nation, and reminding them of the national sacrifice.

enlarged

The spirit of the liberation war and ultimate independence is continuously seeping through the nation as its monument circulates on the Taka50 bill.

History of Bangladesh from Ekhushe through the Liberation War is monumented in a beautiful water fountain called *'the journey to victory' (Bijoy Sharani)*. It is situated at Farm Gate, Dhaka. These postcards (Ideal Products, Dhaka) show day and night scenes of the victory.

Please visit these websites and set yourself a sail in the ocean of the Bangladesh freedom struggle. You will find that your ship soon gets wrecked and you are swimming in the stormy sea of her politics. The website bangla2000.com paid a tribute to Sheikh Mujibur Rahman with historical photographs. The following web clip (http://www.bangla2000.com/News/Resources/ Snapshots/Bangabandhu/default.asp) was taken in 2002. When I revisited there in August 2004 this web page was no longer there. Nevertheless, http://www.bangla2000.com still provides useful information on various aspects of Bangladesh including Ekhushe and liberation war. In March 2005, I found http://www.joybangla.net/ dedicated to Bangabandhu Sheikh Mujibur Rahman and his Awami League.

http://www.bangla2000.com/News/Resources/Snapshots/Bangabandhu/default.asp

www.bangla2000.com

Pictorial Tribute to the Father of the Nation

Shiekh Mujibur Rahman
Father of Nation and the first President of Bangladesh

Sheikh Mujibur Rahman was killed on the night of August 15, 1975, by a group of military officers. Everyone in the house, a total of 17 including his wife, three sons, two daughter-in-laws, and grandchildren were also killed as per http://www.joybangla.net/. His 10-year old son Russel, 4-year old grandson, and pregnant niece-in-law were also killed. It was brutal. Still fortunate, two daughters Sheikh Hasina and Sheikh Rehana survived the massacre as they were in West Germany at that time.

Step by step, he came downstairs talking to the military officers who came to kill him. He asked them to tell their grievances so that he could address them. He sat down on the stairs and continued talking and puffing off his famous cigar there. He was shot dead. He died with his heart blown out by the bullets, but his cigar still in his mouth. I have seen that striking photo of courageous death many times. You may find it in this website if it is still posted there. He was the President of independent Bangladesh when his own soldiers killed him. When I am in the Banani graveyard I always make one round of homage to the graves of Sheikh Mujib and his family. He was a great politician who mobilized 70 million Bengalis into the freedom struggle.

Please visit http://www.bangladesh.gov.org/pmo/introduction/bang_in1.htm#4 for more information.

You can find a number of credible accounts of the biography of Sheikh Mujibur Rahman. The following excerpt is taken from *Sheikh Mujibur Rahman Biography* by Khaleda Zia, which is posted at http://www.polymernotes.org/biographies/BGD_bio_rahman.htm.

"The Bangabandhu is the Father of the Nation. His state philosophy has four pillars: Nationalism, Democracy, Socialism and Secularism. His foreign policy opened up new horizons of peace, cooperation and non-alignment throughout Asia. He visited many countries of Asia and Europe including China and the Soviet Union. Statesmen of many Asian countries were his personal friends. He was awarded Julio Curie Peace Prize for his being a symbol of world peace and cooperation. In the eyes of the people in the third world, he is the harbinger of peace and development in Asia."

Today, Bangladesh remembers him in this 10-Taka bill and with a Sheikh Mujib Monument (Azad Products postcard) in his home district Faridpur.

Sheikh Mujib Monument

Chapter 3. The Return of Pan-Islam

Bangladesh saw the return of Pan-Islam soon after her secular leader Mujib (Sheikh Mujibur Rahman) was assassinated on August 15, 1975. I am not qualified to answer the question why he was killed. But, I shall focus on the consequent rise of Bangladesh Pan-Islam after his death.

Not only Sheikh Mujib but also another four prominent leaders detained at Dhaka jail were killed by the military officers. After killing President Sheikh Mujibur Rahman the military junta that took over imprisoned Vice President Syed Nazrul Islam, First Prime Minister Tajuddin Ahmed, Prime Minister Mansur Ali, and Cabinet Minister Kamruzzaman. They were all killed by the same group of military officers after illegally entering the jail on the night of November 3, 1975. This action after 80 days of Sheikh Mujib's assassination, clearly revealed that it was a planned clean-up of Awami League's leadership. It was not only targeted at Sheikh Mujib, but also Awami League as a whole was the target.

The events that took place between August 15 and November 7, 1975 will never surface in truth. Bangladesh history will remain in the dark for that short period. Khandakar Mushtaq Ahmed, a Awami Leaguer, General Khaled Mosharraf, and General Zia Rahman are the names in the history of those dark days which were characterized by coups and counter-coups. General Zia turned out to be the strongest person who crushed some 20 counter-coups and cleaned up the army. As the Chief Martial Administrator he formed his own political party, amended the constitution, held a general election and emerged as the elected President of Bangladesh on April 21, 1977. He was killed by one of his colleagues, another general, on May 30, 1981. Upon his assassination, Vice President Abdus Sattar took over the presidency. General Hossain Mohammad Ershad quietly removed President Sattar in a bloodless coup on March 24, 1982.

A list of successive Bangladesh governments from 1971 to date is summarized below. This demonstrates gradual but progressive renaissance of Pan-Islam in post-Mujib Bangladesh. The caretaker or acting governments that ruled in the interludes or transitions during the general elections are not included. Only heads of the government who actually weld the power are considered.

1. January 10, 1971 to August 15, 1975: Sheikh Mujibur Rahman, President, assassinated in a military coup d'état. Awami League (AL).
2. August 15 to November 7, 1975: Interlude ridden with coups and counter coups.
3. November 7, 1975 to May 30, 1981: Ziaur Rahman, President. Popularly known as General Zia and later President Zia. Assassinated on May 30, 1981 by a general who was a former colleague. Bangladesh Nationalist Party (BNP).
4. May 30, 1981 to March 24, 1982. Abdus Sattar. President. Disposed by a military coup. BNP.
5. March 24, 1982 to December 6, 1990. Hossain Mohammad Ershad, General, later President.

> "Men of ideas vanish first when freedom vanishes"
> Carl Sandburg
> **1878-1967**
> American Poet

Came to power through coup and later became elected president. Overthrown by a popular uprising. Thrown into jail under the guilty verdict of corruption charges. Now free and active in politics leading his Jatio Party (JP).

6. March 20, 1991 to March 30, 1996, Khaleda Zia (Begum Zia). Prime Minister. Widow of President Zia. Won the 1991 general election. BNP.
7. June 23, 1996 to July 15, 2001: Sheikh Hasina. Prime Minister. Daughter of Sheikh Mujibur Rahman. Won the 1996 general election. AL.
8. October 1, 2001 to date: Khaleda Zia. Prime Minister. Won the 2001 general election. BNP.
9. Tomorrow: ? Next election will be in 2005.

Today, Bangladesh is losing her secularism with the rise of anti-intellectualism. Intellectualism is the main force behind the secularism, which is a component of liberalism. Indeed there are mixed reactions in the society. Dr. Iajuddin Ahmed, a prominent soil scientist, professor and dean of Dhaka University, is honored as the President of the nation.

On the other hand incidents of attacks on the intellectuals are rising. The attacks on Dr. Kamal Hossain, the architect of the 1971 Bangladesh secular constitution, and Dr. Humayan Azad (1947-2004), a professor of Bengali, at Dhaka University, are in the front line news. Especially, the case of Dr. Humayan Azad demands serious attention and analysis. He was attacked and seriously wounded in front of Bangla Academy, inside the Dhaka University campus on February 27, 2004, for his recent book *Pak Sar Jamin Sad Bad* (The Sacred Blessed Land). His novel critically features the role of Pakistanis and their Bangladeshi collaborators before the independence of Bangladesh in 1971. His book was strongly denounced by the Islamist political parties. The assailants wanted to slit Humayun Azad's throat on a *la jihadi* fashion.

An analyst named A.H. Jaffor Ullah wrote, "It may surprise many readers to know that Humayun Azad's attackers wanted to slit his throat on February 27, 2004, a *la jihadi* fashion. A *Murtaad* or apostate is a fair game. Once a person is labeled *Murtaad*, beheading that person is considered no crime. You see, the Islamists in Bangladesh declared Dr. Azad a *Murtaad*. For some thoughts on Dr. Azad's plight in the hands of his assailants, please pursue the rest of my

Government of the People's Republic of Bangladesh

President Dr. Iajuddin Ahmed

Visit http://www.bangladeshgov.org/

Dr. Iajuddin Ahmed is a soil scientist whom his younger colleagues, including my wife (Zoology Department) and I, call *Dulabhai* (elder brother-in-law). His wife, Dr. Anawara Begum, a professor of zoology, is loved and respected as our elder sister, and we call her *Apa* (elder sister) - a very lovingly sweet Bengal culture. Bangladesh has honored many intellectuals as the nation's president - a beauty of respect for intellectualism, unique to Bangladesh. Please visit Dhaka University website http://www.univdhaka.edu/president_of_bangladesh.htm.

I wish this tradition of love and respect for intellectualism and intellectual freedom will not vanish in Bangladesh.

	Bangladesh political killings 2001-2005. The information given here are based on the online BBC news on the given dates and BBC Timeline Bangladesh at http://news.bbc.co.uk/1/hi/world/south_asia/country_profiles/1160896.stm.							
Sl. No.	Name	Profession	Party	Place	death	injury	Date (mmdyy)	How? (method)
1	Ahsan Ullah Master	MP, Trade Union Leader	AL	Tongi	1	na	5/7/04	gunmen
2	General public	New Year Concert goers	na	Dhaka	9	?	4/14/01	bomb attack
3	General public	Roman Catholic Church worshippers	na	Baniarchar	10	?	6/1/01	bomb attack
4	Plotical workers	Party cadres	AL	Narayanganj	22	?	6/16/01	bomb attack
5	Plotical workers	Strikers (hartalers)	BNP?	nation wide	1	>200	4/1/01	bomb attack
6	Plotical workers	AL supporters	AL	Bagerhat (Khulna)	8	>100	9/23/01	bomb attack
7	Plotical workers	Plotical activists	all partes	nation wide	>100	?	2001	elction campaign clashes
8	General public	movie goers	na	Satkhira	2	200	Sept., 2002	bomb attack
9	General public	movie goers	na	Mymensingh	17	200	12/8/02	bomb attack
10	Plotical workers including Ivy Rahman*	Party cadres	AL	Dhaka	22	20	8/22/04	grenade attacks
11	Plotical workers	Party cadres	AL	Sylhet	1	30	8/8/04	bomb attack
12	Anwar Choudhury**	The British High Commissioner	British diplomat	Sylhet	3		May, 2004	bomb attack
13	Shah AMS Kibria and 3 others	Kibria was a MP, minister of finance & diplomat	AL	Laskarpur	4	?	1/27/05	grenade attack
14	Dr. Humayan Azad***	Professor of Bengli	Academician	Dhaka	na	1	Feb. 27, 2004	attckers tried to cut off his neck.
15	Dr. Kamal Hossain	Bar at Law, former Foreign Minister, architect of 1971 Bangladesh Constitution	Statesman	Rangpur	na	1	Oct. 19, 2004	kidnapped and beaten
16	Dr. Badruddoza Chowdhury	Physician & Former President of Bangladesh	Statesman	Rangpur	na	1	Oct. 19, 2004	kidnapped and beaten
				Total	>200	>753		
	*Sheikh Hasina barely escaped. Senior Awami League leader, Ivy Rahman, who gave her body cover died.							
	**Anwar Choudhury was injured. The British diplomat was paying a visit to his home town.							
	*** Professor Humayan Azad later died in Germany.							

Demolition 45-minutes

On the 17th of August 2005, 459 bombs blasted almost simultaneously in the sixty three districts of Bangladesh (BBC News World Edition online, Wednesday, 17 August 2005, and Narinjara News online 8/18/05). With panic and confusion, the nation became to a halt. The blasts began at 10:45 am and ended at 11:30 am, indicating that the group is capable of demolishing Bangladesh within 45 minutes.

Reportedly the bombs are small and homemade. Only two deaths and 50 injuries were so far reported. Suspicion fell upon an outlawed group known as Jamatul Muhajideen Bangladesh. Its leaflets found near the blast sites state that "It is time to implement Islamic law in Bangladesh" and also warned Bush and Blair to get out of Muslim countries, trumpeting its global significance.

article". Please visit http://www.faithfreedom.org/oped/JafforUllah40301.htm to read his full article. Today, the television viewers are familiar with the beheadings of the hostages in Iraq.

On August 13, 2004 he was found dead at his apartment in Munich, Germany. The news was reported by various media in Europe and Bangladesh. A report http://www.drishtipat.org/ nuke/modules.php?name=News&file=article&sid=103&mode=thread&order=0&thold=0, read as follow.

"Humayun Azad found dead in Munich. Writer Humayun Azad, grievously injured in February in a knife attack his family blamed on Islamist extremists, was found dead in Munich in Germany on Thursday morning, prompting his relatives to react in disbelief. "Prof Azad arrived in Germany on August 8 where he intended to do several months of research on romantic German writer Heinrich Heine," a German Embassy press release says. "Prof Azad was found dead in his Munich apartment by a member of the German PEN (Poets Essayists Novelists) Centre when he did not come to an appointment with the PEN member," the release says. "An autopsy has indicated that it (Azad's death) was due to heart failure," AFP quoted police spokesman Dieter Groebner as saying in Germany. "There is absolutely no evidence of any violence," he said. "He died of natural causes." The spokesman said tests for poisons or toxins had been undertaken and the results would be available in a few weeks".

The news adds that he wrote "some 70 books that include 10 novels, seven collections of poems, and seven books on linguistics and two for children. He has received the Bangla Academy Award and Shishu Academy Award for literature".

At the time of writing this page (i.e. on August 18, 2004), the test results for poisons or toxins were not available yet. I believe it was a natural death due to heart failure. Nevertheless, we cannot exclude the probable fact that his heart weakness could have been the aftermath of severe blood loss, injuries to the blood vessels and trauma that he received when his assailants attempted to cut his throat in February. Dhaka University authorities have decided to bear all the expenses of carrying the body of Prof. Humayun Azad from Munich to Dhaka.

Please visit the following web pages for more information. I visited these web pages on August 13, 16, and 18, 2004.

http://www.thedailystar.net/2004/03/02/d4030201022.htm

http://news.bbc.co.uk/1/hi/world/south_asia/3561184.stm

http://www.lainsignia.org/2004/marzo/der_018.htm

http://www.mukto-mona.com/Articles/humayun_azad/hu-mayun_azad_dhormanubhuti.htm

http://groups.yahoo.com/group/mukto-mona/message/14475

http://www.mukto-mona.com/Articles/humayun_azad/death_threat/hu_azad_2.jpg

http://www.mukto-mona.com/Forum/forum.html

http://www.hrcbmdfw.org/bk_news/press_release_02282004.htm

http://www.amnestyusa.org/countries/bangladesh/docu-ment.do?id=80256DD400782B8480256E4D00637FB4

http://www.faithfreedom.org/oped/JafforUllah40301.htm

http://www.welt.de/data/2004/08/14/318806.html

Let us examine how Bangladesh has been making a transition from secularism to Islamism in the coming pages. The rest of this page is dedicated to Professor Humayun Azad. Sadly, his voice is silent now. Could we honor him as *"Socrates of Bangladesh"*?

http://www.mukto-mona.com/Articles/humayun_azad/humayun_azad_dhormanubhuti.htm

মুক্ত মনা
Freethinkers

Dr. Azad returns Bangladesh, blames Jamaat for attack ... .

Dr. Humayun Azad Stabbed, fighting for life

Protest From Mukto-mona

ড: হুমায়ুন আজাদ — আমরা তোমার পাশেই আছি

Prof. Ajoy Roy writes on Humayun Azad

কণ্ঠ আমার রুদ্ধ আজিকে ....

অজয় রায়

The attackers tried to behead Professor Humayun Azad on February 27, 2004. In this picture, he was seen profusely bleeding from the neck as he was brought to the hospital by the passersby's who found him badly injured. The attack was in the evening, and people were in the vicinity of the attack inside the Dhaka University campus.

The Daily Star
Committed to PEOPLE'S RIGHT TO KNOW

Vol. 4 Num 271
Tue. March 02, 2004

Intellectuals for erasing communal forces

Dhaka turns into protest ground on Azad attack

Staff Correspondent

Protesting the attack on Prof. Humayun Azad, writers, litterateurs, teachers, intellectuals and professionals yesterday urged the progressive political parties to forge an alliance to topple the government and get rid of fundamentalist and communal cliques in society.

http://www.thedailystar.net/2004/03/02/d4030201022.htm

BBC NEWS UK EDITION

Last Updated: Friday, 13 August, 2004, 10:21 GMT 11:21 UK

http://news.bbc.co.uk/1/hi/world/south_asia/3561184.stm

Top Bangladeshi author found dead

A top Bangladeshi author wounded in a knife attack in Dhaka in February has now been found dead in Germany, his relatives have said.

German officials in Dhaka told the family that Humayan Azad, 57, had died in his sleep in his flat in Munich.

3.1. Secularism to Islamism. The new born Bangladesh was a secular state with a secular constitution. The original Preamble of her constitution reads as below. Today's amended preamble as per the Proclamations Order No. 1 of 1977 is given in the next page. Please note the Islamization of the Preamble in 1977. Footnotes of the Constitution are also given. Dr. Kamal Hossain was a key figure in drafting the constitution. Full text of the Bangladesh constitution can be read at her government's website, http://www.bangladeshgov.org/pmo/constitution/.

Original Preamble of Bangladesh Constitution 1971

PREAMBLE

We, the people of Bangladesh, having proclaimed our Independence on the 26th day of March, 1971 and through [2][a historic war for national independence], established the independent, sovereign People's Republic of Bangladesh;

(Author's note: I understand that there was an original second paragraph here. I could not find the original version. The substituted second paragraph as per the Proclamations Order No. 1 of 1997, can be read in the next page).

Further pledging that it shall be a fundamental aim of the State to realise through the democratic process to socialist society, free from exploitation-a society in which the rule of law, fundamental human rights and freedom, equality and justice, political, economic and social, will be secured for all citizens;

Affirming that it is our sacred duty to safeguard, protect and defend this Constitution and to maintain its supremacy as the embodiment of the will of the people of Bangladesh so that we may prosper in freedom and may make our full contribution towards international peace and co-operation in keeping with the progressive aspirations of mankind;

In our Constituent Assembly, this eighteenth day of Kartick, 1379 B.S corresponding to the fourth day of November, 1972 A.D., do hereby adopt, enact and give to ourselves this Constitution.

End of the original preamble.

Now let us study the preamble and the Islamic aspects of the amended Bangladesh Constitution. Islamization of the constitution began in 1977 with the Chief Martial Administrator General Zia Rahman's Proclamations Order No. 1 of 1977.

General Ziaur Rahman (1935-1981) was the person who put Bangladesh on the path of Pan-Islam. In this 1993 party's postcard he is presented with his wife who leads the party after his demise.

বাংলাদেশ জাতীয়তাবাদী দল
জাতীয় কাউন্সিল '৯৩

Amended Bangladesh Constitution

[1][BISMILLAH-AR-RAHIMAN-AR-RAHIM

(In the name of Allah, the Beneficent, the Merciful)]

PREAMBLE

We, the people of Bangladesh, having proclaimed our Independence on the 26th day of March, 1971 and through [2][a historic war for national independence], established the independent, sovereign People's Republic of Bangladesh;

[3] **[Pledging that the high ideals of absolute trust and faith in the Almighty Allah, nationalism, democracy and socialism meaning economic and social justice, which inspired our heroic people to dedicate themselves to, and our brave martyrs to sacrifice their lives in the war for national independence, shall be fundamental principles of the Constitution;]**

Further pledging that it shall be a fundamental aim of the State to realise through the democratic process to socialist society, free from exploitation-a society in which the rule of law, fundamental human rights and freedom, equality and justice, political, economic and social, will be secured for all citizens.

Affirming that it is our sacred duty to safeguard, protect and defend this Constitution and to maintain its supremacy as the embodiment of the will of the people of Bangladesh so that we may prosper in freedom and may make our full contribution towards international peace and co-operation in keeping with the progressive aspirations of mankind;

In our Constituent Assembly, this eighteenth day of Kartick, 1379 B.S corresponding to the fourth day of November, 1972 A.D., do hereby adopt, enact and give to ourselves this Constitution.

End of the amended preamble.
Notes:
[1]The words, commas and brackets "BISMILLAH-AR-RAHMAN-AR-RAHIM (in the name of Allah, the Beneficent, the Merciful)" were inserted by the Proclamations Order No. 1 of 1977)
[2]The words "a historic war for national independence" were substituted for the words "a historic struggle for national liberation" ibid.
[3]The second paragraph was substituted for the former second paragraph, ibid)

Please note that *Bismillah-ar-Rahimna-ar-Rahim* (In the name of Allah, the Beneficent, the Merciful) was added at the opening of the constitution and a new second paragraph was added totally deleting the original one. We may moderate by saying that we also use "In God We Trust" and "One nation under God". Therefore, simple addition of *Bismillah-ar-Rahimna-ar-Rahim* and *absolute trust and faith in the Almighty Allah* in the preamble does not necessarily crumble the secular nature of the constitution. Nevertheless, it does compromise the principles of secularism as well as alienate non-Muslims. This is bad enough to crack the national solidarity. We may still note that the notions "In God We Trust" and "One nation under God" are generously used by the US government, though these phrases are not in the US constitution. The Declaration of Independence of the United States of America also uses such phrases as *Laws of Nature and of Nature's God* and *We hold these truths to be self-evident, that all men are created equal, that they are endowed by their Creator"* . However, the legislature is prohibited from indulging in regulating religion in any form. Its Constitutional Amendments I (The Bill of Rights) says, "Congress shall make no law respecting an establishment of religion, or prohibiting the free exercise thereof; or abridging the freedom of speech, or of the press; or the right of the people peaceably to assemble, and to petition the Government for a redress of grievances".

The national anthem of Great Britain is *God Save The Queen (King)*, but she is a nation of tradition with no written constitution. I have come across many Americans who do not know this and become very puzzled, wondering how that nation functions. I do not blame them. It truly is a puzzle. The British democratic norms and social orders are their age-old cultural heritage that exists and manifests in every walk of life. I place this cultural democracy high above the constitutional democracy. The people under the constitutional democracy become un-democratic when the law-enforcement is relaxed or compromised. In other words, they are democratic by law, but in the absence of such law they can become corrupted. This does not happen to a Britisher who is culturally democratic. In the United States democracy is limited by its constitution whereas in Great Britain democracy is limitless. It is a wonder of cultural democracy in the fact that anarchism is absent in that limitless democracy of Great Britain.

We can also educate ourselves with other secular constitutions such as those of India and Japan. The Constitution of India stands out for its absence of any form of religious fervor. Its preamble clearly says, "WE, THE PEOPLE OF INDIA, having solemnly resolved to constitute India into a SOVEREIGN SOCIALIST SECULAR DEMOCRATIC REPUBLIC and ....".

The constitution of Japan in its preface says, "We, the Japanese people, ...do proclaim that sovereign power resides with the people and do firmly establish this Constitution. Government is a sacred trust of the people, the authority for which is derived from the people, the powers of which are exercised by the representatives of the people, and the benefits of which are enjoyed by the people. This is a universal principle of mankind upon which this Constitution is founded. We reject and revoke all constitutions, laws ordinances, and prescripts in conflict herewith".

You can study the US constitution at the US government archives website, http://www.archives.gov/, the Indian Constitution at   http://www.indiacode.nic.in/coiweb/welcome.html, which is the website of India Government Ministry of Law and Justice (Legislative Department), and the Japanese constitution at its prime minister web site, http://www.kantei.go.jp/foreign/government_e.html. However, to learn the British democracy one must live in that country. Fortunately, I had the opportunity to live there four and half years from 1972 to 1976. I gained insight into democracy during that time and became a democratic person dwelling in the abode of liberal enlightenment.

The Bangladesh constitution referred to in this analysis is obtained from her government website, http://www.bangladeshgov.org/pmo/constitution/. Now let us continue with our exploration into the mechanism of Islamization of her constitution.

After a gentle Islamic touch at the preamble by General Ziaur Rahman, the constitution itself was Islamized by General Ershad who initiated it by making Islam state religion in 1988. This was followed by various modifications to the constitution as required by the state religion. The modified version of the constitution is presented below.

"[5][2A. The state religion.

The state religion of the Republic is Islam, but other religions may be practiced in peace and harmony in the Republic.]
........"

Note: [5]Article 2A, was inserted by the Constitution (Eighth Amendment) Act, 1988 (Act XXX of 1988), s,2.

"7. Supremacy of the Constitution.

(1)

All powers in the Republic belong to the people, and their exercise on behalf of the people shall be effected only under, and by the authority of, this Constitution.

(2)

This Constitution is, as the solemn expression of the will of the people, the supreme law of the Republic, and if any other law is inconsistent with this Constitution and other law shall, to the extent of the inconsistency, be void.
......."

Supremacy of the constitution is the standard norm in a constitutional nation. When Islam is constitutionalized as the state religion it subordinates all other religions in the country, making the non-Muslims as the second class citizens. In political context they are alienated because any law that is inconsistent with Islam becomes void. Let us continue to examine how does this effect the fundamental rights of a citizen.

"FUNDAMENTAL PRINCIPLES OF STATE POLICY"

"8. Fundamental principles.

[9][(1)

The principles of absolute trust and faith in the Almighty Allah, nationalism, democracy and socialism meaning economic and social justice, together with the principles derived from them as set out in this Part, shall constitute the fundamental principles of state policy.

(1A).

Absolute trust and faith in the Almighty Allah shall be the basis of all actions.]

(2)

The principles set out in this Part shall be fundamental to the governance of Bangladesh, shall be applied by the State in the making of laws, shall be a guide to the interpretation of the Constitution and of the other laws of Bangladesh, and shall form the basis of the work of the State and of its citizens, but shall not be judicially enforceable.

.......”

Note. [9]Clauses (1) and (1A) were substituted for the former clause (1) by the Proclamations Order No. 1 of 1977.

The provisions in the above constitutional articles strictly confined that the laws of the state, the principles and the actions must be in absolute trust and faith in the Almighty Allah. The principles and action of nationalism, democracy and socialism would be defined within the framework of trust and faith in the Almighty Allah. This clearly dictates the rule of Islam. Let us go ahead with our study.

“11. Democracy and human rights.

The Republic shall be a democracy in which fundamental human rights and freedoms and respect for the dignity and worth of the human person shall be guaranteed [11]* * * [12][, and in which effective participation by the people through their elected representatives in administration at all levels shall be ensured].

Notes:

[11]The comma and words ", and in which effective participation by the people through their elected representatives in administration at all levels shall be ensured" were omitted by the Constitution (Fourth Amendment) Act, 1975 (Act II of 1975), s. 2.

[12]The comma and words ", and in which effective participation by the people through their elected representatives in administration at all levels shall be ensured" were inserted by the Constitution (Twelfth Amendment) Act, 1991 (Act XXVIII of 1991, s.2 (w.e.f. 18-9-91).

12. [Omitted]

[13]* * * * * *

Note: [13]Article "12, Secularism and freedom of religion" is omitted by the Proclamations Order No. 1 of 1977.

“26. Laws inconsistent with fundamental rights to be void.

(1) All existing law inconsistent with the provisions of this Part shall, to the extent of such inconsistency, become void on the commencement of this Constitution.

(2) The State shall not make any law inconsistent with any provisions of this Part, and any law so made shall, to the extent of such inconsistency, be void.

[16][(3) Nothing in this article shall apply to any amendment of this Constitution made under article 142].

......"

Note: [16]Clause (3) was added by the Constitution (Second Amendment) Act, 1973 (Act XXIV of 1973), s.2, which shall be deemed to have taken effect on the 15th day of July, 1973.

In the above provisions, we can see that the Article 12: "Secularism and freedom of religion" is abolished. Under the modified constitution, fundamental rights are governed by the principles and actions in absolute trust and faith in the Almighty Allah, as described earlier.

"27. Equality before law.

All citizens are equal before law and are entitled to equal protection of law.

28. Discrimination on grounds of religion, etc.

(1) The State shall not discriminate against any citizen on grounds only of religion, race caste, sex or place of birth.

(2) Women shall have equal rights with men in all spheres of the State and of public life.

(3) No citizen shall, on grounds only of religion, race, caste, sex or place of birth be subjected to any disability, liability, restriction or condition with regard to access to any place of public entertainment or resort, or admission to any educational institution.

(4) Nothing in this article shall prevent the State from making special provision in favor of women or children or for the advancement of any backward section of citizens.
......"

The above provisions are the originals since 1972 when the constitution was first adopted. However, later Islamization of the constitution not only creates internal conflicts within the constitution but also makes these provisions meaningless. This is because these provisions come under the regulation of the articles "8. Fundamental principles" and "26. Laws inconsistent with fundamental rights to be void". Again, please do not overlook that the fundamental rights are governed by the principles and actions in absolute trust and faith in the Almighty Allah.

"39. Freedom of thought and conscience, and of speech.

(1) Freedom of thought and conscience is guaranteed.

(2) Subject to any reasonable restrictions imposed by law in the interests of the security of the State, friendly relations with foreign states, public order, decency or morality, or in relation to contempt of court, defamation or incitement to an offence-

(a) the right of every citizen of freedom of speech and expression; and

(b) freedom of the press, are guaranteed.
......"

The provisions given in the above constitutional articles read quite logical and are the original since 1972. Nevertheless, the logic falls apart again when we realize that "the security of the (Islamic) State" is gravely compromised by the non-Islamic activities. The principles and practices of secularism such as changing to a new religion, rejecting the religion or atheism, practice of Hinduism and Buddhism, and liberal democracy are non-Islamic. Similarly, teaching of scientific education becomes impossible since the cosmic and organic evolutions form the basic theories, principles, and practices of today's science. Emergence of industrialized techno-logical society based upon scientific principles becomes obscured as Islam prohibits population control. Population control is a crucial strategy in developing a sustainable economy. This is the sphere where the Islamic Bangladesh is facing grave drawback.

"41. Freedom of religion.

(1) Subject to law, public order and morality-

(a) every citizen has the right to profess, practice or propagate any religion;

(b) every religious community or denomination has the right to establish, maintain and manage its religious institutions.

(2) No person attending any educational institution shall be required to receive religious instruction, or to take part in or to attend any religious ceremony or worship, if that instruction, ceremony or worship relates to a religion other than his own.
......"

Here, freedom of religion is subject to law, public order and morality. This provision virtually marginalizes religious freedom in an Islamic society where "absolute trust and faith in the Almighty Allah shall be the basis of all actions". It is not extreme to say religious freedom in an Islamic State is meaningless.

I contrast these provisions from the US Constitutional Amendments I (The Bill of Rights) that says, "Congress shall make no law respecting an establishment of religion, or prohibiting the free exercise thereof; or abridging the freedom of speech, or of the press; or the right of the people peaceably to assemble, and to petition the Government for a redress of grievances".

It is my view that by Islamizing the constitution Bangladesh betrays the very principle of her 1971 liberation war and the blood of her freedom fighters.

3.2. The Process of Islamization. The excerpts of the Bangladesh constitution discussed earlier clearly show the course of her recent Islamization. The Proclamations Order No.1, 1977, is the key to the changes. The most important occurrence was omission of the Article 12, "Secularism and freedom of religion".

How did this happen? Why did this happen? Let us examine the course of its development towards recent Islamization. Leaders play key roles in these developments. As such we shall look into their religious inclinations.

Sheikh Mujib was neither an atheist nor a fundamentalist. He was a Muslim politician, but secular. The Generals, namely Zia and Ershad, who Islamized the constitution cannot be considered as better Muslims than Sheikh Mujib. The difference is Sheikh Mujib has a political philosophy whereas the two generals have none. When Mujib and the four top political leaders were killed the country went silent. A state of ideological bankruptcy set in.

The people of Bangladesh, just like those of Myanmar, understand only four languages namely nationalism, religion, socialism and communism. Even though they talk much about democracy it is not in their culture. Democracy is a culture, not a political ideology. Nothing is defined or confined in or by democracy. Accordingly, democracy is seen as a form of anarchism, especially so in the eyes of the soldiers. Even such a figure not less than the Father of Nation, Bangabandhu Sheik Mujibur Rahman, himself undermined democracy that he fought for his whole life. He formed *Baksal* (Bangladesh Krishak Sramik Awami League, meaning Bangladesh Peasants' and Workers' Awami League), introduced one-party *Baksal* dictatorship and banned all other political parties in February 1975. According to Taj I. Hashmi that was posted on Holiday On-Line, Friday, August 2, 2002, *Baksal*'s act "turned underground, clandestine politics, both secular and Islamic, as the only option for the people." **Then, how does it differ from Yahya Khan's *basic democracy* of military dictatorship?**

I believe he was influenced by General Ne Win of Burma. When I reached Bangladesh in 1977, I had a very hard time explaining that the Burmese Way to Socialism was nothing but a military dictatorship. The Bangladesh people believed me in 1988 only when the democracy uprising broke out. To my amazement, in Bangladesh, General Ne Win was revered as *the Tito of Burma*. I believe you are familiar with Marshal Josip Broz Tito (1892-1980) of Yugoslavia. I had a worst time dealing with the Bangladeshi military officers who held General Ne Win very high as *the crown-commissioned officer*. Indeed, General Ne Win was commissioned by the crown not only once but twice, first by the Japanese Imperial Crown in 1942 and second by the British Imperial Crown in 1945. I realized only then that for a soldier, this truly was a great achievement and honor.

Killing of Sheikh Mujibur Rahman was a consequence of multiple domestic and international political factors. The reader will be able to find a number of books on this subject. I identify only two major factors based on my experience.

1. His alliance with India entering a 20-year friendship pact.
2. His secularism and introduction of *Baksal*.

His alliance with India put Bangladesh in the Moscow-New Delhi axis of that given time and space creating great concern in the West, China, and Islamic Umma. Secularism evaporated the last drop of patience from the hearts of Islamists such as the Muslim Leaguers and Jamaat-i-Islamiers across the world. Please note that I say "across the world". One party dictatorship in the name of the *Baksal* angered the forces of left, right, and center camps. The result was his blood and death.

His one-party totalitarianism was used as an excuse by Lt. Col. Farooq for his miscarried revolution. It was a revolution with no ideology, no leader, and no follower. It simply created chaos. When Awami League returned to power in 2001, he and his colleagues were charged with the murders. The court has made its verdict. Below, I present to you a piece of information on the verdict that I collected from the New Nation Online. I, however, do not believe that the case will end here with the note of "convicted and forgotten"; many questions will still remain and new questions will pop-up seeking the answers.

When Maj. General Zia Rahman emerged as the strongman he understood very well that he could not hold the country under the Marshal Law Administration for long. Reportedly, he faced some 20 counter coups in a duration of some fourteen months between November 1975 and December 1977. He needed a doctrine to quiet the boiling the temper of the country. He needed to recruit cadres to control the angry mass. He found religion as the quieting force. He recruited the rightists to control the angry mass. He was successful since the leftists and the centrists were the scourge of the unquiet nation's anger at that time. Accordingly, he marginally Islamized the constitution just before the general election ensuring his victory. I do not believe that he had intention to Islamize the entire constitution. It was a simple tactical maneuver to quiet the boiling nation and win an election. But, it went out of control. He was killed on May 31, 1981, at Chittagong where he was on an official tour with his cabinet. It appeared that the killing was masterminded by a disgruntled military commander, Major General Abdul Manzoor,

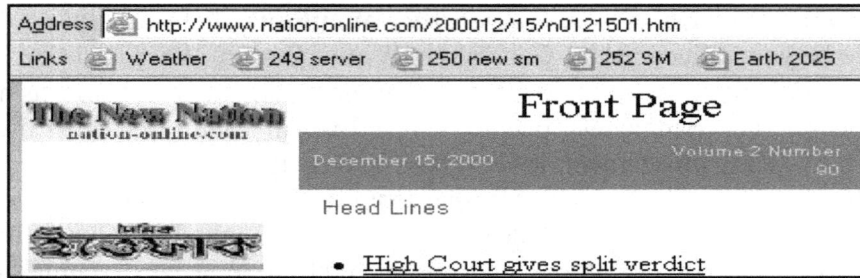

Address 🔗 http://www.nation-online.com/200012/15/n0121501.htm

Links 🔗 Weather 🔗 249 server 🔗 250 new sm 🔗 252 SM 🔗 Earth 2025

The New Nation
nation-online.com

Front Page

December 15, 2000   Volume 2 Number 90

Head Lines

- High Court gives split verdict

Bangabandhu murder case

High Court gives split verdict

Staff Reporter

The High Court Bench of the Bangladesh Supreme Court on Thursday announced its split verdict in the death reference and appeal of Bangabandhu Sheikh Mujibur Rahman murder case in which the lower court sentenced to death 15 former army officers.

Senior Judge Mohammad Ruhul Amin, in his verdict, acquitted five of the 15 persons sentenced to death by the lower court while the junior judge ABM Khairul Huq confirmed the death sentences of all the 15 former army officers.

Those acquitted by the senior judge are: Lt. Col. Mohiuddin Ahmed (Artillery), Major Ahmed Sharful Hossain, Captain Md. Kismat Hashem, Captain Nazmul Hossain Ansar, Risaldar Moslemuddin alias Moslehuddin. Of them, only Lt. Col. Mohiuddin Ahmed (artillery) has been arrested and in Dhaka Central Jail now and others tried in absentia.

The death sentences of the 10 former army officers passed by the lower court and confirmed by both the judges are: Lt. Col. Syed Farook Rahman, Lt. Col. Sultan Shahriar Rashid Khan, Lt. Col. Khandker Abdur Rashid, Major Md. Bazlul Huda, Lt. Col Shariful Haque Dalim, BU, Lt. Col. AM Rashed Chowdhury, Lt. Col. AKM Mohiuddin (Lancer), Lt. Col. SHBM Nur Chowdhury and Lt. Col. Md Abdul Aziz Pasha. Of them, Col. Farooq, Col. Shahriar Rashid Khan and Major Huda are in custody and others are absconding.

who was a former colleague. The Abdul Mansoor was pursued and killed some where in the northern Chittagong hilltracts. Various explanations, such as a personal revenge, an abortive coup, and a mutiny, were given for the killing. It was even charged that General Ershad was behind the abortive coup. But, we will not know for sure since Abdul Mansoor was killed.

General Hossain Mohammad Ershad seized the power in 1982 and again imposed the Marshal Law Administration. He followed the footpath of Ziaur Rahman, got elected as the President, formed a political party and ended his Marshal Law Administration. He was overthrown by a popular uprising in 1991 and later even thrown into jail under the guilty verdict of corruption charges. Now free, he actively leads his Jatiya Party (JP).

We have journeyed through the maze of Bangladesh stormy politics, though very brief. Let us now look at the present stand of the political parties and their scenarios.

For the sake of simplicity and convenience I am giving the clips from the party's web site with some of my notes. Please visit the following web sites for more details.

1. http://www.albd.org/ of the Bangladesh Awami League.

Bangladesh Awami League is the most glorious party of the nation. Sheikh Hasina has been a veteran politician since her student life. She was put at the helm of the party in 1981. Due honor and credit must be endowed to Bangladesh Awami League for its role in leading the nation to independence and introducing a secular constitution.

The big question today: **Is Awami League going to give up its secularism?**

http://www.albd.org/

Bangladesh Awami League

Party President

One Year of BNP-Jamaat Misrule: Sheikh Hasina gave her assessment

Read in Bangla

President
Bangladesh Awami League

- Sheikh Hasina slates Khaleda Zia for celebrating fake birthday
- Sheikh Hasina shocked at death of Prof. Humayun Azad

নমিত হৃদয় আজ দিকে দিকে - পতাকাও নমিত সে শোকে। তেরোশত নদী আজ অশ্রু ঢালে কোটি কোটি

(Author's Note: Sheikh Hasina (b1947) is the present president of Awami League. A graduate of Dhaka University, she married Dr. M. A. Wazed Miah, a scientist, in 1968. They have a son and a daughter. An activist since her student life, she is a seasoned politician as well as a formidable stateswoman credited as the second woman prime minister of Bangladesh (1996-2000). Today being the most powerful Opposition Leader, she is working hard to gain back her premiership. How long and how far she would be able to stand against the surge of Pan-Islam is the question that she alone can answer in the male chauvinist Islamic world of Bangladesh).

---

50 Years of Struggle and Achievements
Bangladesh Awami League
An excerpt from http://www.albd.org (http://www.albd.org/aldoc/50years.htm)

Bangladesh Awami League is the oldest and biggest political party of Bangladesh. It originated in the soil of the country and evolved with the evolving hopes and aspirations of the people living on the Padma- Meghna- Jamuna delta. It is the party that gave leadership in the glorious Liberation War. Awami league is one of those political parties in the world under whose leadership struggles were led and won, tearing apart the chains of domination and servitude. Awami League represents the mainstream of the progressive, non-communal, democratic and nationalist politics of Bangladesh. This half-a-century- old party has a glory of relentless and uncompromising struggle against autocracy and communalism, against political and economic domination. Its greatest achievement is the emancipation of the Bangalee people from the colonial rule of Pakistan. This was the party that both germinated and helped blossom the Bangalee nationalism: the independence won in 1971 is the undying monument of that grand success of Awami League as a political party. Bangabandhu Sheikh Mujibur Rahman, our Father of the Nation, gave the leadership to the people and the party that took us through the glorious War of Liberation. Since then, the party has worked tirelessly to combat autocracy and communalism, to nourish the non communal political tradition and to institutionalize democracy through establishing a constitutionally elected government. Therefore, as a political party, Awami League can claim to have attained success in the overall development of the political history of the country, particularly in the process of building a nation-state for the Bangalee people. It is continuing in its role as the people-oriented political party with progressive and pragmatic political, social and economic agenda for the betterment of the lot of the toiling masses of the country.

General Ziaur Rahman was the first person who changed the secular constitution towards Islamic. He was the man who actually declared the independence of Bangladesh in March 1971 from a Chittagong radio known as *"Shadheen Bangla Betar"* or the Independent Bangla Radio. He must also be credited as the originator of the South Asia Association of Regional Cooperation (SAARC) concept. He also brought about a sense of political stability in Bangladesh. Most strikingly, he ambitiously introduced national family planning with the policy of one family two children. In the screen of my memory, I can still see the billboards that say, "boy or girl two is enough". My family and many urbanites followed his policy. These billboards no longer exist in today's Bangladesh. You can find more about him at his party website http://www.bnpbd.com. At the time of the writing this book, BNP is in power under the leadership of Begun Khaleda Zia. The BNP won the 2001 election in alliance with the Islamist parties.

BANGLADESH NATIONALIST PARTY(BNP)

বাংলাদেশ জাতীয়তাবাদী দল (বি এন পি)

http://www.bnpbd.com/

Home

About BNP

BNP as governme

(Author's Note: Begum Khaleda Zia (b1945), the first woman prime minister of Bangladesh, leads BNP today. She studied at Surendranath College, Dinajpur and married Ziaur Rahman, a Captain then, in 1960. A mother of two sons, she has developed herself from a poetic housewife to a weathered politician and credible stateswoman. This is her second election for the office of premier. How far she will go for Islamization of the country is her well-calculated power game. But, we may just guess!)

Major Objectives of BNP

1. To Protect the Independence, Sovereignty, Security & Territorial Integrity of Bangladesh and Sustain the process of liberal democracy in the country through People's Unity based on Bangladeshi Nationalism.

2. To defend Bangladesh from imperialism, expansionism, neo-colonialism, hegemonism and external aggression through attainment of economic prosperity and self-sufficiency for the united and revitalized nation.

3. To Ensure Human Development and Promote Economic Growth & Social Justice through Politics of Production & People's Participatory Democracy

(p) To protect age-old human values by promoting Islamic education, Islam being the religion of the majority, and teachings of other religions. In particular, expand educational facilities for backward communities and ethnic groups, and provide wider opportunities for their participation in national life.

On March 24, 1982, General Hossain Muhammad Ershad (b1930) led a bloodless uprising, which toppled the government of President Abdus Sattar. You can learn more about him at his party website http://www.jatiyaparty.org. Today, his party is a member of the Islamic Alliance along with Jamaat-e-Islami and other leading Islamist parties. Some policies that distinguish his party from the others are given below. Some landmarks during his rule are discussed in the coming pages.

President Hussain Muhammad Ershad

Reconstruction

a. In place of unitary system of central government, the country may have a few provincial governments as well as the one in the centre. It is extremely difficult for one central government to efficiently rule in a country of 130 million people utterly beset with multifarious problems. Therefore, we propose to divide the country into 8 provinces. Each province will have a provincial assembly and the affairs of the respective province including all development works will be run by the provincial governments.

The Party Chairman, Hussain Muhammad Ershad has elaborately explained his ideas of the provincial system of government in a separate booklet.

Religious

a. Existing laws would be brought in line with the principles of the Quran and Sunnah. Salary will be provided to the Imam and Muazzin of Mosque in 68 thousand villages of Bangladesh.

b. Laws contrary to Quran and Sunnah shall be amended.

c. Shariah laws would be followed as far as possible.

d. Special laws would be made for punishing those making derogatory remarks against the Prophet (sm) and the Shariah.

e. Religious education would be made compulsory at all levels.

f. Right of the followers of all religions shall be safeguarded.

Sheikh Mujibur Rahman brought independence to Bangladesh. General Ziaur Rahman restored law and order in the post-independent era. President Hossain Muhammad Ershad got an opportunity to develop the country in an atmosphere of reasonable political stability. But he failed. Nevertheless, he must be given due credit for his materialization of SAARC (South Asian Association for Regional Cooperation) during his rule. We must also give due credit to late President Ziaur Rahman for his vision of SAARC. As mentioned earlier, the concept and vision of SAARC was originated by Ziaur Rahman. Please visit http://www.saarc-sec.org/ for more information of SAARC.

CHARTER OF THE
SOUTH ASIAN ASSOCIATION FOR REGIONAL COOPERATION

We, the Heads of State or Government of BANGLADESH, BHUTAN, INDIA, MALDIVES, NEPAL, PAKISTAN and SRI LANKA;

....
....

DO HEREBY AGREE to establish an organisation to be known as SOUTH ASIAN ASSOCIATION FOR REGIONAL COOPERATION hereinafter referred to as the ASSOCIATION, with the following objectives, principles,

Another important landmark of President Ershad's work is hosting of the fourteenth Islamic Conference of foreign ministers of the members of the Organization of Islamic Conference (OIC) from 6 - 11 December 1983 (i.e.2-7 Rabiul Awal, 1404 H). This conference carries special significance in subsequent Islamic renaissance in Bangladesh. Here I presented some information on the Conference to make the reader acquainted with OIC. Please visit http://www.oic-oci.org/ to learn more about OIC, which is the biggest world organization, only second to the United Nations.

Please find on the next page the OIC member states and observers that attended the conference so that the reader may get some idea of the OIC's significance in international affairs.

Please visit http://www.oic-oci.org/

Source: http://www.oic-oci.org/

The List of the OIC member States and Observers that attended OIC Conference in Dhaka, 1983.

The conference was attended by People's Republic Democratic of Algeria, People's Republic of Bangladesh, State of Bahrain People's Republic of Benin, United Republic of Cameroon, Republic of Chad, Federal Islamic Republic of Comoro, Revolutionary People's Republic of Guinea, Republic of Gabon, Republic of Gambia, Republic of Indonesia, Republic of Iraq, Islamic Republic of Iran, Hashemit Kingdom of Jordan, Republic of Djibouti, State of Kuwait, Republic of Lebanon, Socialist People's Libyan Arab Jamahiriya, Malaysia, Republic of Maldives, Republic of Mali, Islamic Republic of Mauritania, Kingdom of Morocco, Republic of Niger, Sultanate of Oman, Islamic Republic of Pakistan, Palestine, State of Qatar, Kingdom of Saudi Arabia, Republic of Senegal, Republic of Sierra Leone, Somalia Democratic Republic, Democratic Republic of the Sudan, Syrian Arab Republic, Republic of Tunisia, Republic of Turkey, Republic of Uganda, State of the United Arab Emirates, Republic of Upper Volta, Yemen Arab Republic and People's Democratic Republic of Yemen.

The following attended the Conference as observers

a. Turkish Cypriots, Moro National Liberation Front.
b. The following international organizations

United Nations organization, League of League of Arab States, UNESCO, FAO, UNICEF, WHO, UWDP, UNIDO, Office of the UN High Commission for Refugees. Arab League Educational, Scientific and Cultural Organisation, U.N. Committee for the Exercise of the Inalienable Rights of the Palestinian People.

c. The following Subsidiary Organizations of the OIC also participated in the Conference.

Islamic Development Bank, Islamic Educational, Scientific and Cultural Organization, International Islamic New Agency, Islamic States Broadcasting Organization, Islamic Chamber of Commerce, Industry and Commodity Exchange. Organization of Islamic Capitals, Permanent Council of Islamic Solidarity Fund, Research Centre on Islamic History, Art and Culture, Statistical, Economic and Social Research and Training Centre for Islamic States, Islamic Foundation for Science, Technology and Development - Islamic Centre for Technical and Vocational Training and Research - Islamic Centre for Development of Trade.

Islamic bodies and societies

Rabitat Al-Alam Al-Islami Motamar Al-Alama, Council of Europe, World Federation of International Arab Islamic Schools, Islamic Da'wa Society, International Association of Islamic Banks, World Assembly of Muslim Youth.

In every country there are Islamic political parties striving for the establishment of Islamic society and rule. The Islamic political parties arise in the light of Allah's revelation in Qur'anic verse 3:104. A blueprint of the verse in Arabic is given below. The image is copied from http://www.islamicity.com/QuranSearch/.

وَلْتَكُن مِّنكُمْ أُمَّةٌ يَدْعُونَ إِلَى الْخَيْرِ وَيَأْمُرُونَ بِالْمَعْرُوفِ وَيَنْهَوْنَ عَنِ الْمُنكَرِ ۚ وَأُولَٰئِكَ هُمُ الْمُفْلِحُونَ ﴿١٠٤﴾

The translation of Yusuf Ali, at the http://www.islamicity.com/QuranSearch/, reads as follows. Yusuf Ali's translation is considered among the best.

"3:104 Let there arise out of you a band of people inviting to all that is good, enjoining what is right, and forbidding what is wrong They are the ones to attain felicity".

The Jamaat-e-Islami website (http://www.jamaat-e-islami.org/about/) translates it as below.

"There must be a community among you to invite (people) to the good and to command what is proper and to forbid what is improper. They it is who are the prosperous ones. [Quran 3:104]"

In accordance with this Allah's revelation Jamaat-e-Islami (JI) was established during the time of British India in Lahore on August 26, 1941. As such we may call it the "Grand Old Party" (GOP) of Bangladesh since the Muslim League, formed in 1906, is too weak in Bangladesh for consideration. The Jamaat-e-Islami is the party we have to keep our eyes on for its key role in shaping day's and tomorrow's Bangladesh politics. It has never been in power, but is a partner in the existing cabinet of BNP Khaleda Zia and exerts a great deal of influence on the nation's development. As an active advocate of Pan-Islam it is the main force in Islamization of Bangladesh. Please visit its web site http://www.jamaat-e-islami.org/ for more information. It stands out as the vanguard of the Islamic Movement in Bangladesh. It works for a United Muslim Ummah.

Professor Golam Azam

(Author's Note: Professor Golam Azam (b1922) is the former Emeer and the main driving force of Jamaat-e-Islami. Married to Sayeda Afifa Khatun, they have six sons. A child of a Maulana dynasty he headed Jamaat for 33 long years. A very controversial figure during the 1971 liberation war, he was classified as *the collaborator* with the enemy and denied his Bangladesh citizenship until Bangladesh Supreme Court determined him a citizen of Bangladesh in 1992. A graduate of Madrasa and Dhaka University he surely is a torch-bearer of the Pan-Islamic movement. In his words *Islam is not only a religion, it is the only complete code of human life prescribed by the Creator Himself. It is the divine guidance for regulating human beings in all aspects of their lives private and public, social and political, economic and cultural, religious and spiritual aspects"*. There are millions and millions across the world who agree with him. Please visit his website, http://members.tripod.com/~golam_azam/main.htm).

Today Jamaat-e-Islami is led by another gallant Islamist named Maulana Motiur Rahman Nizami. The party chief is called Ameer. According to http://www.hyperdictionary.com/dictionary/emeer it is pronounced "u'meer" and means "an independent ruler or chieftain". It is Arabic. Its synonyms are "ameer", "amir" and "emir"*.

(Author's Note: Maulana Motiur Rahman Nizami(b1943), Ameer of Jamaat-e-Islami Bangladesh, succeeded Professor Golam Azam in December 2000. He has been a seasoned Islamist politician since his student days. A Madrasa-educated man and a graduate of Dhaka University, he is an Islamic thinker. His wife Shamsunnahar is an educationist and they have four sons and two daughters. Bangladesh liberation forces also classified him as an *enemy collaborator* during the 1971 liberation war. Today, he is the Minister of Industries in BNP Khaleda Zia's cabinet).

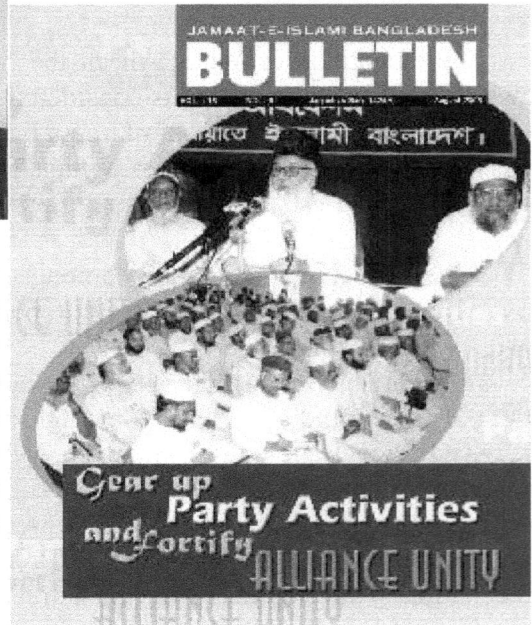

The Jamaat-e-Islami has a very sound party program as given below. Please note Jammat-e-Islami is not just confined to Bangladesh. It exists in every country on our planet. The following are excerpts from http://www.jamaat-e-islami.org/about/anintroduction.html. The reader may visit the website, http://www.jamaat-e-islami.org for more information.

"The Programme"

"The Jamaat-e-Islami Bangladesh aims at bringing about a revolution. But it is opposed to all forms of violence. It aims at channeling the thoughts of the people to

---

*Note: The reader will be familiar with a country named "United Arab Emirates" or UAE in the Arabian Gulf. It is a federation of seven emirates, namely Abu Dhabi, Dubai, Sharjah, Ajman, Umm Al-Qaiwain, Ras Al-Khaimah, and Fujairah. These states or emirates are ruled by the Emirs. If a state is ruled by a Khan it is called a Khanate, and if by a Sultan a Sultanate. Afghanistan was a Khanate and many Indian States used to be Sultanates. The words Emir, Khan, and Sultan are of Arabic, Mongolian, and Persian origin respectively, having the same meaning "ruler" or "Chieftain".

the right direction first. Then people of similar thinking have to be organised and trained up as able leaders and efficient workers of the Islamic movement. They are to be fully acquainted with social problems and equipped with abilities to solve those problems. If Allah, the Lord of the universe, grants opportunity, the Jamaat-e-Islami Bangladesh, backed by the people's support, shall form government and mold the whole society and the state in accordance with the dictates of the Quran and the Sunnah. With this end in view, the Jamaat-e-Islami Bangladesh has chalked out a four-point programme:

i) **Tabligh** and **Dawah** (Propagation and call)

To propagate the real message of Islam to the people at large, to purify and reconstruct their thoughts in the light of the teachings of Islam and to awaken in them an urge to follow and implement Islam in all walks of their life.

ii) **Tanzeem** and **Tarbiah** (Organisation and Training)

To organise those people who are eager to see Islam established in all spheres of life and to train them up as efficient workers equipped with abilities to face the challenges of Jahiliah and prove the superiority of Islam.

iii) **Islah al-Ijtimayee** (Social Reforms)

To try to bring about a change in the social and cultural conditions of society, to effect a normal reconstruction on the basis of Islamic values and to render selfless services to the suffering humanity.

iv) **Islah al Hukumah** (to reform the Government & Administration)

To strive, through constitutional means, to change the Government and to establish the leadership of the honest and God-fearing people at all levels, with a view to ensuring rectification in all state-affairs paving the way for the total implementation of Islam".

3.3. Impact of Islamic Renaissance. The Islamic renaissance in Bangladesh has great impact in every walk of her nation. The following table shows the color of Bangladesh legislature from 1973 to present. Gradual but progressive advancement of the Islamists can be seen. The table is constructed on the basis of the information I collected from the sources that are given on the next page.

Table 3.1. The impact of Islamic Renaissance in Bangladesh Parliament
(For the explanations, please see next page)

Pre-Bangladesh (Pakistan)

Party	1970 (1)
Awami League (Mujib)	167
Jamat-e-Islam	4
Jamiat-e-Olema	7
ML (Con-vention)	2
ML (Council)	7
ML (Qayuum)	9
NAP (Wali)	6
PDP	1
PPP (Butto)	88
Individuals	7

1971 Bangladesh was born through a bloody revolution --1971--

Independent Bangladesh

Party	1973 (2)	1979 (3)	1986 (4)	1991 (5)	1996 (6)	2001 (7)
Awami League	293	39	97**	88	177	62
BNP		207	BC	168	113	201
CPB				5		
Ganotantri Party				1		
Islami Oikya Jote				1	1	2
Jamaat-e-Islami			10	20	3	18
Jatiya Party (Undivided)			203	35	33	n/a
Jatiya Party (Ershad)						14
Jatiya Party (Manju)						1
Jatiya Party (Naziur)						1
JSD (Undivided)		8	4	n/a		
JSD(Siraj)				1		
JSD(Rob)					1	
Muslim League		18	4			
NAP (Bhashani)	1					
NAP (Muzaffar)	1			5		
NDP				1		
Workers Party				1		
Independents/ others	5/0	3/10	5/0	2/0		2/0
Total seats	300	300	300	330*	330*	300

114

Notes and Resource Information for Table 3.1.

Notes:
**1986 election AL 8 -parties Alliance jointly won 97, of which 76 were Awami Leaguers.
*From 1990 to 2000 the parliament had additional 30 non-elected women members who were appointed by the elected members as per the constitutional amendment mentioned. That amendment expired in 2001.
'BC' means boycotted.
'n/a' indicates not applicable since the party was divided into factions.
'BNP' stands for Bangladesh Nationalist Party.
'CPB' stands for Communist Party of Bangladesh.
'JSD' stands for Jatiyo Samajtrantik Dal, a leftist party.
'ML' stands for Muslim League.
'NAP' stands for National Awami Party.
'NDP' stands for National Democratic Party.
'PDP' stands for Pakistan Democratic Party.
'PPP' stands for Pakistan People's Party.
'Independents' mean members without any party affiliation.
'Others' means members belonging to a party that is not identified by the reference source.

Source: (1) Muktadhara, http://members.tripod.com/scohel/page15.html, (2) The Europa World Yearbook 1974, Vol.2, (3) The Europa World Yearbook 1980, Vol.1, (4) World Factbook 1987, (5) &(6) http://www.virtualbangladesh.com/bd_politics.html#parties, see under the elections, (7) World Factbook 2002, http://www.odci.gov/cia/publications/factbook/geos/bg.html.

The NSI. The resurrection of the Islamists in Bangladesh deserves deeper analysis. For this purpose I create a new term, the National Secularism Index (NSI), and define it in the coming pages with tables and figures. Please go through it with a steady speed as you will need time to digest them. The previous Table 3.1 is reanalyzed in the line of theocracy and secularism on the next page. I will group the Bangladesh political parties in a descending scale of the secular points keeping '100' points for secularism and stepping down to '0' (zero) for non-secularism, i.e. Islamic dictatorship in this scenario. The color of the scale becomes darker as the secularism decreases. For example, in the case of Bangladesh the Awami League scores a '100' and the Jamaat-e-Islami scores a '0' (zero).

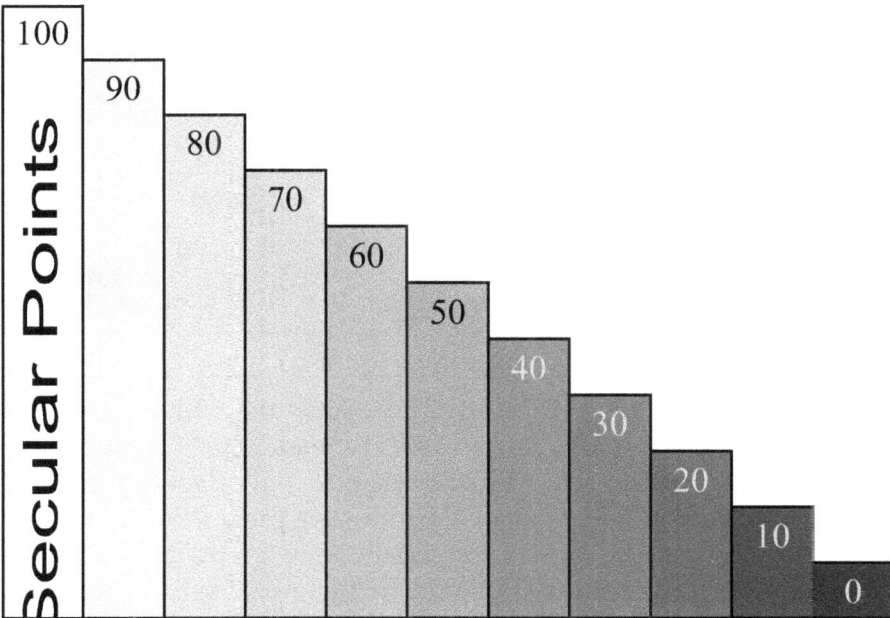

Figure 3.1. Secular Points Scale. 100 points mean most secular.

Table 3.2. The Secular Points scored by the Bangladesh political parties, as determined on the basis of the Secular Point Scale given in the previous page, Figure 3.1.

Party	Secular Points
Awami League	100
BNP	60
CPB	100
Ganotantri Party	100
Islami Oikya Jote	0 (zero)
Jamaat-e-Islami	0 (zero)
Jatiya Party (Undivided)	60
Jatiya Party (Ershad)	40
Jatiya Party (Manju)	60
Jatiya Party (Naziur)	60
JSD (Undivided)	100
JSD(Siraj)	100
JSD(Rob)	100
Muslim League	0 (zero)
NAP (Bhashani)	100
NAP (Muzaffar)	100
NDP	50
Workers Party	100
Independents/others	score not determined

Notes on the NSI values. Of course the NSI values are very relative as much as subjective. The Secularism Score of the Bangladesh political parties as presented in Table 3.3 is the key to the NSI value. Different analysts will give very different scores for the political parties. My scoring is based upon the following performances of the parties.

1. I give 100 to Awami Leagues because it introduced a secular constitution with a clear "Article 12. Secularism and freedom of religion" and still advocates for secularism.

2. I give 100 to the leftist parties because they supported the secular constitution and also manifest secular policy in their party objectives.

3. I give 60 to BNP as it introduced the clause Bismillah and erased "Article 12. Secularism and freedom of religion" with the Proclamation Order No. 1 in 1979.

4. I give 60 to JP (Undivided) since it introduced Islam as the state religion in 1987.

5. I give 40 to JP (Ershad) since he swings more towards Islamism and enters alliance with Islamic hardcore parties like Jamaat.

6. I give Jamaat-e-Islami and other Islamic parties '0' (zero) because their parties' constitutions manifest Qur'anic Islamic rule as their goal.

Moreover, I met and talked to the members, cadres, student fronts and leaders, from top to bottom, of *all* political parties during my years in Bangladesh. I say all political parties. Yes, I have met with all political parties. I have been privileged to meet the innermost circle of the parties.

In Bangladesh I earned a platform as the Chief Scientific Officer of BIRDEM, Diabetic Association of Bangladesh, under the patronage of Dr. M. Ibrahim. Accordingly I was honored as a scientist and granted golden opportunities to meet them, discuss openly with them, and even critique them. After publication of my book - *Burma: Nationalism and Ideology*, University Press Ltd., Dhaka, 1989, I was given even more opportunities by the political parties. I had gone deep to *the right* as well as deep to *the left*. On the top of that I had very good liaison with the minorities communities of the Hindus and the Buddhists. My judgement is also based upon these experiences. I am very confident that the NSI values determined here reflect *the reality of secularism* in Bangladesh.

(I hereby acknowledge my sincere thanks to *all of them* who granted me interviews).

Table 3.3. National Secular Index (NSI) as an indicator of deterioration of secularism in Bangladesh from 1973 to 2001.						
	1973	1979	1986	1991	1996	2001
Total Party Secularism Score (PSS)* (please see the definition below)	29,500	17,120	22,280	22,330	26,560	18,940
National Secularism Score (PSS)**	30,000	30,000	30,000	33,000	33,000	30,000
National Secular Index (NSI)***	98.33	57.07	74.27	67.67	80.48	63.13

Notes on the Table 3.3.
1. *Total Party Secular Score (TPSS) = sum (number of the party's parliamentary members x party secular points).
2. **National Secular Score (NSS) is the product of the total number of the parliamentary seats and the highest secular score, 100. It is the highest possible score in the parliament.
3. ***National Secular Index (NSI) is defined as the percentage of National Secular Score and it equals (TPSS/NSS) x 100%.
4. Independents/others parliamentary members are not included in the calculation for their secularism score cannot be determined with reliable confidence.
5. An example of worksheet for 2001 is given in the next page for better clarity of calculation.

Table 3.4. Worksheet for the 2001 National Secular Index (NSI)			
Party	Secular Score given	Number of parliamentary seats in 2001	Party Secular Score (PSS)
Awami League	100	62	6,200
BNP	60	201	12,060
CPB	100	none	n/a
Ganotantri Party	100	none	n/a
Islami Oikya Jote	0 (zero)	2	0
Jamaat-e-Islami	0 (zero)	18	0
Jatiya Party (Undivided)	60	n/a	n/a
Jatiya Party (Ershad)	40	14	560
Jatiya Party (Manju)	60	1	60
Jatiya Party (Naziur)	60	1	60
JSD (Undivided)	100	none	n/a
JSD(Siraj)	100	none	n/a
JSD(Rob)	100	none	n/a
Muslim League	0 (zero)	none	n/a
NAP (Bhashani)	100	none	n/a
NAP (Muzaffar)	100	none	n/a
NDP	50	none	n/a
Workers Party	100	none	n/a
Independents/others	Not Determined	n/a	n/a

Total Party Secular Score (TPSS) = sum(6,200+12,060+560+60+60) = 18,940
National Secular Score (NSS) = 100 x 300 = 30,000 (i.e. highest possible score x total number of parliamentary seats).
Therefore National Secular Index (NSI) = (TPSS/NSS) x 100%
= (18,940/30,000) x 100 = 63.13%

Values of the National Secular Index (NSI) that are worked out in Table 3.3 can be visualized in a figure below. Please note that the higher NSI indicates the broader secularism. When it approaches a value of 50 the secularism exists only in marginal freedom. Once it goes below 50 it can hardly be said to be secular any more. Since 1979 until 2005 secularism has been greatly compromised with the rise of the Pan-Islamists. With a NSI value of 63.13% from 2001 to date, Bangladesh is at the point of losing her secularism. How did this happen? Let me present you my analysis.

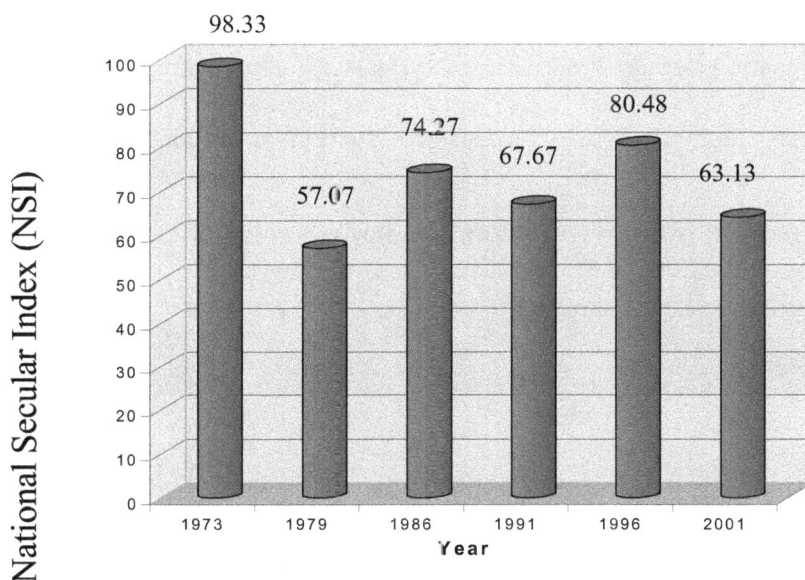

Figure 3.2 . Changes in the National Secular Index (NSI) in Bangladesh from 1973 to 2005. This figure is constructed from the NSA results from Table 3.3 and will remain valid till next parliamentary election.

National Secular Grade (NSG). The secularism of Bangladesh can also be expressed by means of a college grading system. We can simplify the NSI, which is the percentage of National Secular Score, by grading it in the style of an educational institute. When the present Bangladesh NSI, 63.13%, is converted into the grade, Bangladesh scores an appalling Grade D as shown in the Table 3.5 below.

Table 3.5. Bangladesh Secular Grade		
Percentage Score	Equivalent Grade	Bangladesh Grade
90 - 100%	A	
80 - 89%	B	
70 - 79%	C	
60 - 69%	D	D
50 - 59%	E	
40 - 49%	F	

119

3.4.. Factors that influence the Islamic Renaissance in Bangladesh. Now, the question is: Why did Bangladesh swing toward the *'Islamic rule'* or *'Islamic dictatorship'* after the long struggle against the Islamic Republic of Pakistan and subsequent sacrifice of three million people in the liberation war? Why did they betray themselves? The Islamic elements are known as *'the Rajaakars, the Muktijoddhas'* or *'the collaborators'* for their collaboration with the Pakistani army that committed a crime of genocide in 1971. As an example below, there are books and websites, dedicated to the liberation struggle, but they belong to a generation already in the twilight zone. They worry that the 1971 liberation war simply may be buried inside the history books or even rewritten. The rising youths are very Islamic. They just attempted to behead Professor Humayun Azad early in 2004 as I mentioned at the beginning of this chapter. Today the Bangladeshi Nation betrays their own martyrs! Why? *This is a very big question.* Let us ask again. Why?

There are five main factors I identify as causes of the revival of Pan-Islam in Bangladesh.

Lest We Forget - please visit: http://www.virtualbangladesh.com/history/genocide.html.
I visited the website last on the 20th of March 2005.

Virtual Bangladesh : History : Genocide 1971

The New Nation	Deshi Bazar
Bangladesh's Leading English Daily	Bangla Books, DVD, CD, VCD, Grocery
Always To The Point	Buy Phone card to call Bangladesh
	Ads by Google

Lest we forget. A compilation of links and resources about the Bangladesh Genocide of 1971.

External Links

- Genocide 1971 in Bangladesh
- Pakistani-Islam's Global Ploy and Suppression of Bengali Genocide ...
- Case Study: Genocide in Bangladesh, 1971
- Statistics Of Pakistan's Democide - R. J. Rummel
- The Bangladesh Liberation War Museum Home Page
- Genocide of Intellectuals- Bangladesh Liberation War 1971
- Bangladesh The Trial of Henry Kissinger by Christopher Hitchins
- Genocide 1971 - Maintained by Faisal Hossain
- Bangla Nuremberg: 1971 War Archives - A collection of articles focused on war criminals.
- Cry for Justice - A documentary film telling the untold stories of from the survivors of the 1971 Genocide in Bangladesh.

Internal Links

- The Genocide Memorial Museum - images
- The Bengali Genocide - a statistical look

Books

http://www.virtualbangladesh.com/history/genocide.html

- Books on Bangladesh liberation and Genocide.

They are (1) The Silence of Intellectualism, (2) The Islamic Money, (3) The Spirit of Nationalist, (4) Islamic Population Growth, and (5) International Rise of Islam.

Factor No. 1. The Silence of Intellectualism. The first person who unknowingly introduced a system that can silence intellectualism is no less a person than Sheikh Mujibur Rahman himself. Similarly, the first party that compromised intellectualism is none other than the Awami League itself. Sheikh Mujibur Rahman and Awami League initiated the silence of intellectualism when they introduced one-party rule or the socialist proletarian dictatorship in the name of *'Baksal'* in 1975. It was disappointing that after freedom from Yayah Khan and Ayub Khan military dictatorship, another form of dictatorship was introduced in that land.

As I mentioned earlier, I believe Sheikh Mujib and Awami League were very much impressed by General Ne Win and his Burmese Way to Socialism on Burma. Bangladesh adored Burma as a socialist heaven; everybody has food to eat. A great thing for starving Bangladesh!

Although I did my best to convince them that Burmese Way to Socialism was nothing but Burmese Way of Military Dictatorship, it was to no avail. They took me as a petty-bourgeoisie, trained in a western country. Such was Ne Win's influence on Bangladesh. The Muslim exodus in 1978 made them rethink their view on Burmese Way to Socialism. Some 250,000 Burmese Rohingya Muslims were driven out into Bangladesh in 1978. Only in 1988, when BBC broadcast the uprising in Burma the people of Bangladesh were convinced that Burmese Way to Socialism truly was a military dictatorship. Again, 1990-exodus of some 200,000 Rohingya Muslims into Bangladesh strengthened their new-found view of Burmese government as the military thugs. Nevertheless, the neighborly good relationship is well-maintained.

Obviously, Sheikh Mujib and Awami League swung from the extreme right to the extreme left. Please remember they were the Muslim Leaguers until 1949. This does not surprise me since I have experienced that the former colonial peoples believe only in the extreme ideologies such as theocracy, communism, socialist autocracy, militarism etc. This is because these ideologies convey easily understood clear black and white messages. I believe that Sheikh Mujib and Awami League leaders wanted to establish a strong socialist society with moderate Islamic fervor in it, exactly the same thing that General Ne Win attempted in Burma - a strong socialism with moderate Buddhism. The Islamists such as Muslim League and Jamaat-e-Islami want to build a strong Islamic society with moderate socialism in it.

Unfortunately Sheikh Mujib made himself a victim of ideology. In despair, a group of young military commanders killed him and the top leaders of the Awami League (AL). I remember the 1947 killing of Aung San and his Cabinet who were the main architects of Burmese independence. A striking similarity is that Aung San was the first president of Burma Communist party. It is heart-breaking to learn it as a *Third World Phenomenon*. The general concept behind the killing of Sheikh Mujib and the AL leaders is that they betrayed *'the spirit of the Bangladesh liberation War'* which is *'freedom and democracy'*. The rebel military officers maintained that it was a revolution. Lt. Col. Syed Farook Rahman, the leader of the rebellion, is now classified as an Islamist. I am not sure if he was an Islamist at the time of the mutiny. I believe he had no fixed ideology at that time, but was an ideology-less patriotic soldier. I met him three times when he was the President of Freedom Party and a presidential candidate in 1986 presidential election, during President Ershad's rule. He is a very well cultured and sophisticated person, justifying his education and his aristocratic background. At the same time he is a soldier, trained to kill. He maintained that it was a revolution. I believe the circumstances pushed him towards the extreme of the right in the political polarity. **My point here is that it was not the Islamic inspiration that killed Sheikh Mujib, but the belief that he betrayed the spirit of freedom and democracy by introducing a leftist one-party rule**. Please read a different story presented in *The Trial of Henry Kissinger* by Christopher Hitchins in the coming pages.

Detention and assassination of the leaders exerts a powerful negative psychological impact on a nation. I am the victim of such an impact. This is a universal truth. Many intellectual political leaders were shocked and stunned. A good number of them went underground. Baksal as well as the Martial Law Administrations put hundreds of party workers, both the leftists and the rightists, into the jails. As a result, Bangladesh went silent.

I repeat. Bangladesh went silent. **Bangladesh went silent**, in the same way Burma went silent when General Ne Win seized power in 1962.

As I emphasized Bangladesh went silent leaving behind a vacuum of intellectual leadership. The military rulers tried to develop the country with the help of the professionals. When I say the professionals I include the military and civilian bureaucrats, engineers, doctors, and university professors in this classification. The professionals were appointed as cabinet ministers. They are good in executing orders. But they have no imagination since they are narrowly trained in their specialized field. They cannot see beyond the horizon of their specialized microcosm. Most of them do not even have a philosophy. The cabinet minister positions they are assigned to are just prestigious jobs for them. They are paid for that. They were nothing but well-paid technocrats. They have no political will. As a result every government development plan and program failed. This leads to Factor No. 2.

Factor No. 2. The Islamic Money. Overall economic failure was rampant in East Pakistan. When Bangladesh emerged as an independent unit the land and resources were totally devastated. Famine was a day-to-day experience. The economic failure was not only a consequence of hundreds of years of colonialism that exploits Bengal, but also a result of the conservatism of the Bengali people. Whom shall we blame? The colonialists or the backward conservatives?

Sheikh Mujibur Rahman and his Awami Leaguers put the blame on colonialism, imperialism and capitalism. Accordingly they adopted a leftist proletarian dictatorship and nationalized private industries with the immediate effect of crippling the weak economy. Famine became rampant and the national subsistence infrastructure broke down.

When Zia Rahman came into power in 1975, he not only faced a paramount challenge to feed some 70 million starving people but also encountered an agitated populace and soldiers. 'Revolutions' and 'mutinies' were common. As he quenched these *'revolutions'* and *'mutinies,* he was drawn into a religion that he found had miraculous power to quiet the masses as well as the soldiers. The best thing he did was privatization of economy. He reversed the nationalized economy to private economy. At the same time he sought help from the rich western nations and the Islamic countries. The response from the Islamic countries was very timely and helpful to overcome the famine. The Islamic Bank became a major source of relief. The Muslim nations

> "Men of ideas vanish first when freedom vanishes"
> Carl Sandburg, 1878-1967, American Poet

gave great job opportunities to the Bangladeshis, and the remittance of their earnings in foreign currency constituted a major source of national income. Bangladesh exported her doctors, engineers and skilled workers to Malaysia, Indonesia, Brunei, and oil-rich Middle Eastern countries. They were known as the wage-earners and seen as the heroes. The Bangladeshi wage-earners gained great respect and confidence by their employers because of their intelligence, professionalism, skill, and most interestingly, for their humility and humbleness - a very basic, but wonderful human nature of the Bengali people.

As a result Bangladesh infrastructure was re-established with the money of the Muslim nations. It is not wrong to call it *Islamic Money*. Many *cottage and small industries* emerged with the financing of these wage-earners. Business loans from the Islamic Bank generated a good number of medium-sized industries such as textiles, pharmaceutical, aquaculture, construction firms, modern shopping malls, and hotels. Later even small proprietary businesses or limited companies, such as photocopying and binding shops, restaurants, travel agencies, medical/dental hospitals/clinics and nursing homes appeared with the financing of Islamic Bank, through a number of Mosque-based Islamic NGOs and Islamic Foundation. The landscape of Dhaka, Chittagong, and other cities changed with skyscrapers and business centers. Import and export was financed not only by the modern Islamic Bank but by the traditional Islamic trade system as well. It was true that the G7 also gave a good sum of aid to Bangladesh, but the aid mainly went to government expenditure. The private sector was entirely financed by the Islamic money. Thus, the Islamic economy took root in Bangladesh.

Factor No. 3. The Spirit of Nationalist. During this national recovery process in the aftermath of the post-independence disaster and famine, Bangladesh was drawn towards Islam, Muslim Brotherhood and Pan-Islam. At the same time East and West hegemonism pushed Bangladesh Muslims deeper into the realm of religious fundamentalism.

There are three political trends in the developing countries, *videlicet* (1) *pro-East* referring to those who follow the Soviet Russia or Red China system, (2) *pro-West* referring to those who favor the Western or American system, and (3) *nationalist* referring to those who want to develop an indigenous system free from the influence of the East and the West. This is the reason why General Zia Rahman introduced *Bangladeshi nationalism* and called his party *Bangladesh Jatiyo Dal* or *Bangladesh Nationalist Party* (BNP). From the beginning, the party gained great popularity just by its name.

Bangladeshi Muslims do not favor Soviet or Chinese style communism or socialism. It is true many Islamic socialists believe that Islam is a better socialism. The Islamic socialist states like Qaddafi's Libya *(Great Socialist People's Libyan Arab Jamahiriya)* and Sadam Hossain's Iraq are two examples of such Islamic socialism. Accordingly, Islam is considered the indigenous socialism. Sheikh Mujib's introduction of Soviet style socialism was outright rejected.

On the other hand:

The Western dubbing of Bangladesh as a *'Bottomless basket* created a bitterness towards the West and the United States of America in the hearts of the Bangladeshi populace. These are the undiplomatic words of Dr. Henry Kissinger who is regarded as the greatest diplomat and peacemaker of the time. He was even awarded the Nobel Peace Prize in 1973. The Bangladeshis dislike Dr. Kissinger bitterly for these words. With great anger they resolve to develop their nation and prove that she is not a bottomless basket. Please see recently emerging news of Henry Kissinger below.

Now the question is: Did Dr. Kissinger plot the killing of Sheikh Mujib, after dubbing Bangladesh as a *bottomless basket*? Please see the excerpt I present below. How disturbing it is! Especially so in Pakistan and Bangladesh because it is an open secret in Pakistan and Bangladesh that the CIA supported the Pakistani military regimes, the Muslim League and the

Bangladesh
excerpted from the book
The Trial of Henry Kissinger
by Christopher Hitchins
Verso Press, 2001
Cited by http://thirdworldtraveler.com/
Kissinger/Bangladesh_TOHK.html

Note: The book is available at amazon.com and Barnes and Noble

p50

In November 1974, on a brief face-saving tour of the region, Kissinger made an eight-hour stop in Bangladesh and gave a three-minute press conference in which he refused to say why he had sent the USS Enterprise into the Bay of Bengal three years before. Within a few weeks of his departure, we now know, a faction at the US embassy in Dacca began covertly meeting with a group of Bangladeshi officers who were planning a coup against Mujib. On 14 August 1975, Mujib and forty members of his family were murdered in a military takeover. His closest former political associates were bayoneted to death in their prison cells a few months after that.

Jamaat-e-Islami all through the 1950s and 1960s, in a preventive measure against the possible takeover by the communists and socialists.

Riding on the rising tide of anti-West/East feelings, Ziaur Rahman introduced Bangladeshi Nationalism, Islamized the constitution with the addition of "BISMILLAH-AR-RAHMAN-AR-RAHIM" (In the Name of Allah, the Beneficent, the Merciful)" and eliminated Article 12: "Secularism and freedom of religion". Islamic parties that were outlawed by Shiekh Mujib's government were made legal. Once again Islam became a pillar of nationalism standing side by side with *mother Bangla* (*cf.* Islam of 1947 Pakistani nationalism).

Factor No. 4. Islamic Population Growth. Since 1975 domination of Islam over the liberal intellectual thoughts has produced a proportionately large number of Islamic intellectuals and Islamic middle class. This process is accelerated by the growth of the Islamic economy. Please recall the previous information I gave on leaders like Begum Khaleda, Sheikh Hasina, Professor Golam Azam and Maulana Nizami. How many children do they have? Here is a table I made out of the information I collected. Please note that I did not include Prof. Azam in this table because he, being born in 1922, belongs to the older generation that commonly has 4 to 11 children! Begun Khaleda, Sheikh Hasina, and Maulana Nizami were respectively born in

Table3.5 How many children Bangladesh leaders have?			
Leader	Sons	Daughters	Total
Begum Khaleda	2	-	2
Sheikh Hasina	1	1	2
Maulana Nizami	4	2	6

1945, 1947 and 1943; hence they belong to the same generation and can be compared and contrasted. Please note the total number of children the leaders have. It is not sheer accidental that Begum Khaleda and Sheikh Hasina have two children each and Maulana Nizami has six children. The former two leaders cherish modern liberal thoughts whereas the latter dwells in Islamic thoughts. This has been the general trend in Bangladesh for past the 30 years. As a result, the number of children with Islamic thoughts greatly outnumbers those having liberal thoughts. Today, these children are the young leaders enjoying the prime age of early 20s or 30s.

> Boy or Girl Two Is Enough!
> This was very pragmatic policy of President Ziaur Rahman.
> Has Bangladesh abandoned it now?

During the days of Ziaur Rahman big billboards bearing the propaganda - "Boy or Girl Two Is Enough" - were visible all over Bangladesh. Zia Rahman must be duly credited for his pragmatic policy. His hybridization of traditional parliamentary system and US presidential system, his idea of SAARC (South Asia Association of Regional Cooperation), his message of 'Boy or Girl Two Is Enough', his ruthless consolidation of military grip, and his tactful exploitation of civilian power indicate that he is a tactical genius. As he could not be beaten with tact and craft, unhappy military officers just killed him in the same way as they did with Sheikh Mujib. On the other hand, he made a big mistake by initiating the Islamization process in Bangladesh.

Things to ponder

"It is not a question of communism, socialism, capitalism, Hinduism, Buddhism, Christianity, Islam, atheism, totalitarianism or liberalism.
It is a question of what or who gives food,
shelter, dignity, and security of life."
It simply is a struggle for existence.

Bangladesh now has bloomed with Islamic thoughts. Islamic democracy, Islamic economy, Islamic education, Islamic justice, Islamic social order, Islamic administration, etc. are only a few of what modern Islamic thoughts are fruitfully generating these days.

Factor No. 5. International Rise of Islam. The renaissance of Pan-Islam in Bangladesh is not an isolated case. It is being influenced by the international Muslims and Islam. Iranian Islamic revolution broke out in 1978, soon after the Bangladesh Constitution was Islamized by the Chief Martial Law Administrator General Zia Rahman in 1977. This gave great impetus to the Bangladesh Islamists. The impact of Ayatollah (Ruhollah) Khomeini (1902-1989) upon the Bangladeshi Muslims was enormous. In those days, group discussions of Islam and Islamic revolution took place in every Mosque. Especially after the Friday Congregation (Jama'ah), the Faithfuls, 10 to 20 in number, gathered around a speaker and listened to his discourses. These discourses were very inspirational. Now and then, I used to listen to those discussions at Baitul Muqarram National Mosque and Subhanbagh Mosque. The attendants paid serious attention with good discipline and asked logical questions. The speakers were very acknowledgeable.

Such seminars were held in every major Mosque in every city, town, and village. Discussions covered religion, politics, economy and social order of both domestic and international affairs. The Muslim liberation movements across the world were also well focussed. A session would last from thirty minutes to two hours. I would say the speakers, the participants, and the topics were very impressive. One should not undermine them.

International Mujahideen resistance from 1978 to 1989 in Afghanistan against her communist regime and later Soviet occupation also strengthened the Bangladesh Pan-Islamic awakening. A good number of Bangladeshi Mujahids took part in that revolution. Similarly, the independence of the Muslim nations - Azerbaijan, Kazakstan, Kyrgyzstan, Tajikistan, Turkmenistan, and Uzbekistan from the Soviet Union was a great boast to the Bangladesh Pan-Islamic renaissance.

Bangladeshi Islamists rightly sense that the time is ripe for the revival of Pan-Islam.

A Map showing 8 Muslim countries that have stimulated the Pan-Islamic renaissance in Bangladesh in the past two decades. Base map is from Microsoft Encarta World Atlas 97 CD-ROM. Legends are mine.

3.5. Blossoms of Islam. Islamic schools known as the Madrashas are now well-established throughout the country. School policies are guided by the Islamic Foundation of Bangladesh while the schools are attached to a Mosque and administered by an Imam, who usually is an Archmaulana of the Mosque. In general, a Madrasha student graduates at an age of sixteen, provided that he or she starts schooling at the age of six. However, study can go up to the age of twenty one to be graduated as a Maulana. At the age of fourteen a Madrasha student will take the Junior Madrasha Examination and at sixteen the High Madrasha Examination (HME) that is equivalent to Secondary School Certificate (SSC) Board examination under the government modern education system. When a student passes the HME he completes ten years of education. Upon completion a student may go to a college to graduate with a Higher Secondary School Certificate (HSC) in two years. That makes a total twelve years of education. After that, the student may continue to a university. I have met a good number of Maulawi reading for Bachelor or Master degrees at Dhaka University. Please see below for the description of a Maulawi or Maulana.

Most of the students, however, are sent to vocational schools to become electricians,

---

http://www.answering-islam.org/Index/M/maulawi.html

MAULAWI

"Maulawi", "Maulavi" and "Maulana" are all three the same person, idea, and concept. They come from the Arabic word "*maula*", which means "leader, master, lord", and "Maulana" means "Our leader, lord, or master". It is a term generally used for a learned man or a scholar of Islam.

"Maulavi" is the Farsi version of the same word because Arabs pronounce the "vav" as a "w" sound and Iranians pronounce it as a "v" sound.

Maulana "Our Master, our Lord" is the title given to various leaders of Sufi Muslim groups, the most famous being, "Jalal a din e Rumi" or "Maulana", "our (Sufi) leader, "our Sufi Master". Jalal a din e Rumi or "Maulana" is a famous Sufi Iranian poet, born in Balkh, Afghanistan (born 1207 AD) who fled the Mongolian invasions and settled in Konya, Turkey (1215-1220 AD) and founded the Whirling Dervishes Sufi order (died in 1273 AD).

---

mechanics or other skilled workers. These vocational schools are also financed and regulated by the Islamic boards or councils, but administered and run by the professionals.

Curriculum in a Madrasha is broad. It begins with Bengali and Arabic alphabets and basic reading, writing, and arithmetic skills. Reading, reciting and learning of the Q'uran is followed, and by the age of twelve the student gets training in Islamic rules, disciplines, and function by involving the day-to-day running of prayers and mass assembly in the Mosque. Selective students are also trained in business and Islamic laws, administration and economy. Outstanding students in this category are selected to be trained as the Maulanas. A graduate as a Maulana is equivalent to a modern university graduate in Islamic Science. He reads and writes Arabic with good proficiency and is well versed in Q'uran, Hadith, and Islamic laws including economy and administration, also in Basic English. He is also trained to manage a Mosque, a Zakat Fund, control and conduct a Mosque or a religious assembly, teach Islam and establish an Islamic society. As part of the curriculum he also assists the Imam in the religious functions in the given jurisdiction of the Mosque. He is better than a modern university graduate in the respect that he is trained to start a professional life and career immediately upon graduation. I judge that a Mualana graduated from a good Madrasha is well trained like an army commissioned officer. He is ready to start a mission with the backing of Islamic Foundations, Islamic Banks and other Islamic institutions. Above all, he already has a good number of devotees ready to follow his leadership. It is evident that the Islamic schools known as *'Madrasha'* produce leaders whereas the universities produce slaves of bureaucracy.

By the time General Ershad seized power in 1983, the Islamic infrastructure had already taken root. A good number of the Madrasha high school graduates were in universities forming the Islamic Student Fronts, and ideologically challenging the traditional Awami League or other leftist and centrist student organizations. The following is a web clip of the most well-known Islamic student organization, *Shibir*.

BANGLADESH ISLAMI CHHATRA SHIBIR
A CARAVAN FOR TRUTH AND JUSTICE

shibir .org

http://www.shibir.org/

With financial support of the Zakat[1] Fund, numerous small businesses, mainly in service industries, had mushroomed under the proprietorship of the Madrasha graduates. It was a very well-planned, disciplined, honest and excellently executed *Islamic renaissance*. Bangladeshi have found a refuge in Islam not only as a religion but also as nationalism with a discipline of life. Being tired of the daily intimidation inflicted upon them by *the Powerful-and-Rich* they have armed themselves with egalitarian Islamic philosophy and practices on their march towards a new life. On the other hand, even after more than 1,300 years of practice and trial, the questions still exist. How egalitarian would Islam be? How far can it enhance advancement of science and technology? How high can it promote economy? How strong can it establish peace and stability? How extreme could its militancy be?

While we may try to answer these questions —

Today, Bangladesh is ready to take a lead in the global Islamic renaissance. Her only weakness is poverty. This is a crippling weakness. Nevertheless, if she is backed by the rich Islamic nations she will be a gallant Islamic Knight in the front. The main concerns are: **Will Bangladesh poverty and overpopulation push the Islamic renaissance into a realm of Islamic Commune in the pattern of the 1871 Paris Commune? How is her neighbor, Myanmar, reacting toward her Islamic fundamentalism?**

Note: 1. Zakat is the charity amount due by a Muslim. It is commanded by Allah in Q'uran. Some examples of the Qur'anic verses are given here. The verses are N.J. Dawood's translation from his book *The Koran*, Penguin Classics, 1974. The Zakat amount is traditionally set at 2.5%, and the income tax is not considered as Zakat.
2:215 "...Say, 'Whatever you bestow in charity must go to your parents and to your kinsfolk, to the orphans and to the poor man and to the stranger....'"
6:141 "It is He who brings forth all manner of plants; creepers and upright trees, the palm and olive, and pomegranates of every kind. Eat of these fruits when they ripen and give away what is due of them upon the harvest day. But do not be prodigal; Allah does not love the prodigal".
9:60 "Alms shall be used only for the advancement of Allah's cause,................... That is a duty enjoined by Allah".
73:20 "...Attend to your prayers, pay the alms-tax, and give Allah a generous loan...."

Chapter 4. The Revival of Myanmarism

Meanwhile, Bangladesh's eastern neighbor, Burma, has strengthened herself by reviving Myanmarism in the last 17 years. Myanmarism is a powerful *ultranationalism* that has produced the First (circa 1057-1297 CE), the Second (1540-1599 CE), and the Third (1753-1885 CE) Myanmar Empires. The followings are some phenotypes exhibited by the rise of Myanmarism. (*Note:* Phenotype is a biological term that covers the anatomical, physiological characteristics and behavioral phenomena of an organism. It is determined by the organism's genotype, which is the makeup of genetic structure and function. Here I am using the biological term for I, being a Social Darwinist, classify a nation as a living organism). The followings are some characteristics of today's Myanmar ultranationalism or *Myanmarism*.

Our Mother land which Anawrahta, Kyansittha, Bayinnaung, Alaungphaya, Sinbyushin, and Bogyoke Aung San had built up nurtured and consolidated through ages, cannot be allowed to be in disorder and to disintegrate during our time. .... (Sr. General Saw Maung, 1989).

Armed Forces will never betray national cause

Emergence of State Constitution is the primary duty of all Union Peoples

Our three main national causes

Non - disintegration of the Union — Our cause!
Non - disintegration of National Solidarity — Our cause!
Consolidation of National Sovereignty — Our cause!

The person who resolutely revived and strengthened Myanmarism was Sr. General Saw Maung (1928-1997 CE) who inherited General Ne Win's military dynasty in 1988. He was a general at the time of succession to the power. Sr. General Saw Maung addressed the nation on the 23rd September 1988 after his ascension to power on the 18th instant. He promoted himself to a 5-star Senior General in 1989. He was born in 1928 in Mandalay, and was commonly known as a Mandalay-thar, meaning a son of Mandalay - a very common Myanmar expression. Complicated with diabetes mellitus and alcoholism he died of an heart attack at Rangoon, in 1997. {Now just a joke: In Burma we say all sons and daughters of Mandalay (Mandalay-thar Mandalay-thu) are related to Mindon Min, the second last Burmese king, since he is known to have more than 300 wives. Now, this is a fact: More than forty of his sons with different wives were killed by his minor queen Laungshe, a Shan princess, who masterminded to put her son, Thibaw, to the throne. The British dethroned King Thibaw in 1885. Besides King Mindon, was there any other man known to have more than 40 sons in the history?}

The following is a piece of excerpt from the address delivered at the 44th Anniversary of Resistance Day (Armed Forces Day, 1989) by the Commander-in-Chief of the Defence Services, Senior General Saw Maung. This address signifies the rise of Myanmarism. The source is *'General Saw Maung's addresses and discussions'*, published by the Ministry of Information (Government of Myanmar), Department of Newspapers and Journalism, 1989, by U Tin Thwey, License No. 3492, page 93-105.

> **"Comrades,**
>
> Of the three main duties of our Tamadaw at present, the first is that of defending and protecting the State and ensuring its security.
>
> Our State has been in existence as an independent one among the nations of the world for thousands of years. It is a State that had stood tall with its own kings all through the eras of Tagaung, Sriksetra, Pagan, Myinsaing, Sagaing, Pinya, Ava and Konbaung ....
>
> Our Mother land which Anawrahta, Kyansittha, Bayinnaung, Alaungphaya, Sinbyushin, and Bogyoke Aung San had built up nurtured and consolidated through ages, cannot be allowed to be in disorder and to disintegrate during our time. ...." *(Sr. General Saw Maung, 1989).*

His successor, Sr. General Than Shwe, continues to cherish the same Myanmar imperial philosophy by asserting that the Myanmar Empires were the enterprises of all national races of the land. The relevant excerpt from his speech delivered on the February 12, 2003 is given here.

> **State Peace and Development Council Chairman Senior General Than Shwe's Union Day message** (source: http://mission.itu.ch/MISSIONS/Myanmar/03nlm/ n030212.htm#State_Peace_and_Development_Council)
>
> **Esteemed national brethren of the Union**
>
> On the occasion of the 56th Anniversary of the Union Day of the Union of Myanmar, I, with goodwill, wish auspiciousness to all the national races of the Union..............
>
> Thus, the national races were able to found the First Myanmar Empire in Bagan Period, the Second Myanmar Empire in Toungoo Period, and the Third Myanmar Empire in Konboung Period, achieving the glory and winning the respect of neighbouring countries.

Importance of these Myanmar Empires in Burmese nationalism is confirmed by Prime Minister General Khin Nyunt (2003-2004). The speech was given in February, 2003 before he became the prime minister in August. The following is an excerpt from the address of General Khin Nyunt, Secretary-1 of the State Peace and Development Council (SPDC). He delivered the speech in his capacity of the Chairman of the Central Committee for Organizing the 56th Anniversary of Union Day, Yangon, 8 February, 2003, source: the New Light Of Burma, http://www.myanmar.com/nlm/enlm/feb09_h1.html.

.... "In Myanmar history, national unity was consolidated and the first Myanmar Empire was built by King Anawrahta in 1044, the second Myanmar Empire by King Bayintnaung in 1551 and the third Myanmar Empire by King Alaungphaya in 1752. Thus, Myanmar could stand tall in the whole Asia and respected by neighbouring countries. In the time of Konbaung kings, discord and hatred were sown among national races by colonialists, disintegrating unity within the royal family and Union Spirit faded. Thus, the Myanmar was enslaved by colonialists. The colonialists had been manufacturing fabrications and accusations to undermine national unity and drive a wedge among national races resorting to various means and ways with the intention of exploiting the national races. Those evil acts were carried out to undermine the national spirit....." *(General Khin Nyunt, 2003).*

With the above words and slogans Myanmarism revived in 1988 and onwards. The junta annihilated millenium existence of the Mon and the Rakhaing kingdoms with heinous colonial philosophy, strengthening the Myanmar ultranationalism. Please see below. The Myanmarese opposition forces and the world blame the military leaders for the failed state of Burma. On the other hand the military government has been there since 1962, a long 43 years by 2005! Surely this is not an ordinary military government that we see appearing and disappearing in some parts of the world like the shooting stars. Without public support neither a regime nor a dictator can survive that long. Accordingly, Myanmarism deserves due analysis.

Mon source: http://www.geocities.com/Athens/Bridge/1256/monhistory1.htm

The second wave of peoples to come into Burma after the Mon were the Tibeto-Burmans from the north. The Mon's reluctance allowed the infant Burman kingdom to survive and grow. In the process the leadership of the Tibeto-Burmans tribes passed to the Burmans and in 849 AD they founded their own city Pagan. In 1044, the Burmese king Anawrahta came to the throne of Pagan. After he grew his power and influence, he challenged and conquered Theravada Mon in Thaton in 1057. It was a unity not by peaceful means but through force.

U Aungzeya, a Burman leader who is better known as King Alaungphaya, drove the Mon out of upper Burma from Ava and regained other lost territories. By 1757 he defeated the Mon and annexed the Mon kingdom of Hongsawatoi. *The Mon have ever since become a people without a country.*

MRAUK-U: GLORY OF A PEOPLE
KHAING WANTHA
Forty-five miles north of Akyab, the capital of Arakan, lays a city of ruins. Littered with rubbles from the collapsed buildings, this city once stood as a glory of a dignified people. Mrauk-U had been the capital of independent Arakan until 1784, when the Burmese annexed to her domain As the independence of Arakan ceased, the glory of Krauk-U dimmed away into the graveyard of history.

Source: Arakanpost December 2003, p12.

4.1. Myanmar Way and Myanmar Style
Myanmar-hmuu Myanmar-han
(မြန်မာမှု မြန်မာဟန်)

The ideology of Myanmar military junta is Myanmarism since the days of General Ne Win. I have explained to great extent the functional principles of Myanmarism in my earlier book *Burma: Nationalism and ideology*, University Press Ltd., Dhaka, 1989. That book covers the twists and the turns of Myanmarism including Burmese Way to Socialism up to 1988. Post-1988 Myanmarism is more aggressive and assertive. Most distinctly it abandons Ne Win's romantic socialism, but revives nostalgic *Myanmar-hmuu-Myanmar-han* or Myanmar Way and Myanmar Style. Indeed Myanmarism emanates from *Myanmar-hmuu-Myanmar-han* (Myanmar Way and Myanmar Style).

The following cover pages of Myawadi Magazine typically represent Myanmar Way and Myanmar Style.

Front Cover		Back Cover
In the front cover please note the girl's hairstyle, the dress, the necklaces, the object she holds, and the wood art of the background building.		In the back cover please note the architecture, the art, and the *Mandala* on the wall of the building. Explanations are given next page.

Myawadi is a monthly magazine published by the Armed Forces since 1950s. These are the covers of Myawadi Magazine, September 1995. As per information given the Front Cover Photo was by Thingi Thwe (Maan Tatkatho) whereas Ko Myint Thein (Rupa) contributed the Back Cover Photo. These two photos truly represent the Myanmar Way and Myanmar Style, which is the foundation of Myanmarism. The Myanmar Armed Forces' establishment of Myawadi since 1950s signifies that it is the flag bearer and guardian of the Myanmar Way and Myanmar Style. *Myawadi,* as you may know, is a Myanmar-Thai border town. During the Konbaung (Shwebo) dynasty of 17th and 18th century there was a person known as Myawadi Mingyi U Sa. He was the governor of Myawadi Province that probably is the present day Tanessarim division. He was a famous soldier as well as a poet. A governor, a soldier and a poet rolled together into one in him. Please compare this with Plato's *Philosopher Ruler.* Accordingly Myanmar Armed Forces selected the name *Myawadi* for their monthly magazine, which survives as the main strategic organ of psychological warfare unto today.

The photos express the Myanmarese psyche, complete with pride and prejudice, which is the dynamic force of today Myanmarism. Therefore, it is worthwhile to describe the significance of the photos in some details. I want you to notice the uniqueness of the art in these photos. Please observe the girl's hairstyle beautified with flowers. This hairstyle goes back to 18th century Mandalay era. Although the detail fashion of her dress is not clearly visible its richness can be easily determined. Similarly, beauty of the necklaces and wrist bracelets attracts attention. The lacquered container in her hand is called Oap[1]. Mostly commonly it is a Hswan-Oap[1]. This cultural object dates back to the 12th century Pagan (Bama) and Tha Hton (Mon) Era. It is used to carry food or other essential commodities for the monks. Especially in the traditional Novice Induction Ceremony and Ta-saung-dine full moon festival a procession of girls carrying such lacquered containers can be seen along the streets of the village, town and cities. Every Myamarese Buddhist boy[2] has to be a monk once in his life. Ceremonial induction of a boy, typically between 7-12 years of age, into a beginner monk or *Novice* is a most essential part of Myanmar Way and Myanmar Style. Ta-saung-dine full moon festival is also known as Kahtin Pwe where the Buddhist monks are provided with essential commodities that they may need for their pilgrimage and missionary journeys. It marks the end of Monsoon Waso season when the monks are confined to the monastery for four months without making any pilgrimage or missionary endeavor.

The wood arts seen in the pictures are typically Myanmar in style that can be found in the millenium-old as well as most modern religious and royal or government buildings. All together - the person, the style, the dress, the ornaments, and the background in unison stage her as a *Shwe Maanthu* (a damsel of golden Mandalay) upholding the age-old Myanmar Way and Myanmar Style, a sophisticated culture. Side by side the building in the back cover photo shows an establishment that is artful, graceful, strong and magnificent, with a wall-symbol that probably is a form of *Mandala*. The mystic culture is a pillar of Myanmar Way and Myanmar Style. Please note the last Myanmar royal capital is called *Mandalay*. It is also known as *Maan Mandala* or *the City of Mystics*. The capital was built with mysticism for its stability and prosperity. The architectural design and art of the building itself dates back to the 12th century Pagan Era, which was the period of the First Myanmar Empire.

These two photos together represent the glories of the First and the Third Myanmar Empires spanning some 700 years of the Myanmar institutions. From these institutions today Myanmarism emanates.

Dr. Htin Aung, Ph.D., D. Litt, a former professor of history and Rector of Rangoon University defines Myanmar Way and Myanmar Style as a *folk culture*. He was an ethnic Bama (Burman) and a great great grandson of Maha Minhla Mindin Raza, a famous Myanmar imperial bureaucrat and noble of the Konbaung dynasty. His book *Thirty Burmese Tales* earned him a doctoral degree in literature (D. Litt). It was the government prescribed English textbook that I learned in my matriculation. He was the Rector of Rangoon University from 1946-1958. I would agree with Dr. Htin Aung that Myanmar Way and Myanmar Style in its form of folk culture is very lovely and very beautiful. Without any taboo, it is liberal and democratic. Liberalism is lost when it is transformed into the political ideology of today's Myanmarism.

Myanmar Way and Myanmar Style has beauty and quality to make Myanmar a great nation, but the Myanmarese ego, which is bigger than her soul, has reduced Myanmar to vanity.

Notes.

1. Oap (အုပ်), Hswan-Oap (ဆွမ်းအုပ်).

2. I was conducted into a novice along with my two elder brothers in 1963. I also entered monkhood and studied advanced Anarpanar Meditation at Mahasi Monastery, Rangoon, in 1976. I became a Muslim in 1978 and preformed Haj in 1985. I also learned Christian Meditation from the Quakers when I was a graduate student in Great Britain, 1972-1976.

4.2. The Historical Myanmarism. The historical Myanmarism is warlordism and colonialism.

The first person who institutionalized the Myanmar Way and Myanmar Style into a military force was King Anawrahta (1044-1077 CE). He was also known as Anawrahta Soa. Some scholars believe that Anawrahta is the Myanmar version of Indian Srì Aniruddhadeva or Anuruddha. One of the ten top disciples of Lord Buddha was Venerable Mahathera Anuruddha. He was an Arahat, meaning a Bikkhu who has attained Enlightenment (Nibban). He earned fame for his superhuman magic powers. If Anawrahta is the Myanmar version of Anuruddha he must have adopted this name after his conversion to Buddhism in 1057 CE under the teaching of a Mon monk named Arahan. He also converted all his subjects in Pugan kingdom into Buddhism and seized Mon Thuwanna Bhumi Tha-hton kingdom to obtain Buddha Three Pitakts. It is very likely that the peoples of Pugan did not call themselves Myanmar at that time. The term Myanmar was visibly introduced only in 1112 CE by Prince Raza Kumar, the son of King Kyansittha (1084-1113 CE). The presence of *Soa* as his last name also suggests his lineage to a pre-Myanmar ethnic group, probably the Pyu. Regardless of his origin, historical evidence indicates that he seeded the foundation of today's Myanmarism.

He regimented his kingdom by assigning military administrative zones. He categorized the villages as the 'ten-zone', 'hundred-zone' etc. A village which is classified as a ten-zone has to supply ten soldiers to the king when summoned whereas a hundred-zone village has to supply hundred soldiers. As such he raised a strong army and founded an empire that is known today as the First Myanmar Empire. Since then he has been the source of Myanmar sovereignty. Every king after him tries to follow his footsteps. Bayinnaung and Alaungphaya came in par with him. Please see the maps presented in the coming pages.

The first victim of Myanmarism was the Mon kingdom and its king Manuha. Anawratha, in order to obtain the Tripitakt (Three Canons of Buddha), invaded and destroyed the Mon Kingdom in 1057 CE. Newly converted Buddhist King Anawrahta also made King Manuha as the *Buddha Slave (Phya Kyaun)* at the Pugan Pagodas. Later, he was allowed to build his own Manuha Pagoda. Thus, Myanmarsim began with a violent war and slavery some 1000 years ago.

The duty of a Buddha Slave was to clean the Pagodas and he could not be touched by the masters who were the Pugan peoples. Thus King Manuha became *"an untouchable"*. Ironically, King Anawrahta introduced Buddhism as well as slavery into the Central Burma in 11th century. The slavery was officially abolished in 1960 by U Nu, the first and last parliamentary prime minister of the bygone democratic Burma. The slaves who were of the Mon, the Rakhaing, or the Thai origin, were rehabilitated in various parts of Burma. Today, Manuha Pagoda, with grace and solemnity, stands as the millennium-old landmark of Myanmar colonialism and slavery.

Manuha Pagoda
is the millennium-old landmark
of Myanmar colonialism and slavery.

The pagoda is also known as the Manuha Temple. As a matter of fact, it was the prison where King Manuha was confined. Upon Manuha's request, his conqueror, King Anawrahta, allowed him to build the temple for worshipping. When the temple was finished he was confined to the temple. It is logical to construe that King Manuha was privileged to build his own prison. It is *the Tower of London* in Burma.

Manuha: This temple was built in 1059 by Manuha, the Mon King of Thaton, while he was held prisoner in Bagan[1] after Anawrahta's conquest of the Mon Kingdom. It holds three seated, and one reclining Buddhas in very small enclosures, their cramped positions being said to reflect Manuha's unhappiness at being a prisoner. (Photo with caption is by Bernard Cloutier (2000), produced here with his kind permission. Many thanks to Bernard. Please visit his web site at http://berclo.net. He has many wonderful photos.

Notes.
1. Bagan is the current name for the ancient Pugan.

Map-1. The map shows an approximate expansion, in white demarcation, of the First Myanmar Empire (1057-1297 CE)[1], on the top of the present international borders. Rakkhapura (Kingdom of Arakan) was not conquered by King Anawrahta. In the year 1057, King Anawrahta conquered the Mon Kingdom Tha-Hton. Base map is from the Microsoft Encarta 97 World Atlas CD.

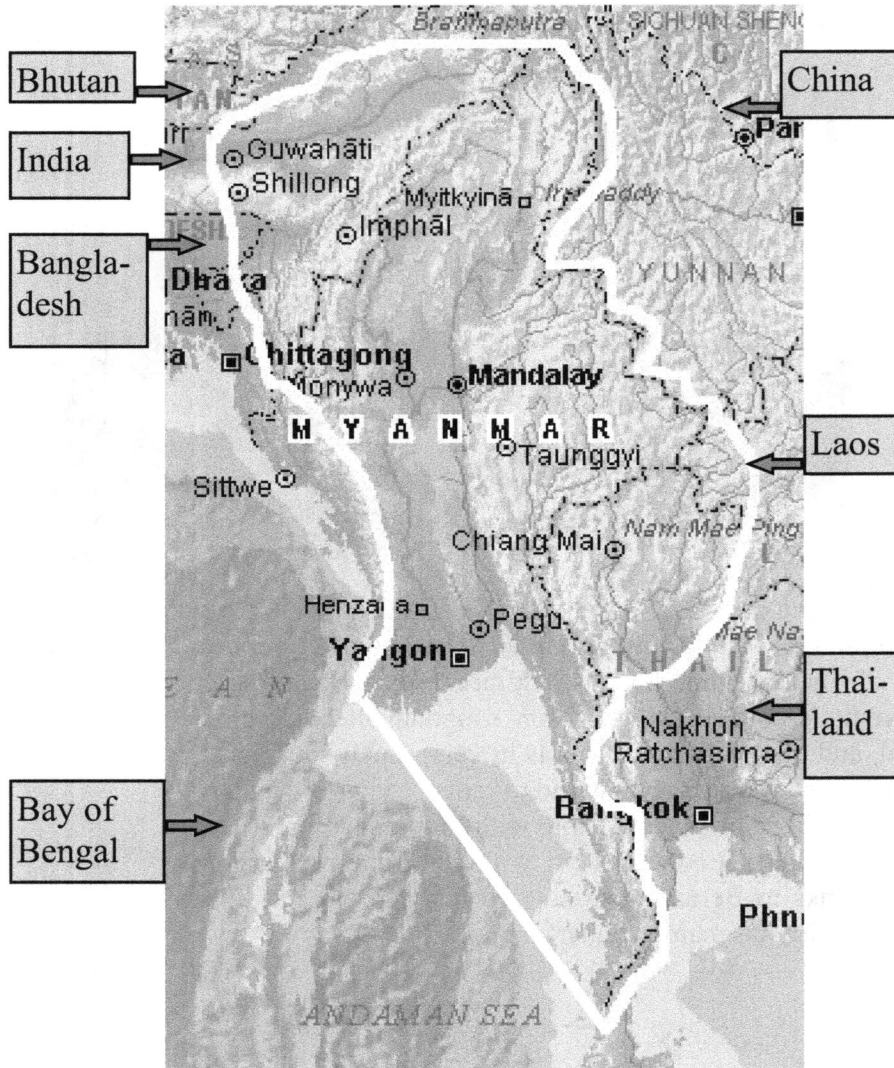

Notes.
1. The historical timeline is based upon the chronology given by Sir Arthur P. Phyare, *History of Burma*, London: Trübner & Co., 1883.

Map-2. The map shows an approximate expansion, in white demarcation, of the Second Myanmar Empire (1540-1599 CE)[1], in addition to the present international borders. The Second Myanmar Empire did not conquer Rakkhapura (Kingdom of Arakan); rather it was destroyed by the Rakkhapureans in 1599. Accordingly, the Rakkhapurean king Raza Gri *alias* Salim Shah is known as the Emperor of Pegu, which was the royal seat of the Second Myanmar Empire. Base map is from the Microsoft Encarta 97 World Atlas CD.

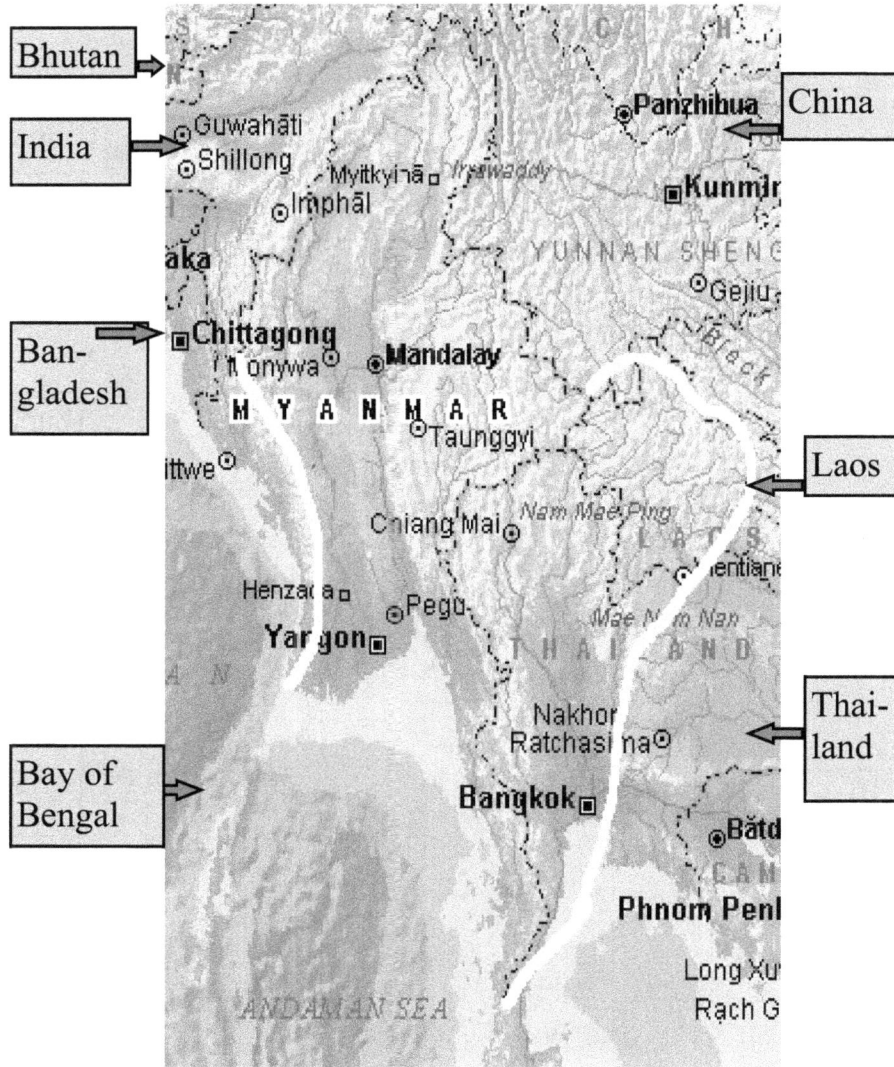

Notes.
1. The historical timeline is based upon the chronology given by Sir Arthur P. Phyare, *History of Burma*, London: Trübner & Co., 1883.

Map-3. The map shows an approximate expansion, in white demarcation, of the Third Myanmar Empire (1753-1885 CE)[1], on the top of the present international borders. Rakkhapura (Kingdom of Arakan) was conquered by the Myanmar king Bodaw in 1784, just 8 years after the United States of America declared independence. While a new nation was born free in the West my kingdom lost her freedom in the East. Myanmar occupation of Rakkhapura violated the demarcated international boundary agreed by the Rakkhapurean king Mun Khari *alias* Ali Khan (r. 1434-1459 CE)[1] and the Myanmar Ava king Narapati[2] (r. 1442-1468 CE)[1]. Base map is from the Microsoft Encarta 97 World Atlas CD.

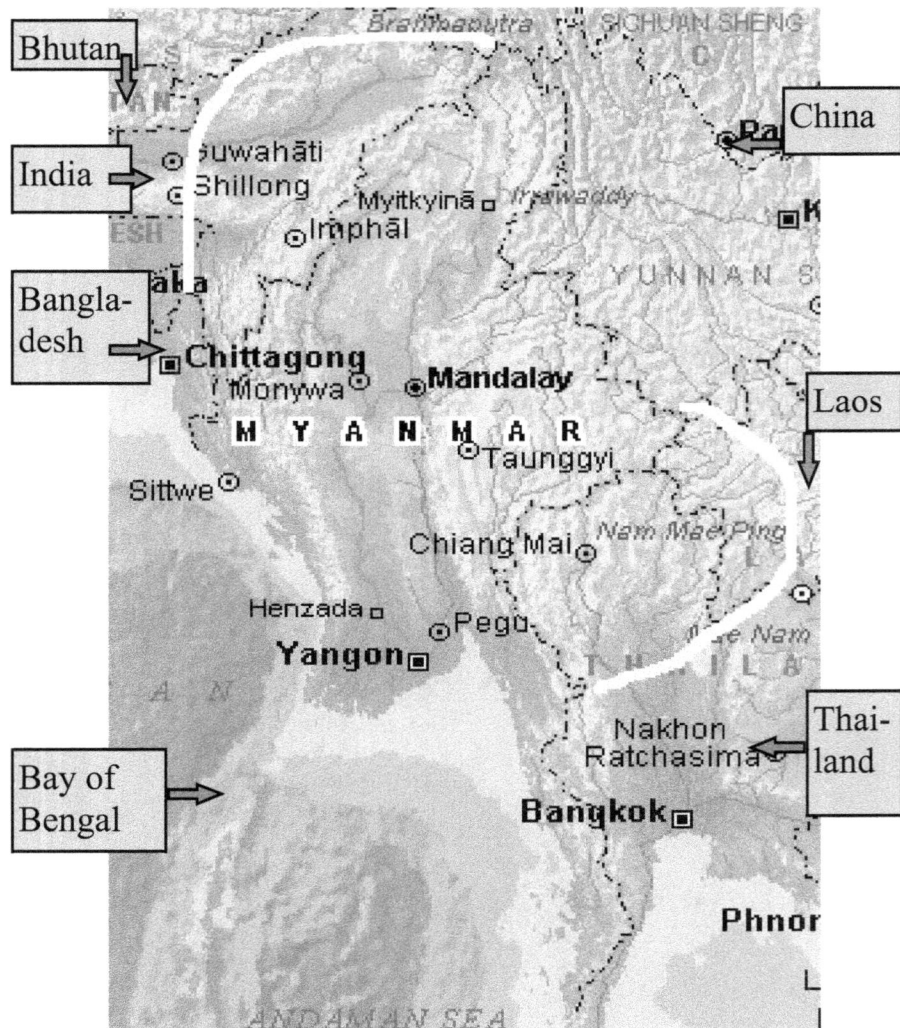

Notes.
1. The historical timeline is based upon the chronology given by Sir Arthur P. Phyare, *History of Burma*, London: Trübner & Co., 1883.
2. Narapati is also known as Thihathu.

As presented in the maps three Myanmar Kings succeeded in colonizing the small neighbors in the past. Firstly, King Anawrahta colonized his neighbors and his empire is recorded to last 139 years from 1058 to 1297. However, based on the Assamese and Chiang Mai histories, it is reasonable to believe that Pugan Kings could not maintain their control of Assam or Chiang Mai for long after the conquest. According to the Indian historians Assam was ruled by the Pala dynasty and Jayapala (1120-1138 CE) was the last ruler of this dynasty (http://www.assamtourism.org/history_assam.htm). The Muslim invasion into Assam took place in 1206 CE and 1226 CE, during the reign of a king called Prithu. In the light of this information it is probable that the Myanmar King Anawrahta conquered Assam but lost control very soon. For sure, Assam was not under the Myanmarese rule up to 1297 CE in the way the Myanmar historians claimed.

Similarly, a piece of information at http://www.lonelyplanet.com/destinations/south_east_asia/chiang_mai/history.htm says that "In 1556 the Burmese captured Chiang Mai for the second time in 500 years. Earlier, before the arrival of King Mengrai, King Anuruddha of Pugan (modern-day Bagan) ruled the area around Chiang Mai in the 11th century. The second period of Burmese control was more successful - they ruled the now-thriving town for over 200 years". According to this description King Anawrahta was unable to rule Chiang Mai for long after his conquest.

For sure, my Rakkhapura Kingdom was not under the rule the Pugan Kings. We have Ley Mrô *(i.e. four cities)* Era from 1018 to 1401 CE, constituted by the Pyinsa, the Parin, the Khrit, and Laung Krak dynasties. I was born in the vicinity of the ancient capital Khrit.

(Note: In my childhood my parents took and showed me the ruins of the palaces, including an Asoka Water Reservoir which was said to be made by Emperor Asoka the Great (b.304 BCE?, r.269-232B CE) of Magadha. The relationship of my Rakkhapura Kingdom and Emperor Asoka is not known except for an interesting fact that, even today, the Bengalis call us Magh or Maghi, meaning the peoples of Magadha. According to the Buddhist chronicles Emperor Asoka built 48,000 water wells, 48, 000 water reservoirs, and 48,000 pagodas. There is also a place that the local people claim to have existed an Asoka Pa-hto. A pagoda that has an entrance into its interior chamber is called a Pa-hto. I also know of another existing pagoda, which our historians claim, was built by Emperor Asoka. I am not identifying it here with fear that the Myanmarese authorities might destroy it. Most of the ancient Rakkhapura historical heritage have been destroyed the ruling Myanmarese).

Therefore, it reasonable to say that the Myanmarese historians' claim of the First Myanmar Empire for more than two hundred years from 1058-1297 CE is nothing but glorification of their feudal past.

The Second Myanmar Empire (1540-1599 CE) was established King Bayinnaung, a king of Taungu (r.1511-1581 CE). He conquered and destroyed Siamese Ayutthaya Kingdom in 1558-59 CE. The Myamarese call it Yodhaya. The Empire was also short lived. The Thai fully regained their independence in 1593 CE when the Thai King Naresuan slew the Burmese crown prince Upraza in their duel riding on the war elephants . Upraza was the second son of King Bayinnaung and younger brother of Burmese King Nanda. The duel fight was staged at Nong Sa Rai near Suphan Buri inside Thailand. The Thai proudly remember their victory in many of their chronicles. One example is given in the next page. The Burmese capital Pegu was finally sacked by the Rakkhapurean (Arakan) King Raza Gri (r.1593-1612 CE), who also adorned a Muslim title Salim Shah Sultan, *The Emperor of Pegu*. Rakkhapura kingdom was never

A mural at the entrance of the Wat Suwandararam in Ayutthaya, painted during the Rattanakosin Period (1782-1868 CE), depicting the 1593 duel of Thai King Naresuan and Burmese Crown Prince riding on the war elephants. The Burmese Prince was killed.	Today a life-size sculpture commemorates the duel at the actual duel site.

conquered by the Burmese kings Tapin Shwehti or Bayinnaung.

The Third Myanmar Empire (1753-1885 CE) was founded by King Alaungpya who established Konbaung Dynasty in 1753. The Myanmarese attacked Thailand many times, but failed to conquer. Alaungpya conquered the Mon Kingdom in 1757. His son Bodawpya conquered Rakkhapura kingdom in 1784. Myanmar occupation of Rakkhapura violated the international boundary demarcated and agreed by the Rakkhapurean king Mun Khari *alias* Ali Khan (r. 1434-1459 CE) and the Myanmar Ava king Narapati (r. 1442-1468 CE) . The two sovereign kings signed the border demarcation agreement with due recognition and respect of each other's sovereignty and territorial integrity in April 1454 CE (Arakanese era: the 6 waxing day of TannKhone AE 816). They met at the Mount Nway Cho Pho Khaung of Arakan Roma Ridge. The border demarcation line was drawn along the crest of Arakan Roma Ridge from the Northern tip down to Mawtin Edge (Cape Negris) at the south into Bay of Bengal. The oceanic island, Haigri, is included in the Arakanese territories. Violating this border agreement Myanmar King Bodaw Maung Wyne annexed Arakan in 1784, under the eyewitness of the British East India Authorities. Upon the victory of the First Anglo-Burman War, Arakan was handed over to the British as per Rantapo Treaty signed by the British and the Myanmar on the 24th February 1826. In that Rantapo Treaty, the territory of our Rakhaingpray (Arakan) was defined according to the 1454-border agreement signed by our Rakhaing king Mun Khari *alias* Ali Khan and Myanmar Ava king Narapati. In this matter of Rakhaing-Myanmar border agreement the reader is advised to consult the native Rakhaing historians and such authoritative book as *Dhannyawadi Razawuntheit* (New Edition of Dhannyawadi History). This agreement is an international treaty that is signed by the two sovereign kings representing their respective kingdoms.

The Myanmarese people and their leaders, both the civilian and the military, deny these facts. For example, Mrs. Aung San Suu Kyi Aris (Daw Suu) remains **silent** about these Mynamar invasions whereas the military leaders openly negate the historical existence of independent Mon and Rakkhapurean kingdoms. Sr. General Than Shwe speech sets an example of such negation.

In his capacity of the Chairman of the State Peace and Development Council Commander-in-Chief of Defence Services Senior General Than Shwe delivered the address at the 57th Anniversary Armed Forces Day Parade in the Resistance Park on U Wisara Road on 27 March 2002. The following is an excerpt from his speech posted at http://mission.itu.ch/MISSIONS/Myanmar/statemnt/57arm.htm) as of February 07, 2004.

"Comrades

Today is the 57th Anniversary of the Armed Forces Day, a day of special significance for our nation.

....

In our country, all the national groups have lived together in harmony since prehistoric times. Even during the feudal period, there was no thought of creating boundaries within the nation according to national groups. The national groups have had the freedom of movement throughout the nation in search of fertile land, and lived together at every location, in every region. ...."

Thus, Sr. General Than Shwe openly denies the existence of the Rakhaing-Myanmar border agreement. This is one more Myanmar colonial practice to erase the history of their victims.

On the other hand, the Myanmarese arrogance and aggressiveness is self-defeating. They lost their territories, and finally independence to the British in three successive Anglo-Burman wars. The First Anglo-Burman War broke out in 1824 and ended in 1826 in favor of the British East India Company. With Ratapo treaty Burma ceded Rakkhapura (Arakan) and Tenessarim to the British East India Company. The following information demonstrates the aggressive behavior of the Myanmar Empire. (Source as of January 20, 2003: http://www.itihaas.com/modern/british14.html).

Lord Amherst[1] became the Governor-General of India in August 1823. During his tenure the most important event which took place was the First Anglo-Burmese War.

Causes for the Declaration of the War

The Burmese had already seized Tenasserim from Siam in 1766, subjugated the kingdom of Arakan in 1784, and also conquered Manipur, near the Surma valley, in 1813. This advance of the Burmese towards the eastern frontier of the Company's dominion made an Anglo-Burmese conflict inevitable. The British were engaged in other parts of India and so they first tried to avoid the direct conflict with the Burmese by sending envoys to Burma - Captain Symes in 1795 and in 1802, Captain Cox in 1797 and Captain Canning in 1803, 1809, 1811 - but it was unsuccessful. Then when the British were fighting with the Pindaris, the King of Ava sent a letter to Lord Hastings demanding the surrender of Chittagong, Dacca, Cassimbazar and Murshidabad. This letter was sent by the Hastings to the Burmese Government stating it as a forged one.

Soon in 1821-1822, the Burmese conquered Assam and in September 1823 the Shahpuri island near Chittagong which was belonging to the Company. The Burmese were then making preparations for an attack on the territories in Bengal. All these events frustrated the British and so finally on February 24, 1824 Lord Amherst declared war on Burma.

Notes.

1. The Governor-General (1823-1828 CE) of India was William Pitt Amherst, the son of Lt. General William Amherst, and nephew and heir of Lord Jeffery Amherst. He was honored as the Earl of Arakan by the British Crown, see Stanley Gordon, *the 1998 Canadian Encyclopedia* at http://www.highbeam.com/library.

In 1852, with the Second Anglo-Burman war the British gained the Lower Burma. In 1885 the British seized Mandalay. From a technical point of view, the Third Myanmar Empire ended in disgrace, losing a war in 1826 to a company, not even to a king. Nevertheless, the Myanmarese historians assert that the Third Myanmar Empire lasted till 1885 when the British East India Company seized Mandalay and imprisoned the Burmese king, Thibaw, at Calcutta. As a matter of historical reality it lasted only 42 years.

4.3. Myanmar Constitutionalism to Colonialism . "The sovereignty of the Union resides in the people," said, the 1947 Constitution of the Union of Burma, in its Chapter 1, article 3. It is from this dialectical constitutionalism that the sovereignty of Union of Burma (*Pyihtaungsu Myanmar Naingan*) derives, not from such feudal kings as Anawrahta, Bayin-naung, or Alaungphya.

The modern independent Burma (Myanmar) was born of a united struggle of the people of the British Burma. The British colonized the territories of so-called Burma through well-planned Anglo-Burman Wars in 1824, 1852, and 1885. In my earlier book *Burma: Nationalism and Ideology* (University Press Ltd. Dhaka, 1989), at Chapter 2.2, I wrote the following:-

"British occupation brought all feudal nations and kingdoms of Burma together under one powerful rule. This, for the first time in the history of Burma, created a common interest among the people of Burma, simply because they faced a common enemy. There appeared a common sense of unity in the struggle of independence. For the first time in the thousand years of rivalry and domination wars, the people of Burma started to try to sink their mutual hatred and discrimination and to forge unity. In such an attempt the common heritage of culture and traditions were highlighted to give the feeling of oneness. The revolutionary elite of all national groups initiated this nationalistic movement."

The movement resulted in an organization named Anti-Fascist and People's Freedom League (AFPFL) in 1944. Bogyoke Aung San (1915-1947), U Nu (1907-1990) and Thakin Than Tun (1911-1986) were the president , the vice-president and the general secretary of the league respectively. Aung San represented the Burma Independence Army BIA), U Nu the *Do Bama Asi-ayone* (We Burman Organization) and Thakin Than Tun the Burma Communist Party. There are also the socialists such as Bo Aung Gyi (later Brig. General), Kyaw Nyein, and Ba Swe etc. The ethnic Rakhaing people were inside the AFPFL; the most prominent leaders were U Aung Zan Wai, U Nyo Tun, and U Ba Saw at the national level and U Pinnya Thiha, Daw Kra Zan, Bogri Kra Hla Aung at the provincial level. U Aung Zan Wai was a Cabinet minister of the Provisional Government of Burma 1947.

Later, the BCP was expelled from AFPFL as the former preferred revolution to negotiation for independence. On the other hand the British government insisted that AFPFL and Aung San must produce credible evidence of the willingness of other ethnic groups, who are referred as the *frontier peoples,* to take independence collectively with the Burmans. As a result, the AFPFL held a conference called Panglong Conference on the 12th February 1947 with the representatives of the Chin, the Kachin, and the Shan. The Mon, the Karen, the Karenni, and the Rakhaing were not present separately in the conference, although it may be said that these peoples are represented by the AFPFL. It was agreed that the frontier people would take independence in unity with the Burman and form a union of Burma in which the frontier people will enjoy full autonomy. It is known as the Panglong Agreement or the Union Treaty.

Based on the strength of this Agreement the British parliament voted in favor of Burma independence and consequence was the Nu-Attlee Treaty leading to the emergence of an independent country in the name of the Union of Burma *(Pyihtaungsu Myanmar Naingan)* on the 4th of January 1948. Evolution of the Union of Burma can be traced in the following political processes.

1. **1937:** Creation of the British Burma separately from the British India in 1937 under the Government of Burma Act-1937. It is commonly known as the 91-Department Administra-

tion. These are the earliest steps taken by the British government for decolonization of her imperial territories. Since 1826 Burma was an administrative unit of the British India. The Government of India Act-1935 paved way to Burma's separation.

2. **1945:** The British Parliament adopted the 'British Government Policy on Burma' in 1945, and committed to grant dominion status to Burma. The people of British Burma united under the umbrella of Anti-Fascist and People Freedom League (AFPFL) and demanded for full independence.

3. **1947, January:** Signing of Aung San-Attlee Agreement in January 1947 guaranteed Burma independence within one year. Aung San was allowed to form a Provisional Government of Burma, which he headed as the prime minister.

4. **1947, February:** Majority of all national groups of the British Burma stood in unity signing the Panglong Agreement in 1947 to take independence in unity and form a federal republic. Please see its complete text in the coming pages. The Panglong Agreement reached by the AFPFL government, and the Federating Nations laid the foundation of the modern Republic of Union of Burma. Thus, the First, the Second and the Third Myanmar Empires have nothing to do with the conception and birth of the Union of Burma; a clear demarcation line of history must be drawn at this point.

5. **1947, May:** The Anti-Fascist People Freedom League (AFPFL), which was the united political front of all national groups of the British Burma, adopted the Draft Constitution of The Burma Union in May 20, 1947. I call this Aung San Constitution as a matter of convenience and simplicity. Bogyoke Aung San and his AFPFL government cabinet members were assassinated due to their concession of a federation to the Frontier Nations. The Frontiers Nations are classified as the tribal subjects of Myanmar by the Burmans (i.e. the Bama). The Burmese authorities found Galon U Saw, a former prime minister of British Burma, guilty of the crime and he was put to death by hanging. It was explained that Galon U Saw killed Aung San and his cabinet ministers out of jealousy. However, my microscopic study shows that the case was not that simple. I will not deal with this issue in this book though, as it is irrelevant with the present subject.

6. **1947, September:** Lawfully elected Constituent Assembly of Burma adopted the Union Constitution on 24th of September 1947. I simply call this U Nu Constitution for the sake of convenience and for contrasting it from Aung San Constitution.

7. **1947, October:** The Union of Burma became constitutionally independent under the Nu-Attlee Agreement that was signed, and came into effect on 17th of October, 1947.

8. **1948, January:** The Union of Burma formally declared her independence at 04:20 O'clock on the 4th of January 1948 in accordance with the advice of her astrological professors. The time of the day provides the best star-alignments for the newborn country as per their star chart.

The full text of the Panglong Agreement, some relevant articles of Aung San Constitution, U Nu union constitution, and Nu-Attlee Treaty are presented in the next pages. U Nu had to scale down the federal constitution to a unitary one. These documents vividly illustrate how the Republic of the Union of Burma was created. It has nothing to do with the First, the Second, or the Third Myanmar Empires.

THE PANGLONG AGREEMENT* (signed February 12,1947)

A conference having been held at Panglong, attended by certain Members of the Executive Council of the Governor of Burma, the *Saophas and representatives* of the Shan States, the Kachin Hills and the Chin Hills:

The Members of the Conference, believing that freedom will be more speedily achieved by the Shans, the Kachins and the Chins by their immediate co-operation with the Interim Burmese Government:

The Members of the Conference have accordingly, and without dissentients, agreed as follows: -

I. A representative of the Hill Peoples, selected by the Governor on the recommendation of representatives of the Supreme Council of the United Hill Peoples (S.C.O.U.H.P.), shall be appointed a Counsellor to the Governor to deal with the Frontier Areas.

2. The said Counsellor shall also be appointed a Member of the Governor's Executive Council, without portfolio, and the subject of Frontier Areas brought within the purview of the Executive Council by Constitutional Convention as in the case of Defence and External Affairs. The Counsellor for Frontier Areas shall be given executive authority by similar means.

3. The said Counsellor shall be assisted by two Deputy Counsellors representing races of which he is not a member. While the two Deputy Counsellors should deal in the first instance with the affairs of their respective areas and the Counsellor with all the remaining parts of the Frontier Areas, they should by Constitutional Convention act on the principle of joint responsibility.

4. While the Counsellor, in his capacity of Member of the Executive Council, will be the only representative of the Frontier Areas on the Council, the Deputy Counsellors shall be entitled to attend meetings of the Council when subjects pertaining to the Frontier Areas are discussed.

5. Though the Governor's Executive Council will be augmented as agreed above, it will not operate in respect of the Frontier Areas in any manner which would deprive any portion of these areas of the autonomy which it now enjoys in internal administration. Full autonomy in internal administration for the Frontier Areas is accepted in principle.

6. Though the question of demarcating and establishing a separate Kachin State within a Unified Burma is one which must be relegated for decision by the Constituent Assembly, it is agreed that such a State is desirable. As a first step towards this end, the Counsellor for Frontier Areas and the Deputy Counsellors shall be consulted in the administration of such areas in the Myitkyina and the Bhamo Districts as are Part 11 Scheduled Areas under the Government of Burma Act Of 1935.

7. Citizens of the Frontier Areas shall enjoy rights and privileges which are regarded as fundamental in democratic countries.

8. The arrangements accepted in this Agreement are without prejudice to the financial autonomy now vested in the Federated Shan States.

9. The arrangements accepted in this Agreement are without prejudice to the financial assistance which the Kachin Hills and the Chin Hills are entitled to receive from the revenues of Burma, and the Executive Council will examine with the Frontier Areas Counsellor and Deputy Counsellors the feasibility of adopting for the Kachin Hills and the Chin Hills financial arrangements similar to those between Burma and the Federated Shan States.

*Reproduced in the *Report of the Frontier Areas Committee of Enquiry,* Government Press, Rangoon, 1947. Also checked with copy of Agreement preserved by U Vum Ko Hau, Minister in Paris, who took part in the Panglong conference as a leader of the Chin Hill Tracts.

This is the full text of Panlong Agreement as mentioned in *Burma's Constitution* by Maung Maung, Martinus Nijhoff, The Hague, 1961, Appendix III.

The Panglong Agreement is a decorative brochure of the ruling junta. Today the official website of the military junta also highlights the importance of it in its own way. According to the http://www.myanmar.com/Union/panglong1.html the following delegates attended the conference.

Delegates who attended Panglong Conference

Bogyoke Aung San and Ministers Bo Khin Maung Gale, U Tin Htut and U Aung Zan Wai, Pha-Hsa-Pa-La delegates Thakin Wa Tin and U Pe Kin, Bo Hmu Aung, Bo Tun Hla and Bo Min Lwin of Pyithu Yebaw delegates, socialist party delegates correspondents club and delegates from daily newspapers attended the conference. Also present were Taungpaing Sawbwa Sao Khun Pan Sein, Nyaungshwe Sawbwa Sao Shwe Thaik, Hsenwi Sawbwa Sao Hon Hpa of Northern Shan State, Mongpon Sawbwa Sao San Htun, Thamongkham Sawbwa Sao Tun Aye and people's delegates from Shan State U Khun Phone, U Tin E, U Tun Myint, U Kya Pu, U Khin Saw, U Khun Hti and Sao Yek Hpa. Kachin delegates who attended the conference were-Sama Duwa Hsinwanaung, U Ding Ra Tang, Duwa Zaw Yit, Duwa Zaw La, Duwa Zaw Lun, U La Bang Garong, La Maw Zaw Taung, Marang Khun Sai, Maung Le Kan and Tin Maung. Chin delegates were U Pon Za Mang, U Taung Chit Tang, U Ko Mang, U Sein Lian, U Hlwa Hmune, U Man Lin, U Taung Za Khok and U Van Ko Hau. Phado Wa Yi Kyaw, Thaton U Hla Pe, Saw San ay and U Chit Tee from KNU attended it as observers. Dominion Secretary Bottomley of delegates from the British government and British officials on hill regions were present as observers.

(Source: http://www.myanmar.com/Union/panglong1.html as of February 15, 2004)

Bogyoke Aung San was the prime minister of the provisional AFPFL government of Burma under the Governor Sir Hubert Elvin Rance. The Panglong Agreement led to adoption of a federal constitution, which I call Aung San Constitution contrasting it with U Nu's Union Constitution. Below I present the first chapter of Aung San Constitution. Dr. Maung Maung documented that "the draft was drawn up by a 111-member committee of AFPFL Convention which met on May 20, 1947, and approved on May 23 when the Convention was dissolved". Please note that Aung San Constitution creates a Federal Union of Burma whereas U Nu Constitution makes the Union of Burma a unitary state with absolute sovereign power vested at Rangoon alone. Under Aung San Constitution the Union States have their own legislatures and governments, in which the residual power rests.

DRAFT CONSTITUTION APPROVED BY AFPFL CONVENTION

THE BURMA UNION AND ITS UNITS
1. Burma should be Proclaimed as an 'Independent Sovereign Republic.'
2. The said Independent Sovereign Republic of Burma shall comprise: -
A. Such territories that were heretofore within the British Burma known as: -

    (i) Ministerial Burma,

(ii) Homalin Sub-Division,

(iii) Sinkaling Khamti,

(iv) Thaungdut,

(v) Somra Tract,

(vi) Naga Hills,

(vii) Salween District,

(viii) Kanpetlet Sub-Division, and

(ix) Arakan Hill Tracts.

B.   The Federated Shan States (including Kokang and Mongpai).

C.   Karenni States.

D.   Kachin Hills, and

E.   Chin Hills District (excluding Kanpetlet Sub-Division)-

3. The said Independent Sovereign Republic of Burma should be known as the 'Union of Burma.'

(1) The status of a *Union State* should be accorded to a people who have: -

(i) a defined geographical area with a character of its own;

(ii) unity of language, different from the Burmese;

(iii) unity of culture;

(iv) community of historical traditions;

(v) community of economic interests; a measure of economic self- sufficiency;

(vi) a fairly large population;

(vii) the desire to maintain its distinct identity as a separate Unit.

(2) The status of an 'Autonomous State' should be accorded to a people who more or less possess the above-mentioned characteristics but lack in economic self-sufficiency.

(3) The status of a *'National* Area' should be accorded to a people who are lacking in all the above-mentioned characteristics except more or less a distinct language, a territory on which it is concentrated in appreciable numbers and the desire to maintain its distinct identity.

(4) The rights of *National Minority* should be guaranteed to a group of persons who -

(i) differ from the Burmese in race, language, culture and historical traditions, and

(ii) form at least one-tenth of the total population of Burma or of any Unit.

4. The jurisdiction of the Union, as represented by its highest organs of state authority and organs of Government, covers the following subjects: -

(1) Constitutional Affairs.

(2) Foreign Affairs.

(3) Defence.

(4) Foreign Trade.

(5) Federal Finance.

(6) National Planning.

(7) Security.

(8) Transport and Communications.

(9) Federal Education.

(10) Federal Health.

5. All power and authority of the Sovereign Independent Republic of Burma, its constituent parts and organs of Government, are derived from the people.

The Chapter 1: The Burma Union And Its Units of Aung San Constitution ends here.

A Union State in the Union of Burma, as per Aung San Constitution, has the following powers. It is very comparable to a State of the United States of America.

THE UNION STATE

1. The Union State shall have its own constitution in conformity with the constitution of the Union and its own specific characteristics and features.

2. It is suggested that the Head of the Union State may be called the GOVERNOR who should be elected by the State Legislature.

3. In the Union State the legislature may exclusively make laws in relation to matters coming within the classes of subjects next hereinafter enumerated: -

(1) Constitutional Affairs: -

   (i) The amendment from time to time of the Constitution of the Union State subject to this Constitution;

   (ii) The conduct of elections to the Union State Legislature and other local bodies;

   (iii) The establishment and tenure of Union State officers and the appointment and payment of State officers.

(2) Finance: -

   (i) Direct taxation within the Union State, other than federal taxes and revenue, in order to the raising of a revenue, for Union State purposes;

   (ii) Land Revenue;

   (iii) Minor minerals as defined in Chapter VIII of the Shan States Manual;

   (iv) Timber other than exportable timber;

   (v) Taxes on luxuries and entertainments;

   (vi) Sale tax;

   (vii) Taxes on professions, trade, callings and employment;

   (viii) Excise duties on alcoholic liquors and narcotic drugs;

   (ix) Shop, saloon, tavern, auctioneer and other licenses in order to the raising of a revenue for State, local or Municipal purposes.

(3) Economic Affairs: -

   (i) Agriculture and Veterinary;

   (ii) Fisheries within the State,

   (iii) Regulation of land tenures;

   (iv) Internal trade and commerce;

   (v) Water Supplies and Irrigations;

   (vi) Unemployment and Relief of the poor.

(4) Security: -

   (i) Police Administration:

   (ii) Administration of justice by Courts subordinate to High Court:

   (iii) The imposition of punishment by fine, penalty or imprisonment for enforcing any law of the Union State made in relation to any matter coming within any of the classes of subjects

---

enumerated in this section.

(5) Communications: -

Local works and undertakings within the State other than Railways, subject to the power of the Union Assembly to declare any work a national work and to provide for its construction and by arrangement with the State legislature or otherwise.

(6) Education: -

   (i) Education, other than higher education;

  (ii) Management and control of all educational institutions;

 (iii) Non-federal libraries, museums and other institutions;

 (iv) Theatres, dramatic performances and cinemas.

(7) Health: -

  (i) Public health and sanitation;

 (ii) The establishment, maintenance and management of hospitals, asylums and dispensaries.

(8) Local Government: -

  (i) Municipalities and other local bodies;

 (ii) Charities and charitable institutions.

The Chapter 11: The Union State of Aung San Constitution ends here.

For full text please see *Burma's Constitution* by Maung Maung, Martinus Nijhoff, The Hague, 1961, Appendix IV. He mentioned that the text was from *The Burmese Review*, May 26, 1947.

Now let us see some articles that deal with the structure of the Union of Burma in U Nu Constitution. Please compare and contrast these with those of Aung San Constitution.

In the Constituent Assembly on September 24, 1947, Prime Minister U Nu moved the draft of Union constitution with an eloquent leftist speech. Since his university days he was a playwright and powerful orator. Leftism was the main philosophy of Burmese independence struggle. This English version is the translation of Dr. Maung Maung from the Burmese article *Burma's Fight for Freedom*, Constituent Assembly Proceedings, vol 3, No. 8, pp.339-345, Government Press, 1948. Here I present some excerpts from his speech.

"Mr. President - Sir, I rise to move that the Constitution of the Union of Burma as amended be adopted.

    ....

    ....Freedom for Burma will be meaningful only when there is freedom for the masses....

    ...., may I say this? The Draft Constitution which is now before the House, contains the seeds of the freedom which is not the freedom of the favoured few but which is the freedom of the Burmese masses. But, however good the seed may be, the gardener must also be efficient. The gardeners in Burma are none other than the hon'ble members of this house........

I firmly believe therefore that they as gardeners, must succeed in raising this tender seedling into Burma's magnificent tree of freedom.

Sir, I beg to move that the Bill of the Draft Constitution for Burma be adopted."

The bill was adopted unanimously. Now let us see some of the constitutional provisions, which are of our interest in this book. Here comes its Preamble and the Chapter 1, Form of State. For full text please see *Burma's Constitution* by Maung Maung, Martinus Nijhoff, The Hague, 1961, Appendix VII.

The Constitution of the Union of Burma

Preamble

WE, THE PEOPLE OF BURMA including the Frontier Areas and the Karenni States, Determined to establish in strength and unity a SOVEREIGN INDEPENDENT STATE, TO maintain social order on the basis of the eternal principles of JUSTICE, LIBERTY AND EQUALITY AND To guarantee and secure to all citizens JUSTICE social, economic and political; LIBERTY of thought, expression, belief, faith, worship, Location, association and action; EQUALITY of status, of opportunity and before the law, IN OUR CONSTITUENT ASSEMBLY this Tenth day of Thadingyut waxing, 13O.9 B.E. (Twenty-fourth day of September,.1947 A.D), DO HEREBY ADOPT, ENACT AND GIVE TO OURSELVES THIS CONSTITUTION.

CHAPTER I

FORM OF STATE

1. Burma is a Sovereign Independent Republic to be known as 'the Union of Burma.'
2. The Union of Burma shall comprise the whole of Burma, including -
    (i) all the territories that were heretofore governed by His Britannic Majesty through the Governor of Burma, and
    (ii) the Karenni States.
3. The sovereignty of the Union resides in the people.
4. All powers, legislative, executive and judicial, are derived from the people and are exercisable on their behalf by, or on the authority of, the organs of the Union or of its constituent units established by this Constitution.
5. The territories that were heretofore known as the Federated Shan States and the Wa States shall form a constituent unit of the Union of Burma and be hereafter known as 'the Shan State.
6. The territories that were heretofore 'known as the Myitkyina and Bhamo Districts shall form a constituent unit of the Union of Burma and be hereafter known as 'the Kachin State.
7. The territories that were heretofore known as the Karenni States, viz., Kantarawaddy, Bawlake and Kyebogyi, shall form a constituent unit of the Union of Burma and be hereafter known as 'the Karenni State."
8. All powers, legislative, executive and judicial, in relation to the remaining territories of the Union of Burma shall, subject to the provisions of section 180 be exercisable only by, or on the authority of, the organs of the Union.

Chapter 1 ends here.

Please note there are three states namely the Shan, the Kachin, and the Karenni States. These states are very different from the Union State of Aung San Constitution. This subject will be brought up again at a later time.

TREATY BETWEEN THE GOVERNMENT OF THE UNITED KINGDOM AND THE PROVISIONAL GOVERNMENT OF BURMA

London, 17th October, 1947

The Government of the United Kingdom of Great Britain and Northern Ireland, and the Provisional Government of Burma;

Considering that it is the intention of the Government of the United Kingdom of Great Britain and Northern Ireland to invite Parliament to pass legislation at an early date providing that Burma shall become an independent State;

Desiring to define their future relations as the Governments of independent States on the terms of complete freedom, equality and independence and to consolidate and perpetuate the cordial friendship and good understanding which subsist between them; and

Desiring also to provide for certain matters arising from the forthcoming change in the relations between them,

Have decided to conclude a treaty for this purpose and have appointed as their plenipotentiaries:-

The Government of the United Kingdom of Great Britain and Northern Ireland: The Right Hon. Clement Richard Attlee, C.H., M.P., Prime Minister and First Lord of the Treasury.

The Provisional Government of Burma: The Hon'ble Thakin Nu, Prime Minister

Who have agreed as follows:-

Article 1

The Government of the United Kingdom recognize the Republic of the Union of Burma as a fully Independent Sovereign State. The contracting Governments agree to the exchange of diplomatic representatives duly accredited.

....

4. In this Schedule the expression "Burma" means the territories which, immediately before the appointed day, were included in Burma.

....

....

Article 15

The present Treaty shall be ratified and shall come into force immediately upon the exchange of Instruments of Ratification, which shall take place on the day on which Burma becomes independent in accordance with the appropriate legislation to be introduced in the United Kingdom for that purpose.

In witness whereof the above-named plenipotentiaries have signed the present Treaty and have affixed thereto their Seals. Done in duplicate in London this 17th day of October, 1947. **(Sd.) Clement Richard Attlee. (Sd.) Thakin Nu.**

I am confident that I have presented adequate amount of information clearly demonstrating the emergence of the Union of Burma (Pyihtaungsu Myanmar Naingan). It is an attempt of the peoples of the British Burma to build a modern nation upon the foundation of the principle that "sovereignty emanates from the people". As described earlier, the Chapter 1, Articles 3 and 4, of U Nu Constitution solemnly constitutionalized this noble principle and was unanimously adopted by the lawful Constituent Assembly. My grandparents and parents surrendered their sovereignty to this constitution. Without demanding the independence of Rakkhapura Kingdom, we, the Rakhaing Nation, also accepted the rule of this constitution and became part of the new nation. Our Rakhaing Nation was a federating nation in the Union of Burma. I was born as a British subject in 1945, but became a citizen of the Union of Burma in 1948 under the U Nu Constitution of the Union of Burma. So were all other peoples of the British Burma. In spite of its negation of the federal structure, federating nations accepted U Nu Constitution with good faith that they would be able to build a federal union through the democratic process that is guaranteed in the constitution.

When this Constitution of the Union of Burma was violently abolished by force on the 2nd March 1962 the Union of Burma ceased to exist. Since then, Myanmar colonialism took over the new republic. The federating nations immediately lost the faith.

Burmese Armed Forces that was known as the Bama Tatmadaw at that time announced that they had to stage the coup d'état because the Shan State was at the point of seceding the Union of Burma. The Shans denied the charge and rebutted that the accusation was nothing but a thin veil of Bama Colonialism. The federating nations agreed with the Shans, and an armed struggle for a Federation of Burma set Burma on fire. I presented a concise account of the armed struggle in the Chapter 5 of my book *Burma: Nationalism and Ideology*, University Press Ltd., Dhaka, 1989. Here, I will give more detail of the event. As you proceed reading please maintain the awareness of the federal structure in Aung San Constitution, and the central monopoly of U Nu Constitution. The federating nations charge that U Nu Constitution is a violation of the Panglong Agreement by introducing a unitary rather than a federal system. When we examine the structure of a State as provided by U Nu Constitution the picture becomes clear. As an example I will present the constitutional provisions that make the Kachin State. U Nu Constitution, Chapter IX, Part II The Kachin State is given here.

PART II. - THE KACHIN STATE

THE KACHIN STATE COUNCIL

166. (1) All the members of the Parliament representing the Kachin State shall constitute the Kachin State Council.

(2) Of the twelve seats in the Chamber of Nationalities six shall be filled by representatives of the Kachins and the other six by those of the non-Kachins of the Kachin State.

(3) Any member of the State Council who shall have ceased to be a member of the Parliament shall be deemed to have vacated his seat in the Council, but may continue to carry on his duties until his successor shall have been elected.

167. (1) A Bill prejudicially affecting any right or privilege which the Kachins or the non-Kachins, as a class or community, enjoyed immediately before the commencement of this Constitution, shall not be deemed to have been passed by the Council unless the majority of the

---

members representing the Kachins or the non-Kachins, as the case may be, present and voting, have voted in its favour.

(2) If any question arises in the State Council whether a Bill is of the character described in the last preceding subsection, the presiding officer shall take the vote of the members representing the Kachins and those representing the non-Kachins in the Council separately on such question and if a majority of either class of members vote in the affirmative, the Bill shall be deemed to be of the character mentioned.

168. The State Council may recommend to the Parliament the passing of any law relating to any matter in respect of which the Council is not competent to legislate.

169. When a Bill has been passed by the State Council it shall be presented to the President for his signature and promulgation. The President shall sign the Bill within one month from the presentation of the Bill, unless he refers the Bill to the Supreme Court for its decision under the next succeeding section.

170. (1) The President may, in his discretion, refer any Bill presented to him under the last preceding section to the Supreme Court for decision on the question whether such Bill or any specified provision thereof is repugnant to this Constitution.

(2) The Supreme Court, consisting of not less than three judges, shall consider the question referred to it and, after such hearing as it thinks fit, shall pronounce its decision on such question in open Court as soon as may be, and in any case not later than thirty days after the date of such reference. The decision of the majority of the judges shall, for the purposes of this section, be the decision of the Court.

(3) In every case in which the Supreme Court decides that any provision of the Bill, the subject of a reference to the Supreme Court under this section, is repugnant to this Constitution, the President shall return the Bill to the State Council for reconsideration and shall decline to sign it unless the necessary amendments shall have been made thereto.

(4) In every other case, the President shall sign the Bill and promulgate the Act as soon as may be after the decision of the Supreme Court shall have been pronounced.

(5) When the President has signed a Bill presented to him under the last preceding section whether without or after a reference to the Supreme Court, the validity of any provision of the Bill shall not be called in question on the ground that it was beyond the competence of the State Council.

171. The signed text of every Act shall be enrolled for record in the office of the Registrar of the Supreme Court and a copy of the same shall be enrolled for record in the office of the Minister for the Kachin State.

172. The Head of the Kachin State may from time to time summon and prorogue the State Council: -

Provided that there shall be a session of the State Council once at least in every year so that a period of twelve months shall not intervene between the last sitting of the Council in one session and its first sitting in the next session.

GOVERNMENT OF THE KACHIN STATE

173. A member of the Union Government to be known as the Minister for the Kachin State shall be appointed by the President on the nomination of the Prime Minister acting in consultation with the Kachin State Council from among the Kachin members of the Parliament representing

the Kachin State. The Minister so appointed shall also be the Head of the Kachin State for the purposes of this Constitution.

174. (1) The Head of the State shall be in charge of the administration of the State, that is to say, the executive authority of the State shall be exercised by the Head of the State either directly or through officers subordinate to him.

(2) Without prejudice to the generality of the provisions of the next succeeding section, the said executive authority shall extend to all matters relating to recruitment to the State civil services, to postings and transfers, and to disciplinary matters relating to these services: Provided that in respect of areas where the non-Kachins form the majority of the population, the I-lead of the State shall act only in consultation with the members representing the non-Kachins in the Cabinet in all such matters.

175. (1) Subject to the provisions of this Constitution, the executive authority of the State extends to the matters with respect to which the State Council has power to make laws, and in all such matters the decision of the Council shall be binding on the Head of the State.

(2) The Head of the State shall consult the State Council in all other matters relating to the State.

(3) In order to facilitate the communication of the decisions and the views of the State Council to the Head of the State, the Council shall at its first meeting after a general election elect from among its members or otherwise a Cabinet of State Ministers to aid and advise the Head of the State in the exercise of his functions:

Provided that not less than one-half of the members of the Cabinet shall be non-Kachins.

176. The Head of the State shall give or cause to be given an account of his work to the State Council in each ordinary session, present or cause to be presented to the Council, a report upon all matters relating to the State, and recommend for the consideration of the Council such measures as he thinks fit for promoting the general welfare.

177. (1) The Head of the State shall prepare or cause to be prepared the estimates of the receipts and of the expenditure of the State for each financial year and shall present them or cause them to be presented to the State Council for consideration.

(2) Subject to any conditions that may be imposed by the Union in respect of any contributions from the Union, the State Council shall have power to approve the budget of the State; and in order to enable the President to satisfy himself that the conditions have been duly observed, such budget shall be incorporated in the Union budget.

178. The provisions of Chapter X of this Constitution shall not apply to the Kachin State.

179. Subject to the provisions of this Constitution, all matters relating to the Constitution of the State including those relating to the powers and duties of the Head of the State, of the State Council and of the Cabinet of State Ministers, and their relations to each other and to the Union Government shall be determined by law.

In 1947, the Federating Nations accepted U Nu Constitution in order to ensure the smooth transition of colonial Burma into an independent republic. In 1950s, they began their Federation Movement inside the Union Parliament to amend the following weakness of the Constitution. Please contrast these features with those of Aung San Constitution.

1. There is no State Legislature. The State Council is virtually powerless as the Union Government holds absolute sovereign power leaving no residual power to the states. This is

termed as the Central Monopoly or the Bama (Myanmar) Monopoly.

2. The Head of the State who is the chief executive of the State Government is not elected, but rather appointed by the Union Government.

3. The head of a State is a only a cabinet minister in the Union Government, who reports to the Union Prime Minister.

4. The above three features violate the Panglong Agreement making the Union of Burma a *Unitary* State deviating from a *Federal* State that is envisaged by the Panglong Agreement.

Embracing the above political analyses the federating nations put up their movement for a Federation of Burma within the framework of the existing parliamentary democracy. This was done because U Nu Constitution is beautified with vital democratic features giving opportunity to create new states, and amend the constitution. Examples are presented below.

PART VI. - NEW STATES

199. The Parliament may by an Act admit to the Union a new State upon such terms and conditions including the extent of representation of the State in the Parliament as may be specified in the Act.

200. The Parliament may by an Act, with the consent of the Council of every State whose boundaries are affected thereby -

(a) establish a new unit;

(b) increase the area of any unit;

(e) diminish the area of any unit;

(d) alter the boundaries of any unit;

and may, with the like consent, make such supplemental, incidental and consequential provisions as the Parliament may deem necessary or proper.

CHAPTER XI

AMENDMENT OF THE CONSTITUTION

207. Any provision of this Constitution may be amended, whether by way of variation, addition, or repeal, in the manner hereinafter provided.

208. (1) Every proposal for an amendment of this Constitution shall be in the form of a Bill and shall be expressed as Bill to amend the Constitution.

(2) A Bill containing a proposal or proposals for the amendment of the Constitution shall contain no other proposals.

209. (1) Such Bill may be initiated in either Chamber of Parliament.

(2) After it has been passed by each of the Chambers of Parliament, the Bill shall be considered by both Chambers in joint sitting.

(3) The Bill shall be deemed to have been passed by both Chambers in joint sitting only when not less than two-thirds of the then members of both Chambers have voted in its favour.

(4) A Bill which seeks to amend -

(a) the State Legislative List in the Third Schedule, or

(b) the State Revenue List in the Fourth Schedule, or

(c) an Act of the Parliament making a declaration under paragraph (iv) of sub-section (1) of section 74 removing the disqualification of any persons for membership of the Parliament as representative from any of the States shall not be deemed to have been passed at the joint sitting of the Chambers unless a majority of the members present and voting, representing the State or each of the States concerned, as the case may be, have voted in its favour.

(5) A Bill which seeks to abridge any special rights conferred by this Constitution on Karens or Chins shall not be deemed to have been passed by the Chambers in joint sitting unless a majority of the members present and voting representing the Karens or the Chins, as the case may be, have voted it in its favour.

210. Upon the Bill being passed in accordance with the foregoing provisions of this Chapter, it shall be presented to the President who shall forthwith sign and promulgate the same.

On the strength the provisions for the creation of new states and the constitution amendments the federating nations were successful in creating the Chin, the Rakhaing and the Mon States in 1961. Forging stronger solidarity the federating nations moved a federation bill to make a radical change in U Nu Constitution. There also came in the air that the states might opt to exercise 'The Right of Secession' if the Bama people bullied to block the federation bill. U Nu Constitution grants 'The Rights of Secession' to the federating nations with the provisions in its Chapter X as follow.

CHAPTER X

RIGHT OF SECESSION

201. Save as otherwise expressly provided in this Constitution or in any Act of Parliament made under section 199, every State shall have the right to secede from the Union in accordance with the conditions hereinafter prescribed.

202. The right of secession shall not be exercised within ten years from the date on which this Constitution comes into operation.

203. (1) Any State wishing to exercise the right of secession shall have a resolution to that effect passed by its State Council. No such resolution shall be deemed to have been passed unless not less than two-thirds of the total number of members of the State Council concerned have voted in its favour.

(2) The Head of the State concerned shall notify the President of any such resolution passed by the Council and shall send him a copy of such resolution certified by the Chairman of the Council by which it was passed.

204. The President shall thereupon order a plebiscite to be taken for the purpose of ascertaining the will of the people of the State concerned.

205. The President shall appoint a Plebiscite Commission consisting of an equal number of members representing the Union and the State concerned in order to supervise the plebiscite.

206. Subject to the provisions of this Chapter, all matters relating to the exercise of the right of secession shall be regulated by law.

Inclusion of the right of secession was a copy of the constitution of the Union of Socialist Soviet Republics (USSR); no other federal states such as the USA, or India, or Switzerland grant right of secession to their federating states. In the case of the USSR it was meaningless since it was absolutely impossible for a state to secede under the communist dictatorship. Indeed, every state seceded when the communist dictatorship, and the USSR collapsed in 1987.

In his 1947-speech to move the Draft Constitution in the Constituent Assembly U Nu called his Constitution a leftist constitution. Upon the assassination of Aung San and his Cabinet in July 1947, the major architects of independent Burma were wiped out. The surviving Minister, U Aung Zan Wai, had no clout since he was an Arakanese. The most dominant group that was left was the East-European style socialists led by Kyaw Nyein, Ba Swe, Brig. Gen. Ne Win, and Lt. Col. Aung Gyi, etc. Later, after 1962 military takeover, General Ne Win was even dubbed as the Tito of Burma. U Nu, a reborn Buddhist and Buddhist Socialist, had no support except for his stand as a unifier opposing the factionalism. On the strength of his neutralism he was accepted as the leader to replace Aung San. Another great asset of U Nu was that he was the only person the British government and Governor Sir Hubert Elvin Rance trusted. The result was that U Nu had to give up most of his belief and accept the socialists' preposition to keep the country intact till independence came officially. He knew it would fall apart after the independence. With great hesitation he accepted the invitation of Governor Sir Hubert Elvin Rance to head the provisional government at the death of Aung San and his ministers. The inclusion of the right of the secession in his constitution was a concession to appease the federating nations who were seriously upset as Aung San federal constitution was virtually trashed by the new Bama leadership. The Red Socialists accepted it taking the example of the USSR. They also wanted to make the constitution a form of socialist dictatorship so that the right of secession could not be practicable. However, they accepted the parliamentary form of constitution simply to satisfy the British parliament, and government. It simply was just a ploy to secure independence. The plan to transform Burma into a socialist dictatorship was an open secret among the well-informed political elite. (For example, upon the adoption of U Nu Constitution, U Nyo Tun told the Arakanese military commander Bo Gri Kra Hla Aung, "You have to go underground and prepare for a guerrilla war; there is no other choice left", because their dream of a federation of Burma was crushed. As an Arakanese political leader U Nyo Tun was in the Burmese secret delegation that negotiated with the Allied Supreme Command for the military alliance to oust the Japanese from Burma. He politically supervised the Arakanese guerrilla forces in 1944 anti-Japanese war in Arakan, hand in hand with the Allied Forces. Bo Gri Kra Hla Aung was the commander-in-chief of the Arakanese guerrilla army. This is what Bo Gri Kra Hla Aung told me when I was a member of his party's central committee in 1966-67.

Now, let us get back to the main theme of the right of secession. In February 1962 the Kachin, Shan, Karenni, Karen, Mon, Rakhaing, and Chin leaders who represented the federating nations gathered at Rangoon to celebrate the 15th Anniversary of Panglong Agreement and Union Day. After the celebration they all remained in Rangoon to finalize the bill of Federal Constitution that they planned to move in the parliament. On the 2nd of March 1962, General Ne Win arrested all of them at Rangoon, seized the power from U Nu, dissolved 1947 U Nu Constitution, and abolished the parliament, its government, and all democratic institutions. His reasons were (1) the Union of Burma was at the brink of breaking up due to the secessionist federation movement and (2) U Nu had deviated from the socialist path. On that day, General Ne Win and the hardliners revived Myanmar colonialism in disguise as the Burmese Way to

Socialism under the strong military socialist dictatorship. In 1988, Sr. General Saw Maung boldly introduced naked Myanmarism after peeling of the socialist cloak. His successors, Sr. General Than Shwe and General Khin Nyunt have strengthened it by solidifying the military rule. They achieve the task by (1) inheriting the state sovereignty from the First, the Second, and the Third Myanmmar Empires, (2) modernizing and enlarging the armed forces to a strength of 500,000 personnel from its original 180,000 in 1988, and (3) brutally crushing any form of opposition that stands in their way. Today Myanmar colonialism is being constitutionalized under the program of the junta's roadmap to democracy as General Khin Nyunt revealed last year[1]. In this Myanmar colonial democracy, pluralism will be allowed, but (1) 25% of the People's Assembly seats will be occupied by the appointed military officers, (2) the president of the country must be a military officer, (3) the elected government has no authority over the armed forces, and most importantly (4) the sovereignty is derived from the First, the Second, and the Third Myanmar Empires. These are the basic characteristics of modern Myanmar colonialism.

As presented above, a Myanmar colonial constitution is being made under the gunpoint. General Ne Win was successful in making his socialist military constitution at gunpoint in 1974 after ruling the country by military decree for 12 years. It lasted 14 years till 1988 when the people rose and rioted against it. Similarly, after ruling the country for 16 years by decree since 1988, the present the military junta has pointed the gun at the people at large and asked them to draft a constitution as per given outline mentioned above. The present junta will be as much successful as General Ne Win. But, how long will it last? This surely is a big question.

Notes.
1. Please also see Shwe Lu Maung *alias* Shahnawaz Khan, *The Arakanese Student and Youth Movement, Series 5: The strategies and tactics after 8.8.88. Arakanpost*, Issue-6, November-2004, Narinjara News, p17.

Myanmarism is a Burmese variety of colonialism. It is an ethnocentric colonialism, in which the larger ethnic group rules the smaller ones with the sovereign power emanating from the Bama National Race. It exists and functions as an inverted pyramid that is illustrated below.

Classification of the national races is adopted from the Myanmar government official web site, myanmar.com. (http://www.myanmar.com/gov/tourist/pop.html, as of November, 2004).

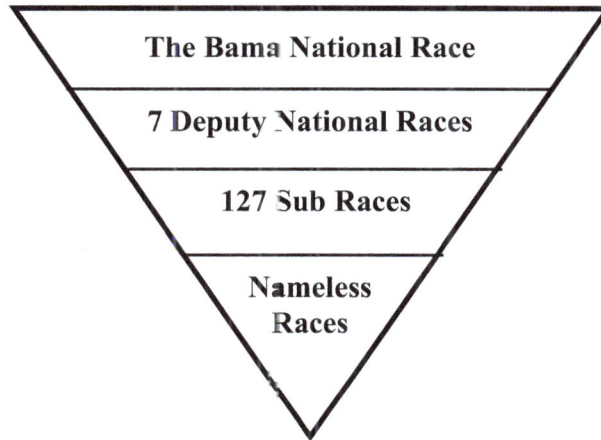

The Bama National Race

7 Deputy National Races

127 Sub Races

Nameless Races

The Bama National Race
The Bama National Race constitutes the First Class Citizens and is the ruling class and colonial masters. Myanmar.com lists a total of 9 sub races in this class.
They constitute 40% of the total Burmese population, 49 millions in 2004. Their powerhouse is known as the Burma Proper that consists of 7 administrative Divisions.

7 Deputy National Races
The Second Class Citizens or the Deputy Ruling Races are made up of seven major national races namely, 1. Kachin National Races (with 12 sub races), 2. Kaya National Races (with 9 sub races), 3. Kayin National Races (with 12 sub races), 4. Chin National Races (with 51 sub races), 5. Mon National Races (with no sub race), 6. Rakhine National Races, (with 7 sub races), and 7. Shan National Races (with 34 sub races). Populations of the Kachin, the Kaya, the Kayin, the Chin, the Mon, the Rakhine, and the Shan vary from 2 to 7 millions and in total they together constitute about 40% of the total Burmese population. The new constitution, which is being drafted, will empower them as the autonomous states, with limited power to formulated their culture and local administration.

127 Sub Races
The Third Class Citizens are constituted by the 127 small sub races, which make up about 15% of the total Burmese population. Each of these sub races is less than 0.5% of the total population. They virtually have no political clout. Even if Burma becomes an ideal democratic country their votes will not make any change in the Burmese racial *status quo*.

Nameless Races
Fourth Class Citizens are classified as the immigrants from India sub continent and China. They make up about 5% of the total Burmese population and are known as the Kala and the Tayut respectively. They are classified as the guest-citizens. The Muslims of the Rakhine State strongly dispute this classification and they identify themselves as the Rohingyas, natives of Arakan. Some of the Rohingya people are in armed rebellion in quest of an independent Arakan or Rohang. Such other Indian descendants as the Sikhs, the Gurakhas, the Bengali, the Tamil, etc. stay very low profile. The Chinese people are wealthy, educated and live wisely by simply minding their business, without indulging in politics.

4.4. Scientific Myanmarism. The revival of Myanmarism gets a boost from an unexpected corner. Discovery in the Pondaung Formation of some 45-million-year old fossils by a Myanmar-French scientific team leads to the euphoria that Myanmar is the origin of human kind. The finding has been reported in a prestigious American journal, Science, volume 286 of 15 October 1999, page 528, by J.-J. Jager and his colleagues. Please see the scanned image showing their article. This academic interest has not only been escalated to the national interest but also incorporated into Myanmarism. Euphoria is such that the regime stands just one step short of declaring that 'Myanmar is the father and Myanmar is the mother of humankind'.

Pondaung Formation is rich in fossils. Fossilized primate bones have been discovered as early as 1914 by the India Geological Survey. Such species known as *Pondaungia cotteri* (1927), *Amphipithecus mogaungensis* (1937), *Myanmarpithecus yarshensis* (1998), and *Bahinia pondaungensis (1998)* are well known these days. You can simply search 'pondaungensis' in the web to find a host of websites dedicating to this newfound 'super star'. The international research teams are being encouraged by the junta. Prime Minister General Khin Nyunt himself patronizes the exploration. Some pieces of impressive scientific publications are presented here as evidence.

A New Primate from the Middle Eocene of Myanmar and the Asian Early Origin of Anthropoids

J.-J. Jaeger,[1] Tin Thein,[2] M. Benammi,[1] Y. Chaimanee,[3] Aung Naing Soe,[4] Thit Lwin,[4] Than Tun,[5] San Wai,[5] S. Ducrocq[1]*

A new genus and species of anthropoid primate, *Bahinia pondaungensis* gen. et sp. nov., is described from the Yashe Kyitchaung locality in the Late Middle Eocene Pondaung Formation (Myanmar). It is related to *Eosimias*, but it is represented by more complete remains, including upper dentition with associated lower jaw fragment. It is interpreted as a new representative of the family Eosimiidae, which corresponds to the sister group of the Amphipithecidae and of all other anthropoids. Eosimiidae are now recorded from three distinct Middle Eocene localities in Asia, giving support to the hypothesis of an Asian origin of anthropoids.

Anthropoid primates are represented during the Eocene in Southeast Asia by three derived genera, which belong to a monophyletic group, the Amphipithecidae (1). Two of them, *Amphipithecus* and *Pondaungia*, are recorded from finities with tarsiiformes (6). Some have even doubted its anthropoid nature (7).

During the November 1998 fieldwork organized in the frame of the Myanmar-French Pondaung Expedition Project, we recovered

A new anthracotheriid artiodactyl from Myanmar, and the relative ages of the Eocene anthropoid primate-bearing localities of Thailand (Krabi) and Myanmar (Pondaung)

Stéphane Ducrocq, Aung Naing Soe, Aye Ko Aung, Mouloud Benammi, Bo Bo, Yaowalak Chaimanee, Than Tun, Tin Thein, and Jean-Jacques Jaeger, *Journal of Vertebrate Paleontology,* 2000, 20(4):755-760

A fragmentary maxillar of a small anthracotheriid has been discovered in the middle Eocene locality of Kyawdaw in the Pondaung Formation (Myanmar). This specimen represents a primitive new species (*Siamotherium pondaungensis,* sp. nov.), possibly ancestral to *Siamotherium krabiense* from the late Eocene of Krabi (Thailand). The occurrence of *S. pondaungensis* in Myanmar suggests that Krabi is younger than the localities of the Pondaung Formation, and it further supports the role that southern Asia played in the origin and evolution of several groups of mammals. (Source: http://www.vertpaleo.org/jvp/20-755-760.html)

PNAS | **July 3, 2001** | vol. 98 | no. 14 | **7672-7677** ; Anthropology-BS

Primate postcrania from the late middle Eocene of Myanmar

Russell L. Ciochon[*], Philip D. Gingerich, Gregg F. Gunnell, and Elwyn L. Simons[§]
[*] Department of Anthropology, University of Iowa, Iowa City, IA 52242; Museum of Paleontology, University of Michigan, Ann Arbor, MI 48109; and [§] Duke University Primate Center, Durham, NC 27705

Contributed by Elwyn L. Simons, January 2, 2001

Fossil primates have been known from the late middle to late Eocene Pondaung Formation of Myanmar since the description of *Pondaungia cotteri* in 1927. Three additional primate taxa, *Amphipithecus mogaungensis, Bahinia pondaungensis* and *Myanmarpithecus yarshensis,* were subsequently described. These primates are represented mostly by fragmentary dental and cranial remains. Here we describe the first primate postcrania from Myanmar, including a complete left humerus, a fragmentary right humerus, parts of left and right ulnae, and the distal half of a left calcaneum, all representing one individual. ....

....

Overall, *Pondaungia* humeral and calcaneal morphology is most consistent with that of other known adapiforms. It does not support the inclusion of *Pondaungia* in Anthropoidea. (Source: http://www.pnas.org/cgi/content/full/98/14/7672

The Myanmarese may be already formulating a new evolutionary line of humankind as follow.

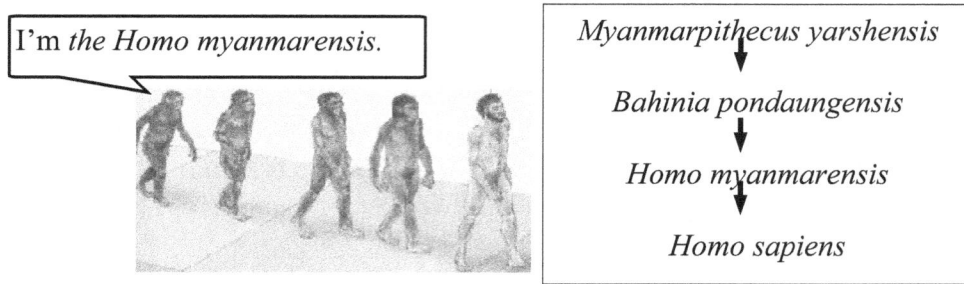

The above human evolution parade is from http://hannover.park.org/Canada/Museum/man /evnman3.html. The caption "I am *the Homo myanmarensis*" and the word diagram are my creation.

The above mockery represents my bias, I must admit. Nevertheless, the following speculative analysis is valid.

Since 1988 Myanmar cities, towns and villages are filled with the billboards that says 'Armed Forces is the Mother; Armed Forces is the Father'[1]. It means the Armed Forces is the mother, and the father of the people. Myanmar authorities might venture to sell similar billboards that say 'Myanmar is the Mother; Myanmar is the Father'[2]. Here it will mean Myanmar is the mother and the father of humankind. Politicization and racialization of science is a menace of Myanmarism. Why does the regime infuse politics and nationalism into evolutionary science? This question is especially relevant since Buddhism, like any other religions, simply falls apart in the face of the evolutionary theory and prevailing scientific evidence. The answer lies in the concept of Myanmar Supremacy, which is the same as the Aryan Supremacy of the Aryan Nations originated by Adolf Hitler (1889-1945). Let us explore into the depth of this issue.

Myanmar Supremacy found its roots in the word *Myanmar* itself. Please keep in mind that the scholars believe the word Myanmar is a derivation of the word Brahma, who is the Lord and Creator of the Universe. Myanmarese cosmology says that when the world was formed the Brahmas came down to the earth to check it was inhabitable or not. The Myanmarese concept of Brahma is different from that of Hinduism. In Hinduism there is only one Brahma. In the Myanmar concept there are the Brahma Worlds (*Brahma Bhun*), in which the heavenly beings known as the Brahmas inhabit. There are 21 Brahma Worlds. The Brahma Worlds are in a higher level than the Devata Worlds (*Nat Bhun* or *Nat Pyi*) in the heaven. There are 6 Devata Worlds. The king of the Brahma Worlds is known as the Brahma King or *Brahma Min* whereas the king of the Devata Worlds is known as *Thigya Min* (i.e. King of All-Knowing-All-Hearing). The Brahmas are the Creators whereas the Devatas are the Guardians of the world, religion, and human activities.

Notes.

1. Armed Forces is the Mother, Armed Forces is the Father. (တပ်မတော် သည် အမိ၊ တပ်မတော် သည် အဖ)။

2. Myanmar is the Mother, Myanmar is the Father. (မြန်မာ သည် အမိ၊ မြန်မာသည် အဖ)။

Brahmas and Devatas are also mortal like human. Their kings, i.e. Brahma king and Devata king also die. Their thrones are occupied by the new kings, just like in the human world. The mortal Brahmas and Devatas are in line with the Buddha's teaching. In his final farewell to his followers, Bikkhus, Buddha said, "Behold now Bikkhus, I exhort you: Impermanent are compound things; strive with earnestness," as described in *Maha-parinibbana Sutta*. This is the summation of his Dhamma - *Anicca, Dukkha, Anatta*. After these words, he passed away into Nibbana.

The Brahma and Devata Worlds never come to an end, but they are all mortals like human. Despite of their mortality human believes they are immortal because of their extraordinary long life span. One hundred days in human world make one day in Devata World and one hundred days in Devata World makes 1 day in Brahma World. Thus, 100 years in Brahma Worlds is equal to 1,000,000 years of human world and a Brahma lives minimum 100 human worlds. One human world, or one *kappa*, is the duration from the time of the formation of earth to its final dissolution in the flames of fire. After the fire that destroys every compound thing it rains from the heaven to cool off the heat and revive the earth. The new earth is filled with such aroma and fragrance that it attracted the Brahmas down to the earth. Failed to resist the temptation of the fragrance, the Brahmas happen to taste the earth. At this point the Brahmas lost their heavenly power and become earthlings to be known as the Myanmars[1]. Such is the Myanmar Supremacy.

The evolutionary theory makes this Myanmarese faith into a myth. Especially so, because it says that human originates from Africa. This cannot be since it negates Myanmar Supremacy. Even if the evolutionary theory is correct human origin must be from Myanmar only so that no question arises to Myanmar Supremacy. This is why the Myanmarese rulers infuse politics into the evolutionary science.

On the other hand, whatsoever I may say and no matter what my opinion is, it is true that *Bahinia Pondaungensis* has given a big scientific boost to Myanmarism. After all, it gives scientific evidence to nourish Myanmar Supremacy.

Note.
1. Erich von Däniken, the author of *Chariots of the Gods,* Putnam & Bantam Books, 1968, might like to call them E.T. Please visit http://www.daniken.com/e/index.html to know Erich von Däniken and his *Chariots of the Gods.*

4.5. Sacred Myanmarism. Sacred mysticism is a prime constituent of Myanmarism. I mentioned it briefly under the heading of mythical culture in the chapter 8.6 of my book *Burma: Nationalism and Ideology*, University Press Ltd., 1989. One aspect of Myanmar mysticism is the worship of Sacred White Elephant. A White Elephant, is considered holy and divine. This belief is probably originated from the ten Buddha birth stories known as *jetaka*. The following is a piece of information on the Bodhisatta Chaddanta elephant from http://www.ignca.nic.in/jatak004.htm. Please do not confuse the White Elephant and the biological albino. For example a white man is not a human albino. The same applies to a white elephant. Existence of white lions and white tigers have also been reported by the biologists. Thus, it is a normal phenotype of variant skin color.

Buddhist literatures known as *the birth stories* say the Buddha was reborn for 4,000,100,000 (i.e. four thousand millions and one hundred thousands or *ley thunshey* and *ta thein* in Burmese counting) *kappas* before he attained Enlightenment and became a Buddha. One *kappa* is a period of formation and dissolution of our world. With the resolution that he would be a Buddha and the Bodhisatta accumulated the virtues of *Ten páramitá* that would lead him to Nirvana . Bodhisatta Chaddanta perfected *síla-páramitá*. The followings are the ten páramitá or ten perfection that are needed for a person to attain Nirvana and Buddhahood. The terms are in Pali.

1. Perfection in Giving and Generosity *(dana parami)*, 2. Perfection in Morality *(sila parami)*, 3. Perfection in Renunciation *(nekkhamma parami),* 4. Perfection in Wisdom *(panna parami)*, 5. Perfection in Energy *(viriya parami)*, 6. Perfection in Patience *(Khanti parami)*, 7. Perfection in Truthfulness *(sacca parami)*, 8. Perfection in Resolution *(adhitta parami)*, 9. Perfection in Loving Kindness *(metta parami)*, 10. Perfection in Equanimity *(upekka parami)*. Pali Source: http://monsite.wanadoo.fr/ayubovan/page7.html

The worship of the white elephant might have been originated from the Bodhisatta Chaddanta elephant. A piece of web clipping of the Bodhisatta Chaddanta elephant is given below. The white elephant is a representative of the Bodhisatta Canddanta who perfected síla-páramitá. He was caught in Rathedaung Township of western Myanmar Rakhine State, in the third week of October, 2001. With royal honor and ceremony the white elephant was brought to Yangon and now housed in its palace at Min-dhamma Hillock Garden, Insein Township, some 12 miles north of Yangon. He is named *Yaza Gaha Thiri Pissaya Gaza Yaza,* which

---

The Illustrated Jataka & Other Stories of the Buddha by C.B. Varma

004 - The Story of Chaddanta Elephant

 Once the Bodhisatta was born as the king of Chaddanta elephants. [Chaddanta (literally "having six tusks") and Uposatha were the two highest classes of elephants often referred to in the Pali sources]. The body of the elephant king was pure white with red face and feet. He lived in a golden cave (Kanchana-guha) on the bank of a lake. He had two queens, namely, Mahasubhadda and Chullasubhadda. Source: http://www.ignca.nic.in/jatak004.htm.

means 'royal accompany glorious entity elephant king'. Junta Chairman Sr. Visit: http://www.myanmar.com. Welephant
General Than Shwe himself takes care of him in person. The welcoming
ceremony was complete with the traditional royal coronation, featuring
recitation of the Seinta Mani Mantra three times, hoisting of the Teingya
Sacred Umbrella above the elephant, blowing of the sacred conch shells,
and beating the gongs to mark the successful completion of the ceremony.
For more information please visit http://www.myanmar.com/Welephant.

Emergence of a white elephant makes Myanmarism divine. In the history
the Burmese kings even invaded Thai Ayutthaya to seize the Thai king's white elephants;
Bayinnaung (r.1511-1581) looted four in 1559 and Sinphyushin (r.1763-1775) one in 1767.
Sinphyushin means lord of the white elephant. He ruled Burma with this name abandoning his
former name Myedu Meng. "Why should not he change?" Once a friend of mine who was a
history student asked in a discussion group with mockery while I was at Rangoon University.
"Myedu Meng means 'earth-digging king'! Who would like to be a king with such a stupid
name?" He ended his question. "It was good that he changed his name," we agreed with him.

Why does the military junta bother so much with the white elephant? Myanmar mystic
belief says that white elephants emerge only in the days of righteous and powerful kings who are
endowed with the blessing of the Devata king, *Thigya Min,* about whom I described in the
previous section. The Myanmarese believes that the emergence of the white elephant is a sign of
Heaven in favor of Sr. General Than Shwe and his military junta. As a result, the land of
Myanmar has become sacred again and will prosper with power like in the old days of Myanmar
Empires.

I shall give some more description of Burmese mystic belief in the next section.

4.6. Mystic Myanmarism. The revival of Myanmarism is impossible without the support of Myanmar mysticism, which is the main spiritual power in Mynmarese politics. In the Chapter 8.6 of my book - *Burma: Nationalism and Ideology* (University Press Ltd., Dhaka, 1989) I presented some account of the Burmese mythical culture. Mysticism is the skeleton of that mythical culture. Fully aware of this important cultural institution, the military junta undertakes a series of actions that will exert mystic powers upon the masses. The followings are what I consider significant mystic moves in post-1988.

1. From Bama to Myanmar. Every Myanmarese name has a form of mystic meaning and power. The country's present capital Yangon means 'end of the foes'. Its ancient capital Mandalay is a derivative of Sanskrit word 'mandala'. When the city was built the icons, which were the geometric representation of the cosmic, spiritual, and mystic power, were buried at the four corners of the city and the palace. These geometric icons that are made in order to achieve a desired power and success are known as the mandalas. The city's name Mandalay is derived from the numerable mandalas that are buried around the city and the palace to achieve the power, strength, peace, and prosperity. Even today, the mandalas are widely used in mystic Hinduism, and Buddhism.

The word 'Bama' from which the English colonialists manufactured the name 'Burma' has no literal or mystic meaning. It is a corrupted version of Brahma. Thus it is ill-fated. It was never used in the official literature in the days of the kings. It gained popularity during the British rule only. General Ne Win was born and brought up as a Bama. As a result he could not shake it off. It was *the Bama Tamadaw* that he founded in the company of the blood-comrades[1] or the Thirty Comrades. In 1941, a group of 30 Burmese was trained and commissioned by the Japanese Imperial Army as the officers of Burma Independence Army[2], BIA, or *Bama Tamadaw* in short. When I was a student at Rangoon University I attended many political meetings and met a good number of BIA veterans. They told me that there was a discussion whether to call *Bama Tatmadaw* or *Myanma Tatmadaw* at the beginning. The term *'Ba'mâ'* was opted with injunction that it carries stronger *'military power'* than *'Myan'mâ'*, in terms of Burmese phonetics[3] or *Htan-ka-rhine*, which is a special way of reciting a word or a verse to provoke its mystic power. Before the Thirty Comrades marched into the British Burma to drive out the British colonialists they made a blood pool by bleeding themselves, drank the pooled blood and sworn as the comrades to remain faithful and loyal unto death. Such comradeship is known as *'blood comrade[1]'*. Aung San was the leader and Ne Win was one of them. This tradition is as old as Mount Popa in Burma. The inactive volcanic peak, Mount Popa, some 1800 meters (~6000 feet) above the sea level, is situated at the center of Burma and is invested with paramount mystic power.

There was a drive to replace the word Bama with Myanmar in the independent Burma. It was resolutely resisted by the *Bama Tatmadaw*. In 1988, the Burmese Vedic professors

---

Notes.
   1. The blood-comrade (သွေးသောက်) or the Thirty Comrades.
   2. Burma Independence Army, BIA, (ဗမ့္ာလွတ်လပ်ရေးတပ်မတော်) or *Bama Tamadaw* (ဗမ့္ာတပ်မတော်).
   3. Burmese phonetics or *'htan-ka-rhine'* (ဌာန်ကာရှိင်း).

determined that Burma was deadly ill and needed a quick recovery to avoid her death. It was then that *'Myanmar'* came in without any resistance because *'Myan'* means *'quick'* and *'mar'* stands for *'recovery'*. Here comes *'Myanmar'* or *'quick recovery'*. This is in agreement with the Burmese mystic principle that says - "Reality follows relativity"[1]. Accordingly ailing Burma is replaced with 'Myanmar' for quick recovery and Bama Tatmadaw becomes Myanma Tatmadaw. Please note it is not *Myanmár* Tatmadaw, but *Myanmâ* Tatmadaw.

2. Rakhaing Tha Kyaw. The Presidency of National Unity Party (NUP) that is the political front of the ruling junta was entrusted to U Tha Kyaw. Why? Because he was a BIA veteran, a trusted person[2] of Ne Win and army. He was a minister of the ministry of transportation during the BSPP regime; nothing more. Nonetheless, U Tha Kyaw (a relative of my comrade-friend Khaing Saw Tun, 1944-1995) can be best classified as a 4th class politician. There are many other capable persons with greater political caliber than him. If so, why U Tha Kyaw? Because he is a Rakhaing!! Mystic occult says, "*Ya* ya may *khine* ya may; *yakhine* phyit ya may,"[3] meaning "Must get, must last, and it must be a lasting acquisition". In Bama dialect it is *'yakhine'* as spoken, but is *'rakhaing'* in written form as the *'r'* sound and *'y'* sound are interchangeable. For example *'Rangoon'* is now written as *'Yagon'* reflecting the Bama linguistic sound. If you say it in Rakhaing dialect it is straight forward. It will say, "*Ra* ra may *khaing* ra may; *rakhaing* phrite ra may". The Burmese word 'ra'[4] means *'get or acquisition or procurement'* whereas 'Rakhaing'[4] means *'lasting or strong or permanent'*. Therefore, *'lasting acquisition'* means 'Rakhaing'[4]. As such we have a Rakhaing as the president of the National Unity Party, which is the political organ of the ruling junta in order to procure the power and to make it lasting once procured.

Do you get lost? If so, please re-read this section again. You may say, "What a rubbish!". Nevertheless, please take my words. It is *not rubbish,* but a very important practice known as *'yetra' (yetya)* in Burmese culture. Please see the section 8.6 *Mythical Culture* in my book - (*Burma: Nationalism and Ideology*, University Press Ltd., Dhaka, 1989).

3. Lawka Chantha Abhaya Labha Muni Buddha. Indeed, it is a standard practice of the Burmese kings to build a pagoda or Buddha image during their reign. It is nothing new. U Nu built Peace Pagodas *(Aye Zedi)* across the nation to overcome the multi-colored armed rebellion. General Ne Win built *Wizaya* Pagoda to ensure his victory over the enemies. *Wizaya* (Vijya of Bengal) conquered the Ogres[5] in Lanka Dipa (presently Sri Lanka) and established a Buddhist kingdom. Thus *Wizaya* signifies victory.

Present military regime constructed the largest Buddha image in Burmese history and named it 'Lawka Chantha Abhaya Labha Muni Buddha'. The name signifies the force of 'yetra'.

Notes.

1. "Reality follows the relativity" (ပည်းညပ်သွားရာ ဓါတ်သက်ပါ).

2. A trusted person (လူယုံ).

3. "Ya ya may *khine* ya may; *yakhine* phyit ya may" - ("ရရမယ် နိုင်ရမယ်၊ ရနိုင်ဖြစ်ရမယ်").

4. The Burmese word 'ra' is 'ရ', and and Khaing is 'နိုင်'. The Rakhaing is 'ရခိုင်'. The Myanmar junta official spelling is *'Rakhine'*, but *'Rakhaing'* is closer to the Arakanese dialect. The word 'ra' is pronounced 'ya' in Burmese dialect, e.g. *'Rangoon'* is pronounced *'Yagon'*. But, in the alphabets 'ya' actually is 'ယ'.

5. Ogre is a *Belu* (ဘီးလူး).

It is not just simply naming it. A complicated series of mystic occult practices that are called *ain, ein, mentra, pattra, yetra*[1], and relevant Buddhist recitations known as the *pareit tara*[2] are incorporated into the Buddha image in order to enforce the designated power. At the end a process known as the *Anaykaza*[3] is performed. Once the religious rites of *Anaykaza* is finished the Buddha image attained equal status of a living Buddha. Thus *the image* is nothing less than

Visit: http://www.myanmar.gov.mm/religious/buddha2002/feb/feb27.html

Buddha himself, worthy of worshipping. Present Buddha Image is named **Lawka Chantha Abya Laba Muni**. The name carries the mystic occult power. Do you believe in *the sound effect*? Combination of certain sounds produces well defined effects. The Buddhist *Pareit tara* are written on this principle. They are not prayers. A name has to be called, a verse has to be recited, or a prayer has to be said with correct tone and sound, known as the *htan-ka-rhine*[4], to produce desired occult effect.

Let us see:-

'Lawka' means *the world*.

'Chantha' means *richly peaceful*.

'Abya' means *victorious* or *free of danger*. It is Pali.

'Labha' means *good tiding* or *benevolent*. It is Pali.

'Muni' means *priceless jewel*.

This Rakhaing family is homeless, half-naked, and hungry while the Burmese temples shine with gold. (See Arakanpost issue-6, November 2004, page 11; Photo courtesy: Arakanpost).

Therefore, it can be adaptively translated as *'the World-Peaceful-Victorious-Benevolent Jewel Buddha'*. The most significant mystic power is embedded in two Pali words - *'Abya'* and *'Labha' in* this case.

The name of Buddha image reflects the new objectives of the military junta that puts on a brand new cloak known as the State Peace and Development Council (SPDC) ending the era of the Slorc (State Law and Order Restoration Council) after the death of Sr. General Saw Maung. Please visit Myanmar official web site http://www.myanmar.gov.mm/religious/buddha2002/feb/feb27.html to view more news and images of Lawka Chantha Abya Labha Muni.

Across the countries thousands of golden temples thrive beginning with Mon Shwedigon, and Rakhaing Maha Mrat Muni. Hundreds of Pagan temples in central Burma gives the evidence of active Buddhism in this beautiful land. Nevertheless whenever one pays a visit to a temple one always remembers the age-old saying[5] - *"golden temple shiny shiny, stomach though empty empty"*. Please visit http://www.myanmar.gov.mm/religious/buddha2002/feb/feb.html to see living Buddhism in Mynamar. It is filled with mysticism, which is the main spiritual power of Myanmarism.

Notes.

1. The *ain, ein, mentra, pattra*, and *yetra* (အင်း၊ အိုင်၊ မန်တြား၊ ပတ် တြာ၊ ယတ်တြာ).

2. The *pareit tara*' (ပရိတ်တရား).

3. The *anaykaza* (အနေကဇာ).

4. The *htan-ka-rhine* (ဌာန်ကာရှိင်း).

5. *golden temple shiny shiny, stomach though empty empty"* (ရွှေကျောင်းပြောင်ပြောင် ဝမ်းခေါင်ခေါင်).

4.7. Ideological Myanmarism. Traditional Myanmarism has been Buddhism and militarism since the days of King Anawrahta (r.1044-1077 CE). Myanmar Buddhism, though claimed as the Theraveda in its essence, is filled with animism. U Nu introduced parliamentary democracy into that fabric with the note that Buddhism is liberal and liberal democracy should work in Burma. Before he could make any impression of liberal democracy he was forced out of the office by his own general whom he entrusted with the national armed forces. As such, militarism prevails over democracy. General Ne Win introduced the Burmese Way to Socialism. The philosophy of his Burmese socialism is sold in the book *The Correlation of Man and His Environment*[1]. As I mentioned in the Chapter 6.2 of my book *Burma: Nationalism and Ideology* (University Press Ltd., Dhaka, 1989) the philosophy was a synthesis of Buddhism and socialism. He failed; the people forced him out through a violent and bloody uprising in 1988. He handed the power down to his trusted man, General Saw Maung.

After quenching the uprising, General Saw Maung announced that he would rule the country according to the *Lauka-thara-pyo* or *Essence of the World.* This is a new beginning of old Myanmarism in modern days. He said this in 1990 as he flatly refused to transfer power to the elected people's representatives, but asked them to convene a constitutional assembly and draft a new constitution. The election winner National League for Democracy (NLD) put up a strong protest. The West and India stood by the winner. Nobel Peace Prize was awarded to Mrs. Aung San Suu Kyi Aris (Daw Suu). At this junction that Sr. General Saw Maung Announced, "I will rule the nation in accordance with the *Lauka-thara-pyo*."

This was a more powerful move than the adoption of Burmese nomenclature 'Myanmar'. The outsiders including the professors and journalists who are honored as the Burma Experts totally lost in this move and could not figure out its head or tail. I do not blame them. Even, the Burmese cannot understand its significance.

In order to understand the significance of the *Lauka-thara-pyo,* a person must be well educated in the Burmese historical dynastic affairs, and connected with the aristocratic circle of the country. A person will have a deeper insight of the role of the *Lauka-thara-pyo* if he or she is involved in the politics and bureaucracy. In short, a person must belong to the aristocracy and bureaucracy. The *Lauka-thara-pyo* surely is a dynastic affair. When Sr. General Saw Maung said these words, I was at Maenarplaw, a liberated Karen area near the Thai border, where the Democratic Alliance of Burma (DAB) was configuring to set up a parallel government. The moment I heard what he said I realized that NLD, DAB, and all other opposition parties and organizations were finished. The *Lauka-thara-pyo* is that powerful. In one sense it is the Burmese version of *the Prince* of Niccolo Machiavelli (1498-1527 CE). The *Lauka-thara-pyo* or 'Essence of the World' is a book of verses written before or around 1327 CE by a Rakhaing Buddhist Bikkhu, known as Rakhaing Thu Mrat or Rakhaing Holy Man, to teach his students. It was a summary of his teachings. Being the teacher of King Mun Hti (r.1279-1385 CE, Laung

---

Notes.

1. This was the primary book that a Burmese elite in the government service had to learn in the training courses of the Burmese Way to Socialism. I attended a two-month training course at Inyalay Ideological Training School, Rangoon, in 1970. I was a junior faculty known as the demonstrator at the Rangoon Institute of Medicine No. 1, in that year. In Burma, schools and higher education institutes are under the Ministry of Education. The demonstrators in science subjects and the tutors in arts subjects are selected through the examinations and interviews by the Public Service Commission.

Krut Dynasty) he was entrusted with the education of three Burmese princes namely Saw Son, Saw Pru, and Saw Tu. They were the sons of King Lyin Saw who was the king of the Chakma (*Thet*)[1]. His kingdom Thayet or Thet Yet[2], meaning the Chakma Province, was seized by the Rakhaing King Mun Hti as the Chakma people marauded the Rakhaing border villages. The City of Thayet[3] is at the border of central and lower Burma. King Lyin Saw and his family were taken to Rakhaing while the Rakhaing Minister Razasithu Thungran was charged as the Governor of Thayet. This conquest left behind the Rakhaing saying, "Thayet is our eastern border"[4]. Rakhaing King Mun Hti was famous for his honesty and promise keeping as a devout Buddhist. He looked after King Lyin Saw and his family well, thus giving good opportunity for the young Burmese princes to pursue education. (Note: Even though the historians refer to them as the Burmese princes their first name *Saw,* which is the last name of their father, indicates that they were not Burmese, but most probably the Pyu. Remember the names of earlier generations of Pagan kings in pre-Anawrahta era - Pyu Saw Hti, Hti Min Yin, Yin Min Pike, Pike Thay Lay, Thay Lay Kyuw, Kyuw Du Rit?. The father's last name becomes the children's first name! It is interesting to see that Saw Tu later became King of Ava with the title of Sao Swa Ke. '*Sao*' is a Shan title and *'Saw'* today is a Karen title!).

In the days of Rakkhapura dynasties the Buddhist monasteries were the universities, designed after the ancient Taxila, which was the biggest Buddhist university established by Emperor Asoka in western India, now Pakistan. Traditionally, sixteen subjects, including the science of war and Buddhism, were taught to the children of nobles and kings, regardless of sex, in a Buddhist University. Rakhaing Thu Mrat was the head monk, or Professor and President, of such a university. When the three princes grew up they became dukes (Myo Hsar) of Myin Sai Myo, Pyi Myo, and Amyint Myo respectively. Later Amyint Myo Hsar Saw Tu (Taraphya Saw Ke) was elected by the ministers and nobles to the throne of Ava in the name of King Sao Swa Ke (r.1367-1404 CE), at the death of the founding King Thadoe Minphya (r.1364-1367 CE). He was elected on the merit that he was a descendant of Pagan Dynasty (1044-1279 CE) and Shan Dynasty (1298-1364 CE). The interlude between the end of Pagan Dynasty and the beginning of Shan dynasty is due to the Mongol Chinese Emperor Kubali Khan's occupation of Burma.

On the 16th year of his reign King Sao Swa Ke invited his aging teacher Rakhaing Thu Mrat to his kingdom. He worshipped and honored him with the title of *Maha Thingha Raza,* which means *Great Lord Sanga.* Thus *'Lauka-thara-pyo'* reached Burma from Rakkhapura and became a royal handbook of the Burmese Kings as well. It is then that the Rakhaing and the Burmese merged into a common written heritage of cultural norms, and royal administrative philosophy. It was a source of unity between the two historically hostile peoples - the Rakhaing

---

Notes.

1. Chakma (သတ်မ) and *Thet* (သက်). Our Rakhaing chronicles tell us that a king of Vāranāsi (Banares, Northern India) came and lived as a hermit in Northern Arakan. One *Hsatma* (သတ်မ) happened to drink the water that was contaminated with his urine and later gave birth to a human boy. The boy became the founder king of Rakkhapura in the name of Marayu. The word *Hsatma* is wrongly interpreted as a doe in modern Rakhaing dialect. Please see Sir Arthur Phyare's *History of Burma*, Trübner & Co, London, 1883, p43. I believe the *Hsatma* actually was a Chakma woman who gave birth to a boy through her union with the hermit king. Our chroniclers hid this act of the hermit.

2. Thayet or Thet Yet (သက်ရပ်).

3. The City of Thayet (သက်ရပ် > သရက် > သယက်).

4. 'Thayet is our eastern border' (အရှေမှာသရက်).

and the Bama. It was the first time since 1784 that the Bama admitted *'Maha Thingha Raza'* was none other than *'Rakhaing Thu Mrat'* erasing the cause of a 200-year dispute.

The junta's announcement to rule the nation in accordance with the *Lauka-thara-pyo* strategically refreshes not only the golden era of Ava but also pacifies the hostility between the two historical rivals. This pacification is so crucial because 30% of the fighting force of the Burmese armed forces, that is approximately 150,000 in the present strength of 500,000, is made up of the Rakhaing youths. The only way the Burmese armed forces can be broken up is to split off the Rakhaing loyalty. With full understanding of this vital tactical issue, the leaders of the armed forces made a radical move to strengthen the cement of the Rakhaing loyalty.

Introduction of the *Lauka-thara-pyo* as the nation's ruling formula and the junta's due acknowledgement of its author, Rakhaing Thu Mrat, as the teacher of the Burmese kings was a great success. Also remember that Myanmar Ava King Sao Swa Ke was a Tagaung and Pyu origin with a Shan title who revered a Rakhaing teacher. This surely is the solidification of the Myanmar national races. This is the craftiest move made by the Burmese military junta. A modern edition of the *Lauka-thara-pyo* was published with an authoritative interpretation and explanation by none other than Min Thuu Wun (Sayagyi U Wun) who is a *guru*, i.e. more than a professor, of Burmese literature, a pioneer of modern Burmese, and a patriot decorated with the national honors of *Wunna Kyaw Htin* and *Thiri Pyanchi*. I salute Sr. General Saw Maung for this move. Within one year of this announcement DAB broke up. Later, its headquarter Maenarplaw fell into the hands of junta. Inside the political arena, heads rolled out from the election winners like NLD (National League for Democracy), ALD (Arakan League for Democracy), and UNLD (United Nationalities League for Democracy). It was a battle won simply with a word - *Lauka-thara-pyo*. Beyond doubt, the Rakhaings were effectively incorporated into Myanmarism. For those Rakhaings who accepted the defeat of 1784 and simply prayed to get a slice of sympathetic cake it was a blessing whereas it was the most lethal blow to a Rakhaing rebel who fought for self-determination. A fresh national solidarity was brought about by that soldier known as Sr. General Saw Maung. General Ne Win tried to become a philosopher, but turned out to be a brute. On the contrary, Sr. General Saw Maung came in as a brute, but turned out to be a philosopher. The *Lauka-thara-pyo* no doubt is the skeleton of Buddhist political ideology. By adopting it as the ruling philosophy Sr. General Saw Maung gave the Myanmar military junta new impetus in the 21st century.

Some quotations of Sr. General Saw Maung (1928-1997), Myanmar's first 5-star general, a soldier-ruler-philosopher who paved way to the modern Myanmarism. The photo is by MNA, the Ministry of Information, on the occasion of his press conference at the Ministry of Defence Guest House, on July 05, 1989.

"Our military science is more advance than political science"

"People told me to settle the matters by negotiation. I am a soldier, not a politician. There is no negotiation in military science".

Rakhaing Thu Mrat was the kings' teacher in the 14th century during the Laung Krut Dynasty of Rakkhapura Kingdom. He summarized his teachings in his poems that he called *Lauka-thara-pyo* or 'essence of the world'. This is the first written evidence of ideological Buddhism that has been in practice in the ancient Rakhaing, Mon, and Bama kingdoms. Sr. General Saw Maung was the first Bama ruler to acknowledge that *'Maha Thingha Raza'*, the author of *Lauka-thara-pyo,* was none other than Rakhaing Thu Mrat. In 1990, he announced that he would rule Myanmar in accordance with this ideological Buddhism. After the announcement the book was published with explanations of Min Thuu Wun who is a poet, *guru* and professor of Burmese literature, rolled into one. See the main body of the text for more information.

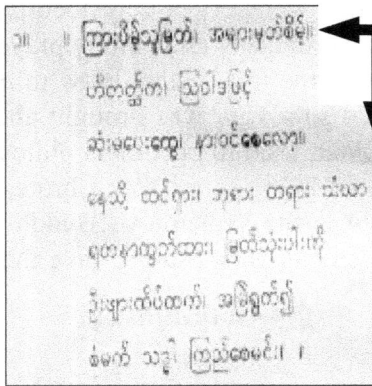

This is the opening verse of the *Lauka-thara-pyo*. English version is my translation.

I, Thu Mrat, shall speak; so people may learn. This is a beneficial teaching; give ear with due attention. Brilliant as the sun are the Buddha, the Dhamma, and the Sangha. Always carry these three jewels on the apex and cherish them with serene mind and heart.

Rakhaing Thu Mrat
Lauka thara pyo

Min Thuu Wun
presents with explanations

4.8. Dirty Myanmarism. Wars, genocide, and human rights violation are dirty. In a political process it is vital to clean up the dirtiness, heal the wounds of wars, overcome the genocidal hatred, and respect everyone's right to self-determination. This is the only way that can bring about justice, peace, harmony, and national unity in a land. This is also the only path that will lead to a happy and healthy nation. The Myanmarese fail to do so. Myanmarism remains as dirty as it was in 11th century, making Burma's republic a failed nation. Myanmarese intoxication with the glory of the tyrannical Myanmar Empires has kept the rotten feudal wars alive even in this 21st century.

The Mons were the first victims of the Myanmarese dirtiness. They claim that many were killed, and some 30,000 Mons were captured and driven to Pagan where the Myanmarese forced them to build the pagodas. Their King Manuha was made a Slave there as mentioned in the preceding section "Historical Myanmarism". In 1757, the Myanmar King Alungphaya invaded and devastated the Mon kingdom, killing tens of thousands of Mon. The killing included learned Mon priests, pregnant women, and children. A Mon source, at http://www.geocities.com/Athens/Bridge/1256/monhistory1.htm, wrote as below.

"U Aungzeya, a Burman leader who is better known as King Alaungphaya, drove the Mon out of upper Burma from Ava and regained other lost territories. By 1757 he defeated the Mon and annexed the Mon kingdom of Hongsawatoi. The Mon have ever since become a people without a country. The conquering Burman leader U Aungzeya persecuted the Mon by massacring over 3,000 learned Mon monks near Rangoon; by burning down holy scriptures and monasteries; by proscribing Mon language and literature; and by genocidal mass executions whereby thousands of Mon were exterminated in several stockade-inferno holocausts. Racial discrimination was rife and hundreds of thousands of the Mon fled to Siam (Thailand) for safe haven. In modern human rights terminology, it was a drastic "ethnic cleansing" process."

The reader may also visit http://www.albany.edu/~gb661 for a similar information.

Similarly, the Rakhaing people were also depopulated by the Myanmarese at least twice. Between 1403-1430 CE, our Rakhaing population was nearly wiped out. Probably, entire male adult population of soldier age was killed. In 1403 CE, the Rakhaing King Narameit Hla took refuge with Sultan Ghiasuddin Azam Shah(r.1399-1409 CE), at Gaur. He became renowned there for his wisdom and knowledge, and widely known as King Solomon (Mun Sawmon) in the Islamic Palace of Bengal Sultan. After 27 years of his service as a minister and soldier, Sultan Jalal Uddin (r. 1415-1433 CE), a Hindu-convert-Muslim, gave him a 30,000-strong Muslim Army to restore his throne in Rakkhapura. Why a Muslim army? Because there virtually was no Rakhaing of prime age left to be soldiers. Such was the history. Again in 1784 the Myanmarese invaded and depopulated our Rakhaing kingdom. How many were killed? Exact head count is not known, but the Rakhaing historians assert that some 250,000 were killed. The readers may visit the ancient Rakhaing capital Mrauk-U and ask some one to show them the mountain of the bones. A knowledgeable resident will be willing to show you discretely. According to my maternal grandmother Daw Hnun Phru (1871-1970) entire adult male members of her ancestors

My grandmother and mother (front row) with friends and relatives in 1965. The hairstyle, with jasmine coronet, of my mother dates back to 18th century.

sacrificed their lives in defense of their king Maha Thamada in Kyein Province. Her great great grandfather was killed in combat along with his clan. His wife founded a village in the battlefield,

rehabilitated the surviving family members and raised the children. The ancient battlefield also witnessed serious Anglo-Japanese battles in WWII. According to my parents I was born in that historical battlefield. My ancestor eventually became the matriarch of the clan and known as *the Anaukshunma* or *the matriarch of Western (Kyein) Territory.* The Anaukshunma was the elder sister of Nga Thandwe. Thus, she was an aunt of the foremost Rakhaing resistance leader, Bo Chunbyan (King Bering). They were the descendants of Danda Bo[1] Dynasty (1710 CE -1777 CE).

My parents, sister, and brothers in 1963.
Left to right, front row: Myself and cousin.
Middle row: My father, mother, and sister
Back row: My two brothers.
My father has a cane in his hand and traditional head-dress, Gaungbaung, a classic fashion.

My father, U Maung Tha Pru (1909-1987), told me a similar story about his ancestors who fought to death in defense of their kingdom against the 1784 Burmese invasion. His ancestor whom we know in the name of Saite-ké Aung, governor of Urittaung Province, commanded the major defensive battle against the Burmese invaders in the 1784 Arakan-Burma War. I believe a Saite-ké[2] in the Arakan Royal Army is equivalent to a major general of a modern army. He led a combined land and naval force of 3,000 men. At the month of Kissapanadi River, he confronted the 30,000-strong Burmese forces led by the Burmese crown prince. He died in the combat along with most of his men. The place where he confronted the Burmese invasion was known as Saite Twêy[3], meaning 'the place where the war meets'. When Arakan came under the British Administration in 1826, the British established a city known as Akyab[3] in Saite Twêy. Akyab is the British version of Ahkyaib-daw[4], which is a very ancient pagoda, at the head of Saite Twêy. Today, in Burmese it is known as Sittwe[5]. The Rakhaing people still call it Saite Twey[5]. In the First Anglo-Burman War the British Forces stopped their pursuit of the Burmese forces at Kissipanadi River. That was why the river was nicknamed Kaladan River, which means the river where the foreigners stopped. The nickname later became the official name of the river in the British time. The British occupation in 1826 was a heaven for my ancestral clan. My grandmother and my father told me this history of my clan when I came back home from my guerrilla life, in 1968. Although, I came back home as a defeated man they told me the history

---

Notes.
1. As per information disseminated to me by my grandparents, parents, and their generation Danda Bo was a warrior and lost one eye in combat. He left the royal service because he did not like the palace formalities, but prefer to be a wild man. He lived as a gardener in a remote place with his followers. Danda Bo was not his original name. He was a martial art master and very good at staff-fighting. Accordingly he was known as Danda Bo or Martial Art Commander. The word *Danda* is classified as Old Burmese (Purana), but it is still alive in today's Indian and Bengali literature. He was put up as the leader to quench the rebellions in the kingdom by the nobles. When he became a king (Sandawizaya Raza, r. 1710 CE -1731 CE) he wasted his royal career by marauding the neighbors, and minting silver coins bearing his name.

1. Saite-ké (စစ်ကဲ); 2. Saite Twêy, (စစ်တွေ့) or (စစ်တွဲ့) means 'the place where the war meets'.

3. Ahkyaib-daw (အာကျိုတ်တော်) >Akyab.

4. Sittwe or Saite Twey (စစ်တွေ). The Burmese and the Arakanese spell the words in the same way, but pronounce different.

with a philosophical note, "The blood never dries."

As such, the atrocity inflicted upon us by the Burmese is not just a history in the books. It is the history of my family and my clan. I know of many Rakhaings who live with the similar family histories. Today, some 30% of the present young generation, who were struggling against the Myanmarese colonial rule, has faced the arbitrary imprisonment and even torture in the detention centers. Another 20% told me that their parents were killed, tortured, or imprisoned by the Myanmarese rulers.

In the 1784 conquest, the Myanmarese drove away more than 100,000 Rakhaing captives including learned monks, carpenters, artisans, and skilled laborers. They were forced to dig Meik-hti-la water reservoir and build Mingun Temple in the central Burma. Mingun bell that weighs about eighty tons is the work of the Rakhaing captives under the Myanmar King Bodawphaya.

In my childhood I grew up seeing the dead bodies of both the Myanmarese soldiers and the Rakhaing guerrillas in Munbra (Minbya). Now and then, as the school children we were lined up to see the guerrilla dead bodies with a lesson that the guerrillas must die in that way. Similarly, we were lined up to see the dead bodies of the government soldiers with the lesson that we must kill the bad insurgents who killed the good soldiers. I can still see the blood oozing out from the mouth of a dead guerrilla. In 1951, our family was caught for three hours in a battle of the guerrilla and government forces. Many times, I also saw twenty or thirty villagers being arrested inside the army cantonment and some were tied to the trees. In general, these villagers were from the places where the soldiers believed there were the guerrillas. Time to time, I wonder that this childhood experience might have conditioned my anti-government attitude.

Here, I present some reports on the dirtiness of contemporary Myanmarism. How true and genuine are these reports? It is up to the reader to judge. I grew up experiencing the discrimination by my own self, seeing the dirtiness with my own eyes, and hearing with my own ears from the victims of the dirtiness. Accordingly, when I read or hear it from a secondary source I incline to believe most of them. I may be bias; the reader is urged to use his or her discretion.

The news of Myanmarese forced labor and conscription of child soldiers fill the international atmosphere with foul smell. Some pieces of the news are presented to the reader as the examples. The worst news in the recent days is a report from the Shan Human Rights Foundation, which is given in some details in the coming pages.

Children's Rights and the Rule of Law
Source: http://hrw.org/doc/?t=asia_pub&c=burma. (Note: Human Rights Watch (HWR) is the biggest and the most credible human rights watch dog).
Burma acceded to the Convention on the Rights of the Child (CRC) in 1991. Since then, however, there has been little progress toward the implementation of the convention, and the underlying problems which impede implementation have not changed. These include a total lack of the rule of law and accountability of the government, as well as draconian restrictions on freedom of expression, association and peaceful assembly, which prevent local reporting and monitoring of the human rights situation of children.

The following is a table showing 2 of 68 results that popped up when a web search was done for 'forced labor in Mynamar. The list is from the Exite-Search at http://msxml.excite.com/info.xcite/search/web/forced%2Blabor%2Bin%2Bmyanmar.

1. CNN.com - Myanmar still using forced labor: UN - November 16, 2001
   Forced labor is still widespread in Myanmar even though it was officially abolished last year, says a UN labor group. ... Myanmar still using forced labor: UN. ...
   http://www.cnn.com/2001/WORLD/asiapcf/southeast/11/15/myanma...

2. Amnesty Says Myanmar Using Forced Labor, Torture
   Amnesty Says Myanmar Using Forced Labor, Torture. ... Forced labor had been outlawed in Myanmar but the order was being flouted by the military, it said. ...
   http://www.commondreams.org/headlines02/0717-06.htm

These days boy soldiers as young as 14 years are common. Many of them are the Rakhaing village boys from western Burma. They are conscripted and taken away to the northern Kachin land, eastern Shan area, or southern Karen and Mon territory, more than one thousand miles away from home and parents. This is how Myanma Tatmadaw has built up its strength to 500,000 from its humble 180,000 in 1988. Earlier there was only one General Ne Win. Now there are Sr. General Than Shwe (a 5-star General), Vice Sr. General Maung Aye (a 5-Star General), General Thura Shwe Mann, and General Khin Nyunt (4-Star General) and a number of 3-Star Generals. The armed forces expanded too fast and too quick in terms of quantity. This poses questions in regard to its quality.

A 2002-publication *License To Rape* by the Shan Human Rights Foundation highlights the dirtiness of sexual abuse being practiced by the Myanmar military personnel. It can be read online at http://www.shanland.org/HR/HR_Frame.htm. It is an extensive report. In the coming pages I present some excerpts. The reader is urged to read the full report online.

The Maynmarese junta has officially responded to the reported allegations. You can find the junta official responses at http://www.myanmar.com/today/SHRF.html. Excerpts are also presented here.

It will be good if an independent international body can look into the matter in order to establish the truth and justice. On the ground of excessive Burmese oppression an exiled Shan group in Canada led by Sao Surkhanpha, eldest son of Burma's first president, Sao Shwe Thaike, declared the independence of the Federated Shan States on the 17th of April 2005.

The Excerpt-1 from *License to Rape* contents from
http://www.shanland.org/HR/Publication/LtoR/license_to_rape.htm.

LICENSE TO RAPE
the Burmese military regime's
use of sexual violence in the ongoing war
in Shan State
By
The Shan Human Rights Foundation (SHRF)
&
The Shan Women's Action Network (SWAN)
May 2002

CONTENTS

The excerpt-2 from *License To Rape.*

Please read the dull text on line at http://www.shanland.org/HR/Publication/LtoR/systematic_and_widespread_incide.htm.

Sexual violence during four decades of civil war in Shan State and international law terminology

".....Most of the information collected in this report covers cases of rape committed by the Burmese military in the past six years. However, sexual violence has been commonplace in Shan State during the past four decades, since the Burmese military began operations against the ethnic resistance forces in the late 1950s.

The context of the civil war has given Burmese troops licence to practice sexual violence against local ethnic women with impunity. As potential supporters of the resistance, women are perceived as legitimate targets for violence. Sexual violence serves the multiple purpose of not only terrorizing local communities into submission, but also flaunting the power of the dominant troops over the enemy's women, and thereby humiliating and demoralizing resistance forces. Furthermore, it serves as a "reward" to troops for fighting in the war......"

The Excerpt-3 from *License to Rape.*

Please read on line at http://www.shanland.org/HR/Publication/LtoR/systematic_and_widespread_incide.htm.

The systematic and widespread incidence of rape

It should be noted that because of the stigma attached to rape, many women do not report incidents of sexual violence. Furthermore, since much of the information about human rights abuses in Shan State is gained from refugees arriving at the Thai-Burma border, news of many incidents may not have reached SHRF. Therefore the figures in this report are likely to be far lower than the actual figures.

The Excerpt-4 from *License to Rape.*

Please read on line at http://www.shanland.org/HR/Publication/LtoR/officers_committing_rape.htm

Officers committing rape

One fact that shows clearly that rape is condoned by the military authorities is that 83% of the cases of rape documented in this report were committed by military officers, from the ranks of corporal to major as the following list of perpetrators shows:

In the vast majority of these cases (85%) the officer was on duty with other troops, and made no attempt to hide his crime. In fact, in 10 of the cases, the officer actually passed on the victim(s) to his troops either to let them gang-rape her, or to let them kill her.

According to a table presented in the report the Myanmarese army committed a total number of 168 rapes victimizing 92 girls, and 527 women in 17 townships in the Shan country in the period spanning from 1996 to 2001. A total of 139 military personnel breaking down into 48 commanders, 14 majors, 63 captains, 5 lieutenants, 6 sergeants, and 3 corporals were mentioned in the report. Please visit the website cited above for the details.

License To Rape of the Shan Human Rights Foundation gives case by case detail as well. The report is well known among the Myanmar watchers. The reader may visit the web site http://www.shanland.org/HR/HR_Frame.htm for the details.

The Myanmar military government has downplayed the report saying that it is a propaganda to tarnish the image of the Myanmar Armed Forces. However, the junta responded the allegations at its official web site http://www.myanmar.com/today/SHRF.html. Some excerpts are presented here. My objective here is to simply present the scenario in black and white, but not to judge which report is correct.

The Excerpt-1 from the Myanmar military junta official response.
Please visit http://www.myanmar.com/today/SHRF.html for the information in detail.

Inquiries Conducted Concerning Allegations Made By The Shan Human Rights Foundation (SHRF) That Myanmar Army Troops Sexually Assaulted Shan Women In The Shan State.

Allegations

1. The Shan Human Rights Foundation, (SHRF) which is an illegal organization made allegations on the Internet that between the period 1991 to 2001, 173 cases of sexual assault on Shan women was committed by troops of the Myanmar Armed Forces, and that it was a racist attack systematically planned by the Myanmar Armed Forces Government. It alleged that troops of the Myanmar Armed Forces had committed rape of young Shan women in the 8 townships of Kengtung, Tachilek, Monghsat, Mongtung, Mongyaung, Mongyan, Mongkhat and Mongpyin of Shan State (East); in the 11 townships of Nyaungshwe (Yawnghwe), Hopong, Loilem, Laichar, Mongkong, Kyaythee, Namsan, Kunheng, Moe Nai, Lin Khe, Mongpan in Shan State (South) and in two townships, Narnkhan and Namtu in Shan State (North). inquiries conducted concerning these allegations.

2. In order to make thorough inquiries and investigations to reveal the real facts of the case, concerning allegations made by the Shan Human Rights Foundation (SHRF), the State Peace and Development Council authorized the formation of inquiry teams to work in collaboration with the National Intelligence Bureau headed by Brig. Gen. Than Tun (BC-12013), Head of Department of the Office of the Chief Military Intelligence.

The Excerpt-2 from the Myanmar military junta official response.
Please visit http://www.myanmar.com/today/SHRF.html for the information in detail.

(b) Case No. 53 reported in the book "Licence to Rape" that took place in Mongtung Township. A soldier whose name remains unknown from a battalion stationed in the area of Mongtung Township, raped one Ma Nar Show (not her real name) aged 29 years of the Lahu ethnic group and of the Christian faith, residing in Lahu village, on 17 July 1998. Investigations revealed that such an incident did not take place at the time specified, but that on 17 April 2002, such a case of rape occurred at Gaw Taw Lahu village, located on the Mongton-Tarhsan motor road, 12 miles distant from the town of Mongtung on 17 July 2002. A Lahu woman by the name of Ma Lon Shay of Gaw Taw village accompanied by another woman Ma Nar Pwint had come to the well near Gaw Taw Village to fetch some water. At the time private Aung Aung of the combined platoon detachment of Mongtung Cantonment forcefully carried off Ma Lon Shay and raped her beside some bushes. The young woman was said to have fainted for 15 minutes. The villagers hearing of this incident reported it to Platoon Commander Captain Aung Lwin who then initiated an inquiry. When private Aung Aung was summoned for questioning he used the rifle he had brought in an attempt to shoot his senior officer and aides. Orders had to be given to return fire in order to capture Aung Aung. He died from his wounds and could not be bought to trial. His remains now lie buried at the Gaw Taw Village Cemetery.

The Excerpt-3 from the Myanmar military junta official response.
Please visit http://www.myanmar.com/today/SHRF.html for the information in detail.

(e) Case No.69 in the book " Licence to Rape " that took place in Mongtung Township. According to this allegation a 25 year old woman of near Khon Hmu Village in Mongtung Township was at home on 21-11-98 while her husband was away working as a porter for the military unit in the township when Maung Win and Oo Kyaw of No. 225 Light Infantry Regiment both raped her at gunpoint. Investigations into this case showed that no such incident occurred that day. But further inquiries revealed a case, which occurred near Tarlay (Palaung) Village in Pon-parkyin Village Tract in Mongtung Township on 27-8-95. Private Maung Hlaing , members of a company of the No.225 Infantry Regiment led by Lt. Ne Win Aung, raped one Ma Ei Nyee near Tarlay Village. The private who committed this crime was tried in accordance with article – 71 of the Defence Services Act and articles – 276/372 of the Penal Code and sentenced to life imprisonment. His accomplices, Lance Corporal Kyaw Tun and private Thein Htay were also tried and sentenced to 3 years imprisonment each, with hard labour. Lt. Ne Win Aung forfeited a year from his service as the senior officer-in-charge.

> **The Excerpt-4** from the Myanmar military junta official response.
> Please visit http://www.myanmar.com/today/SHRF.html for the information in detail.

> **Conclusion**
>
> 8. A review of the findings from the investigation and inquiries conducted, will show clearly that the allegations made by the SHRF are false and without foundation. Its goal is to provoke racial hatred and resentment. The so-called report has just exploited a few incidents from the past and together with love affairs that will often arise between young people, stirred and mixed them into exaggerated and fabricated accounts. It will also be seen that authorities at all echelons do not condone the behaviour of those members of the Armed Forces who violate rules and regulations and action is always taken and appropriate punishment meted out. The Myanmar Armed Forces is thus the most well organized and disciplined force with a pledge to protect the people of Myanmar, including the ethnic groups. There is no intent to dominate the ethnic races and there never has been. In fact it gives priority to the development of border areas and the national races. Thus to allege that the Myamnar Armed Forces Government encourages systematic rape as a weapon to oppress the ethnic minorities is not only false, but also a ridiculous accusation.

These are the allegations and responses. It will be good if there could be an impartial international commission to investigate into this matter. Under the existing international laws a citizen cannot sue his or her government in the international courts such as the International Criminal Court. Similarly, the United Nations cannot take any action since it is purely a domestic concern. On the other hand, in my view a citizen must have the right to sue his or her government in an international court when there is a reason to believe that the *State* itself is directly or indirectly involved in the given crime and he or she cannot get justice under the country's judicial system.

The news are very disturbing. Therefore, the reader is advised to practice due discretion. Another piece of news from Kaladan News Agency is given here. Full text is reproduced after the web image.

YAHOO! Mail   Yahoo! - My Yahoo! - Help

Date: Wed, 12 Nov 2003 05:27:01 -0800 (PST)
From: "Kaladan Press" <kaladanpress@yahoo.com>
Subject: A Cowboy Boy Sodomized by Army
To: burmese@bbc.co.uk

KALADAN NEWS

Dated: Wednesday November 12, 2003

A Cowboy Boy Sodomized by Army

Buthidaung, Novemver 12: An army in Buthidaung Township in Arakan State sodomized a victim.

The victim, named Deen Mohamed, 12, son of Noor Boshor Deen hailed from Kyakma Taui State was sodomized by an army of Battalion No.556 on October 28, 2003, he further added.

Full news read as below.

Date: Wed, 12 Nov 2003 05:27:01 -0800 (PST)
From: "Kaladan Press" <kaladanpress@yahoo.com>
Subject: A Cowboy Boy Sodomized by Army
To: burmese@bbc.co.uk

KALADAN NEWS

Dated: Wednesday November 12, 2003

A Cowboy Boy Sodomized by Army

Buthidaung, November 12: An army in Buthidaung Township in Arakan State sodomized a Rohingya cowboy, according to a relative of victim.

The victim, named Deen Mohamed, 12, son of Noor Boshor Deen hailed from Kyakma Taung village of Buthidaung Township in Arakan State was sodomized by an army of Battalion No.556 on October 28, 2003, he further added.

The story in brief was that the victim accompanied by other boys were grazing their cattle in a lawn nearby Battalion No. 556 and `were playing football in the lawn with the said army. In one stage, the ball was shooting at jungle by the army and all the football players were going to the jungle for searching the ball. By taking this advantage, the army forcibly took away the cowboy to a hillside solitary place and sodomized him there, a villager said to our source.

When the cowboy screamed out, all the players rushed to the spot and saw the culprit with him. But, they didn't dare to do anything against the army and took the victim to his house. While all the boys were going to their village with their cattle, the culprit asked them not to expose the matter to anyone, if you told it anyone you will be not allowed to graze your cattle in the lawn, he further said.

The following day, father accompanied by his son went to the concerned battalion commander and he was apprised of the matter but no action has been taken against the culprit. The commander also said, " This is done by mutual understanding and without accepting it is not possible to commit sodomy. Nobody can bar this kind of sodomite, if anyone makes obstacle, he will be accused as a culprit," said another relative of the victim to our source.

The father of the victim wasn't satisfied by the Battalion commander's explanation and proceeded against the culprit to the higher authority, Military Operation Command (MOC) -15 and appraised it in detail again. The MOC-15 commander said, "Our Burmese army is well-known in the world about their courage, well discipline, polite behavior, sympathy to people. By knowing this, why do you come to vilify our soldiers? Don't come again." After hearing, father of the victim returned home with great frustration, he further added. ##

For further information, please contact Kaladan Press at:
E-mail: kaladanpress@yahoo.com
Mobile: (+880) 11 227 138

In addition to this case, I have received a number of reports of sexual violation, physical abuse, confiscation of land and properties, and harassment by the soldiers and officers of Myanmar Army in the Rakhine State. Although I believe there is substance in the reports there is no way that I can verify and confirm them. Only one systematic record has been published in

Burmese by Khaing Aung Kyaw (Sittwe) in his book *Human Rights Violations in Arakan State*, Series 2, *Uncontrollable Tears From The Jail*. For a copy of the book reader may contact the National Committee of Arakan, WZ, 57, Opp DGII, Dodella Village, Vikaspuri, New Delhi-110018, India, telephone 91-11-5517158. I do not know if they still exist or not. India government has been crushing the Burmese oppositions since 2001 when it re-initiated the traditional friendship with Burma after some 13 years of hostile diplomacy.

Khaing Aung Kyaw (Sittwe) has documented women rights abuses of the Myanmar military junta in the Rakhine State, which is the most neglected backwater of Burma.

Human Rights Violations
in Arakan State
(Series 2)

Khaing Aung Kyaw (Sittwe)

Uncontrollable Tears From The Jail

This book accurately presents heart-breaking stories of the Rakhaing women whose lives were ruined by SLORC military junta's violation of human rights.
Distributor
Arakan National Committee (India)

I know in person of a woman who was arrested by the Myanmar military intelligence service (MIS) because her husband was involved in antigovernment rebellion. She was isolated and detained in a military base. Everyday, one MIS man came in for interrogation. However, she was never asked any questions, but instead was raped. This continued for a few months till she became sick and subsequently was sent to the prison without any charge, trial, or conviction. The reader may find and ask a man named Christopher Gunness, a BBC correspondent, who reported a similar case that occurred in Insein Prison in 1987-88. A large number of Rangoon University female students were victimized in the prison.

I shall narrate an incident that I faced when I was in the Yakin College of Rangoon University in 1960. One evening as I came out of the dining hall after the diner I met Ko Thein, Ko Kyaw Oo and Ko Htu Myint. These are false names I use here. They were 3 to 4 years older than me by age. Yakin College Hostel hosted some 500 students. The unforgettable dialogue took place as follow.

Ko Thein: "Shwe Lu! How would you like to come with us for a visit to a Yodyama?"

I: "Who is Yodyama? I do not know her."

They laughed at me and Ko Htu Myint interrupted the laugh saying, "Let us go. Leave that kid alone".**

(**Note: My parents sent me to school at the age of three when actual school age was five. Most parents sent their children to school when they were seven or eight, in general. As a result I ended up as a kid in the college.)

For a while, I stood there in a puzzle. Confused and upset for laughing at me, I narrated the incident to a senior student. He smiled at me and said, "Shwe Lu, Yodyama is a common name for the prostitutes. They laughed at you because of your innocence. Just ignore them."

Later, I learned that Yodya is Burmese for Ayuthaya of Thailand. When the Bama King Nayinnaung conquered it in 16th century he brought back hundreds of Ayuthaya women into Burma and made them slaves and prostitutes. From that time on Yodyama, meaning Ayuthaya women, became a trade name of the prostitutes in Burma.

The above case of the slavery and forced prostitution could be ignored as the feudal past. Nevertheless, the following piece of news is recent and very disturbing.

A Modern Form of Slavery. (Source: http://hrw.org/doc/?t=asia_pub&c=burma). *Trafficking of Burmese Women and Girls into Brothels in Thailand.* Thousands of Burmese women and girls are trafficked into Thai brothels every year where they work under conditions tantamount to slavery. Subject to debt bondage, illegal confinement, various forms of sexual and physical abuse, and exposure to HIV in the brothels, they then face wrongful arrest as illegal immigrants if they try to escape or if the brothels are raided by Thai police. (Note: Human Rights Watch (HWR) is an international human rights watch dog).

Now, I would like to tell you a story. The following story serves as a window into the secrets of how women are viewed and treated in Myanmar society. I learned it when I was a Rangoon University student. The story begins below in quotes.

"......It happened in a remote rural village of northern Burma. One morning, Khin May was on her way to paddy field carrying breakfast for her father who ploughed the paddy field. She met Nga Htu, the local youth, as she passed a paddy field. He pulled her down behind a straw bale and raped her. Khin May yelled and shouted, to no avail. When she was free she continued with her chores . In the afternoon she went to the mountain to collect vegetables and firewood. She met Nga Htu again and he raped her again. The same thing happened for the third time when she went to fetch water from the river in the evening. Furious for being victimized repeatedly, she reported the case to the village *elders* at the end of the day when her household work was done. Immediately, *the elders* called a village meeting and summoned Nga Htu, the youth. Khin May narrated the accidents of the day to *the elders* and the villagers in the meeting. *The chair of the elders* asked.

"Nga Htu, is it true that you raped Khin May three times?"

"Yes. It is true". Nga Htu answered.

The elders looked at each other and nodded. Then the chair of the elders announced.

"Nga Htu is found guilty of raping Khin May three times. According to the law of village Nga Htu is ordered to pay Khin May three quarters accounting one quarter for each rape. 'Now, Nga Htu, give Khin May three quarters, *right now'*."

Nga Htu handed out a one dollar bill to Khin May and said, "Give me the change".

Khin May replied, "I have no change". Truly, she was penniless.

Nga Htu reported the case to elders saying, "She did not give me the change".

The chair of the elders ordered Khin May to give the change to Nga Htu. Khin May again said, "I have no change".

Nga Htu yelled, "I want justice!"

The elders looked at each other and nodded. Then, the chair of the elders announced.

"Since Khin May does not give the change let Nga Htu rape her once more and let her keep the change."

The story ends here.

There is more irony than truth in this story. It is a rhetoric that tries to draw attention to the neglected rural women who are completely occupied with household chores, since they reach the age of 12 or 13 years. Nevertheless, I would like to ask, "How far has the Myanmar society advanced from this irony and rhetoric?".

As long as there lacks a credible evidence to satisfy this question it will be difficult to discard these reports of Myanmarese dirtiness.

On the other hand, recently on 19th November 2004, Prime Minister Khin Nyunt, who was also the chief of the National Investigation Bureau (NIB) that includes the Military Intelligence Services (MIS), was discharged from the post and arrested. The NIB, including MIS, was also dismantled with the message that the unit was no longer relevant as the country moved towards democracy. The State Peace and Development Council (SPDC), which is the ruling body of the Myanmar military government, appointed Lt. General Soe Win as the Prime Minister. General Thura Shwe Mann, who is the third in the military hierarchy after Senior General Than Shwe and Vice-Senior General Maung Aye, gave a lengthy explanation of the development on the 24th instant. General Khin Nyunt was charged with corruption and creating discord within the Myanmar Armed Forces. Reportedly, a good number of the top MIS ranks and files were also arrested and put under the investigation of the teams that were made up of the armed forces officers, police officers and civilian officers. Narinjara News reported that the former NIB's jobs, authority and jurisdiction were transferred to the Police Department. This will mean that no body can be arrested or detained without a warrant or permit issued by a judge. This will also mean that the accused will have the rights to a lawyer and due legal procedure. In November, 2004, the junta released 9248 prisoners including some leading political activists. The ruling junta found that the NIB committed *irregularities* and *improperly* imprisoned them. I determine this trend of development is very healthy and gives a ray of hope for a better human rights situation in the future.

On July 22, 2005, BBC online world news reported that former prime minister General Khin Nyunt was found guilty of the corruption charges in a closed court trial and sentenced to forty four years of suspended imprisonment. I hope and pray that "Dirty Myanmarism" comes to an end very soon. Let Myanmar be an Enlightened Country.

Chapter-5. Behind the Rise of Myanmarism

The manifestations of Myanmarism, which I described in the previous chapter, are *the effects*, but not *the causes* of the rise of Myanmarism. In every phenomenon there is a cause that leads to the manifestation of the effect. In biological world, there always is a genetic factor that modulates the phenotype of an organism. In the case of Myanmar, I identify three factors that create and modulate the form of Myanmarism that we see in post-1988 Burma.

Factor-1. East-West Confrontation.
Factor-2. Communist Danger.
Factor-3. Islamic Expansionism.

Prior going into the details of these factors I must make the reader acquainted with the Myanmar transition from pre-1988 to post-1988. I presented a concise account of the transition from pre-1988 to post-1988 in the 'Preface' of my book, *Burma: Nationalism and Ideology*, University Press Ltd., Dhaka, 1989. With some grammatical polish, I am reproducing it here so that the reader will get well acquainted with Burma's 1988.

'Preface' of my book, *Burma: Nationalism and Ideology*

Preface

This book presents an analysis of Burmese society, culture and politics in a search for the root causes of the events in Burma.

Tens of thousands of Burmese including school girls and boys gave their lives in the streets of Rangoon, Mandalay, and other cities across the country during the Great Democratic Movement which took place from March to September 1988. The democratic world, regardless of ideology, religion, and culture, watched with dismay when the military regime brutally crushed the Movement. Once again 'Might' won over 'Reasons' and a civilization was put to death in Burma.

The Burmese political volcano has been building up pressure for the last 26 years under the repressive heat of the military government. Its eruption in 1988 shooting out the lava of blood across the nation is a major landmark in the political history of the world.

The eruption took place as the millions of people, with the students in the front marched along the streets of Rangoon, Mandalay, and forty other cities demanding democracy and multiparty system, resignation of the military government, dissolution of the so-called Burmese Socialist Program Party and formation of a neutral interim government to oversee the election and transition to democracy.

General Ne Win resigned on 23rd July 1988. The Burmese Socialist Program Party (BSPP), the organ of the military regime, on 26th July appointed the former General Sein Lwin as the chairman of the Party and President of the Government. Sein Lwin earned the notorious name 'Butcher' when his ruthless suppression of the movement left well over 70,000 (seven thousand) dead across the nation. Despite the bloodbath the students and populace stood up against the guns bravely and boldly upholding their demands. As a consequence, after 17 days in power, Sein Lwin was removed and a week later, Dr. Maung Maung was put up as the new Chief.

'Preface' of my book, *Burma: Nationalism and Ideology*

Dr. Maung Maung revised the 1974 Constitution giving room for a multiparty system, terminated all members of the armed forces from the membership of the ruling BSPP, declared the Army apolitical and formed the Election Commission with the proposal of a general election. The students and populace were not satisfied with his concession and stood firmly by their original demands for the dissolution of the BSPP and formation of a neutral interim government. On 23rd of August they mounted massive demonstration and took over all the BSPP offices. The government employees joined the Movement resulting in the total collapse of the government's administration. The civil administration was taken over by the People's Committees formed by the students, monks, and strikers. The crisis deepened further as the entire police force and a good number of the servicemen from Navy, Air Force, and Infantry defected to the people. Then the government was non-functional.

At that junction it was believed that General Ne Win formed an Anti-Strike Committee with himself as the Chairman and worked to disrupt and break up the Movement by creating dacoities, lootings and assassination attempts targeted at the popular leaders, especially at Aung San Suu Kyi, the daughter of the national hero General Aung San. There were news of the Military Intelligence Agents poisoning the food supplies to the hospitals and drinking water at the cities. In anger and confusion the people arrested and beheaded the troublemakers whom they believed to be Military Agents. Major anti-government demonstrations and riots broke out in the jails of Akyab, Moulmein, and Insein. On 26th and 27th of August as many as 3000 inmates, including many political detenues, were believed to be killed at the Insein Jail which was totally gutted down by fire. As a result many, rather almost all, inmates were set free. Looting of food godowns and commodity warehouses took place. Anarchy prevailed all over Burma. While the people believed that the anarchy was systematically created by General Ne Win and his cronies they failed to materialize their political programs. Despite the popular demand, the opposition leaders failed to unite and form an interim government even when the entire civil administration was taken over by the people across the country. On the 9th of September U Nu declared that he was still the legally elected Prime Minister of Burma and that his government legitimate as the 1947 Constitution had never been dissolved. Accordingly he resumed his Premiership, revitalized his government, declared Maung Maung's government illegal and Army the rebel, and asked them to surrender to him. Before the people could understand the political significance of his move the Association of Former Military Commanders denounced U Nu as an opportunist who tried to rebuild his throne on the blood of the students. Actually those military commanders were frightened to get themselves prosecuted as they were not only part of the 1962 military coup but also responsible for the killings of students in July 1962 and December 1974 (see section 6.1). As the great expectation had been placed upon such former military leaders as Brigadier Aung Gyi and General Tin Oo, the students and people failed to consider with proper logic and rationale the significance of U Nu's move. For the second time the populace was deceived and tricked by the military leaders and U Nu again fell victim to the infantile disorders of Burmese politics (see sections 8.6, 8.7 and 9.1).

On the other hand the illustrious Aung San Suu Kyi could not detach feelings and sympathy towards the Army that was founded by her father, General Aung San. As she had been out of touch with Burma and had lived apolitical life since her teens she could not realize that the national army, which was given life by her father, was no longer there but it had been reconstituted with the anti-people military adventurists. In fact, in view of the political tactics, U Nu's move was based upon very sound constitutional considerations and he could emerge as an alternative government which could have served as the interim government with due international recognition had the people stood by him.

While U Nu was being discredited Brigadier Aung Gyi, Aung San Suu Kyi, and General Tin Oo, who were together known as Aung Suu Tin, could not reach any consensus and disagreed with the people to form an interim government. Thus the Democratic Movement reached a dead end and became frustrated with indecision. The failure of the people at large and the newly emerged leaders was due to their lack of experience in political tactics for Burma as a whole had been a prison of darkness for last 26 years under Ne Win's military dictatorship.

Amidst such political chaos and confusion, the crisis further deepened as famine loomed over the cities. The food supply from the rural areas could not reach the cities since not only the national transport system but also the production of fuel was paralyzed by the nation-wide strike.

This situation was again exploited by the army on 18th of September to seize the power under the name of State Law and Order Restoration Council using exactly the same reasons given by General Ne Win in his 1962 coup. The Great Democracy Movement failed to break the backbone of the military culture (see section 8.5).

The military take-over was well orchestrated. Dr. Maung Maung, the 3rd BSPP ruler, announced on 14th of September that Armed Forces, Police and Government employees were no longer members of the ruling Party. The next day, General Saw Maung, Chief of the Staff, from radio and television, directed the armed forces that they were no longer party members and their duty in that condition was to defend the country, and protect lives and properties of the people. Citing the 1958 General Ne Win's speech to armed forces at the event of the military take-over as the care-taker government at that time, he instructed the rank and files to be neutral in the politics and to uphold the spirit, moral, and discipline of the Burmese People's Army. On the 18th of September. he seized the power. Earlier in the second week of September. he had transferred many officers and soldiers of the most loyal, and battle-hardened Light Infantry Division 22 to various key regiments and battalions across the country to exert and ensure his control. In the speech to the nation he declared that the multiparty democratic election would be held soon after the law and order, and functional stability of general national life restored. He asked the people to maintain law and order as he had already given them democracy which was their demand.

The students, monks and people, with anger and frustration, resisted the military takeover mounting pitch battles in the streets and defending their Strike Camps with such primitive weapons as swords, spears, *jinglees* (i.e. catapult which shoots 4- inch special nails), and with guns which they seized from the police stations. Serious street battles took place at Rangoon, Mandalay, Moulmein, Pegu and few other cities on 18th, 19th and 20th of September. Their weapons were no match to the military automatic rifles, and by the first week of October the resistance was crushed, leaving behind about 2000 dead. The Democratic Movement was further subdued by massive arrest and summary executions. The strike leaders of the government employees were sacked en masse. In the second week of October the civil administration was normalized to a great extent as the civil servants and workers returned to work. However, almost all industries including the oil fields and refineries became non-operational as these had been sabotaged by the workers during the resistance.

Later, the military government allowed formation of the political parties which must be registered with the Election Commission in order to go for the polls. Under the new decree known as the Registration Law of Associations and Organizations, formation of the Trade Unions and Employees' Union are banned. The employees of the Government are prohibited from joining any political party. As all the factories are owned and operated by the government the decree technically puts the workers and other employees who constituted the major effective fighting force during the Democratic Movement into isolation from politics. Thus the political force is greatly weakened.

On the other hand General Saw Maung's Military Government is seen as a manipulation of General Ne Win and hard to be accepted as the interim government by the people. At the same time Saw Maung himself is not acceptable to the people as they believe that he was the accomplice of Sein Lwin. As his hand is stained and Burma remains pungent with the blood of thousands of peaceful demonstrators it will be impossible for Saw Maung and his Army to gain credibility of a care-taker government in the line of Ne Win's stand in 1958-60.

Meanwhile, the so-promised multiparty election presents an illusion as the election will be for the People's Assembly under the 1974 Constitution enforced by the BSPP which has now transformed itself into the National Unity Party under the leadership of the old guards of Ne Win. Despite the withdrawal of the membership from the BSPP Saw Maung and Army will never be able to identify themselves independently of the Party and Ne Win's militarism. The people are apprehensive that Ne Win, his BSPP and Army are working together to stay in power by introducing a sort of military democracy instead of the military socialism.

Under these circumstances the opposition forces have been divided into two factions, *pro*-election and *pro*-revolution. Up to January 1989 those of the pro- election factions have formed more than 160 political parties and registered with the Election Commission. Noteworthy among those are:- 1. National Unity Party (NUP) which is the reincarnation of the BSPP; 2. National League for Democracy (NLD) led by Aung San Suu Kyi who claimed to have more than a million membership; 3. Democracy Party (DP) which is the brain-child of U Nu and led by Bo Hmu Aung, one of the Thirty Comrades and a close associate of U Nu; 4. Party for People's Democracy (PPD) led by Widura Thakin Chit Maung who was the President of the National Unity Front before; 5. Party for Peace and National Development (PPND) which is patronized by Thakin Soe, the former General Secretary of the Red Flag Burma Communist Party; and 6. Union National Democracy Party (UNDP) led by the former Brigadier-General Aung Gyi after he broke off from the NLD. These parties have expressed the intention to participate in the election provided that the election is certainly going to be free and fair. They, however, have declared that they will not betray the blood of the students, monks, and people who have sacrificed their lives in the recent Democratic Movement.

The pro-revolution faction is led by the students, the General Strike Committee and the Monks. They have called for the final assault to achieve full democracy by staging an armed revolution which will annihilate the BSPP-militarists. If they fail to do so they have to live like animals for years to come under the militarism, All Burma Students Democratic Front (ABSDF) warns the people. They have made it clear that they have been compelled to resort to armed struggle by the brutal killing of the peaceful demonstrators by the BSPP-militarist. The ABSDF is about 7,000 (seven thousand) strong at present. The General Strike Committee (GSC) is estimated to compose about 3000 members. The Young Monks Union of Burma(YMUB) is believed to have about seven hundred monks at the border areas. These three revolutionary organizations are encamped along the border areas controlled by the guerrillas of the National Democratic Front (NDF). In addition, other revolutionary parties namely All Burma Muslim Union (ARMU), Chin National Front (CNF), National Unity Party for Democracy (NUPD), Overseas Burmese Liberation Front (OBLF), and Overseas Karen Organization (OKO) have emerged.

These eight revolutionary organizations join the ten members of the National Democratic Front (NDF) and People's Patriotic Party (PPP), Committee for Restoration of Democracy in Burma (CRDB), Muslim Liberation Organization of Burma (MLOB), National United Front of Arakan (NUFA) and People's Liberation Front (PLF) to form the 23-member Democratic Alliance of Burma (DAB) (see section 5.1). In a conference called the 'General Conference of Opposition to the Rangoon Military Regime' held at a liberated area from 14th to 18th of November 1988 the newly formed DAB declared their main objectives as to overthrow the Rangoon Military Regime, to establish a democratic form of government, to end the civil war and restore internal peace, and to bring about national reconciliation and creation of a genuine federal union. With these political programs the DAB having a membership of more than seventy thousand including a sixteen thousand strong fighting guerrilla force is by far most solidified politico-military opposition to the Rangoon military regime. Thus it can be contrasted distinctly from the city-based political parties whose party-structure still needs crystallization and their political objectives clarified.

In the overview, it seems that the final act of Burma's drama is yet to be played. The people of Burma want democracy. Whether that DEMOCRACY will come through the ELECTION or the REVOLUTION is the big question.

The 'Preface' ends here.

**Things to ponder
Wisdom of a Red Comrade**

In the last week of August 1988, when the Burmese pro-democracy uprising was at its peak, my good friend Red Comrade U Oo Khin Maung, a politburo member of the Arakan Communist Party and Joint Secretary of the National United Front of Arakan walked into my office in Dhaka. After exchanging pleasantries he took a seat in front of me and put on his standard humble and gentle smile. Then, I realized that a rosy silver bullet was on its way. He said, "So! *Brother* Shwe Lu Maung, you believe that the Bama military government will be thrown out this time?"

"Brother' or *'Ako'* is our Rakhaing traditional civility used to address to each other among men. 'Bama' is the indigenous word for the Burmese.

I replied, "It is so *Ako* Oo Khin Maung. I believe that the Bama military government will be overthrown this time."

"How can you believe so when what is going on is nothing but the *'Paris Commune'* in Burma?", He stunned me with these words.

"How can you say that!?", was all that I could say.

Today, I worship him just for that discourse. One should never undermine the wisdom of a *Red Comrade*.

(Note. My article *The Third Dimension of 8.8.88*, Arakanpsot, Issue-5, July 2004, gives detail account of the 'Paris Commune in Burma'. You may read it at http://shwelumaung.org/publications/series4.pdf).

5.1. East-West Confrontation. It is an undisputed universal and historical fact that the external threats and dangers bind the peoples of a clan or tribe. Similarly, the common and greater external threats and dangers drive the different clans and tribes into the bondage of nationhood. Since the British occupation the western threat has been a major source of Myanmarese unity.

'....British occupation brought all feudal nations and kingdoms of Burma together under one powerful rule. This, for the first time in the history of Burma, created a common interest among the people of Burma, simply because they faced a common enemy. There appeared a common sense for unity in the struggle of independence. For the first time in the thousand years of rivalry and domination wars, the people of Burma started to try to sink their mutual hatred and discrimination and to forge unity. In such an attempt the common heritage of culture and traditions were highlighted to give the feeling of oneness. The revolutionary elite of all national groups initiated this nationalistic movement....' (Shwe Lu Maung, *Burma: Nationalism and Ideology*, University Press Ltd., Dhaka, 1989, Chapter 2.2).

I wrote the above cited statement some 14 years ago, but I conceived it since I was 12 years old when I attended a political rally held by the then Rakhaing National Unity Organization (Ra-Ta-Nya) in 1957. This statement is our national consensus. Today, I stood by this statement stronger than ever before. The Great Britain was a powerful external force that served well as a binding glue. When the British Masters left Burma the binding glue also vaporized into the humid tropical air. Internal strife took in such ferocity that Burmese Armed Forces aka *Bama Tatmadaw* found a very good excuse to stage a coup d'état in 1962 and set up the military dictatorship that lasted up to today.

General Ne Win and his military commanders Colonels Aung Gyi, Kyi Maung, Maung Lwin, etc. declared that the Federating Nations (ethnic minorities) were working to secede from the Union of Burma with the help of a certain western power. In Burma, even an unborn child knows that 'a western power' is a pseudonym of the United States of America. Another Burmese slang for the Americans is *'Nga Pwa Gyi'*[1], meaning 'inflated big thing'. By charging American interference in Burma's domestic affairs General Ne Win motivated Burmese patriotism in a classic fashion. The West was charged of instigating secessionism.

How effective was the American-sponsored secessionist propaganda? Its effectiveness goes further than the limit you can imagine.

In terms of the historical internationalism the Burmese are afraid of two enemies namely (1) the Chinese *(Tayut)*[2], and (2) the Indians *Kula*[3]. 'Kula' is pronounced 'kala'. The Kula are of two kinds namely the White or European Kula and the Asian Kula. The Burmese populace, including the communists, immediately and firmly stood by General Ne Win. As such the military junta succeeded in consolidating its power with one propaganda in 1962.

Exactly in the same manner, Sr. General Saw Maung charged the West with interfering in Myanmar's internal affairs and took refuge in the folds of ASEAN and China. The Burmese

---

Notes.

1. Nga Pwa Gyi (ငွပြီး)။ 2. The Burmese call the Chinese *Tayut.* Originally, the *Tayut* (တရုပ်) means a Tartar and the *Tayat* (တရတ်) is a Turk. The Mongol Emperor Kublai Khan's army invaded Burma and destroyed the kingdom of Pagan in 1297 CE. His army was made up of the Tartars and the Turks. Since then the Burmese call the Chinese *Tayut.* 3. *Kula* (ကုလား) is pronounced *kala* (ကလား).

http://www.myanmar.com/Union/interference.html

American interference in internal affairs of Myanmar

CIA (a) Central Intelligence Agency of American

Today, the United States of America is interfering in the internal affairs of other nations. Interference jointly made by CIA of America and MI 5 of the British can be seen obviously in international events. Therefore, it is necessary to keep a watchful eye with national vigil on insincere acts of American CIA, dangers which is probably posed to the nation and interfering acts.

American interference in internal affairs of Myanmar - *CIA (a) Central Intelligence Agency of American - Interferences and meddlings of CIA - Foreign spies - US involvement in nationalist Chinese intrusion into Myanmar - US scheme to separate Shan State from the Union - US support for U Nu's expatriate group*

US interference in 1988 disturbances - *Assistance provided to anti-government groups - America's obstruction against Myanmar's entry into ASEAN - America's economic sanctions on Myanmar - American leaders' assessment on the economic sanctions*

http://www.myanmar.com/Union/union.html

military junta openly put up charges against the United States of America. The reader may visit http://www.myanmar.com/Union/interference.html and http://www.myanmar.com/Union/union.html for the details of their viewpoint. The followings are major points of the scores made by the Rangoon junta.

(1). The US involvement in nationalist Chinese intrusion into Myanmar from 1950-57: There is some truth in this. The US wanted the Nationalist Chinese (Kuomintang) to establish a stronghold in the Shan State of Burma and stage counter offensive against the Chinese Communists. No country, let alone Burma, will accept such an unscrupulous scheme. This is one reason, across the world, why there are many people who hate the United States of America. Furthermore, Burma recognized the Chinese Communist government from the very beginning of 1950 whereas the US did so only in 1970.

(2). The US scheme to separate the Shan State from the Union: This Myanmarese propaganda is baseless and wrong in the light of my experience. Since 1966, I and my colleagues have approached the regional and international powers soliciting aids for toppling the military junta, establishing a federation of Burma or, if necessary, an independent Arakan Republic. We reached the diplomats, cabinet ministers, military high commands, and intelligence sources. Everyone of them gives moral support for democracy. All are indifferent to the issue of a federation of Burma, but condemn the idea of secession without any reservation. The followings are the examples of some typical answers.

US: "Burma is not Nicaragua. Whatever happening there is totally your domestic affair". This typical US policy is true as long as the communists are not in power.

USSR: "Revolution cannot be exported". The USSR was pretty sour with the Chinese who gave some marginal support to the Burma Communist Party just to use it as a leverage against the Rangoon junta.

India: "You are a secessionist, and you have contact with the Mizo and the Assamese rebels!". India is very sensitive of her Northeastern Mongolian people as their pre-independent dream of a United States of Tribal Nations has not totally evaporated yet.

China, Thailand and Bangladesh: "We are good neighbors". I believe in Thailand only. I do not trust China and Bangladesh.

The point here is to illustrate that no one in this world wants Burma to get disintegrated. The Myanmarese's charges against the US do not have any substance. It could be that some CIA field agents in late 1950s might have suggested to slice off the Shan Plateau for the Nationalist Chinese (Kuomintang). This surely was not and still is not the US government's policy. On the other hand the Shan people or their leading Sawbwas did not and still do not want or have a plan to secede from the Union of Burma[1]. If they had such thinking they would have opted to demand independence separately from the beginning. It is also wrong to say that the federal policy of the Shan Sawbwas was instigated by the US. The federation was envisaged during the British rule, finalized in the 1947 Panglong Agreement, and consequently constitutionalized in Aung San Constitution, which was trashed by the Myanmarese after killing Aung San in 1947.

(3). The US support for U Nu's expatriate group: I do not agree with this charge. The US government was not involved in Prime Minister U Nu's insurrection of 1970-1972. He was financially supported by some businesses that incurred great loses due to General Ne Win nationalization of all private, both foreign and domestic, enterprises. They supported U Nu who promised to denationalize and compensate the losses. What U Nu got was too small to pose any major threat to the military junta.

(4) The Western support of 1988 pro-democracy uprising in Burma: I discuss this issue in the next page.

(5) The US and European assistance to the anti-government groups: This is a standard practice of the western democratic countries. So far, their assistance in humanitarian aid is a very minute amount. In fact, I call it negligible. Especially so when we take into the account that the Communist China gave Myanmar 1.2 billion US dollar military grant to enlarge and upgrade her armed forces between 1989 and 1991. All what the US Congress gave to the Myanmarese dissidents was 1 million US dollars for resettlement and education. It is just a broken piece of peanut, amounting to 0.083% of 1.2 billion dollars of the Chinese aid. At present the Chinese grant must have come up above 2 billion US dollars. I will pick up this point again at a later session. With the Chinese aid Myanmar armed forces are the strongest and largest in the Southeast Asia with a strength of 500,000 fighting force today. This is the main reason why all the anti-junta rebel armed forces have surrendered or entered into cease-fire agreement to the advantage of the junta. We have more reason to complain about the Chinese interference in Myanmar domestic affairs.

(6) The Western support of, and showering awards on Mrs. Aung San Suu Kyi Aris (Daw

---

Notes. 1. As I write this book an exiled Shan group in Canada led by Sao Surkhanpha, eldest son of Burma's first president, Sao Shwe Thaike, declared the independence of the Federated Shan States on the 17th of April 2005. This is their recent decision in response to 43-years of oppression by the Bama military dictatorship. In 1962, Sao Surkhanpha was only 24 years old, and neither he nor his father had a thought of secession.

Suu), including Nobel Peace Price in 1990: Daw Suu is married to a Britisher, Dr. Michael Aris, who was an Oxford don. He died from prostate cancer in 1999. In Myanmar, a marriage to a foreigner is seen not only as a lack of patriotism but also as treason to the nation. "Just think of a Britisher sleeping with your Prime Minister!", the propaganda says. It wins instant support from the armed forces personnel, and the patriotic Myanmarese. In my view the western support to Mrs. Aung San Suu Kyi Aris is more beneficial to the military government than to herself or the Myanmarese democracy movement. I do not consider that kind of support as interference in politics. It is just a matter of expression of different political values.

(7). The US rejection of Myanmar and tutoring her in English grammar: This is very amusing to me. Please see next page where I presented a comparison of the US and the UN. I find the US showing infantile disorder in this matter. The original Burmese version is 'Pyi-htaung-su-myanmar-nai-ngan'[1] whereas the English version is The Union of Burma. In 1988 the original Burmese version was restored and The Union of Myanmar became the English version. It was officially changed at the United Nations. This produced a significant change in political psychology the Burmese mind with a boast on patriotism. The boast is further supplemented unexpectedly by the United States when she declined to recognize *'Myanmar'*[2], making herself a villain in the eyes of the Myanmarese and the Asians. In Myanmar, anything that is anti-US is a hero in its face value because the Myanmarese never bother to look into the substance. The US officially adopted a spelling of 'Myanma'[2], but not 'Myanmar', asserting that *'r'* is redundant. This created a conflict of authority. The Asians believe that Myanmarese government has every authority to spell it in the way it sees it right and the international community is obliged to respect the Myanmarese sovereign authority. For example, the Myanmarese do not come and tell the Americans that they have to spell l-a-b-o-u-r, but not l-a-b-o-r. Despite my opposition to Myanmâ[2] colonialism, I accept that Mranmar is the correct spelling and pronunciation. I also see US government's stance as a violation of international norms. Unfortunately, the US has an obsession of defying and irritating the world with prejudice. The US neither have the stomach to openly announce that she does not recognize Myanmar and the Myanmarese military junta, nor does she know that she is simply making the Asians angry just by creating an issue out of a *name*. What does it matter? It is just a name. Believe it or not, this infantile disorder of the US created a good mind among the ASEAN to accept Myanmar as its new member.

Now let me present my analysis on the above charges.

How true was the Western or American interference in Burma's domestic affairs? It was something there, but I do not call it 'interference'. I call it love-hate-relationship of the Myanmar and the West. I will try to give a relevant and concise account of West-Myanmar flirtations here.

Always, there exists controversy and contradicting story. When I look at the other side of the coin, the West and the US have been at the side of the Myanmarese ruling junta from the onset. It is convenient to present the theories in chronological order.

A school of the analysts assert that the 1948 pro-West Karen rebellion (Karen National Democratic Organization, KNDO and later Karen National Union, KNU) was a brain child of the Allied Forces in agreement with the Burmese and Thai authorities. The West planted the KNDO as a buffer zone so that the Burmese and the Thai-Malaya communists could not join

---

Notes. 1. Pyi-htaung-su-myanmar-nai-ngan (ပြည်ထောင်စုမြန်မာနိုင်ငံ).

2. Myanmar (မြန်မာ); Myanma (မြန်မ); Myanmâ (မြန်မာ).

geographically. This theory renders some credibility in the light of the fact that Burmese Armed Forces and the KNU entered into a kind of cease-fire agreement whenever the fight with the Burmese Communists grew serious. The Burmese forces never tried to eliminate the Karen rebels even though they were thirty six times stronger with superior weapons (i.e. 5,000 Karen fighters versus 180,000 Burmese soldiers) at the height of the rebellion. The KNU got Arms, ammunitions and other logistic supports through Thailand. It is a common sense that illegal arm purchases and transports for many years, in this case 50 years, could not occur without the cooperation of the authorities concern. Obviously, the Thai high command knew everything, but kept a close eye to these activities in their strategic interest of preventive measure against a possible united front of the Burmese, the Thai and the Malaya communist parties. Post-1988 events that I will present in the coming paragraphs render credible substance to this theory.

The Chinese were the main enemy that bound the peoples of Burma together from 1962 to 1988. 'The Chinese are coming' was the patriotic song. The Burmese fear of the Chinese came into daily life when the Great Kublai Khan, Emperor of Yuan dynasty, sent his army and

---

The US vs. the UN
On the name of Myanmar
The underlined emphasis is mine to draw your attention.

US

US rejected the name Myanmar.

Source as of February 16, 2003: -
(CIA World Fact Book 2002)
http://www.odci.gov/cia/publications/
factbook/geos/bm.html

conventional long form: Union of Burma
conventional short form: Burma
local short form: Myanma Naingngandaw
local long form: Pyidaungzu Myanma Naingngandaw (translated by the US Government as Union of
Myanma and by the Burmese as Union of Myanmar)
former: Socialist Republic of the Union of Burma
note: since 1989 the military authorities in Burma
have promoted the name Myanmar as a conventional name for their state; this decision was not approved by any sitting legislature in Burma, and the
US Government did not adopt the name, which is a
derivative of the Burmese short-form name Myanma
Naingngandaw

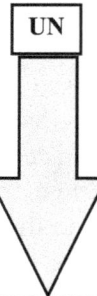

UN

The United Nations accepted the term 'Myanmar'.

Source as of February 16, 2003:
http://www.un.org/Overview/
unmember.html

Mongolia -- (27 Oct. 1961)
Morocco -- (12 Nov. 1956)
Mozambique -- (16 Sep. 1975)
Myanmar -- (19 Apr. 1948)
Namibia -- (23 Apr. 1990)
Nauru -- (14 Sept. 1999)
Nepal -- (14 Dec. 1955)

Author's Notes: (1) 'မြန်မ' will be pronounced and written 'Myanma', but 'မြန်မာ' is 'Myanmar'. Again, if the word is 'မြန်မာ့' it is pronounced 'Myanmâ'. In Burmese standard translation into English when the stress is placed at the ancillary alphabet 'ာ' the letter 'r' is suffixed. (2) There was no sitting legislature in 1989 since the 1974 Socialist Constitution was abolished by the military regime in 1988 and the country was ruled by decree.

crushed the First Myanmar Empire in 1279, as the Burmese king failed to present annual tribute to him. Up to today the Burmese are afraid of the Chinese. If Burmese say I am wrong they are simply deceiving themselves. The 1950 Myanmarese refusal to allow the Nationalist Chinese establishment inside Burma was simply because they were afraid that the Chinese Red Army would just march into Burma just like Kublai Khan's army did. The Chinese Red Army would not take more than one month to occupy Burma.

After Burma's independence in 1948 the Chinese claimed a large chunk of Burma's northern territory covering the area of presently Kachin and Shan States. The Burmese government settled it in 1960 by giving away a large part of the claimed land to China avoiding a war with the fear of repetition of 1279. After that experience Burma balanced of the Chinese menace by flirting with the Union of Soviet Socialist Republics (USSR) and the United States of America (USA). In 1989 I wrote as follow.

".......Mainly the throne of Ne Win is propped up by a strong tripod. The first leg of the tripod is the Union of Soviet Socialist Republics, the second leg is the United States of America, and the third one is the People's Republic of China. The tripod is standing on the Foundation of the Third World Colonialism which is submerging the minorities as hidden colonies or the Fourth World." (*Burma: Nationalism and Ideology*, University Press Ltd., Dhaka, 1989, Chapter 9.2).

The subject of international politics in Burma and her recent clone, Myanmar, is vast and complicated. I dealt it very briefly giving only the essential points in my 1989 book. Similarly, I do not intend to give an extensive account, but I must present adequate information for the sake of clarity.

Modern international game was designed by my one-time colonial master, the Great Britain. She and her allies decided that the key was to keep the communists out of power in Burma. By the time she left the colony the Burmese Communists had been split into two - Red Flag and White Flag Burmese Communist Parties, CPB and BCP respectively. In 1947, U Nu's provisional government outlawed both communist parties. Most important point that has not appeared in the political archives is that the Allied Forces had trained a bunch of loyal Burmese military commanders who are highly politicized and anticommunist. The training continued up to today!

The Western powers did not like prime minister U Nu (1901-1993) who was very independent and became an architect of the Bandung Agreement and Non-Aligned Movement along with such figures like Jawaharlal Nehru (1889-1964) of India, and Ahmed Sukarno (1901-1970) of Indonesia. The West argued that he was weak whereas the truth was that they viewed his independent non-aligned policy as a threat to the West. They were afraid that U Nu might end up making peace with the Burmese communist parties and made them legal leading to a communist-dominated Burma. After all the communist leaders were U Nu's college pals and colleagues in Burma's struggle for independence under the banner of the Anti-Fascist and People's Freedom League (AFPFL). In contrast General Ne Win was a sort of lone wolf in those days. In 1962, a good number of the political analysts in Burma argued that the General Ne Win and his military takeover of the prime minister U Nu's government was orchestrated by the Western governments with the view of preventing the communists power in Burma. On the other hand the military government of General Ne Win as well as the present generals charged that the US supported U Nu's armed insurrection against them. Let us examine these two arguments.

For sure, all high ranking Burmese military intelligence service (MIS) personnel were (and still are) trained by the West. For example, former MIS Chief Colonel Tin U *(Lanky)* as well as the later MIS strongman General Khin Nyunt (Prime Minister of Myanmar August 2003 to October 2004) were trained by the US-CIA, the British HM Secret Service, and the Israelis in Diego Garcia. It is a British territory in Indian Ocean, which hosts a Western military strategic command center having a strong UK-US military base. In late 1960s and early 1970s when *Lanky* Tin U was the Chief it was even said that the Burmese MIS shared the information of the Red China with their CIA counterparts. In those days the Burmese Military Socialist regime sent many missions to the People's Republic of China on various good-will programs ranging from the youth training to industrial and military training. The observers in Rangoon charged that these missions were implanted with the CIA-MIS moles. I do not think anybody can prove or disprove these charges due to its dubious nature. Nevertheless, intelligence-sharing is a common agreement among the governments. It is nothing irregular.

Therefore, in the days before 1988, there lacked credible reasons to agree with the military junta's charges against the United States interference in Burma's domestic affairs. It was rather a mutual relationship benefiting each other.

On the other hand it is reasonable to view that 1988 pro-democracy uprising in Burma at a time when the USSR was at the brink of total collapse was not a sheer coincidence. Mikhail Sergeyevich Gorbachev's newfound policy of openness *'Glasnost'* and the soviet liberalism *'Perestroika'* had already signaled the fall and disintegration of the communist giant. The West had inflicted a cultural lethal wound upon Gorbachev with its powerful weapon 'Nobel Peace Prize' in 1990. Accordingly, of the three legs (i.e. USA, USSR, and China) of the tripod that supported the Burmese military regime only two were left.

Since 1974, beginning with her Pin Pong diplomacy, the USA has been cultivating the Red China as a strategic friend of post cold war era. The great revolutionary and theoretician, but a bad economist (e.g. Great Leap Forward, 1958) and tactless politician (e.g. Cultural Revolution 1966-1976), Chairman Mao Ze Dong (1893-1976) died at the peak of his radical cultural revolution leaving the Chinese door open for a new era. His successor, French-educated Deng Xiaoping (1904–97) pragmatically reformed Red China and effectively terminated her hostility towards the West, developing receptivity towards capitalism. Most importantly Beijing completely stopped its logistic supports to the communist parties of Burma, Thailand, and Malaya. This was a key regional development that bore global impact in post-Mao Ze Dong era.

In early 1980, the West determined that communism was no longer a danger at Southeast quarter of the planet. With this determination the fortune of its proxies military dictators across the world instantly changed. Please see the table in the next page. In this global strategy of political change, Burma was no exception. Counting, China as a *'friend'*, under the given circumstances, the US activated her *'sleepers'* in Burma. The first pawn was the MIS Chief Colonel Tin U , nicknamed *Lanky*. His Western Gurus overlooked that General Ne Win was one of the best soldier-rulers (*cf.* Plato's philosopher-ruler), if not number one, on this earth. Ne Win sensed it out and sent *Lanky* Tin U to the infamous Insein Prison. His life was spared on account of Ne Win's promise to *Lanky* Tin U's mother. Want to know what the promise was? Please see it on page 198.

Since 1988, it is true that the US, Europe, India, Australia, and Canada openly denounce the present military junta and give moral support to the non-violent pro-democracy forces, especially to the winning parties of the 1990 election. Exploiting this situation, the junta smartly provokes the Myanmarese patriotic psychology by painting a picture of Western conspiracy against Myanmar's sovereignty. It also charges the pro-democracy activists and Mrs. Aris as the Western stooges. The psychological warfare elevates Myanmarese patriotism and the Myanmarese look at the military government not only as the hero of the modern Myanmarism but also as the defender of Myanmar Sovereignty.

While Myanmar tries very hard to stay free of Western grip, she also woos the Western support in her defense against the communism and the Burma Communist Party (BCP). Since the Burma Communist Party is seen as an appendage of the Soviet Russia or the Red China, every move against the communists or communism has a positive impact on the rise of Myanmarism. We shall see this in the next session.

Lurking in a corner of many minds across the world the following disturbing question will remain for many years to come. The question is: Are the military regimes of the 1960s through 1970s the brainchild of CIA to deter the communist domination of the Third World? The table presented below will serve you as food for thoughts.

(Also see:http://www.shwelumaung.org/OutlawMG/page2.html, February 02, 2003)

Global Citizens Suffering Under the Military Rule
(Source: %world population under the military rule is from http://users.erols.com/mwhite28/. Actual head count is calculated from the world population data found at http://www.un.org/popin/).

Year	% World Population under the military rule	Actual Head Count In Millions (approximate)
1950	<5	107.90
1962	5	151.01
1967	15	500.00
1972	15	553.65
1977	20	813.20
1982	20	**885.94 (the peak)**
1987	15	723.68
1992	10	525.48
1997	5	283.10

Ne Win's Promise

General Ne Win may be politically considered as a bad guy. Nonetheless, he was a promise-keeper strictly following the traditional rule of the Burmese Kings. He is believed to be a descendant of King Bayinnaung, the Destroyer of Thai Ayutthaya, (r.1551-1581). The rule of the country says, "Man must be loyal whereas king must keep promise". Most people in Burma agree that survival of Ne Win as a ruler was due to his adherence of the promises he made.

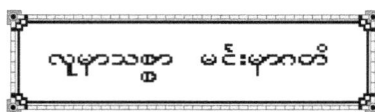

လူမှာသစ္စာ မင်းမှာကတိ

We were told that Colonel *Lanky Tin* U was the youngest of the three brothers who were the commissioned officers in Burma Army. His two elder brothers were killed in action in the post independence internal war. The mother successfully secured an audience with General Ne Win and asked him to see personally that the last of her sons did not get killed. With great admiration of the mother's patriotism and courage he promised. *Lanky* Tin U was transferred to the intelligence unit, trained and eventually made chief of the Military Intelligence Service (MIS). Being good at work he earned the title 'MI Tin U'. He was a 6-footer (6 feet 2 inches or 185 cm), a tall figure in Burma where the average height is 5 foot 6 inches (165 cm). So, he was also known as *Lamba* (meaning *lanky*) Tin U. I have told you the story.

An apology. I have used his nickname *Lanky* to distinguish Colonel Tin U from General Tin U and many other Tin U's. There are many Tin U's in Burma army holding very high ranks. He was also known as MI Tin U because he was the chief of military intelligence (MI). Now there is also another MI Tin U. Therefore, I have used his distinguished nickname *Lanky* that he earned due to his extraordinary height 185 cm (6 feet 2 inches) among the Burmese. I do not mean to be rude. From a professional point of view he was an honorable soldier and excellent MI.

5.2. Communist Danger. The communists pose both external and internal danger. As a matter of fact, it is more real than the western threat. Soon after the 1962 coup d'état there came a rumor saying that the military takeover was a job of US-CIA. I did not trust the rumor because those who said it were the pro-BCP students. However, it became refreshed in my mind in 1983. In that year, I came to the United States of America as a post-doctoral fellow at the University of Missouri, Columbia. In many occasions, during the small talks with my American colleagues, friends, and students I happened to mention the above rumor to them. Surprisingly, they inclined to believe it saying, "Yeah, CIA could have done that". As they said, they also smiled with fishy twists. In those days, US news was filled with the Contras and Nicaragua. I even remember reading a piece of news reporting that the CIA agents were selling drugs in the streets of San Francisco to raise fund for the Contras! In 1985 I went back to Bangladesh, and again came to the USA in 1994, and back to the University of Missouri in 1995. Again, I told the same rumor to my new friends, colleagues, and students. To my amazement, they also inclined to believe it. It was then that I re-analyzed the rumor. Here I present some reasons that favor the rumor.

More interesting part is shown on the map of communist powers and insurrections in the period from 1950 to 1980s on the next page. In the given time and space it was argued that the 1962 Burmese military takeover had tacit consent of the West. From late 1960s through the end of 1988 Burmese patriotism was kept throbbing and rallying around the military government with the effective whispering campaign saying *"The Chinese are coming"*. These words were not said aloud, nor were announced in public, but whispered in the pubs, restaurants, teashops, snack parlors, military officers and privates mess, etc. In Burma, it is the most effective way of making people believe. Once a piece of news or information is announced publicly the Burmese do not believe it any more. (Also see my book - *Burma: Nationalism and Ideology*, University Press Ltd., Dhaka, 1989, Chapter 8.1). Secrecy means reality in Burma. This secrecy even resulted in a Burmese-Chinese riot in 1967 killing a good number of Chinese. It was also said that the Chinese fired rockets from their Embassy compound. This coincided with the onset of the Chinese Cultural Revolution, Mao's export of his Revolution to Southeast Asia, and establishment of BCP headquarter in Beijing. My high school friend, Ako Maung Aye, a cadre of BCP (Arakan), was trained in Beijing and became prominent as the Beijing-trained Maung Aye. He was killed in action in central Arakan. Similarly, the Cultural Revolution ignited a series of overseas Chinese uprising in Southeast Asia to such an extent that Beijing had to call her overseas compatriots **"to be loyal to their country of residence"**. This message of Chinese wisdom cooled off the overseas Chinese unrest in Burma and other Southeast Asian countries. However, the Burmese, the Thai and the Malaya communist parties gained a good number of new recruits. At the same time, a rise of the Shan and Karen organizations, in particular the armies of General Khun Sa and General Bo Mya, was observed along the Burma-Laos-Thai border, stretching a distance of 2,250 km (1,400 miles). The rise of their military power at the border areas can be construed as a planned operation to prevent the possible links between the Burmese and the Thai-Malay communist armed forces. This development rendered credibility to the theory of an anticommunist buffer zone that I discussed earlier. The military might of the Shan and Karen rebels remained strong and effective until the year 1997.

Is the commies' threat much exaggerated? No!
My experience with communism and communist parties

I grew up amidst the Burmese civil war. My home town Munbra (Minbya) was attacked by the guerrillas quite often between 1950 and 1955. Dead bodies of the government soldiers and guerrillas of anti-government armed parties were displayed very frequently. We, the school kids, were lined up to see the bodies. Even today, I can still see the blood stained dead bodies in my eyes, especially the ones that had blood oozed out from mouth and nose. It is probable that these dead bodies created political interest in my childhood heart and mind. I took part and attended political rallies and processions since I was 9 years old. When I read Lenin's *State and Revolution* I was only 13 years old. The students' cry at that time was 'Give us peace, only peace, please'.

The song "Give us Peace" was composed, and sung by the Rangoon University student

> **The Chinese are coming!**
> **The Chinese are coming!**
> **The Chinese are coming!**
> **The Chinese are coming!**

"The Chinese are coming" was the national glue that bound the Burmese people from 1962 to 1988 while the military government maintained its declaration that the Burmese Army seized the power to prevent a US-sponsored secessionist movement. The map below explains why.

> **Communist Power Map.** A map of Burma and her neighbors showing the communist powers and armed insurrections from 1950 to 1980s, linked with the proletarian flags.

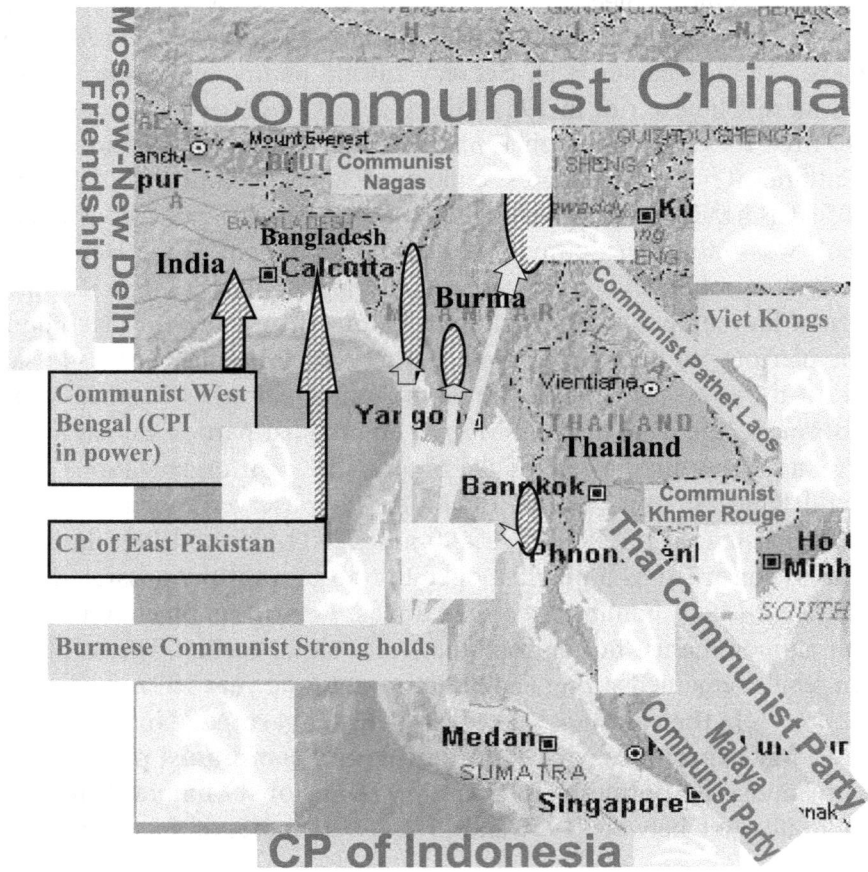

Part of the lyric of the students' song crying for peace in late 1950s and early 1960s

ငြိမ်းချမ်းရေးသာ ပေးပါ ပေးကြပါ
စစ်ဖြစ်လာပြီဆိုမှဖြင့်
မိခင်တကွဲ သားတကွဲနဲ့ သေပွဲဝင်ချာ
စစ်ကိုမလိုပါ စစ်ကိုမလိုပါ
ငြိမ်းချမ်းရေးသာ ပေးပါ ပေးကြပါ

Give us peace, only peace please
When war breaks out
Mother dies here and son dies there
We don't want war
We don't want war
Give us peace, only peace, please

artists and musicians around 1956. This was when Burmese civil war and international Cold War were at their peaks. I cannot remember all lyrics. My sister, Daw Phwa May, now a retired high school principal, and brother Shwe Kyaw, now a retired major of Burma Navy, were at Rangoon University at that time. When I came there in 1960 the song was still alive. I used to join in the chorus in the student processions. This tradition died in 1965 as entire Burma went silent at the event of the military dictatorship. My sister retired in 1985 and brother was compelled to retire in 1978 due to *my undesirable activities* against the junta.

What is my experience with Burmese communism and communist parties? I list my experience below.

1. When I was 6 years old I learned that my uncle, my father's elder brother, was killed by the communist insurgents in his home town, Ponnagyan. We were in Munbra[1], some 60 miles away northwest. It was about 8 O'clock in the evening. Like every day, my father was at the point of telling my second elder brother, Tha Zan Maung, and me a good night story in our bed when a telegram was delivered to us. As he read he yelled aloud, " Oh, Father" and buried his face in the pillow. My mother read the telegram said, "Oh, Buddhaw". My brother read it and said to me, "Senior Uncle is killed". I did not quite understand and still asked, "Papa, won't you tell us the story today?". My brother scolded me. My father hugged me and said, "Tomorrow I will tell you. Go to sleep now, son". I will never forget it. My father, a government officer, was shot at by the unidentified guerrillas forces in many occasions while on his field trips as the Inspector of Land Records having a duty of looking after the entire township. (He retired as the Superintendent of Land Records in 1964). Later, I understood that my uncle was killed as he did not pay the tax to a local communist party. I am not sure my father's status as a government officer also contributed or not.

2. Communism was everywhere as I grew up. The Students' Union was dominated by the procommunist students. They led National Day processions that I joined raising my fisted arm with every slogan. They boycotted the government Independence Day Rally that I attended with my father. Does the solution of our Burma's illness lie in communism and proletarian dictatorship? This question haunted me until 1964. I read Lenin's *State and Revolution*, Karl Marx's *Capital, Dialectical Materialism, The Manifesto of Communist Party, Mao Ze Dong's Selected Works,* and a good number of communist and leftist books. I became active in the students' politics that was dominated by the procommunists such as Ako Maung Aye, see page 193.

I did not have any ideology formed in my mind, though in 1963 I became a Zoology

Notes.
1. Munbra (မင်းပြား) means Mangroves of the King or King's Mangroves. The city was a suburban during the ancient days and the local historical sites date back to the days of Emperor Asoka the Great (r.269-232 BCE) of Magadha.

Honours student with much attraction to Darwinism. (Now I identified myself as a Social Darwinist). It was in 1964 that I made my decision that *'Communism and BCP are not the solution'*. I said this to Ko Cho (Ko Myint Thu) who was a BCP cadre in the campus and a good friend of mine. By then a good number of university students had left the campus to join BCP. Please also see Chapter 5, Notes 1, in my book- (*Burma: Nationalism and Ideology*, University Press Ltd., Dhaka, 1989). Ko Cho needed some one to work in the campus and came to recruit me as he knew my interest in communism. When I gave a 'no' he asked me why. I explained my thoughts to him that can be summarized in three points as follow.

(1). I don't believe that proletarian dictatorship will be any better than military dictatorship.

(2). I don't believe that socialist economy is better than capitalist economy.

(3). I don't believe that proletarian dictatorship under BCP will bring about liberation of my Rakhaing people.

Sadly, Ko Cho left me with best wishes for my studies. Later that year he was arrested and sent to Ko Ko Island concentration camp in the Adamans Islands.

Although I abandoned communism and dismissed BCP as a possible alternative ideological institute I still gave a helping hand to my friends who were the BCP members in Pegu Yoma. After all they were my friends. Up to today I remember helping three of them get treatment for malaria at Rangoon and I even managed to get one of them hospitalized at Rangoon University hospital in 1964. These communist friends of mine were killed in combat or their party internal purge during that fateful BCP's Cultural Revolution (1967-68). By 1968, when I returned Rangoon from my guerrilla life they were all dead. My best friend, Khaing Saw Tun, a lawyer who worked for DAB with me in 1989 and died in 1995, said the following words to me.

" Shwe Lu, I am glad that you are back alive. May be only you and I are left now. Those who are in Pegu Yoma are all gone."

Ironically, he happened to tell these sad words when we were accidentally walking pass the ruins of Rangoon University Students Union Building that was dynamited, after killing more than 100 students on the 7th of July 1962, by General Ne Win, Brig. General Aung Gyi, Colonel Kyi Maung, Colonel Maung Lwin, and their clique[1]. Upon his words we spontaneously happened to stop a moment and looked around the wreckage and weeds where the magnificent Students Union Building once stood with grace. It was a moment of silence that I never find words to describe. (Please take a look back at the Students Union Building on the page 7 of the Preface). In 1963, we built a bamboo cottage and reestablished the students union just to have it crushed within 3 months, with a consequent student uprising and closure of the universities for long nine months. It was at that time that a number of Rangoon University students, somewhere between 150 and 200, went and joined the Burma Communist Party. Only a few who managed to reach China survived the Rangoon offensive or the internal Cultural Revolution. The 7th-July

---

Notes.

1. Colonels Kyi Maung and Maung Lwin became the leader of the main opposition party known as the National League for Democracy in 1989. Colonel Kyi Maung resigned from the post of NLD Chairman in 1997 and Colonel Maung Lwin is the present NLD Chairman. Unto my death, I will uphold our verdict that they are the criminals, guilty of the military coup d'état and killing of the university students in 1962. I will never believe in their democracy. The verdict was reached by the Rangoon University student assemblies that were held in 1962 and confirmed in the 7th-July Anniversary in 1964. On this ground, I also charge Mrs. Aris (Daw Suu) being guilty of collaboration with the 1962 criminals.

Part of a lyric that commemorates the 7th July

နေ့လိုလလို ဘုန်းသမ္ဘာအရှင့်အမာ
ငါ့လိုမင်းမှ ဒင်းဒိုက မာန်ဇီလာ
ဒေါသပုန်ပွားကာ
ကျောင်းသားယူနီယံကြီး ကိုဖြုတာ
သေနပ်နဲ့ပစ်ရာ
ကျောင်းသားတွေမှာ အတုန်းအရုန်းသေချာ
ရာဇဝင်ကြေလဲ မသဲမကွဲ ရှိမြဲရှိမှာ
သဲသဲကွဲကွဲ ရှိမြဲရှိမှာ
ယူနီယံအဆောက်အဦးဟောင်းတနေရာ
ယူနီယံအဆောက်အဦးဟောင်း အေဒီတနေရာ

"Like the sun and the moon,
Strong and powerful I am;
To such a king as I, they pose a challenge",
Thus aroused with anger
He destroyed the Students Union Building
Under the gunfire
Students fell dead piles after piles
History may come to an end
But there will exist in haze or in daze
The ruin of the Students Union Building
Right there, the Students Union Building in ruin.

killing of the students was the key factor that made our generation anti-military junta. I believe Ako Khin Myunt, now His Excellency Prime Minister General Khin Nyunt[1] was still at Rangoon University when the killing took place. I do not believe that he has forgotten it.

3. In 1966-67, I was a nationalist guerrilla holding a high rank as a Central Committee Member of Arakan National United Organization (ANUO) led by Bogri Kra Hla Aung, a WWII veteran with a Myanmâ Gonyi Class III decoration by the Rangoon Government. It was a very sad event. I stood against my own eldest brother, Shwe Kyaw who at that time was a *Bogyi* in Burma Navy, an equivalent commissioned officer position of a Lieutenant in the British Naval ranking system. My friends Nee Lay Maung (Army), Ako Tha Tun Aung (Navy) etc. are newly commissioned officers in Burma Armed Forces and I counted myself in a guerrilla force against them! I still cannot overcome the sadness of *'brother-against-brother'* and *'friend-against-friend'* as the causes of the hostile conflict still exists.

At that time entire ANUO leadership including Bogri Kra Hla Aung and I were sentenced to death in absentia by the local Kyauktaw Township BCP(Arakan) with the charges that we were the capitalist American stooges. *The* Cultural Revolution was already in Burma. They came and attacked our political head quarter where I was stationed. We were about 12 men with 5 rifles of WWII origin. They were well equipped with motors, automatic rifles, and Bren Guns. We retreated deep into a mountainous area crossing a series of high mountain ridges for 3 days. They chased us. Getting the news Rangoon forces marched into the areas looking for both parties. It was good for us. BCP fled and Rangoon forces followed their trail. After 4 days of hiding in a very deep mountain valley and surviving on wild banana plants we could come out safely. It was sometime in February 1967. Man! I hate these White Flag commies.

4. A month earlier I met Arakan Communist Party Chairman Red Comrade Kyaw Zan Rhwee who was famous for his fight for the establishment of People's Republic of Rakhaing-pray (Arakan). I would say he was a nice guy. We reached a kind of alliance agreement with him and his party. ACP split off from Thakin Soe's Red Flag CPB. Red Comrade Kyaw Zan Rhwee was also a WWII veteran. At the age of 16 he joined the Rakhaing Patriotic Forces that fought alongside the Allied Forces in 1944 to drive out the Japanese from Arakan. By December 1944

Notes.
1. General Khin Nyunt was arrested and detained by the junta with the charges of corruption and creating discord within ranks and files, on 19th October 2004. He was sentenced to forty four years of suspended jail terms in 2005.

Arakan was free of the Japanese. Bogyoke Aung San joined the fun only on the 27th of May 1945. Some academicians and journalists classify the Red Flag Burmese Communist Party as the *Trotskyites*. In my experience, they are the Marxist-Leninist-Stalinists. They celebrate the birthdays of Karl Marx, V.I. Linen, and J. Stalin and denounced Trotsky as a traitor. When our Arakan National United Organization delegation led by President Bo Gri Kra Hla Aung reached the ACP headquarter they just finished celebrating 87th birthday of Stalin in 1966. The communist town was still decorated with big posters of Stalin and his philosophy. I got opportunity to go through their primary school text book and to my amusement I found that at one page it reads, "Trotsky is a traitor; U Seinda is a traitor; Kra Hla Aung is a traitor." I showed this to my President Kra Hla Aung and he, without any emotion or sentiment, simply told me, "I have read that many times; these Red Flags will never change."

5. My friend Red Comrade U Oo Khin Maung whom I mentioned in page 189 is a democratic communist in the sense that he now believes the proletarian dictatorship is obsolete. He believes that a communist welfare state can be established within the frame work of multi-party democratic system. Am I still right calling him a communist?

Even today, I do not believe that communism has disappeared from Myanmar. General Ne Win's Burmese Way to Socialist Programme Party was manned by the ex-communists. Many communists are still there. General Tin U who presently is a Vice-President of the NLD is a disciple of Brig. General Kyaw Zaw, a hard core BCP member. General Kyaw Zaw is one of the Thirty Comrades. Just when I am finishing this part of writing I get a copy of an email from an unexpected source. To my great surprise it contains a message from Comrade Uncle Kyaw Mra who is a politburo member of the Burma Communist Party (BCP). Also known as Thakin Kyaw Mra, he is contemporary with Bogyoke Aung San, Thakin Than Tun and U Nu and together studied at Rangoon University. As the only Rakhaing national politburo in the BCP he is very well known in Burma. I came to know his name since I was 13 years old. He managed to survive the BCP cultural revolution (1967-78) when many of the newly recruited university students of my generation got killed in the internal party purge of the *reactionaries*. We learned that he was also in the list of *the reactionaries*. He was in charge of the BCP (Arakan Division) and stationed in western Burma. The BCP Chairman, Thakin Than Tun, summoned him to his headquarter in Pegu Yoma where the party tribunals were held and executions were done. We at Rangoon learned that he came from Arakan, crossed Irrawady River and proceeded to China directly without going to the Pegu Yoma BCP headquarter where Thakin Than Tun was waiting for him. We believed that he was tipped off *the reactionaries* list and got a chance to escape to China. It was in 1968 that I learned about his escape to China. The Military Intelligence Service (MIS) had published the full account of BCP cultural revolution and assassination of Thakin Than Tun by one of his bodyguards in the book *The Last Days of Thakin Than Tun*. In 1977, at Rangoon I learned from a friend that he was keeping well at Beijing. The Rakhaing people, including myself, have great respect for him though we do not like the BCP. I have never heard of, seen or read a letter of his own in my life; this was the first time. He must be 87 years or older now. It surely is an extraordinary move for the BCP to let him write such a letter to the Rakhaing National Conference that, I learned, was held in India in the first week of March 2004. I interpret his communication as the BCP's attempt to make a comeback. This wooing of the Rakhaing nationals by the BCP renders credibility to the claim of the military junta and its excuse to hold on to power. Interestingly, the letter does not mention anything of communist ideology. Although leftist in pre-WWII Burmese literacy style it rather sounds like the BCP is advocating

The following is the brief excerpt of Comrade Kyaw Mra's letter that is 4-page in Burmese. The letter is dated the 20th December, 2003, indicating that he knew quite in advance and wrote it in good time so that it would reach India from Beijing on time for the Rakhaing National Conference held in the first week of March 2004. English version is my translation.

ရခိုင်ပြည်နယ်ရှိ တကွဲတပြားစီဖြစ်နေသော ပြည်ချစ်ဝါဒီရဲဘော်များသို့
ရခိုင်ရဲဘော်ဟောင်းတစ်ဦးထံမှ ပန်ကြားလွှာ

ခင်မင်လေးစားအပ်သော ရဲဘော်တို့-

၁၊ ယနေ့ ရခိုင်ပြည်နယ်ရှိ လူမျိုးပေါင်းစုံ၊ ပြည်သူလူထုတရပ်လုံးမှာ စစ်အာဏာရှင် အစိုးရ. ဖက်ဆစ်ဆန်စွာ ဖိနှိပ်ညှဉ်း ပန်းမှုကို မခံမရပ်နိုင်ဖြစ်ကြသဖြင့် ရဲဘော်တို့အနေနှင့် ကိုယ်ကျိုးစီးပွားဟူသမျှကို စွန့်လွှတ်ကာ ပြည်သူ လူထုဘဝ လွတ်မြောက်ရေး အတွက် ပြည်သူလူထုနှင့်အတူ လက်တွဲကာ တိုက်ပွဲဝင်ရန် တော်လှန်ရေး နယ်ပယ် သို့ ခြေစုံပစ်ဝင်ရောက် လာဘကသည်ကို လှိုက်လှဲစွာ ခိုးကျူးဂုဏ်ပြုကြိုဆိုအပ်ပါသည်။

ရဲဘော်တို့ အားလုံး တခုတည်းသောရည်မှန်းချက်ပန်းတိုင်မှာ ပြည်သူများကိုညှဉ်းပန်းနှိပ်စက်နေသော စစ်အာဏာရှင် အစိုးရကို ဖယ်ရှားပြီး ဒီမိုကရေစီအစိုးရတရပ်ကို ထူထောင်ရေးဖြစ်သည်ဟု ယုံကြည်ပါသည်။

....

ရဲဘော်တို့. သဘောထားအမြင်။ ဝေဖန်ချက်များကို စောင့်မျှော်လျက်ရှိပါသည်။

အဖိနှိပ်ခံပြည်သူတို့. ဘဝလွတ်မြောက်ရေးတိုက်ပွဲ မုချအောင်ရမည်။
ပြည်သူကို နှိပ်စက်ညှဉ်းပန်းနေသော စစ်အစိုးရ မုချကျဆုံးရမည်။

ခင်မင်လေးစားစွာဖြင့်
ရဲဘော်ကျော်မြ
၂၀-၁၂-၂၀၀၃

A Communication from a Rakhaing Veteran
to the Divided Nationalist Comrades of the Rakhaing State

Dear Respected Comrades,

1. Today, all national races and people of the Rakhine State cannot stand the oppression of the fascist military dictatorial government. With this view, you abandon every bit of your personal interest, and resolutely enter the revolutionary arena to fight hand in hand with the peoples for the liberation of the peoples. I delightfully welcome and honor you all.

I believe that your united goal is to remove the oppressive military dictatorship and establish a democratic government.

....

I would be looking forward to receiving your opinions and comments.

Oppressed peoples' struggle for liberation must win.
Oppressive military junta must fall.

Sincerely,
Comrade Kyaw Mra
December 20, 2003.

for a democratic government. He did not sign in his capacity of a BCP Politburo, but simply appended as Comrade Kyaw Mra. On the previous page I presented a brief excerpt of U Kyaw Mra's letter. The letter became very suggestive when the Rakhaing people formed an Arakan National Council with U Thein Phay and U Maung Maung as its Chairperson and General Secretary respectively, in 2004. U Thein Phay is a former member of the Red Flag Arakan Communist Party whereas U Maung Maung is a BCP member. The ANC was established in a Rakhaing National Conference that was convened with a fund made available by the European Union through its program called "Ethnic Initiative" for democracy in Burma. A statement from ANC can be read at http://www.mizzima.com/Solidarity/07-mar04-06.htm, as of November 26, 2004.

As long as the Myanmarese communists are breathing and the China remains *Red* and apparently a nice next door neighbor the Myanmar Armed Forces will ever remain in power with a sound excuse of the communist danger. Such propaganda of the military junta as presented below will always serve as a strong pillar of the ultranationalistic Myanmarism.

Please visit http://www.myanmar-information.net/bcp/bcp.htm for more information.

Burma Communist Party's
Conspiracy to take over State Power

Reference: State Law and Order Restoration Council Secretary (1) Brig-Gen Khin Nyunt's Statement, Special Press Conference held on 5th August 1989.

State Law and Order Restoration Council Secretary (1) Brig-Gen Khin Nyunt held a special press conference with the local and foreign journalists at the Guest House No. 2 of the Ministry of Defence at 9 am on 5th August 1989.

I would like to conclude this section with a tale of a Burmese Communist Monk. In Burma there were many Buddhist monks who became communists and vice versa. There are many jokes and tales about them. Here is the one I like most.

A Tale of Burmese Communist Monk

There were two true friends, Kyaw Min and Htoo Shwe. When they passed the Intermediate (which is US equivalent of a General Education Certificate) Kyaw Min told Htoo Shwe.

Kyaw Min, "Htoo Shwe, this is between you and I; don't tell anyone. I am going underground to join the BCP and live a proletarian revolutionary life. I do not want to become an intellectual petty bourgeoisie and serve the capitalist. What do you say for yourself?"

Htoo Shwe, " I want to be an engineer and serve the people in the way I can."

Kyaw Min, "Well, then, Htoo Shwe. When proletarian dictatorship is established in our land I will reeducate and make a good worker out of you. Farewell!"

After some twenty years U Htoo Shwe, a distinguished District Engineer, at southern

Burma, came to learn that a well-famed new acetic monk named U Tehzawwuntha of Sagaing Valley was none other than his friend Kyaw Min. He took a leave of absence from work, bought essential commodities that an acetic monk would need and traveled with his wife and three children more than 700 miles to Sagaing Valley at the north, which had accommodated many famous ascetics in the long history of Burma. At last the two friends met each other again.

U Htoo Shwe gave due respect to the Friend Monk, presented the charitable commodities, introduced his family to him, and the two friends entered into a long nostalgic conversation. At the end U Htoo Shwe asked his friend monk.

U Htoo Shwe, "Well then, Sir Monk, please tell me this. After all these years of proletarian revolution you came back with no skill to earn a honest living. Is that why you adorn yellow robe, become a monk, beg for food and live a life of parasite in the society?"

Friend Monk, "You are a communist! Aren't you?".

The tale ends here, but I may need to explain a bit more so that you can feel the punch. Since the beginning of communism the Burmese communists attack the monks calling them parasites and promise that monks would have to live a regulated life under the proletarian dictatorship when they come to power. I believe this anti-Buddhism is the main cause of the fall of Burmese communists and their party. As the vanguard of Buddhism the Burmese military will always remain in power.

5.3. Islamic Expansionism. The danger of Islamic Expansionism is considered real and present in contrast to the East-West Confrontation and the communist danger. The East-West Confrontation is a classic phenomenon and the Myanmarese, like any other South and Southeastern Asian people, do not believe that the West will again make any military adventure in their region. They believe that the presence of three Asian nuclear powers, namely China, India and Pakistan, has effectively deterred possibility of a Western military adventure in their region.   To their great satisfaction these three countries, which have fought a series of war in the past 50 years have now made peace. India made strong friendship with China with a series of border treaties and cooperation agreement in 2003. Recently, she just declared that there would be no more war with Pakistan, after the historic Cricket Policy in April 2004.   Similarly, the Myanmarese understands that the Burmese communists are nothing but paper tigers being soaked in the tropical rain. Their final destruction will come very soon since the USSR is gone quite a while ago and Red China is gradually becoming pinkish white. The Myanmarese knows very well that the danger of Burmese Communist Party is greatly exaggerated by the military junta for its survival. I have met a number of ex-communists who have become Buddhist monks, trying to erase their past sins with Anarpanar Meditation. The 'commies' are not a threat anymore. On the other hand, every Myanmarese I have met in past twenty years, regardless of their political affiliation, profession, ethnic origin, education, location, or country of residence, believes that Islamic Expansionism is a real and present danger.

I determine the following determinants contribute in making Islamic Expansionism a real and present danger in Burma AKA Myanmar.

Determinant 1: Historical Muslim-Buddhist War.

Determinant 2: Global revival of Pan-Islam.

Determinant 3: Bangladesh's Pan-Islamic renaissance and rapid Muslim population growth.

Determinant-4; Muslim's traditions in the Myanmarese Rakhine State (Arakan).

In the Chapters 2 and 3 of this book I have given a good account of the determinants 1, 2, and 3. I shall now present the determinant 4: 'Muslim's Claim of Myanmarese Rakhine State'.

Muslim's traditions in the Myanmarese Rakhine State (Arakan). Existence of strong Muslim's traditions in the Myanmarese Rakhine State (Arakan) complicated politico-religious issue. Lost in the complexities of the modernity it demands understanding of the past history of the Rakhine State as well as contemporary Burma.

Past History of the Myanmarese Rakhine State. The word 'Rakhine' is the Burmanized version of Rakhaing, which derives from Rakkhapura. As I mentioned earlier the Rakhine State was the main land of ancient kingdom of Rakkhapura. I would refer the reader to the classic book of Sir Arthur P. Phyare's *A History of Burma* (London: Trübner & Co., 1883).   The relevant part of her historical will be given here with a critical outlook, in chronological order.

Ancient Rakkhapura. The ancient kingdom of Rakkhapura probably originated as an defense outpost of Brahmaputra civilization some 5,000 years ago. Through thick and thin she survived as a small *Rajadom,* as the southern most kingdom of the India Subcontinent. In 1403 CE the Myanmarese invaded, occupied and committed genocide. Her king,   Mun Saw Mwan, took refuge in then independent Bengal under the kind accommodation of Sultan Ghiasuddin Azam Shah in 1403 AD. As a matter of fact he was not alone. Entire royal clan and their followers took refuge there. The King's original name was Nareikmeithla. According to the oral traditions I learned from my parents, local historians, and history books he served the Bengal Sultan well with loyalty and sincerity. Serving as a minister as well as a general he successfully defeated an enemy of the Sultan and stabilized the administrative institution of Bengal Sultanate. He spoke Persian, Hindi, and Bengali on the top of his mother tongue Rakhaing. A Muslim tradition claimed that Saw Mwan is the corruption of Solomon. I was told by a knowledgeable Arakanese Muslim that due to his wisdom and knowledge the court of Gaur Sultan honored him with the biblical name Solomon. The word "Mun" is the Rakhaing word for king. Therefore, the Rakhaing version Mun Saw Mwan stands for King Solomon in the Muslim tradition. After years of exile he regained his throne with the aid of Sultan Jalaluddin Muhammad Shah, a Muslim-convert Hindu king, in 1430 AD. The first Muslim general Wali Khan betrayed Mun Saw Mwan and seized the throne for himself. Sultan Jalaluddin Muhammad Shah gave a new Muslim army under the command of General Sidikh Khan to the Rakhaing king to restore his throne. General Sidikh Khan remained loyal to Mun Saw Mwan and served him for the rest of his life. The Rakhaing King also honored him well as a minister and general and built Sidikh Khan Mosque in his capital Mrauk U in the same year. This was the first Mosque built in all of Burma. It was destroyed during Myanmar occupation of Arakan in 1784 . Mrauk U palace was manned mostly by the Muslim officials and Persian became royal international language. Accordingly Rakkha-pura entered into the world with her Persian name Arakan in 1430. The Muslim tradition says that it is Al-Rakhon in Arabic and later it evolves into Arakan.(Note: The Rohingya Muslims of present Myanmarese Rakhine State are believed to be the descendants of Al-Rakhong. Their popular name Rohingya is the Burmanized version of Ro{k}hongya, with k-sound silent. The people of Dhaka are also called *Dhakaya* in the Chittagonian dialect). Later the British adopted the Persian name Arakan in their literature.

It is believed that Mun Saw Mwan entered into a tributary relationship with the Bengal sultan, as a debt of gratitude. The Arakan kings also minted coins bearing Kalima in Persian and their names in Rakhaing language. In his article published in the journal of Asiatic Society Bangladesh (Hum.), Vol. XXXI (I), June 1986, Alamgir M. Serajuddin, a professor of history, mentioned that nine Rakhaing kings took the Muslim titles as mentioned below.

1. Mun Khari is Ali Khan (1434-1459 CE).
2. Basawphru is Kalima Shah (1459-1482 CE).
3. Gadzabadi is Ilyas Shah Sultan (1523-1525 CE).
4. Tha Tsa Ta is Ali Shah (1525-1531 CE).
5. Mun Ba Gri (Mun Bun) is Zabuk Shah (1531-1553 CE).
6. Mun Phalaung is Sikander Shah (1571-1593 CE).
7. Mun Raza Gri is Salim Shah (1593-1612 CE)[1].
8. Mun Kha Moung is Hossain Shah (1612-1622 CE)[2].
9. Thiri Thu Dhamma Raza is also Salim Shah (1622-1638 CE) , same title as Mun Raza Gri.

In the light of the above historical fact, *some* Muslims assert that Arakan was a Muslim Kingdom and the Myanmarese Buddhists occupied it in 1784. Therefore it is the duty of the

Notes.
1. Mun Raza Gri conquered Myanmarese Pegu in 1599, and hence known as the Conqueror of Pegu.
2. Mun Kha Moung seized and ruled Dhaka in 1615.

Muslim world to liberate Arakan from the hands of infidels. *This view is seen as the Islamic Expansionism.*

The Islamic Arakan is summed up by a Mohamed Ashraf Alam in his article 'The Rohang (Arakan)', as posted at http://rohingya.com/rohang.htm, as of March 11, 2003 and at http://www.rohingyatimes.i-p.com/history/history_maa.html as of April 04, 2004 highlights the Muslim's version of Arakan. It is a very interesting Arakanese Muslims version of history. Mr. Alam has a master degree in history from Rangoon Arts and Science University. It is a full-length 16-page article with 93 references. The reader is urged to visit the website mentioned above for the full text, including the references. Some excerpts of the article are given below.

Some excerpts from the article of Mohammed Ashraf Alam at http://www.rohingyatimes.i-p.com/history/history_maa.html as of April 04, 2004.

A Short Historical Background of Arakan

Mohammed Ashraf Alam

Introduction

ARAKAN, once a sovereign and independent State, is now one of the states of the Union of Burma. The Arakan State comprises a strip of land along the eastern coast of the Bay of Bengal from the Naf River to Cape Negaris and stretches north and south touching Bangladesh on the Northwest. The river Naf separates it from Chittagong region of Bangladesh. It is cut off from Burma by a range of near impassable mountains known as Arakan Yomas running north to south, which was an obstacle against permanent Muslim conquest. The northern part of Arakan, today called the "North Arakan," was point of contact with East Bengal. These geographical facts explain the separate historical development of that area – both generally and in terms of its Muslim population until the Burmese king Bodaw Paya conquered it on 28th December 1784 AD. Under different periods of history Arakan had been an independent sovereign monarchy ruled by Hindus, Buddhists and Muslims.

....

Mohammed Hanifa and Queen Kaiyapuri

The Arab Muslim traders had good contacts with Arakan (Rahambori Island), Burma, Indochina, Indonesia, Malay etc. with their trade and they propagated the religion of Islam in those countries. The arrival of Mohammed Hanif son of Hazarat Ali (R.A) to Arakan is also narrated in a book written in 16th century by Shah Barid Khan named Hanifa O Kaiyapuri.

"In 680 AD after the war of 'Karbala' Mohammed Hanofiya with his army arrived at Arab-Shah Para, near Maungdaw in the Northern Arakan, while Kaiyapuri, the queen of Cannibals ruled this hilly deep forest attacking and looting the people of Arakan. Mohammed Hanif attacked the Cannibals and captured the queen. She was converted to Islam and married to him. Her followers embraced Islam en masse. Mohammed Hanif and the queen Kaiyapuri lived in Mayu range. The peaks where they lived were still known as Hanifa Tonki and Kaiyapui Tonki. The wild cannibals were tamed and became civilised. Arakan was no more in danger of them and peace and tranquillity prevailed. The followers of Mohammed Hanif and Kaiyapuri were mixed up and lived peacefully." The descendants of these mixed people no doubt formed the original nucleus of the Rohingya Muslims in Arakan.

....

The Origin of Rohingya

Rohang, the old name of Arakan, was very familiar region for the Arab seafarers even during the pre-Islamic days. Tides of people like the Arabs, Moors, Turks, Pathans, Moghuls, Central Asians, Bengalees came mostly as traders, warriors, preachers and captives overland or through the sea route. Many settled in Arakan, and mixing with the local people, developed the present stock of people known as ethnic Rohingya. Hence, the Rohingya Muslims, whose settlements in Arakan date back to 7th century AD are not an ethnic group which developed from one tribal group affiliation or single racial stock. They are an ethnic group developed from different stocks of people. The ethnic Rohingya is Muslim by religion with distinct culture and civilisation of their own. They trace their ancestry to Arabs, Moors, Pathans, Moghuls, Central Asians, Bengalis and some Indo-Mongoloid people. Since Rohingyas are mixture of many kinds of people, their cheekbone is not so prominent and eyes are not so narrow like Rakhine Maghs and Burmans. Their noses are not flat and they are a bit taller in stature than the Rakhine Maghs but darker in complexion. They are some bronzing coloured and not yellowish. The Rohingyas of Arakan still carried the Arab names, faith, dress, music and customs. So, the Rohingyas are nationals as well as an indigenous ethnic group of Burma. They are not new born racial group of Arakan rather they are as old an indigenous race of the country as any others.

....

The emergence of Mrauk-U Empire

This independent kingdom turned westward, toward Bengal, as a result of the growing power of the Burmese court of Ava. In 1404 AD, the king of Arakan, Narameikhla (1404-1434 AD), was forced to flee to Gaur, capital of Bengal Sultanate, which 86 years earlier had already become independent of the Mogul Emperor in Delhi. Ahmed Shah, Sultan of Gaur, welcomed the refugee king. Narameikhla remained at the court of Gaur, where he served as an officer in Ahmad Shah's army and fought in his wars. After the victory of the war, king Ahmed Shah handed over the throne of Gaur to his son Nazir Shah (according to Bengal History it was not Nazir Shah but Sultan Jalaluddin Mohammed Shah) in the year 1426 AD. Then Naramaikhla pleaded help from the king to regain his lost throne at Launggyet in Arakan. According to Rakhine Razawin (Rakhine History), the Sultan of Bengal agreed to do so when Naramaikhla agreed to abide the following 6-point conditions. They are: -
1. To return the twelve towns of Bengal.
2. To receive Muslim title for the kings of Arakan from Bengal.
3. The court emblem must be inscribed with Kalima Tayuba in Persian.
4. The coins, medallions must be inscribed with Kalima Tayuba in Persian and to mint them in Bengal.
5. To use the Persian as court language of Arakan.
6. To pay taxes and presents annually.

....

The Arakanese Kings with Muslim names and titles

According to former Chairman of Historical Commission, Burma, Lt. Col. Ba Shin's "Coming of Islam to Burma 1700 AD", Min Sawmon as Solaiman Shah, the founder of Mrauk-U dynasty and his successor were greatly influenced by Islamic culture. The practice of adopting a Muslim name or title by the Arakanese kings continued for more than two hundred years (1430 – 1638). This titles which appeared in Arabic script / Persian Kufic on their coins is given below:

No.	Names of the Kings Muslim Names	Reigning period
1.	Narameikhla (a) Sawmon Solaiman Shah	1430-1434 AD.
2.	Meng Khari (a) Naranu Ali Khan	1434-1459
3.	Ba Saw Pru Kalima Shah	1459-1482
4.	Dawlya Mathu Shah	1482-1492
5.	Ba Saw Nyo Mohammed Shah	1492-1493
6.	Ran Aung Noori Shah	1493-1494
7.	Salimgathu Sheik Abdullh Shah	1494-1501
8.	Meng Raza Ilias Shah - I	1501-1513
9.	Kasabadi Ilias Shah - II	1513-1515
10.	Meng Saw Oo Jalal Shah	1515
11.	Thatasa Ali Shah	1515-1521
12.	Min Khaung Raza El-Shah Azad	1521-1531
13.	Min Bin (a) Min Pa Gri Zabuk Shah	1531-1553
14.	Min Dikha Daud Khan	1553-1555
15.	Min Phalaung Sikender Shah	1571-1591
16.	Min Razagri Salim Shah - I	1593-1612
17.	Min Khamaung Hussain Shah	1612-1622
18.	Thiri Thudama Salim Shah - II	1622-1637

End of the excerpt.

Major Points of the Muslim's Traditions. Here, I will highlight major points of the Muslim's traditions, which are construed as the assertion of Islamic Expansionism. It is important to focus on Harazat Ali, his son Mohammed Hanifa, and the Battle of Karbala. I shall present the focal points one after another in the given order. Numerous books and web sites can be found on the topic of Hazarat Ali, but the information on his son Muhammad Hanif is scattered. Nevertheless, I am confident that I can present the reader with a logical account. In addition to the Internet sources the following books are consulted. (1) *The History of al-Tabari*, Vol. XVI, The Community Divided: The Caliphate of Ali I, translated and annotated by Adrian Brockett, State University of New York Press, 1997. (2) *The succession to Muhammad*, A study of the early Caliphate, Wilfred Madelung, Cambridge University Press, 1997. (3) *The Shi'ite Religion*, a history of Islam in Persia and Irak, Dwight M. Donaldson, Luzac & Company,

Ali is The Lion of Allah (Asadullah).

"Ali Ibn Abu Talib, radiya' llah Ta'aala anhu wa-Karrama wajhahu." (Ali Ibn Abi Talib, may God Almighty be pleased with him and honor him.) The script is **Tawqi'** (an art of cursive Arabic Calligraphy), structured into the shape of a lion. (Source:http://www.amaana.org/contents/contents.htm).

London, 1933. (4) *An Advanced History of Islam*, Mohammad Arshad, Ideal Publications, Dacca, 1967. (5) *History of Arakan (Burma)*, Moulvi Nur Ahmad, Department of Dawah, World Muslim Congress, Karachi, 1978.

1. Hazarat Ali (599 CE-661 CE). The key is Hazarat Ali, who is formally known as Ali ibn AbuTalib. He is the most loved and respected person by the Muslims, only second to the Prophet himself. Prophet Muhammad affectionately called him the 'Father of Dust' (Abu Turab) and later, after a series of Jihad, honored him as the 'Lion of Allah' (Asadullah). The saying "No one fights like Ali" has been a household word in the realm of Islam since the days of Prophet Muhammad. In the bottom of his Islamic warrior's heart he was a human being. Please read some of his words in the next page. In the Shiite world he is the *First* Caliph, 'Commander of the Faithful', and Imam. They regard the First, the Second, and the Third Caliphs (Abu Bakr, Umar, and Uthman, respectively, as the usurpers. In the entire Muslim world he is the Fourth Caliph and the Fourth Commander of the Faithful. (Note: "The word 'Caliph' is the English form of the Arabic word 'Khalifa,' which is short for **Khalifatu Rasulil-lah**. The latter expression means **Successor to the Messenger of God**, the Holy Prophet Muhammad (peace be on him). The title 'Khalifatu Rasulil-lah' was first used for Abu Bakr, who was elected head of the Muslim community after the death of the Prophet". This quotation is from http://www.darulfalah.org/article/caliphs.shtml). In modern political terms, Caliph is a all-in-all king who holds executive, legislative, and judicial powers. The Shiites believe that the Muslim World (Islamic Ummar) must be led by a Spiritual Leader or Imam. Prophet Muhammad was the spiritual leader, but not a king, and the Q'uran is the legislative laws or constitution given by God (Allah). Accordingly, they rebelled against the Caliphate or system of the all-in-all kingship, and invested the power of Imam on Hazarat Ali. He is also considered the great Imam of Tasawwuf (Spiritual Science or Mysticism). Many Muslims honor him as *Ali, The Magnificent*. I view him as a good example of Plato's 'philosopher king'. In the coming few pages I present some of his values to give the readers a glimpse of his greatness in Islam and Muslim World. A son of his landing in Arakan is of great significance in Pan-Islam.

The Commander of the Faithful Hazarat Ali was born inside the Holy Kaaba in Mecca on Friday the 13th Rajab, 30 Amulfeel or year of the Elephant (i.e. 24 BH) 11th October 599 CE. to the Abu Talib and his wife Bibi Fatima Binte Asad (source: http://www.amaana.org/ali/hazratali.htm). As of March 2004, the author at http://www.sunnah.org/publication/khulafa_rashideen/caliph4.htm mentioned his genealogy as "Ali ibn Abu Talib `Abd Manaf ibn `Abd al-Muttalib ibn Hashim ibn `Abd Manaf, Abu al-Hasan al-Qurashi al-Hashimi". He is popularly known as Hazrat Imam Ali Ibn e Abu Talib among the Shiite. Hazrat is a title that can be interpreted as 'His or Her Holiness'. Among Sunni Muslims he is famous, honored and respected as Ali ibn Abu Talib, the Fourth Caliph of the Muslims. His father Abu Talib and Prophet's father Abdullah were brothers, sons of Abdul Muttalib from the same mother. Prophet also married him to his youngest daughter Fatima az-Zahra (Fatima Zahra). Accordingly, Hazarat Ali is popular and famous as the cousin and son-in-law of the Prophet. Shiite Muslims recognize only Hazarat Ali and his descendants as the Caliph and Commander of the Faithful.

Some Words of Hazarat Ali

1. The ignorant man does not understand the learned for he has never been learned himself. The learned man understands the ignorant for he was once ignorant himself.
2. Knowledge gives life to the soul.
3. To teach is to learn.
4. Honesty is Divine language.
5. To fulfill promises is the highest form of integrity.
6. Friendship is impossible with a liar.
7. Lying spoils news.
8. Enmity is the occupation of fools.
9. To fight against one's own desires is highest wisdom.
10. The wise aim at perfection.
11. The foolish aim at wealth.
12. To separate oneself from things of time and to connect oneself with things of eternity is highest wisdom.
13. He is really wise whose actions reflect his words.
14. Humility is the product of knowledge.
15. Pride mars greatness.
16. Humility is one of the nets spread by real greatness.
17. Boasting issues from small minds.
The above sayings of Imam Ali (A.S) are taken from *Du'a-e Kumail*, trans. N. Hussein Mardi, Chehel Sotoon Theological School: Iran, 1989. (Source: http://www.al-islam.org/masoom/sayings/sayings.html).

18. Like your body your mind also gets tired so refresh it by wise sayings. (Source: http://www.mubai.cc/sayings.htm).

19. "...do not begin a battle even if the enemy so desires unless you have explored every avenue of amity and good-will and have exhausted all the chances of a peaceful settlement". (This is part of his instruction to Ma'qil bin Qays Riyahi when he sent him with an army of 3000 soldiers to Syria; source: http://www.al-islam.org/nahjul/letters/letter12.htm#letter12).

20. "After invoking Allah and praising the Holy Prophet (s) be it known to you that villagers and farmers of the provinces under you, complain of your harshness, arrogance and cruelty. They complain that you consider them mean, humble and insignificant and treat them scornfully. I deliberated over their complaint and found that if, on account of their paganism they do not deserve any favourable treatment of extra privileges, they do not deserve to be treated cruelly and harshly either. They are governed by us, they have made certain agreements with us and we are obliged to respect and honour the terms of those agreements." (First part of his letter to one of his governors; source: http://www.al-islam.org/nahjul/letters/letter19.htm#letter19).

Some examples of Hazarat Ali's nobleness

Live like 'Ali

Excerpts from Nahzul Balaga

(Source: Editorial, The Bohra Chronicle March 1988, http://www.dawoodi-bohras.com/chronicle/mar98/index.htm)

In the battle of "Siffeen" Moavia reached the river Euphrates (Furaat) before the army of Hazarat 'Ali and took position at the river. When 'Ali's army reached there he was informed that they would not be allowed a drop of water from the river. Hazarat Ali sent a messenger to Moavia saying that his action is against the canon of humanity and tenets of Islam. Moavia's reply was that "a war is a war therein one cannot accept the principles of humanity and doctrines of Islam. My sole aim is to kill 'Ali and to demoralise his army and this stoppage of water will bring these results easily and quickly." Hazarat 'Ali ordered Imam Hussain to attack and gain access to the river. In the attack that followed, Imam Hussain recaptured the river. It was now Moavia's turn to beseech permission to get water from the river. His messenger arrived and 'Ali told him to take as much water they liked and as often as they required.

When 'Ali's officers told him that those were the very people who refused water to them, should they be allowed have a free run of the river? Hazarat 'Ali replied, "They are human beings and, though they have acted inhumanly, I cannot follow their example and refuse a man food and drink because he happens to be my worst enemy."

Once, one of Imam Ali's favourite and trusted companions, Usman ibn Hunayf, told him that by introduction of the principle of Equal Distribution of wealth and bringing important persons down to the level of commoners, and by raising the status of Negroes, and Persians to that of Arabs, by allotting shares to slaves equal to their masters, by depriving the rich persons of their land-holdings and by stopping special grants apportioned to them according to their status, he had done more harm to himself and his cause, than good. Continuing he said, "Look Sir! These are the reasons why the influential and rich Arabs are deserting you and are gathering around Muawiyah. Of what use these poor persons, disabled people, aged widows and Negro slaves are to you? How can they help and serve you?"

He replied, "I cannot allow rich and influential persons to exploit the people of this Islamic State and to run an inequitable and unjust system of distribution of wealth and opportunities. I cannot for a moment tolerate this. This is Public wealth, it comes from the masses it must go back to them. The rich and powerful persons have not created any wealth, they have merely sucked it out from the masses and after paying the taxes, etc. what is left to them is many times more than what they pay to the State and they are allowed to retain it. Had all this been private property, I would have gladly distributed it in the same manner. So far as their desertion is concerned, I am glad they have deserted me. So far as the usefulness or services of these disabled persons and have-nots is concerned, remember that I am not helping them to secure their services, I know thoroughly well that they are unable to serve me. I help them because they cannot help themselves and they are as much human beings as you and I. May Allah help me to do my duty as He wishes me to do." (Source: http://www.geocities.com/Tokyo/Spa/7220/iman-ali.html#a17).

It appears that the principles of the Geneva Conventions were first laid down by Hazarat Ali some 1300 years ago!

Imam Ali (a) did not tolerate mere mercenaries but did not let the services of volunteers go unpaid. He hated murder and bloodshed and desired his soldiers to be soldiers in the service of Allah and religion. His strict orders to the army were,

"Always keep fear of Allah in your mind, remember that you cannot afford to do without His Grace. Remember that Islam is a mission of peace and love. Keep the Holy Prophet (s) before you as a model of bravery, valour and piety. Do not kill anybody unless in self-defence. Take care of your mounts and your arms, they are your best guards. Work hard while you are at it and then devote some time to rest and relaxation. Rest and relaxation are as much necessary for you as hard work. Do not let one overstep the time limit of the other.

Do not pursue those who run away from an encounter, and do not kill fleeing persons.
Do not kill those who beg for life, and mercy.
Do not kill civilians.
Do not outrage the modesty of women.
Do not harm old people and children.
Do not accept any gifts from the civil population of any place.
Do not billet your soldiers or officers in the houses of civilians.
Do not forget to say your daily prayers.

Fear Allah. Remember that death will inevitably come to everyone of you sometime or the other, even if you are thousands of miles away from a battlefield; therefore be always ready to face death."

(Source: http://www.geocities.com/Tokyo/Spa/7220/imam-ali.html#a17)

Ali did not kill defenceless enemy. Enemies are, "but human beings".

Talha-Ibne-Abi Taha was not only a bitter enemy of Islam, but was a personal enemy of the Holy Prophet (PBUH) and 'Ali (A.S.). His exertions to harm these two and their mission is a legion. He was the flag-bearer of Quresh in the battle of Ohad. 'Ali faced him and in a hand-to-hand encounter dealt him such a severe blow that he reeled and fell down. 'Ali left him there and walked away from him. Many Muslim warriors ran up to 'Ali and advised him to finish Talha, saying that he was 'Ali's worst enemy. 'Ali replied "enemy or no enemy he cannot defend himself now, and I cannot strike a man who is not in a position to defend himself. If he survives he is free to live as long as his life lasts."

In the battle of 'Jamal' in the thick of encounter 'Ali's slave Quamber brought some sweet syrup saying "my lord the sun is very hot and you have been constantly fighting, have a glass of this cold drink to refresh yourself." Ali looked around and replied, "Shall I refresh myself when hundreds of people around me are lying wounded and dying of thirst and wounds? Instead of bringing syrup for me take a few men with you and give each of them a cold drink." Quamber replied "My lord, they are all our enemies." 'Ali said "Maybe, but they are human beings. Go and attend to them."

The Bohra Chronicle, February 1998.

**The following Ali's saying shows
that he envisaged 'The United Nations' some 1300 years ago.**

"Mankind" said Ali, "with all its spiritual faults and vices would move to a crisis of the nations and could only survive by a corporate sense of responsibility. Individual responsibility would positively avouch solidarity." (Source: http://www.karbala-najaf.org/abuturab/social.html).

Ali stands out as the best law giver in the history as testified by his Famous Epistle To Malik Ashtar, Governor of Egypt in 658 CE (38 A.H.). "Hazarat Ali is credited with not less than 480 treaties, lectures and epistles on a variety of subjects dealing with philosophy, religion, law and politics, as collected by Zaid Ibn Wahab in the Imam's own life time", Rasheed Turabi, at http://www.amaana.org/ismaali.html.

"Remember, Maalik, that amongst your subjects there are two kinds of people: those who have the same religion as you have; they are brothers to you, and those who have religions other than that of yours, they are human beings like you. Men of either category suffer from the same weaknesses and disabilities that human beings are inclined to, they commit sins, indulge in vices either intentionally or foolishly and unintentionally without realizing the enormity of their deeds. Let your mercy and compassion come to their rescue and help in the same way and to the same extent that you expect Allah to show mercy and forgiveness to you."

(An excerpt from Hazrat Ali's Famous Epistle To Malik Ashtar, Governor of Egypt. Ali appointed him as the Governor of Egypt in place of Muhammad bin Abi Bakr. Source: http://www.al-islam.org/nahjul/letters/letter53.htm#letter53)

The above Arabic writing is somewhat differently translated by another author below, but carries the same essence of meaning.

"Remember that the citizens of the state are of two categories. They are either your brethren in religion or your brethren in kind. They are subject to infirmities and liable to commit mistakes. Some indeed do commit mistakes. But forgive them even as you would like God to forgive you."
....
Beware! Fear God when dealing with the problem of the poor who have none to patronize, who are forlorn, indigent and helpless and are greatly torn in mind - victims of the vicissitudes of Time......For God's sake, safeguard their rights; for on you rests the responsibility of protection. Assign for their uplift a portion of the state exchequer (Baitul-mal), wherever they may be, whether close at hand or far away from you.
....
Meet the oppressed and the lowly periodically in an open conference and, conscious of the divine presence there, have a heart-to-heart talk with them, and let none from your armed guard or civil officers or members of the police or the Intelligence Department be by your side, so that the representatives of the poor might state their grievances fearlessly and without reserve.
........"

(Source: Hazrat Ali's Famous Epistle To Malik Ashtar, Governor of Egypt, translated By Rasheed Turabi at http://amaana.org/ismaali.html).

May Allah take all of us to IMAM ALI (A.S) shrine for ziyarat (AMEEN).
A prayer at http://www.14masumeen.com/html/21ramazan

ZARI-E-HAZRAT IMAM ALI (A.S.)

Source: http://www.rafed.net/towns/english/najaf.html   Source: http://www.14masumeen.com/html/21ramazan

Hazrat Ali (A.S) was buried at Najaf, Iraq. Today his magnificent shrine still stands there and is filled with devotees. (Source: http://www.14masumeen.com/html/21ramazan and http://www.rafed.net/towns/english/najaf.html.)

It was the fortieth year of Hijra. A fanatical group called Kharijites, consisting of people who had broken away from 'Ali due to his compromise with Muawiya, claimed that neither 'Ali, the Caliph, nor Muawiya, the ruler of Syria, nor Amr bin al-Aas, the ruler of Egypt, were worthy of rule. In fact, they went so far as to say that the true caliphate came to an end with 'Umar and that Muslims should live without any ruler over them except Allah. They vowed to kill all three rulers, and assassins were dispatched in three directions. On the 20th of Ramadan, 40 A.H., while he was absorbed in prayers in a Mosque in Najaf a Kharijite named Ibn-e-Muljim killed him with a poisoned sword.
(Source: http://www.islamknowledge.faithweb.com/ali_ibn_abi_talib.htm)

The Internet sources as well as the books I consulted testifies that Hazarat Ali and Hazarat Fatima had five children namely Hassan, Hussain, Zainab, Umm-e-Kulsoom, and Mohsin (still birth). Another author at http://www.ismaili.net/Source/hist/full.txt wrote:-

"His first wife was Fatima, the only daughter of Muhammad, during whose lifetime, he did not marry any other lady. By Fatima, he had three sons, Hasan, Hussain and Mohsin, who died in infancy; and two daughters, Zainab and Umm Kulsum. By his wife, Ummul Banin bint Hizam, Ali had four sons, viz. Abbas, Jafar, Abdullah and Uthman. By Layla bint Masud, he had Ubaidullah and Abu Bakr. By Asma bint Umyas, he had Yahya and Muhammad Asghar. By Umm Habiba bint Rabia, he had one son, Umar and a daughter, Ruqaiya. By Amama bint Abil Aas, he had a son, named Muhammad al-Awasat. By Khawla bint Jafar bin Qais al-Hanafiya, he had Muhammad Akbar, who was known as Muhammad ibn Hanafiya. By Umm Sa'id bint Urwa bin Masud, he had Ummul Hasan and Ramla." (Source: http://www.ismaili.net/Source/hist/full.txt).

Muhammad Ibn al-Hanafiya (638-700 CE). As described above the person referred to as Mohammed Hanifa by Mohamed Ashraf Alam is none other than Muhammad Ibn al-Hanafiya, a celebrated and famous son of Hazarat Ali and his 5th wife Khawla bint Jafar bin Qais al-Hanafiya. He is widely known as Muhammad Ibn al-Hanafiya (also Muhammad ibn al-Hanafiyya); I will address him in this name. Still then, please keep in mind that different writers refer him in various synonyms such as Muhammad Ibn Ali, Muhammad Hanif, Muhammad Hanifiah, Muhammad Hanafia, Muhammad Hanafiya, and also as Muhammad Akbar. He is popularly known as the son of al-Hanafiya, in honor of his mother's tribe.

A great personality by his own deeds, he left behind a blazing trail in the history of Islam. I can list the following honors of his. According to a Muslim tradition the Prince of Believers, 'Ali, told his son Muhammad ibn al-Hanafiya: "Your courtesy, due to innate nobility, is more excellent than mere noble lineage" (source: http://www.sicm.org.uk/suduk/Suduk41.html). This clearly highlights the personality of Muhammad ibn al-Hanafiya. Let us study more about this noble person.

1. He was a great Islamic warrior (Mujahid). According to the Muslim chroniclers (eg. http://www.al-islam.org/kaaba14/6.htm) Hazarat Ali always put him at the front line and it was his duty to protect his elder brothers, Hasan and Hussain, who were born of Fatima, and thus the direct descendants of Prophet Muhammad. He is honored as the 'hero of the Battle of Naharwan'. A group of followers withdrew their allegiance to Ali and mutinied. These mutineers were known as the Kharijites or Kharijis. They encamped at Naharwan, which was a township situated on a canal of the same name, a few miles east of the Tigris near Madain and between Baghdad and Wasit. In 37/658, Ali marshaled his forces and led the final assault against the Kharijis in the memorable battle of Naharwan, which took place in Shaban, 38/January, 659. (Source: http://ismaili.net/histoire/history03/history343.html). The mutineers were defeated. Two years later, a Kharijite assassinated Caliph Ali.

2. He was a "Ahl-Ul-Hadith", who are "those who proceed upon the way of the Companions and those who followed them in righteousness, in clinging to the Book and the Sunnah,..... (i.e., the Qur'aan and the Sunnah) take precedence over any statement or code and conduct - whether in belief, or acts of worship such as dealings and transactions, mannerisms, politics or social life". Please read full definition by Shaikh Rabee' bin Haadee al-Madkhalee from Makaanat Ahl ul-Hadith, translation by Bilal Davies, in salafipublications, at http://www.allaahuakbar.net/scholars/al-madkhalee/so_who_are_ahl_hadith.htm. In the Islamic hierarchy there are three main authorities, firstly it is Prophet Muhammad himself, secondly His Companions, eg. Hazarat Ali, and thirdly the Ahl-Ul-Hadith. Shaikh Rabee described as follow:- "They after all of the **Companions** - and at the head of them the rightly guided Caliphs - are the leaders of the taabi'een and at the head of them: **Sa'eed ibn al-Musayyib** (d. 90H), **'Urwah ibn Zubair** (d. 94H), **'Alee ibn al-Hussain Zain al-'Aabideen** (d. 93H), **Muhammad ibn Hanafiya** (d. 80H), **'Ubaydullaah ibn 'Abdillaah ibn 'Utbah ibn Mas'ood** (d. 94H or later), **Saleem ibn 'Abdillaah ibn 'Umar** (d. 106H), **Qaasim ibn Muhammad ibn Abee Bakr as-Sadeeq** (d. 106H), **al-Hasan al-Basree** (d. 110H), **Muhammad ibn Sireen** (d. 110H), **'Umar ibn 'Abdul-'Azeez** (d. 101H) and **Muhammad ibn Shihaab az-Zuhree** (d. 125H)".

3. He was a source of Hadith, which are the sayings of Prophet Muhammad and His Companions. The following are some well known Hadith duly credited to him.

(1). Muhammad ibn Hanafia said from, 'Mustadrak', "We were in the presence of Imam Ali (a.s.). A person asked the Imam some question about the Mahdi. The Imam (a.s.) replied:

"Alas! and he repeated this seven times and then said: Mahdi will emerge at the end of time when those who would call out the name of Allah would be killed."

(2). Narrated Muhammad bin Al-Hanafiya: I asked my father ('Ali bin Abi Talib), "Who are the best people after Allah's Apostle ?" He said, "Abu Bakr." I asked, "Who then?" He said, "Then 'Umar. " I was afraid he would say "Uthman, so I said, "Then you?" He said, "I am only an ordinary person. (Volume 5, Book 57, Number 20: , http://www.masmn.org/Hadith/ Sahih_Bukhari/057.htm). (Note: Uthman is also referred as Osman by many authors; he was the Third Caliph, after Umar).

(3). Muhammad ibn al-Hanafiya (638-700 CE), a close relative of Prophet Muhammad, is quoted denigrating the notion that the prophet ever set foot on the Rock in Jerusalem; "these damned Syrians," by which he means the Umayyads, "pretend that God put His foot on the Rock in Jerusalem, though [only] one person ever put his foot on the rock, namely Abraham."[17].

{Sources: http://www.meforum.org/article/490 and http://www.tzemachdovid.org/Facts/ claim.shtml; ([17]Quoted in Joseph van Ess, "'Abd al-Malik and the Dome of the Rock," *Bayt al-Maqdis: `Abd al-Malik's Jerusalem*, ed. Julian Raby and Jeremy Johns (Oxford: Oxford University Press, 1992), vol.1, p.93.)}.

4. He was also a source of history. He was quoted nine times in the History of al-Tabari, Volume XVI, the Community Divided, translated by Adrain Brockett, State University of New York Press, 1997. The famous historian Abu Jafar Muhammad bin Jarir al-Tabari (839-923 CE) recorded the history in his famous book *The History of Prophets and Kings* (Ta'rikh al-rusul wa'lmuluk), which is the most extraordinary and authoritative exploration of the ancient Islamic World. A modern author Wilfred Madelung quoted Muhammad Ibn Hanafiyya fourteen times in his book *The succession to Muhammad*, Cambridge University Press, 1997, although all of his references are from al-Tabari.

5. He was the Imam of a sect of Shiite majority in later part of his life. The Shiite historians recorded as follow.

"The nucleus of his following, though, was not formed before 73/692, the year which marks the death of Ibn az-Zubayr and a complete collapse of the political aspirations of the peoples of the Hijaz and Iraq. The majority of the Shi`is, however, continued to recognize the Imamate of Ibn al-Hanafiya and later on his son Abu-Hashim `Abd Allah". (Source: http:// www.karbala-najaf.org/shiaism/235-258.htm).

Please note the date, 73 AH/692 CE, in the above citation. The significance of this time factor will be a major point of discussion in next pages. Islamic Era known as After Hijra or AH began in 622 CE when Prophet Muhammad and his followers migrated to Medina. Hijra in Arabic means migration or flight.

His Imamate is explained by another author as below.

"While the Tawwabun had known that the Prophet (pbh) had declared that his religious and political successor or Imams, would be his descendants through his daughter Fatima, most of the wavering common Arabs and the new converts were carried away by the talented eloquence of Mukhtar and his successful propaganda for Ibn al-Hanafiya as the *Mahdi* or Deliverer from the tyranny and injustice of the Ummayad. This, even without Ibn al-Hanafiya's own consent. They were not able to make the distinction between the son of Ali and the son of Ali and Fatima, thus the descendants of the Prophet.

Although he maintained his quiescent policy like his grandfather Ali ......, Imam Zayn al-'Abidin made known the truth to the people concerning his position as the rightful Imam and

Mukhtar's proclamation of Ibn al-Hanafiya as an usurpation of his rights.

The Imam's quiescent policy did not stop Caliph (Abdulla) Ibn Zubayr though, who was in power for nine years, from holding the Imam in Mecca under his supervision. Caliph Ibn Zubayr also imprisoned Ibn al-Hanafiya at *'Arim*. The period of Imam Zayn al-'Abidin saw growing interest in Medina in Prophetic traditions and the learned circles of lawyers and scholars held the Imam in high esteem". (Source: http://www.themuslimhistory.info/INenglish/ImamN-cal/Chap11.htm).

Caliph Abdulla Ibn Zubayr (61-73 AH or 678-692 CE) ruled from Mecca in parallel with the Umayyad Caliph at Syria. It was recorded that the Kaisánís horsemen freed Muhammad Ibn al-Hanafiya, whom they recognized as the rightful Imam.

It needs to present the history of succession after the death of Caliph Imam Ali (Hazarat Ali) in order to clarify the time frame of the event and the events referred in the above account. After his death the Caliphate and Imamate was handed down to his eldest son, Hasan. The rival Umayyad Caliph, Mu'āwiya, of Syria challenged his Caliphate. Hasan abdicated Caliphate in 661 CE in order to avoid the war and the split of Muslim world, but remained as the Imam of the Shi'ite Muslims. Still then, Mu'āwiya successfully plotted to poison him through Hasan's wife Asama (ja'dah bint al-Ashath Ibn Kais). Dwight M. Donaldson gives a good account of the poisoning in his book *The Shi'ite Religion*, Luzac & Co., London, 1933, pages 76-78. Imam al-Hasan died in 50 AH(670 CE).

After his death his brother al-Husain (also spelled as al-Husayn) succeeded him as the Third Imam. The Imamate was legitimately passed onto al-Husain's surviving son Ali Asghar, or 'Ali the younger', the elder brother, Ali Akbar, being killed in the Battle of Kerbala. He was popularly known as Imam Zayn al-'Abidin, a title meaning the *Ornament of the Pious*. The legitimacy of Imam Ali Asghar Zayn al-'Abidin was considered rightful on the ground that he was the direct descendant of Prophet Muhammad as his mother was Prophet's daughter Fatima, whereas Muhammad Ibn al-Hanafiya's mother was a Hanafite.

Nevertheless, a faction of the Shi'ites, who were known as the Kaisánís, an Arabian tribe, recognized Muhammad Ibn al-Hanafiya as the rightful and legitimate Imam, as he was the son of Imam Ali. This, according to some analysts, was due to the fact that Muhmmad Ibn al-Hanafiya was a more capable person with stronger character, who could lead them against oppression of the Umayyad Caliph. At the death of Muhmmad Ibn al-Hanafiya, the Kaisánís put up his son Abu Hashim Ibn Muhammad ibn al-Hanafiyya (also known as Abu-Hashim `Abd Allah) as their Imam. Later, he was poisoned by the 10th Umayyad Caliph Hisham (105-125 AH, i.e. 723-742 CE) of Syria, (see page 123 of Dwight M. Donaldson's book *The Shi'ite Religion*, Luzac & Co., London, 1933). The followers of Imam Muhmmad Ibn al-Hanafiya are also known as Kaysaniyya Sect. The Islamic historians also agree that Muhmmad Ibn al-Hanafiya never claimed his being Imam.

According to Shahrasáni the Kaisánís believe that there dwelled in Prophet Muhammad a divine spirit that passed to Imam Ali and after his death, to his sons, Imam Hasan, Imam Husain, and Imam Muhammad al-Hanafiya. Another Shi'ite tradition tells us that the Kaisánís believe Imam Muhmmad Ibn al-Hanafiya is Imam Mahdi, the Savior or the Just Leader of Humanity, and he will return from Mount Radwa, where they believe that he is living, and not dead (Shahrastani, Milal wa nihal, Vol. 1, p. 232; Nawbakhti, Firaq al-shi'a, Najaf edition, p. 27., cited by http://www.al-islam.org/mahdi/nontl/Chap-2.htm#n1). The poem below, which is reproduced from Donaldson's *The Shi'ite Religion*, page 101, testifies the hope of a Shi'ite sect, the Kaisánis, for the arrival of Mahdi Muhammad Ibn al-Hanafiya on his horse and lead his horse men to liberate them from the evils of oppression.

Four complete are the Imams,
of Kuraish, the lords of Right:
Ali and his three good sons,
each of them a shining light.
One was faithful and devout;
Kerbala hid one from sight;
One, until with waving flags,
his horsemen he shall lead to fight,
Dwells on Mt. Radwa, concealed;
honey he drinks and water bright.

Imam Muhmmad Ibn al-Hanafiya was buried at Jabal Radwa, but a Shi'ite sect, the Kaisánis, believes that he is Imam Mahdi and is still alive, living there and waiting for the right time to emerge again for the salvation of humankind. Jabal Radwa is west of Medina in Saudi Arabia. Map is from Microsoft Encarta 97 World Atlas.

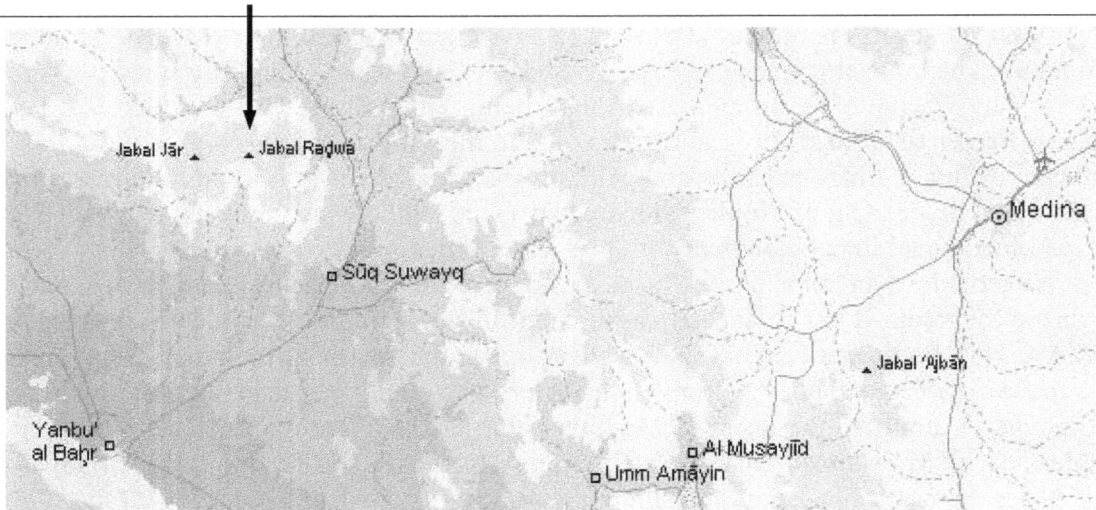

The Battle of Kerbala (61AH/680 CE). It was the battle that made the decisive division of the Sunni and the Shi'ite, never to be friends again. In recent days, Iran(Shi'ite)-Iraq(Sunni) War (1980-1988) left an estimated 1.7 million wounded and 1 million dead as per Microsoft Encarta 97 Encyclopedia, CD. Estimates of the number of dead range up to 1.5 million according to The Columbia Encyclopedia, Sixth Edition.2001, (quoted by http://www.bartleby.com/65/ir/IranIraq.html). Accordingly the eventful Battle of Kerbala is well recorded in all standard history books of Islam. It took place at the plains of Kerbala along the western bank of the famous river Euphrates that, along with its twin Tigris, gave birth to the ancient civilizations of Assyria (7th millenium to 609 BCE), Babylonia (18th to 6th century BCE), Sumer (5th millenium to 18th century BCE). (Note: The time frame of the civilizations are taken from Microsoft Encarta 97 Encyclopedia CD). The battle lasted about 10 days in the month of Muharram in 61 AH

(October, 680 CE). The last battle scene that took place on the 10th day of Muharram, 61 AH (12th October, 680 CE) is graphically presented by Dwight Donaldson in the Chapters VII and VIII of his book, *The Shiite Religion*, Luzac & Co., London, 1933. He described the death toll as follows.

"......And those who died with Husain, on the tenth day of Muharram, were eighty-seven people. Among them was his oldest son, Ali Ibn al-Husain. Hasan's sons, Abdulla and Kasim and Abu Bakr, were also killed. And the brothers of Husain that were killed, all of them sons of Ali (but not of Fatima), were Abbas, Abdulla, Ja'far, Uthman, and Muhammad the Younger.

............On his (Husain's) body they counted thirty-three strokes of the lance and thirty-four blows of the sword............Umar ibn S'ad (the commander of Yezíd's army) ordered his horsemen to trample the body of Husain underneath their horses' feet, for he had lost eight-eight men in the conflict....

.....At last, Sinán ibn Aws al-Nakha'í came forth against him and thrust him with a lance, and he fell. Ḥawlí ibn Yazid a-Aṣbaḥi then fell upon him to cut off his head, but his hands trembled, so his brother, Shibal, cut off the head and handed it over to Ḥawlí."

It was recorded that his head was finally buried in Cairo, Egypt. The Mosque of Hasaneym was built centering the sacred tomb where, unto today, devotees circumambulate paying respect and mourning for the Imam. His body was buried in Kerbala. That is why the poem mentioned in the previous page says, "Kerbala hid one from sight."

Imam Husain became a martyr because of his legitimate stand and noble intention. He challenged the legitimacy of Umayyad Caliph Muawiya's unilateral decision of making his son, Yezíd, the successor. Umayyad Caliph Muawiya betrayed the tradition of Prophet Muhammad and former Caliphs. Prophet Muhammad did not designate any successor, but left the issue to his Companions. The Companions of Prophet elected among themselves the successor known as the Caliph. This tradition was followed by Abu Bakr, Umar, Uthman (Osman), and Ali. The ruling Caliph can nominate a candidate who may or may not be elected. Muawiya betrayed this tradition, made his son his successor, and forced the governors and people of Islamic Empire to swear allegiance to his son. The *Alids* (i.e. the descendents of Caliph Imam Ali) and the household of Prophet refused to do so.

Mohammad Arshad wrote as follow.

"In 679, Muawiya nominated his son Yazid as his successor. This was certainly a deviation from the principle followed by the Pious Caliphs........He invited deputations ....from all provinces and important cities to take the oath of allegiance to his son. Iraq and Syria submitted. Muawiya then preceded to Medina and Mecca to secure the convent of the people of Hijaz. In Medina the leading citizens including Hussain the son of Ali, Abdullah the son of Caliph Umar, Abdur Rahman the son of Abu Bakr, and Abdullah the son of Zubair refused to take an oath on any condition. Abudllah ibn Zubair was of opinion that 'It could be left to the free choice of the citizens as was in the case of Abu Bakr. There could be nomination by the reigning Caliph provided the nominee was best by all criteria and not related to the ruling sovereign. That was what Abu Bakr did regarding Umar. There could still be a third course, that is, the appointment of a board of electors for the selection Khalifa. That was what Umar did.' But Mu'awiya was not convinced by these arguments. Ultimately he exacted an act of fealty to Yazid from the Meccans and Medinites." (*An Advanced History of Islam*, Mohammad Arshad, Ideal Publications, Dacca, 1967, page174).

Imam Husain was killed in the battle of Kerbala in 680 CE, and his headless body was buried there. His Shrine erected at his burial site is sacred to the Shi'ite Muslims and Kerbala is a Holy City.

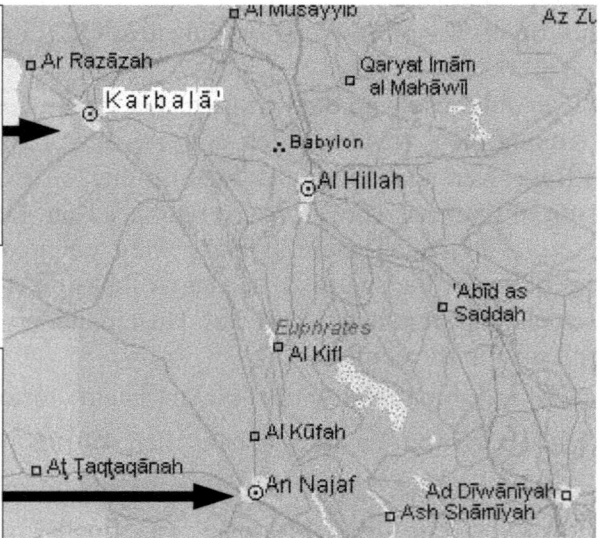

Some 130 km (~80 miles) to south is the Holy City of Najaf where Imam Husain's father Imam Ali was killed and his Shrine testifies his righteousness.

The location of Kerbala in relation to Najaf.
In Kerbala Imam Husain was killed and buried whereas his father Imam Ali was killed and buried in Najaf.
(Map from Microsoft Encarta 97 World Atlas)

Ashura Day, the day whereby millions of Muslims all over the world commemorate the martyrdom of Imam Husain (A.S.) which took place in Kerbala, Iraq on the 10th of Muharram 61 A.H. (680 AD), creates a historical symbol of unity and struggle against evil, injustice, and oppression.

http://www.jana.org/ashura/ashura.html

Imam Husain Shrine, Kerbala, Iraq
In 680 Imam Husain was killed here. Today, there still exists violence.
This web clip from online Shia News dated 17 October 2003.
(Source: http://www.shianews.com/low/middle_east/news_id/0001001.php)

Thus, at the death of Mu'āwiya, the Caliphate went to his son, Yezíd. His name is also spelled as Yazid. The people of Kufa city from Iraq offered allegiance to al-Husain and tempted him to challenge Yezíd. When al-Husain and party went to Kufa they were intercepted by Yezíd's followers at a place called Kerbala. He was killed and beheaded in the battlefield and later his body was buried there, but his head in Egypt some time later. The tragedy occurred on 10th Muharram 61, AH (12th October, 680 CE).

The Islamic chronicles described that Imam Husain's campaign against Yezíd's caliphate was not supported by his most trusted brothers and cousins. The author at http://www.victorynewsmagazine.com/ImamHassanMadePeaceWhyDidImamHussainFight.htm wrote:-

"Imam Hussain (AS) ....made a testament to his brother Muhammad bin Al-Hanafiya in which he declared:

'This movement of mine is not on account of stubbornness, rebellion, worldly passions or instigation by Satan. It is also not my object to create trouble or to oppress anyone. The only thing which invites me to this great movement is that I should reform the affairs of the followers of my grandfather, eradicate corruption, undertake enjoining to do good and restraining from evil, and follow the tradition of my grandfather, the Prophet of Allah and my father Ali'........"

A similar account that took place between Husain and his cousin Ibn Abbas is described by Donaldson as follows in page 81 of his book that has been cited earlier:-

"......... 'At any rate, if you refuse my warning and are determined to go, I pray you not to take the women and the children, for I solemnly declare that I am afraid that you will be killed as Uthman was killed, and his women and children saw it happen." "If in deed I die on the battlefield," said Husain, "I witness before God that that will be better than to live in dishonour in Mecca.'

When Ibn Abbas got this final answer, he left his presence, distressed and disheartened."

The course of the early Islamic history illustrated above clearly shows that Muhammad Ibn al-Hanafiya and his army never landed in Arakan in contrast to the Muslim traditions of Arakan. He was buried at Jabal Radwa, but the Kaisánís believe he is still alive to return as Imam Mahdi. Nevertheless, the tradition is part of the cultural life of the Rohingya Muslims.

In real life, factual history is simply confined to the scholars and academicians. In general, social, cultural, and political life of the common people are mainly guided by the traditions, tales, beliefs or myths, rather than facts. This is especially true in such closed and underdeveloped societies like Myanmar. Accordingly, the Arakanese Muslim oral history of 'Kaya-pari', Kaira-pari, and Hanifar Tonkies (shrines) as mentioned by Moulvi Nur Ahmad (*History of Arakan (Burma)*, Department of Dawah, World Muslim Congress, Karachi, 1978, page 5), and Mohammed Ashraf Alam must be given due attention. Under this tradition, the Arakanese Muslims, especially those who identify themselves as the Rohingyas, proudly claim that they are the Arabian descendants; some even claim to be the direct descendants of Prophet Muhammad. They scrupulously maintain and follow the Arabian Islamic traditions, in which the Arabs are the most holy people, Arabic is the tongue of God (Allah), and Islam is the only right religion. *This tradition is seen as the Islamic expansionism.* Needless to say, the concept of the Arabian-Islamic supremacy collides head on with the ideology of Buddhist-Myanmar supremacy. The result is a Muslim-Buddhist war and Neo-Nazism in Arakan.

Chapter-6. Muslim-Buddhist War and Neo-Nazism in Arakan

In my earlier book, *Burma: Nationalism and Ideology* (University Press Ltd., Dhaka, 1989), chapter 6.4. *Religions in War*, I wrote, "Each and every religion preaches peace, love and brotherhood among mankind, and each and every religion fights with every other. In Burma there is no exception." Also in chapter 3.7, *Islam vs. Buddhism,* of the same book I mentioned, "The upheaval of a group of Arakanese Muslims under the banner of the Mujahidens brought about the religious ambitions of the Muslims in Burma."

According to the Burma Centre Natherlands, "the core problem of the Rohingya people is still the discriminatory and repressive policy of the Burmese junta (SPDC) in Arakan State." This is a symptomatic diagnosis. I will try to present to the world that *the core problem of the Rohingya people is* a result of the Muslim-Buddhist war and Neo-Nazism in Burma. Denial of citizenship accompanied with systematic oppression of the Rohingya Muslims is a preemptive action of the Myanmarese to prevent the anchorage of Pan-Islam inside Burma.

In fear of Pan-Islam, the Rakhaing people render full support to the discriminatory and

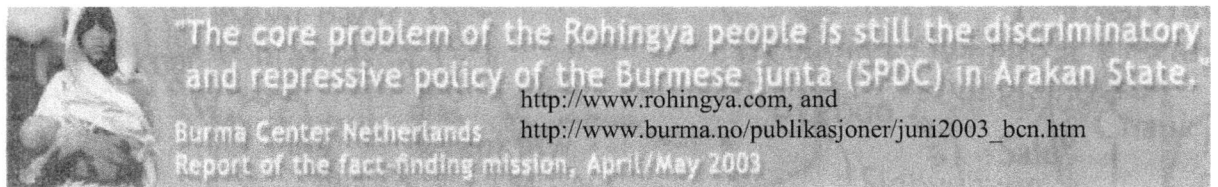

"The core problem of the Rohingya people is still the discriminatory and repressive policy of the Burmese junta (SPDC) in Arakan State."
http://www.rohingya.com, and
http://www.burma.no/publikasjoner/juni2003_bcn.htm
Burma Center Netherlands
Report of the fact-finding mission, April/May 2003

repressive policy of the successive military governments, from the very beginning with General Ne Win to today's Sr. General Than Shwe. In political reality, they have become neo-Nazis in the core, with the belief that Pan-Islam can be stopped with the practice of ultranationalism. In good faith, the United States of America and European countries, including Netherlands, have given political asylum to a number of the Rakhaing activists in the name of democracy. Their pathetic promotion of Neo-Nazism is reflected in their words and actions of war against Muslims. In the previous chapters I have described the historical Muslim-Buddhist war across the world. Now, I shall present its scenario in Arakan of Burma.

6.1. Burma Citizenship Law (1982). Under the Citizenship Law of Myanmar 1982, two million Muslims of Arakan lost their citizenship and became stateless aliens. This is the most visible characteristic of the Muslim-Buddhist war in Arakan. The underlying cause is the Myanmarese failure to build a modern nation, in which sovereignty will emanate from the citizens. Today, sovereignty emanates from the Buddhist Bama national race, which is the majority of the 135 national races. The Bama ruling race is assisted by the seven deputy national races, which are the Kachin, Kayah, Kayin, Chin, Mon, Rakhine, and Shan National Races. These eight national races rule the 127 sub-races and a number of nameless races. The Muslims of Burma is a nameless race. Please use Chapter 4.3 and page 159 as a reference in this context.

This racial hierarchy is the force that kicked out parliamentary Prime Minister, U Nu, in 1962. From the day he was forced out, imprisoned and then exiled, the colonialistic-feudal power structure, in which sovereignty originates from hierarchical religio-racial groups, has been gradually reinstalled. Today, the religio-racial ultranationalism has evolved into a form of Neo-Nazism in Myanmar. Political institution of citizenry is non-existent, only the religio-racial institutions play a role in the society under the military rule. As a result, the Muslim-Buddhist war that begun to subside in U Nu's era, has been escalated in her western Rakhaing province. Amidst the oppression, the Arakanese Muslims stand firm hoisting the flag of the Rohingya

A civilian victim of the Muslim-Buddhsit War in the Rakhine State of Myanmar?

Author's Note: Please note the face and the back of the body. Torture marks are easily visible. Lower panel shows his funeral.

Kaladan News
Dated: April 28, 2004
Barbaric Killing of a Religious Teacher in Nasaka Custody
Maungdaw, April 28: A barbaric killing of a religious teacher in Nasaka (Border security Force) custody was occurred on 21st April 2004, in Maungdaw township, Arakan State, according to our sources.

On 1st April 2004, Maulavi Sayed Ahmed, 35, son of Sayedul Islam of Duden village of Maungdaw Township was arrested by the Nasaka from his Madrasa (Religious School) and carried him to Ngakura Nasaka Sector No.5 camp, a place about 12 miles north of Maungdaw town. He was a young religious teacher and the Head of the Academic Affairs of the religious school of "*Madrasa Tauhidia*" of the village of *Ye Twin Pyin* in Maungdaw Township, said a villager of the village who participated in funeral prayer.

On that day, together with him, three others namely Maulavi Abdullah son of Haji Khalilur Rahman, who is Burmese and English teacher of Longdun Madrasa, Obaidullah son of Abdus Salam, a clerk of the same Madrasa and Mohammad Amin son of Sultan Ahmed, a former village chairman of Duden village. They were all arrested from the Lundun Madrasa by a team of 30 Nasaka forces from Sector No.5 camp of Ngakura village, he further added.

All of them were arrested under false and fabricated charges of having link with an insurgent group and running the Madrasa with fund of the insurgents, said a Village Peace & Development Council (VPDC) member of nearby village who is very close to authorities and prefers not to mention his name.

From April 1 to 21, they had been inhumanly tortured them day in, day out in the Nasaka camp to extract confession. As a result, Maulavi Sayed Ahmed succumbed to his injuries in the fateful night of 21st April 2004, he further reported.

Next morning, on 22nd April, the Duden villagers came to know about the custodian killing, the surrounding villagers in grief went to get the corpse for burial, but the Nasaka denied to hand it over to them. When more villagers with students were headed towards the camp in confrontational mood, the situation became very tense the Nasaka threatened to shoot at the public. After sometime, the Nasaka under instruction of the Nasaka Hqs handed the dead body over to the angry villagers.

The deceased body was covered in blood with marks of serious injuries and bruises. His tongue was cut off and sex organs were destroyed while testicles were squeezed. The deceased was declared a "*Shaheed*" (martyr) by religious leaders. On the same day, this dead body was buried at the graveyard of Duden village without giving it funeral bath as a martyr needs not be given funeral bath according to *Shari'a* (Islamic Law). The funeral prayers were joined by thousands of Rohingya villagers.

However, on 22nd April, the three other victims were brought to Nasaka Hqs and were released on 23rd April from the headquarters of Kyigan Pyin of Maungdaw Township as innocents. Dr. Nurul Haque, the Chairman of the Islam Thathanaye Council (*Islam Propagating Council*) of Maungdaw Township received them.

According to an elite Rohingya from inside Arakan, " We have no choice to practice our religion under the present ruling military regime. They have been carrying out various kinds of humiliating attacks on the religious institutions, centers and persons, as well as religious sentiments of the Muslims. It is a part of the SPDC's design to threaten the entire Rohingya Muslim community in Arakan. There is no specific law for the Nasaka forces towards Muslim Rohingya community in Arakan." ##

For further information, please contact at:

Mobile: +880-11227 138
E-mail: kaladanpress@yahoo.com

nationalism and upholding their Islamic traditions, as discussed in the previous chapter. They do not yield to the alienation and subordination, but demand equal rights as one of the Burmese National Races.

"You cannot step into the same river twice, for fresh waters are ever flowing in upon you," said Greek philosopher Heraclitus (540?-475? BCE). His words, "All things are flowing," becomes proverbial (http://www.thebigview.com/greeks/heraclitus.html). In a river, new water flows constantly; yesterday's water is always being replaced by today's water. Tomorrow, a fresh supply of water will arrive and today water will be no longer there. It may already have reached the ocean, by then. Therefore it is a new river everyday, though it may carry the same name. Still then we may say it is logical to claim that it is the same river because the mass of the water is all continuous from the beginning of the river down to the ocean. In the same manner today's Myanmar is not the same as yesterday's Myanmar. Nevertheless, she cannot be separated from her past. It is continuous, generations after generations. In the light of this universal truth, I define that a nation is a river of people, flowing and refreshing with new people forever. The Myanmar ultranationalism treats the nation like a lake. As a result, Myanmar is drying up with the heat of unsolved cultural and political conflicts. I love looking back and peeping forward, with the thought that future is more important than the past. I shall tell what I see to the readers.

6.2. Myanmar Ultranationalism. The Myanmar's 1982 citizenship law is the mirror of the Myanmar ultranationalism. It is based upon the feudal history of the nation whereas the 1947 Union of Myanmar's constitution guarantees the people's citizenship right on the ground of the socio-political prevalence of the British Burma, which is governed by the Government Act of Burma 1935. The 1947 Constitution of the Union of Burma, in its Chapter II Fundamental Rights, states the citizenship as follow.

CITIZENSHIP

10. There shall be but one citizenship throughout the Union; that is to say, there shall be no citizenship of the unit as distinct from the citizenship of the Union.

11. (i) Every person, both of whose parents belong or belonged to any of the indigenous races of Burma.

(ii) every person born in any of the territories included within the Union, at least one of whose grand-parents belong or belonged to any of the indigenous races of Burma;

(iii) every person born in any of the territories included within the Union, of parents both of whom are, or if they had been alive at the commencement of this Constitution would have been, citizens of the Union;

(iv) every person who was born in any of the territories which at the time of his birth was included within His Britannic Majesty's dominations and who has resided in any of the territories included in the Union for a period of not less than eight years in the ten years immediately preceding the date of the commencement of this Constitution or immediately preceding the 1st January 1942 and who intends to reside permanently therein and who signifies his election of citizenship of the Union in the manner and with the time prescribed by law, shall be a citizen of the Union.

12. Nothing contained in section 11 shall derogate from the power of the Parliament to make such laws as it thinks fit in respect of citizenship and alienage and any such law may provide for the admission of new classes of citizens or for the termination of the citizenship of any existing classes.

In the context of the above constitutional provisions, (1) a person who is a descendant of the 135 indigenous races of Myanmar is a citizen of the Union of Burma in 1948, and (2) a person, who is not a descendant of the indigenous races, becomes a citizen if he or she is born and has lived eight of ten years immediately preceding the 1st of January 1942. This dates to 1932, five years before Burma became a separate unit of British colony, detached from the British India in 1937, under the Burma Government Act 1935. Accordingly, an immigrant who settled in Burma in 1932 became the citizen of the Union of Burma. The Constitution's Citizenship Article 10 says, "There shall be but one citizenship throughout the Union".

Henceforth, all citizens are equal. This is the noblest and humanistic feature of the 1947 constitution.

Now, let us have a look at the 1982 **Burma Citizenship Law** (Pyithu Hluttaw Law No. 4 of 1982). The essential articles of the Chapter II given here is as published by the Working People's Daily, Saturday, 16 October, 1982, which is posted at http://www.ibiblio.org/obl/docs/ Citizenship%20Law.htm. The government newspaper's special supplement wrote, "The Chairman of the Council of State on 15, October promulgated the Burma Citizenship Law which was approved and passed by the third session of the Third Pyithu Hluttaw. The following is the English translation of the Burma Citizenship Law.

Burma Citizenship Law
(Pyithu Hluttaw Law No. 4 of 1982)
The Pyithu Hluttaw enacts the following Law:

Chapter II
Citizenship
3. Nationals such as the Kachin, Kayah, Karen, Chin, Burman, Mon, Rakhine or Shan and ethnic groups as have settled in any of the territories included within the State as their permanent home from a period anterior to 1185 B.E., 1823 A.D. are Burma citizens.
4. The Council of State may decide whether any ethnic group is national or not.
5. Every national and every person born of parents, both of whom are nationals are citizens by birth.
6. A person who is already a citizen on the date this Law comes into force is a citizen. Action, however, shall be taken under section 18 for infringement of the provision of that section.
7. The following persons born in or outside the State are also citizens:
(a) persons born of parents, both of whom are citizens;
(b) persons born of parents, one of whom is a citizen and the other an associate citizen;
(c) persons born of parents, one of whom and the other a naturalized citizen;
(d) persons born of parents one of whom is (i) a citizen; or
(ii) an associate citizen; or
(iii) a naturalized citizen; and the other is born of parents, both of whom are associate citizens;
(e) persons born of parents, one of whom is
(i) a citizen; or
(ii) an associate citizen; or
(iii) a naturalized citizen; and the other is born of parents, both of whom are naturalized citizens;
(f) persons born of parents one of whom is
(i) a citizen; or
(ii) an associate citizen; or
(iii) a naturalized citizen;
and the other is born of parents, one of whom is an associate citizen and the other a naturalized citizen.
8. (a) The Council of State may, in the interest of the State confer on any person citizenship or associate citizenship or naturalized citizenship.
(b) The Council of State may, in the interest of the State revoke the citizenship or associate citizenship or naturalized citizenship of any person except a citizen by birth.
9. A person born in the State shall have his birth registered either by the parent or guardian in the

prescribed manner, within year from the date he completes the age of ten years, at the organizations prescribed by the ministry of Home Affairs.

The two striking features of the 1982 Burma Citizenship Law are the provisions of Chapter II, articles 3 and 4. Under these two provisions some two million Muslims lost the citizenship and became stateless. The law violates the UN Charter Chapter 1, Article 1, Section 2 reads as follow.

"To develop friendly relations among nations based on respect for the principle of equal rights and self-determination of peoples, and to take other appropriate measures to strengthen universal peace;"

Please read full text of the UN Charter at http://www.un.org/aboutun/charter/index.html. The main point here is *the right to self-determination of peoples*. Definition of the right to self-determination can be found in many writings. Here are some exhibits that you may read.

Exhibit 1. (Please read full text at http://www.unhchr.ch/tbs/doc.nsf/(Symbol)/ f3c99406d528f37fc12563ed004960b4?Opendocument)

"General Comment No. 12: The right to self-determination of peoples (Art. 1) :
13/03/84.
CCPR General Comment No. 12. (General Comments)
Convention Abbreviation:

CCPR GENERAL COMMENT 12
The right to self-determination of peoples
(Article 1)
(Twenty-first session, 1984)

1. In accordance with the purposes and principles of the Charter of the United Nations, article 1 of the International Covenant on Civil and Political Rights recognizes that all peoples have the right of self-determination. The right of self-determination is of particular importance because its realization is an essential condition for the effective guarantee and observance of individual human rights and for the promotion and strengthening of those rights. It is for that reason that States set forth the right of self-determination in a provision of positive law in both Covenants and placed this provision as article 1 apart from and before all of the other rights in the two Covenants. 2. Article 1 enshrines an inalienable right of all peoples as described in its paragraphs 1 and 2. By virtue of that right they freely "determine their political status and freely pursue their economic, social and cultural development". The article imposes on all States parties corresponding obligations. This right and the corresponding obligations concerning its implementation are interrelated with other provisions of the Covenant and rules of international law."

Exhibit 2. (Please read the full text at http://www.webcom.com/hrin/parker/selfdet.html)

" Understanding Self-Determination: The Basics

BY KAREN PARKER

DEFINITION OF SELF-DETERMINATION

The right to self-determination, a fundamental principle of human rights law, (1) is an individual and collective right to "freely determine . . . political status and [to] freely pursue . . . economic, social and cultural development." (2) The principle of self-determination is generally linked to the de-colonization process that took place after the promulgation of the United Nations Charter of 1945. (3) Of course, the obligation to respect the principle of self-determination is a prominent feature of the Charter, appearing, inter alia, in both Preambles to the Charter and in Article 1.

The International Court of Justice refers to the right to self-determination as a right held by people rather than a right held by governments alone. (4) The two important United Nations studies on the right to self-determination set out factors of a people that give rise to possession of right to self-determination: a history of independence or self-rule in an identifiable territory, a distinct culture, and a will and capability to regain self-governance. (5) …."

Now what rights does a human have? The human rights are prescribed by the Universal Declaration of Human Rights (http://www.un.org/Overview/rights.html). Some excerpts are given here.

PREAMBLE (http://www.un.org/Overview/rights.html)
"Whereas recognition of the inherent dignity and of the equal and inalienable rights of all members of the human family is the foundation of freedom, justice and peace in the world",

…………..

Article 2.

"Everyone is entitled to all the rights and freedoms set forth in this Declaration, without distinction of any kind, such as race, colour, sex, language, religion, political or other opinion, **national or social origin**, property, birth or other status. Furthermore, no distinction shall be made on the basis of the political, jurisdictional or international status of the country or territory to which a person belongs, whether it be independent, trust, non-self-governing or under any other limitation of sovereignty."

…………..

Article 15.
(1) Everyone has the right to a nationality.
(2) No one shall be arbitrarily deprived of his nationality nor denied the right to change his nationality.

In the light of the United Nations Charter's guarantee of 'the right to self-determination of people' and the Universal Declaration of Human Rights, it is not wrong to say that Burma Citizenship Law (1982) is a crime against humanity.

6.3. Rakhaing's Neo-Nazism[1]. Neo-Nazism is here defined as the contemporary body of political and economic doctrines, which espouses totalitarian principle of government, state control of economy, predominance of groups assumed to be racially superior, and supremacy of the racial-military dictatorship. The enactment of the Burma Citizenship Law (1982) was greatly influenced by the Rakhaing's interest, which is expressed by their distinguished intellectual leader Dr. Aye Kyaw, a professor of history in a New York City University. Dr. Aye Kyaw presented *a position paper of the Arakanese perspective*, at the Oslo Burma Seminar on January 15-17, 2004. The position paper, *The Burma We Love,* is published in Arakanpost, Issue-5, July, 2004, p13. An ethnic Rakhaing, Dr. Aye Kyaw, now a US citizen, is a professor of history and highly respected in the Rakhaing as well as Myanmarese community abroad and at home. He is a key figure in the formulation of ALD and ANC racial policy, which is purely based upon the feudal and colonial events of the 18th century. An excerpt from his article is presented below.

> *"Ethnic Minorities vs. Non-ethnic Minorities*
>
> With respect to the definition of an ethnic minority, Dr. Maung Maung, a lawyer and a State Councilor, who later became president of Burma invited Professor U San Tha Aung, Director General of the Department of Higher Education, and myself as Rakhaing representatives in 1979. Present at that meeting in his office was U Kyaw Nyein who later became Minister of Education. I submitted my proposal that those people who appeared in the Inquest (census) of King Bodawpaya taken in the 1880s[2] ought to be regarded as ethnic minorities. Through the discussion, we agreed that those people who were in Burma before the end of the First Anglo-Burmese War in 1826 should be regarded as ethnic minorities. Those people who came along with the British colonial administration were regarded as non-ethnic minorities.
>
> This definition is in line with the principle defined by General Aung San, father of the Nobel Laureate Daw Aung San Suu Kyi. This definition is historical valid and sound, thereby not creating any further problem.
>
> We have accepted this definition. In April 2001, the Arakan League for Democracy (in Exile) held its third conference in New Delhi, India. This conference laid down, among others, a principle, which was very important for shaping the destiny of Burma. This principle is called the *Bhumi Rakkhita Putra Principle*. Bhumi means land; Rakkhita taking care of, Putra sons and daughters. Those who were in Rakhaingland, and who have been cherishing, maintaining, and taking care of this land generations after generations before the end of the first Anglo-Burmese War ought to be given priority and preference." The excerpt ends here.

From this presentation it is clear that the citizenship demarcation at 1823, one year before the commence of the First Anglo-Burman War in 1824, is the original idea of Dr. Aye Kyaw.

Notes.

1. Please analyze the development of the Rakhaing Neo-Nazism in comparison with the origin and evolution of European Fascism as discussed by Professor Myra Moss at http://gould.claremontmckenna.edu/publications/ monograph/pdf/Moss.pdf. She wrote in her introduction: "The development of European fascist ideology was influenced by the nineteenth- and twentieth-century Romantic rebellion against Enlightenment philosophies. Intellectually, fascism represents a profound shift from an Enlightenment to a Romantic view of nature and humanity: this shift involves the rejection of a realist theory of an independently existing universe, as composed of distinct and separable material atoms, along with the denial of an a-historical essence of humankind, which remains the same regardless of historical circumstance and differs fundamentally from nature and from the state; and the acceptance of an idealist conception of a spiritual yet historical, evolving, organically unified reality, which includes the self as a necessary part of it."

2. The year 1880 must be a typesetting error. It must be 1780. King Bodawpaya died in 1819. He brutally annexed Arakan in 1784. The First Anglo-Burman War broke out in 1824, with victory to the British in 1826. Arakan was handed over to the British under the Rantapo Treaty in 1826.

This complicated the racial and political situation in Arakan, which is rich in strong Islamic traditions from as early as 1430 CE, when the Rakhaing King Narameit Hla restored his throne in Arakan with a 30,000-strong Muslim Army. (As far as the Muslim settlement in Burma it is recommendable to consult Moshe Yegar's *The Muslims of Burma,* Wiesbaden, O. Harrassowitz, 1972). King Narameit Hla is popularly known as Mun Sawmon in the chronicles. According to the Muslim's tradition Sawmon is a corruption of the name Solomon, as I mentioned in Chapter 4.8. Upon the conquest of his throne, King Sawmon allowed his Muslim followers to build the Sidikh Khan Mosque, which was the first Mosque ever built in Burma. It was destroyed during the Burmese occupation of Arakan in 1784. It is also assumed that all Muslims were killed at that time. Thus, Arakan was free of the Muslims until British occupation in 1826. The British East India Company brought in Bengali Muslims to the depopulated Arakan and revitalized her agriculture. Under the British management, Burma became number one rice exporter in the world with an export record of 3.6 million metric tons in 1936, of which Arakan contributed 20%. With the 2002 rice export of 730,000 metric tons, independent Burma is far away from achieving the colonial record. The British brought along not only the Bengali skilled farmers, but also soldiers, businessmen, and government civil servants into Burma. On this ground, Dr. Aye Kyaw, a professor of history, proposed the citizenship cut-off point at 1823 CE. General Ne Win happily accepted it and the Rakhaings became the partners of the Burmese military dynasty up to today. My clan even boosted two cabinet ministers during Ne Win's rule, one is Colonel Min Kyi, a cousin of my late brother-in-law U Tun Yi (a school superintendent), and Colonel Kaung Hla Pru, a cousin of mine from my father's side. Colonel Min Kyi is a brother-in-law of Professor Aye Kyaw who is married to his sister, Daw Htway Shin, also a faculty of the philosophy department at Rangoon University. I have great respect for both Dr. Aye Kyaw and Daw Htway Shin as my teachers, even though I was a biology student. They are good academicians. Dr. Aye Kyaw and I attended the same training course in Burmese Way to Socialism at Inyalay campus of Central Institute of Political Science in 1970. The training was a compulsory for every scholar who was selected for higher studies abroad.

In Burma, the university faculty and staff are government employees. Therefore, in the context of General Ne Win's Burma, Dr. Aye Kyaw's was simply doing his job as a government servant. It was one reason why I abandoned Burma in 1977. I argued with myself as follows, "Serving General Ne Win and his military government is not the same as serving the nation and the people, but I will be an instrument of oppression." This reason facilitated my plan to abandon Burma. Now, both of us are the US citizens. We have taken the advantage and privilege of US liberal policy and live as the citizens with equal rights to the May Flowers' descendants. As a US citizen, I am dismayed to see that Dr. Aye Kyaw is still advocating for the special rights of a group of people whose ancestors were believed to have lived in the pre-1824 Third Myanmar Empire, and to keep a group of people, who came into Burma during the British rule in post-1826, as the second class citizens to be known as non-ethnic minorities.

I do not believe that Professor Aye Kyaw had any idea where his academic view would lead. As a pure academician he is proud that his proposal was accepted by none other than General Ne Win, and was incorporated in the citizenship law. This surely is a significant achievement for an academician. The Rakhaings are very happy with the government's decision and the Burma Citizenship Law of 1982. Nevertheless, I simply believe that neither Professor Aye Kyaw nor the Rakhaing populace foresaw the political consequences of the academic view, which is based purely upon certain historical records. It is beyond doubt that the explosion of Muslim-Buddhist war and neo-fascist ultranationalism in Arakan is detonated by the Burma Citizenship Law of 1982., but the explosives were given by a Rakhaing academician. Professor Aye Kyaw is supported by his student, Dr. Chan Aye, another outstanding Rakhaing historian.

Dr. Aye Chan's article, *Who are the Rohingyas?*, is posted at the scholar's column of http://rakhapura.com/ as of April 10, 2005. He asked the question in response to a piece of BBC Burmese program news about a Burmese Rohingya, Zaw Min Htut, who was granted political Asylum by the Japanese government. The Rohingya published a book, *The Union of Burma and Ethnic Rohingyas,* in Japan in 2001. In his book, Dr. Chan Aye, charged Zaw Myint Htut for the distortion of Arakanese history by depicting Arakan as a Rohingya kingdom. Dr. Chan Aye also pointed out that Zaw Myint Htut and the Rohingyas are the direct descendents of immigrants from Chittagong District of East Bengal (present day Bangladesh) and the British Colonial officials called them Chittagonians in their administrative records. In his article, *Who are the Rohingyas,* he described the atrocities inflicted upon the Rakhaing Buddhist population during the Kala-Rakhaing (i.e. Muslim-Buddhist) riot of 1942, and the Mujahid uprising of 1950s. He put the blame on the British colonial masters. While he strongly denounced Zaw Myint Htut, he wrote, "This, of course does not mean that they do not deserve the equal rights that other ethnic groups of Burma should enjoy regardless of whether or not democracy is restored." Dr. Chan Aye, a supporter of Mrs. Aung San Kyu Kyi Aris, actively participated in the 1988-pro-democracy uprising in Burma, and was imprisoned by the junta for two years. I knew him as a Rakhaing student when I was working as a junior faculty, *demonstrator*, at the Department of Zoology, Rangoon Arts and Science University in late 1960s.

With the support of the two celebrated Rakhaing academicians, the Rakhaings sway towards the historical nationalism and their umbrella organization, the Arakan National Congress (ANC), recognizes the Rohingyas as the Arakan Bengalis or the illegal immigrants. I have mentioned the formation of ANC in the chapter 5.3 of this book. Recently, ANC drafted an Arakan State Constitution. According to the draft constitution Arakan is a republic and it will be voluntarily associated a unit of the Federal Union of Burma. Although the draft is very rudimentary it has agitated the Rohigyas for the clauses mentioned below.

"-The citizenship of the Republic of Arakan shall be determined and regulated by law. The citizen of Arakan shall be known as Arakanese."

"-Buddhism shall be the state religion."

"-Only Arakan legal entities and citizen of Arakan nationality shall have the right to own land."

"-In order to be a candidate for the presidency or the vice-presidency of Republic, any citizen of either sex must meet the following conditions.

(a) Be an Arakan National by birth;

(b) Be born of parents who are Arakan Nationals;

"- The Senate shall consist of;

(a) ---------------- representatives of the ethnic nationalities of Arakan, and

(b) ---------------- members to be nominated by the President in accordance with the provisions of clause (3).

To each ethnic nationality of Arakan specified in the first column of the following table, there shall be allotted the numbers of seats specified in the second column there of to that ethnic nationality of Arakan, as the case may be.

Table
1. Rakhaing (Rakhine) .... *(—)*
2. Mro (aha) Khumi .... *(—)*
3. Maramagree (Barua) .... *(—)*
4. Kaman Muslims .... *(—)*
5. Thauk .... *(—)*
6. Daingnet .... *(—)*
7. Other Linguistic or religious group ..... *(—)"*

"*- A person shall, subject to the provisions of clause (2) be qualified to be elected as, and to be a member of House of Representatives if he is a citizen of Arakan and has attained the age of twenty five years.*"

In the light of the clauses presented above, the proposed Republic of Arakan is not a secular state, in which only an Arakan national by birth is eligible to be the President or Vice President. Similarly, a specific number of the senators will be allocated to each ethnic nationality. The question of ethnic nationality and citizenship still remains unsolved. According to Professor Aye Kyaw's *a position paper of the Arakanese perspective*, those people who were in Burma before the end of the First Anglo-Burmese War in 1826 should be regarded as ethnic minorities whereas those who came along with the British colonial administration were regarded as non-ethnic minorities, in the context of Burma. When we consider it in the context of Arakan it can be interpreted that the ethnic nationality of the proposed Republic of Arakan is conferred to those people who were in Burma before the end of the First Anglo-Burmese War in 1826. Since the Rohingyas are classified as Arakan Bengalis they will be subjected to a second class citizenship and alienation due to their foreign origin and religion; they may not have the right to own land either. As per Professor Aye Kyaw's definition of *Bhumi Rakkhita Putra Principle 2001,* "those who were in Rakhaingland, and who have been cherishing, maintaining, and taking care of this land generations after generations before the end of the first Anglo-Burmese War ought to be given priority and preference." The *Bhumi Rakkhita Putra Principle* is the Rakhaing's version of the notorious Malaysia's *Bhumiputtra.* I shall present some views of the Rakhaings who are the members or the supporters of ANC and its racist constitution.

(1). The Rakhine Security Association. On January 27, 2001, All Arakan Students and Youths Congress (aasyc@yahoo.com) sent an email to 43 recipients with a subject *a report on the conditions and sufferings of the Rakhaings in Maungdaw (The original homeland of Rakhaings or Arakan).* The AASYC is a founding member of ANC. The report gave an extensive account of the Chittagonian Bengali Muslims' aggression and urged all Rakhaings to support the 1982 Burma Citizenship act and contain the Muslims. The report was a translated version from its original publication in Burmese by the Rakhine Security Association, Maungdaw, Rakhine State, on the 9th October 1988 It can be found at http://www.arakan.homestead.com/files/Articles/Report.htm. The excerpt I present below will help you form your own view.

"In that way, the Chittagonian Bengalis are trying to-
    i. To have recognition of Rohingya as a nation within Burma by changing the real history of Rakhaing state.
    ii. After becoming as a nation of the country, a Muslim state will be created with

90% of Maungdaw, 80% of Butheedaung as per its geographical position and population condition etc.

iii. After successful completion of above plans, with the help of outside, a separate state with sovereign power will be established. Later, it will be made a confederation state with Bangladesh.

.... the then Burmese minister Brig. Sein Lwin in his above quoted new citizenship law, 1981 *(i.e. 1982)* returned the Rohingyas of Maungdaw and Butheedaung to be Bengali descendants. U Sein Lwin and U Ne Win Govt. commented that they are descendants of Chittagonian Bengalis only.

.... According to the above mentioned facts, Chittagonian Bengalis, who have been living in Maungdaw and Butheedaung (Kula) started entering into our country since the year 1852. And it revealed that they have been settled here for the last 180 years only. Observing the history of a country, they should not have equal rights with the original people of the origin. So, the foreigners Act, 1982 should be welcomed and accepted. In that law, every person coming from outside will be treated as a foreigner. As per Sec. 3 of that law, those who have been settling in any part of the country before 1823 (i.e. 1185 R.E.) along with Kachin, kayah, karen, Chin, Mon, Shan, Rakhaing be treated as the national of the country. Accordingly, this law should be enforced strictly failing which, the country will surely be turned into a Muslim country without any doubt. If we accept them, then they will suck our blood and our properties will be taken by all those Chittagonian Bengalis (Kula). Moreover, in some occasions, all those Bengali would marry Burmese girls by way of introducing themselves as Rakhaing Buddhists of Arakan. Moreover some of them using the Burmese wife occupied all the facility of business to earn much money to build large mosques......" Quote ends.

(2). Moe Kyaw Tun's view. While the Rakhine Security Association advocates in favor of the Burma Citizenship Law (1982), Moe Kyaw Tun put up a proposal to determine the citizenship on the basis of the DNA test. Based upon his communication in the Arakan People Unity Forum (APUF@yahoogroups.com), he is a Rakhaing engineer settled in Netherlands. He is a citizen of Netherlands. The APUF started with a view to forge unity between the two major communities of Arakan, namely the Buddhist Rakhaings and the Muslim Rohingyas. However, due to the refusal of the Rakhaings to recognize the Rohingyas as the ethnic people of Arakan or Burma, a hot email exchange took place. One of the most incredible piece of neo-nazi's view was put up by Moe Kyaw Tun. Below, I present to you his neo-nazi's view and the responses by Aung Tin and Shah Arkani. Some essential excerpts of Aung Tin and Shah Arkani, but full text of Moe Kyaw Tun is given so that the reader can get the whole picture of his vision.

To: "moe kyaw tun(kma)" <k_m_aung@yahoo.com>, apuf@yahoogroups.com, burmese_rohingya@yahoogroups.com, burmesemuslim@yahoogroups.com, democracy_forburma@yahoogroups.com.au, nldmembrsnsupportersofcrppnnldndassk@yahoogroups.com, "Rohingya Youth (RYDF)" <rydf2003@yahoo.com>, rohingyanet@yahoogroups.com, sycburma@yahoogroups.com
From: "Tin Aung" <aungtintoronto@yahoo.ca> Add to Address Book
Date:Mon, 21 Feb 2005 01:50:22 -0500 (EST)
Subject:[APUF] Re: " Save our Land even as Hitler if necessary....instead of losing out in foreign

Dear MKT

Please, take my sincere thanks for your kind response. I also like to admit that you are a strong, bright, intelligent, but, sorry to say, dangerous. .... I can sense your hatred. Your logic is strong and articulate, but cruel, inhumane and one sided, not fit for widely accepted main stream culture in today's world........

As for Hitler, even the extremists except for very few do not praise Hitler not to mention Germans themselves. It is shocking to read you dare to praise Hitler.

Aung Tin, Toronto.
****
"moe kyaw tun(kma)" <k_m_aung@yahoo.com> wrote:

Hitler is evil only for jews. He got good vision for his own people. Because of his partiotic propagations, german race became more cautious about foreign illegal immigrants problems and thats why until now majority germans are not welcoming foreigners for residing in their country. Thats why german can now proud of being monoethnic country. Their strong partiotic spirits and intelligent mindsets help their country to recover within short time after World War II. Patriotism and ethnic identity are very important for a country in long run. If you learn about G8 (G7+ russia), all are found as monoethnic ones except USA and Canada which two are formed with white immigrants from Europe on virtually no man land.
Please check our nearest neighbours. Why china and india now developing very fast and china even faster. There are very few ethnic problems facing in china. Almost all minorities except a few percentage had been successfully absorbed into main stream han chinese and therefor they can do development job efficiently. In india, different states got various ethnicity and they speak loudly about their voices. This is infact obstacles in development. I don't want to elaborate too much about that. You can carefully study these cases. What are the most developed countries in South East Asia. Sinapgore in which chinese dominate in almost all areas and act as monoethnic country, but they cleverly disguised as cosmopolitan country giving equal rights to others. In reality, there is no equal rights. If others ask for their rights, they (chinese) simple turn down by democratic means(by voting out). The second most prosperous country in south east asia is Malaysia, where chinese and indian are positively discriminated by constitution.
In Thailand and Indonesia, minority (chinese) control around 70-80% of business. And now these countries are legging behind malaysia although they were wealthier than Malaysia in the past century (during the era when no chinese were there).
What I mean is the country should be monoethnic and majority race should control almost all so that the country can be developed easily. If the minority could grib firm power in politic or economy, they will do for their own (this is common sense, people will do for their own first, then family and then friends, as mentioned in Buddha' teachings or Confucian's teachings.)
Therefore, there should be no compromise on rights of ethinc rakhine who is the decedents of Tibeto-Burman tribes(not Bangali or Indo-Aryan). If not, so called Rohingas or Bangalis who are traditionally better in saving money than ours will dominate all our economy first, then our political power will be bought through some corrupted Arakanese and then they will import their culture also. This evidences can easily be found in modern Burma (Myanmar) where Chinese gradually control our economy and then politic. There are many majors, generals and high ranking official of chinese decedents in myanmar now and they help lobbying government to do favours for china. Now , they even trying to import chinese culture.
" Save our Land even as Hitler if necessary....instead of losing out in foreign hands "
****

Shah Arkani <shah_arkani@yahoo.com> wrote
Dear respected APUF members:
Please allow me to write a few lines for sometimes it is necessary to kick-back if bigotry undermines everone overtly. This would-be technocrat seems intended to go beyond the call of duty to bring injustice and destruction into his own society. Well, initially, I inteneded to write a bit longer, but after reading Ako Mra Wa's emial taht titled "Look before You Jump", I beleive i do not need to elaborate my thought any further because it (that email) covers a great detail of waht intended t wrote.
****

"Tin Aung" <aungtintoronto@yahoo.ca> wrote:
I wonder what Hitler was saying at his time.

The above communications are the sequels of Moe Kyaw Tun's proposal to undertake DNA tests for citizenship of the Rohingyas. He wrote as follow.

"moe kyaw tun(kma)" <k_m_aung@yahoo.com> wrote:

Dear Friends,

Nowadays, technology can help us a lot in differentiating Rakhine from Rohinga or Bangali. If Rohinga is to be recognized as indigenous race, any one who claim himself should take DNA test. This can be easiest way for him to prove. If his DNA is different from those of Bangali, he or she should be accepted as ethnic Arakan citizen. If not, he should be chased out to Bangladesh or anywhere else away from our land.

This will be the main factor in differentiating illegals from ethnic races and I am sure it will be key factor in issuing citizenship documents.

Our fatherland (Arakan) and our nation (Burma) is now in danger of illegals from neighbouring bangladesh and china. These aliens not only came her illegally but also grabbing our lands and properties, degrading our blood and bringing illicit cultures.They all should be barred from integrating into our culture.Otherwise our traditions and cultures will be eradicated.

Regards,
****

The view of Moe Kyaw Tun's is a clear reflection of the *Bhumi Rakkhita Putra Principle* Professor Aye Kyaw presented in his *position paper of the Arakanese perspective*, at the Oslo Burma Seminar on January 15-17, 2004. His proposal to apply the DNA tests for the citizenship and his words, "Save our Land even as Hitler if necessary" are widely agreed by the Rakhaings. Examples are given below.

A Rakhaing named Ran Nin Soe wrote in the APUF in February 2005 explaining his view of the conspiracy being plotted by the Rohingyas and Muslims, in reply to Sayed Hussein (shussein72@hotmail.com) and Thiha Aung (aungthiha8888@yahoo.com)

Rannin Soe <ranninsoe@yahoo.co.uk> wrote:

Dear Thiha Aung,

We respect Human Right but they are not fighting for Human Right. They are fighting for occupied our land by Islamic Backbone. Do you know what is called Rohingya? Who are they? Where they come from? And what they demand? I believe you already know what is called Jeehad (killed for all of non-Muslim). Mujaheed Protest to Muslim and fighting for non -Muslim. My friend they are fighting for Independent make a Islamic State. How can Bangali fight to Burma/Arakan? They are Islamic behind the Mask. For Example more than (200) Bangali gave name as Rohingya themselves checking for Asylum. They can't speak any language from Burma Ethnic groups. So how can we accept they are from Burma. If you want to say Human Right please tried to know about what is called Rohingya. You can lie to Burmese people about (Rohingya behind the Mask) but please don't tried to lie us.
1947
The Mujaheed Party, Arakan
Jeehad Council
ON August 20, 1947, the Mujaheed Party, Arakan was formed under Dobboro Chaung Declaration. It was led by Mr. Jafar Hussain popularly known as Jafar Kawal. The Mujaheed Party of guided Jeehad Council consists of the then Rohingya elders who supported Jeehad movement in Arakan.

1964

Rohingya Independent Force (RIF)

Rohingya Independent Force (RIF) was formed on 26 April 1964 at Maungdaw, Arakan under the leadership of Master Sultan Ahmed and Mr. Jafar Habib popularly known as B.A. Jafar. In 1969 the name of RIF was changed into AIR (Rohingya Independent Army) and led by Mr. Jafar Habib.

1973

Rohingya Patriotic Front (RPF)

On 12 September 1973 near Sack Dala on Burma-Bangladesh border the name of AIR was changed into Rohingya Patriotic Front (RPF) and led by Jafar Habib. After the independence of Bangladesh there were many changes in RPF and finally in June 1974 RPF was reconstituted and was led by Mr. Jafar Habib, President, Mr. Nurul Islam, Vice

President and General Secretary was Master Shabbir Hussain.

The Chittagonian Bangalis are trying to -

1-To have recognition of Rohingya as a nation within Burma by changing the Real History of Rakhing State.

2-After becoming as a nation of the country a Muslim state will be created with Islamic Backbone.

3-Aftersuccessful completion of above plan, with the help of outside (Islamic radical countries) a separate state sovereign power will be established. Later it will be made a confederation state with Bangladesh.

With Best Wishes

Ran Nin Soe

From a message posted by an APUF member I learned that Ran Nin Soe is a Bangladeshi Rakhaing, who has taken political asylum in Netherlands with a forged identity of a Burmese democracy activist and in disguise as a supporter of the opposition leader Nobel Laureate Mrs. Aung San Suu Kyi Aris. It is a well-known fact that many Bangladeshi have sought political asylum with forged identity of the Burmese Rakhaings or Rohingyas in the United States and European countries.

The Rakhaing Neo-Nazism is not an isolated small group, but it is an wide spread phenomenon led by the umbrella organization, Arakan National Congress (ANC), and supported by the intellectuals and professionals alike Their writing can be read at www.rakhapura.com, which posts the articles and news of Rakhaing Buddhist's interest. Recently, it also has one of my articles, *Rakhaing nation demands 'Decolonization of Burma*, posted. I recommend the reader to take a look at the articles of Kyaw Zan Tha, MA, U Shwe Zan's *Study of Muslim infiltration into Rakhine State*, and U Tha Hla's *The Rakhaing-5*.

In addition to an array of the intellectuals and professionals, there exists a good gang of Fifth Columnists among the Rakhaing Neo-Nazis. Some examples are given below.

(1). Anonymous. A Rakhaing person proposed to put the Rohingyas in a concentration camp under the UN supervision and to settle them in a third country. Dr. Yunus presenting his concern at the Arakan People Unity Forum (APUF). Please pay attention to my emphasis in bold letters. Dr. Yunus, M.B.B.S., a Maungdaw native, is a friend of mine since my days at Rangoon University in 1960. He is considered as an extremist. I shall have talk about him more in the coming pages. His message reads as follows. I have deleted the the name of the accused.

To: APUF@yahoogroups.com

From: "rsoyunus" <rsoyunus@yahoo.com> | This is spam | Add to Address Book

Date: Tue, 29 Apr 2003 04:14:51 -0000

Subject: [APUF] Before we unite!

Hello my Arakan compatriots,

It is very good idea and important factor to forge an unshakable unity and solidarity of people of Arakan to free ourselves from the subjugation of Burman corrupted military rule...............

The Rakhine say Rohingyas are foreigners in Arakan and there was no Rohingya in the history of Arakan,a few of them say they have the right to live in Arakan as permanent residents after completion of immigration process or to become naturalized citizens in a free Arakan. xxxxxxxxx **wrote in his article that all so-called Rohingya should be put in concentration camp under the supervison of UN body and later be resettled in a third country.**

So far, the accused Rakhaingthar, a US citizen from New York City, has denied he said such a thing, upon my enquiry. I believe him. Nevertheless, I had frequently heard such words from the Rakhaingthars. I will not be surprised to read these words in the world wide web.

(2). Arakan Students Association (ASA). A group that called themselves Arakan Students Association (ASA) claimed that they "have the arrangement to clean ---------for father land of Arakan". I believe the blank (————) is meant for the Kala, and I am included in it as a 'Dear Brother-in-law of Kala', since my recognition of the Rohingyas as the native compatriots in Arakan. The Muslim Rohingyas have been in Arakan since 7th or 8th century and in large population serving the Rakhaing king since 1430, spanning some 600 to 1,400 years in Arakan. How many generations does a person have to live in a land to be called 'native'? Please use Moshe Yegar's The Muslims of Burma (Wiesbaden, O. Harraaowitz, 1972) as cross reference for the Muslim settlement in Arakan and Burma.

Cambridge International Dictionary of English, Cambridge University Press, 1995, described 'native' (noun) in a sentence- *'The missing person is believed to be native of Monaco* (=person born in Monaco)'. Therefore, if a person is born in Myanmar Rakhine State he or she is a native of Rakhine State as well as of Myanmar. This is confirmed by the Random House Webster's College Dictionary, Random House, 1991, which defines 'native' as '1. being the place or environment in which a person was born or a thing came into being: *one's native land,* and ..4. born in particular place: *a native Chiacagoan'.* Since the 1947 constitution, in article 10, says, "There shall be but one citizenship throughout the Union". According to this they are all Myanmarese by citizenship, but may belong to a different ethnic group depending on the origin and culture. As they call themselves the Rohingyas, then they are the ethnic Rohingyas and for sure they are not the Rakhaings or the Bamas. They have every right to give a name they like to their ethnic identity. Freedom of expression is a basic human right. Denial of this right is nothing but racism. For my recognition of this basic human right, which is recognized internationally under the Universal Declaration of Human Rights, some Rakhaing students who claimed to be the members of the Arakan Students Association in USA want to kill me. This is the irony.

Although the threat posed to me is not formidable it reflects the mind of the general populace of the Rakhaings who are being guided by the ultranationalism or Rakhaing neo-Nazism. This is unfortunate. One of his communications is given below. I do not mean to blow the issue out of proportion, but this deserves due attention as it underlines the prime cause of the ethnic conflict not only in Arakan but in all Myanmar also. The email messages are reproduced without any modification of content or spelling correction.

From: "Aung Soe" <asa7974@msn.com>

To: skhans@yahoo.com, aldaustralia@hotmail.com, aldmalay@hotmail.com, aldyouth@yahoo.com, arakan5@juno.com, arakan999gold@yahoo.co..1k, arakanone@yahoo.com, thaiald@hotmail.com

CC: drkyaw@mail.pcmagic.net, kokophoto@yahoo.com, meemeekhine756@hotmail.com, mizzima@del6.vsnl.net.in, moechery@yangon.net.mm, nkeefer@uclink4.berkeley.edu, nyinyilwin8@yahoo.com, zarni@mail.essential.org
Subject: Warning for Dr.Shwe Lu Maung
Date: Sat, 28 Jun 2003 09:55:18 -0700

To Dear Brother law of Kala,

You distroyed Arakan nationality. You wrote two kinds of Arakan about the story at the online.(Khaw Taw Kala Muslim Rakhine and Buddhist Arakan. Please stop to write the Arakan history without your brain and destroy your story. We have the arrangement to clean ---------for father land of Arakan.

Regards,
Khaing Min Soe
Freedom fighter of Arakan

The above email is one of many that were sent to me by a person in the name of Khaing Min Soe, a Freedom fighter of Arakan, from ASA. It appears that other members of ASA agree with him. Please see another email that I got from a person styled as Than Htay.

Date: Tue, 1 Jul 2003 14:22:00 -0700 (PDT)
From: "Than Htay" <arakanone2000@yahoo.com>
Subject: Re: We agree to move the Dr.Shwe Lu Maung to other life.
To: skhans@yahoo.com, aldaustralia@hotmail.com, aldmalay@hotmail.com, aldyouth@yahoo.com, asa7974@msn.com, arakan999gold@yahoo.cz.uk, thaiald@hotmail.com
CC: arakanone@yahoo.com, drkyaw@mail.pcmagic.net, kokophto@yahoo.com, mizzma@del6.vsnl.net.in, moechary@yangoon.net.mm, nyinyilwin8@yahoo.com, zarni@mail.essentail.org
Than Htay <arakanone2000@yahoo.com> wrote:
To Dear comrades,
We will support the patriot (Ko Khin Min Soe) to move Shwe Lu Maung. We don't care any kind of Kala students,association and party. We know that Shwe Lu Maung reported to Kala group. We have the alot of information of kala group. But Shwe Lu Maung are the first enemy of Rakhine and Kala.

Regards,
Than Htay

The last email from Than Htay demonstrates the Rakhaing's hatred toward the Rohingyas who they call Kala or *nigger*. It is sad to see that the leading Rakhaing intellectuals are supplying oxygen to the fire of hatred rather than trying to extinguish it.

Date: Wed, 9 Jul 2003 17:38:43 -0700 (PDT)
From: "Than Htay" <arakanone2000@yahoo.com>
Subject: Re: Warning. From negative to positive.
To: "Shahnawaz Khan" <skhans@yahoo.com>, "RSDA" <rsda9999@yahoo.com>
CC: nupafa@yahoo.com, narinjara@yahoo.com, aasyc@bdonline.com, kaladanpress@yahoo.com, hamid@rohingya.com, haroon_bur@hotmail.com

To,
U Shwe Lu Maung,

I will never change my target for you. You are not educated because you changed target to your brother in law(Kalar). When you got the email from me, you reported to Kalar group. You should be think about that Rahine never afraid Kalar. If you are educated and hero of Rakhine, you need to challenge with me to discuss Rakhing history. **I recognize Khua Taw Kalar from Bengali as a human. But I can't recognize as our ethnic group and I can't share with him to live at Rakhine.** One day, I will come your home without your invitation.

Regards,

Than Htay

In my judgement, the threat to my life through these emails do not carry substance. Later, I learned that these two young seamen, Khaing Min Soe and Than Htay, were landed immigrants in USA, seeking for political asylum. It was unfortunate that they happened to threaten the life of a US citizen. Their community leader Ven. Bikkhu Dr. Nayaka, whom I knew since 1988 and with whom I have cooperation for the advancement of democracy and peace in Myanmar, was kind enough to make them understand it was a wrong doing. I present it here, not with ill-feeling, but to illustrate the feelings that dwell in the mind and heart of the Rakhaing people. As per information in his email Than Htay is from Maungdaw, which is the Muslim-dominated city of Myanmarese Rakhine State at the Bangladesh border.

Now, please pay attention to the high-lighted bold sentences in Than Htay's last email. He honestly expressed his mind, in writing, that he recognized the Khua Taw Kalar (i.e. the worst form of nigger, if translated in American racist language) as a human, but in his heart he could not recognize the Kala, i.e. Rohingya, as a compatriot ethnic member and share the land with him to live in Rakhine State. This mixed feeling is shared by the general populace of the Rakhaing people. This is a sad state of hatred. This hatred is the basis of the Muslim-Buddhist war in Arakan. It is a hate-war. It is the devil. Instead of terminating the devil the Myanmar military junta has been domesticating it since 1962. Today in 2005, the devil is huge and indestructible. Very soon, it will devour the entire nation of Myanmar. This may sound rhetoric. Nevertheless, it surely is a war that exists at the grassroots level. This is dangerous because this is the war that will ignite a bigger and greater Muslim-Buddhist war with international significance.

The ANC's adoption of *the Bhumi Rakkhita Putra Principle,* which espouses the Rakhaing special rights and alienates the Rohingyas as illegal immigrants from Bangladesh, infuses new toxins into the blood of Rakhaing Neo-Nazis across the world. Consequently, a rise of vocalist Rakhaing Neo-Nazis is witnessed attacking the Rohingyas in the world wide web, with a special target at myself, who bestows due respect and recognition to the Muslim Kala Rohingyas. I do not mean to personalize this presentation. However, there always is sensational politics surrounding a personality, which creates *political tsunami* in the society. On the other, my recognition of the Rohingyas as an ethnic group of Arakan and Burma is purely based on the simple philosophy that sovereignty emanates from the people and everyone has the right to self-determination in a civilized human society.

6.4. Historical Background of Rakhaing Neo-Nazism. The Rakhaing Neo-Nazism is the last attempt of the Rakhaing people to prevent ultimate extinction of their fading glory. According to the geological text books, the land known as *Rakkhapura* (3000 BCE to 1784 CE) was formed some 12 to 65 million years ago, during the middle or late Tertiary period. At that geological time the tectonic Indo-Australian Plate moved to the north and collided against the stationary Asian landmass on the Eurasian Plate, creating the Himalayas mountains and its southern ridges that are known as the Rakhaing Roma or Arakan Mountains. It was a great geological upheaval. The abyssal floor of ancient Tethys Sea became Mount Everest or *Chomo Lungma* (Tibetan meaning Mother-Goddess), the highest mountain, 8848 m (29,028 ft), in the world. Later, a crescent delta was formed at between the Rakhaing Roma and the Bay of Bengal.

6.4.1. Her Origin. Based upon our chronicles, archaeology, regional histories, and *my own experience* in Burma, Bangladesh, and India I believe that my Rakkhapura kingdom originated around BC 3000 (some 5,000 years ago), as part of Brahmaputra Civilization. It prospered in parallel with Indus Civilization of the western India, Ganges Civilization of north central India and Deccan (*dakshina,* Sanskrit meaning south) Civilization of south India some 5000 years ago. With the retreat of Himalayan Glaciers as the climate warmed, these Civilizations emerged some 10,000 years ago, reaching a peak some 3000-5000 years later. The Brahmaputra Civilization is the most neglected, least explored, and is overshadowed by the Ganges Civilization. Rakkhapura probably originated as a defense outpost of Brahmaputra Civilization. Present day Indian word *'Bharat Rakshak'* (Indian Military), and Bengali words *'Proti-Rokkha'* (National Defense) and *'rokkhi bahini'* (Defense Militia) strongly testify that *'Rokkha'*[1] and its variant *"Rakkha"* means military *'defense'*. The word *'Rakkha'* is Pali version of Sanskrit *'Rakshak'.* whereas *'Pura',* or its variant *'Para'*, is a well known word meaning 'land', 'township', 'village', 'settlement', etc. Thus, *'Rakkhapura'* originally must have been a *defense village* or *military outpost*. It probably was later upgraded to a *Rajadom* under the patronage of a *Maharaja* or by a rebel prince of the *Brahmaputra* Civilization. In the course of literacy evolution *'Rakkha'* mutates expressing its meaning as *'Patriot'*. Today, in Rakhaing and Burmese language *'Rakkhita Tara'* means the *'duty of patriotism'*. On the other side of the coin, it is remarkable to note that the Bangali got their name from the Mongolians. The Bangladeshi intellectuals believe that the name Bangal itself derives from a Mongolian word 'Vanga' or 'Banga' meaning flat plains. Bangali means 'people of the plains'. This tallies with a Mongolian Rakhaing word *'ban'*, which means a flat tray. The word *ban* is also used in such terms as *'laong ban'* meaning flat plate and *'Lan Ban'* meaning 'roads and plains'. *Banga* (i.e. ban + ga) will mean 'wide plain'. This shows existence of a cultural relationship in the region long before the days of recorded history.

6.4.2. Her Peoples. The peoples who are arbitrarily called as the Indo-Aryans, the Dravidians and the Mongolians met in this warm coastal area known as Rakkhapura, most probably during the last ice age. I would like to call them the Rakkhapureans. The descendents of these ancient Rakkhapureans constitute the Rakhaing Nation or today's Rakkhapureans. The name 'Rakhaing' is a derivative of the Pali word 'Rakkhi', or its variant

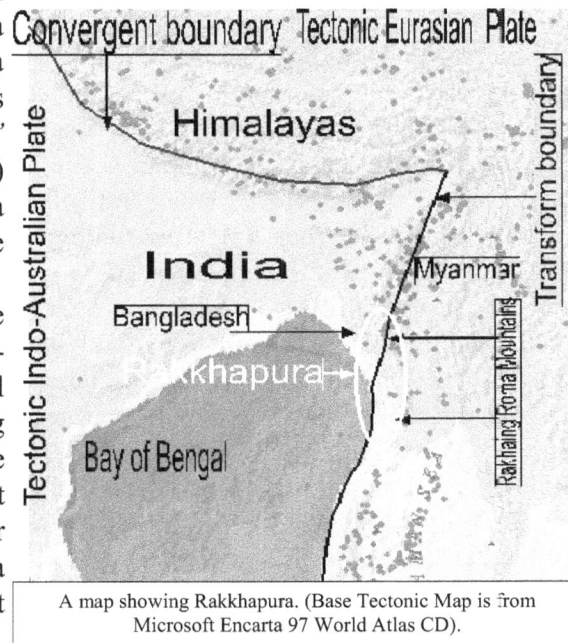

A map showing Rakkhapura. (Base Tectonic Map is from Microsoft Encarta 97 World Atlas CD).

Notes. 1. Here, editor Sabiha Khan made a note that says,"We use this word in everyday language as well without any military meaning attached. e.g. 'The dcotor Bacchaki Rokkha Korlo' means 'The doctor saved the child'." Bangla is Sabiha's mother tongue.

pronunciation 'Rokkhi', which originally means a 'soldier or militia'. It is also interesting to note Bangladesh archaeological history that states that the origin of the Bangali is from "three ethnic groups of Ariyan, Drabid and Mongolian tribes dates back to some 10,000 years". (Please visit Ethnological Museum at Chittagong.)

Today, the Rakhaing peoples inside Myanmar are officially classified as the Rakhine races under the racial Myanmarism, which in made up of 135 races. In 1947-48 the British colonial masters divided the land into three geographical parts, 75% inside the Union of Burma (Myanmar), 15% inside East Pakistan (now Bangladesh), and 10% inside India. People of the Rakhaing Nation inside Bangladesh and India live the life of the most neglected minorities at the backwater of these countries. The Rakhaing inside Myanmar are nothing more than the colonial slaves in the context of 21st. century civilization. But, their ego is still very big.

6.4.3. Historical Internationalism. A Bangladeshi intellectual Dr. Fasiuddin Mahtab, D.Sc., a former minister of the Ministry of National Planning during President Ershad's regime, once told me in 1986, "See, Longyi culture ends in Bengal; it will be very interesting to study it". Only then, I noticed for the first time that Longyi culture begins in Philippine and south pacific islands and ends in Bengal of South Asia. As such, wedged between the South Asia and Southeast Asia, our land is the meeting as well as melting point of the two subcontinental cultures, with the rounds of wars and interludes of peace resulting in cultural integration amidst hatred. Last 600 years of our land had a history of turmoil although our ancestors were able to hold it strong for some two hundred years. Heavy burden of defense against the advancing Mogul Muslim Empire and the menace of Myanmar Imperialism exhausted our national resources, both in terms of manpower and natural resources. In 1666, the Mogul Empire seized our western territory, consisting of Chittagong and its Hill Tracts. In 1784, the Myanmar Empire brutally occupied our main land of Rakkhapura. In that brutal and savage invasion the Bama Nation killed 250,000 or a quarter of our total population. Another 100,000 were chained and driven to Mandalay. My grandparents and parents told me that only women and children of both my maternal and paternal ancestral clan survived the war, and I was born in a village that was built on the last battle ground by my matriarchal ancestor who lost her husband in that battle. (Please cross reference to Chapter 4.8.) The most painful event was that the Rakkhapurean captives had to carry their Maha Mrat Muni Rakhaing Buddha, the greatest booty of the Bama, to Mandalay. Since then Rakhaing Buddha has been kept as the Prisoner of Mandalay. It will be 221 years on the 31st December 2005.

The Myanmarese occupation of Rakkhapura nakedly violated the 1454-border Agree-ment of my Rakkhapurean King Mun Khari *alias* Ali Khan and Myanmar Ava King Narapati. The two sovereign kings signed the border demarcation agreement with due recognition and respect of each other's sovereignty and territorial integrity in April 1454 CE (Rakkhapurean era: the 6 waxing day of TannKhone 816 RE). They met at the Mount Nway Cho Pho Khaung of Rakhaing Roma Ridge and the border demarcation line was drawn along the crest of Rakhaing Roma Ridge, from the Northern tip down to Mawtin Edge (Cape Negris) at the south into Bay of Bengal. The oceanic island, Haigri, is included in the Rakkhapurean territories. Violating this border agreement Myanmar King Bodaw Maung Wyne annexed Rakkhapura in 1784, under the eyewitness of the British East India Authorities. Upon the victory of the First Anglo-Burman War, Rakkapura was handed over to the British as per Rantapo Treaty signed by the British and the Myanmar on the 24th February 1826. In that Rantapo Treaty, the territory of our Rakhapura was defined according to the 1454-border agreement signed our Arakanese King Mun Khari and Myanmar Ava King Narapati. The British called Rakkhapura in her Persian name *Arakan*. In

> ### A treasure of Rakhaing Nation
> A Rakhaing gold coin in archaic Rakhaing script. At the top is 1014 Rakhaing Era, the year of accession. The second line probably bears the title of the king. I am pretty sure that the third and the fourth lines make up *'San-da-thu-dhamma-raza'* (r.1014-1046 Rakhaing Era, 1652-1684 CE). The another side of the coin bears the same writing, but shows more wearing.

1947-48 Rakkapura was divided into three parts as described above. (**A question:** Under the violation of the 1454 Rakkapura-Myanmar border treaty can the Rakkhapureans bring their case to the United Nations or to the International Court of Justice?).

Today, once again, with the change of the regional and international affairs, the Rakkhapureans face the danger of total annihilation and extinction. In the international arena, revival of Pan-Islam is observed in every part of the world, including in the United States and Europe. With the rise of Islamic States in the Middle East and former Soviet Union, the glory of the Mogul Islamic Empire has been prominently rekindled in Bangladesh for last 10 years. Chittagong presently is the center of Pan-Islamic activities in the region. The Myanmar Imperial power was revived in Burma in 1962 and strengthened in 1988. Thus history is repeating again, endangering the ancient land Rakkhapura. History has shown that *Pan-Islam or Myanmar Imperialism spares no one*. Rakkhapura along with her people faces the last stand. Having been caught in the crossfire of the Muslim-Buddhist War, they do not know what is to be done. Her chance of survival will depend upon her tact and intelligence simply because she has no other strength, but only love for her land and her people. This is a struggle for their simple existence.

The prevailing Muslim-Buddhist war in Arakan is a cold war, characterized by the words and actions of alienation towards each other. The Muslims claim that the name of the land in Rosang, or Rohong, and her people are known as Rohongya. The Rohingya is a corrupted Myamarese dialect. I incline to believe that the term *Rasang* or *Rosang* is the derivative of the Sanskrit word *Rakshak* whereas the word Rakhaing or Rakhine is the Pali version as mentioned the earlier section 6.4.1. 'Her Origin'. The Rakhaingthars charge the Rohingyas are the illegal Bengali immigrant from East Pakistan, which is now Bangladesh, and prepare to contain them in a style of neo-Nazism.

Therefore, Muslim-Buddhist war in Arakan is a war of alienation of each other on the basis of (1) lingua-ethnic , and (2) religio-ethnic differences. This has its roots in the past history that may not be seen by a historian, but can be visible to a political analyst. I will list the significant historical events that have led to this communal division in this small crescent coast of the Bengal Bay.

6.5. Lingua-Ethnic Division. The Rohingyas speak Chittagonian Bengali, which is a synthesis of Bengali and Arabic, whereas the Rakhaing language is a Pali-based Mongolian dialect. Gautama Buddha used Pali in his teaching. Pali was the language of the commoners as an easier version of Sanskrit, which was used by the Vedic Brahmin priests of his time in 6th century before the common era (BCE). Thus a new religion in a new language emerged some 2600 years ago, defying the priestly class. In the course of time, the Pali version of Buddhist Cannons spread to Sri Lanka and Southeast Asia whereas its Sanskrit version remain in India and also disseminated to the Far Eastern countries such as China and Japan. As a result, the languages of Sri Lanka and Southeast Asian nations have their origin in Pali. Similarly, the Rakhaing language is a derivative of ancient Pali. Bengali language appears to me somewhere between Sanskrit and Pali, even though the scholars say it had roots in Sanskrit. In Vrandra Museum, in the city of Rashahid, northern Bangladesh, I saw a chart depicting pre-Bengal alphabets that are very similar to those of Rakhaing and Myanmar. I believe Sanskrit hybridization of Pali-based Bengal alphabets could have occurred at the fall of Pala Dynasty in the 12th century, with the revival of Sanskrit-based Brahminism over the fall of Pali-based Buddhism. This event strikingly coincided with the rise of Pali and Buddhism in the Central Burma (Pagan Era-1050-1297 CE).

As I mentioned earlier Rakkhapura is the meeting point of the South and Southeast Asia. Thus we have this division of peoples in the line of languages in this land. The language-based division becomes more complicated with the arrivals of the Arabs and later the Qu'ran, the Bible of Islam. The international trade in the Bay of Bengal has brought the seafaring Arabs to south and Southeast Asia since before the time of Islam. The Bengal port Chittagong has been there more than two millenniums. In this port area the Arab traders and sailors settled and a new dialect, which is a synthesis of Bengali and Arabic developed. This is known as Chittagonian dialect in Bangladesh. This Chittagonian Bengali dialect is the language of the Rohingya, with a tint of Arabic. One of its distinct characteristics is the word 'ya'. It is used as a suffix to the name of a place to identify its people, for example Dhakaya means people of Dhaka. In our case Rohingya means peoples of Rohang. Again, Rohingya is the Myanmarese pronunciation of Rohangya. The Chittagonian suffix 'ya' is equivalent to the 'thar' of the Rakhaings and Myanmarese, for example Dhaka-thar, Rakhaing-thar, Mandalay-thar, etc. If you speak some Bengali, Rakhaing and Myanmar (Bama) dialects it will be easier to understand this language complications. It is complicated as you can see and under such complication of language-based ethnicity there is a division of peoples in Arakan forming two major communities known as the Rohingya and the Rakhaing. Ironically, though, both terms 'Rohingya' and 'Rakhaingthar' refer to the people of the country that is known as Rakkhapura or Rakhaingpray or Arakan depending on the ethnic bias. Since Chittagong and its hill tracts were under the rule the Rakhaing kings for two hundred years from 1460 to 1666 it is natural that there would and will be a good number of Chittagonians everywhere inside Arakan or Rakkhapura. Based on their dialect they call themselves the Rohingyas, which simply translates into Rakhaingthars in the Pali-based Mongolian dialect. Unfortunately, the lingua-ethnic diversity forms a source of hatred and war, which is compounded by the differences in religious belief.

6.6. Religio-Ethnic Division: the Magh and the Kala. The Rohingyas are the Muslims while the Rakhaings are the Buddhists. The Rohingyas and the Bengalis discriminate against the Rakhaingthars as the *Magh(s)* or *Maghi(s)*, while the latter despised the formers as the *Kala(s)*. Let us talk about the Magh first. The discrimination under the term of Magh is a sharp two-pronged attack.

6.6.1. The Maghs. In Bengali language 'magh' means 'pirates'. The Rakhaings used to raids the Bengal delta in the early days of 16th century. A Bengal historian Shihabuddin Talish recorded that: "They (the Rakhaings) carried off the Hindus and Muslims, male and females, great and small, few and many that they could seize, pierced the palms of their hands, passed thins canes through the holes and threw them one above another under the deck of their ships". This is cited by a Chittagong University history professor Alamgir M. Serajuddin in his article *Muslim influence in Arakan and the Muslim names of Arakanese kings*, Journal of Asiatic Society of Bangladesh (humanity) Vol. XXXI (1), June 1986. This is a well-known fact that I knew since I was small in my Rakhaing land. The captives were sold as slaves to the Portuguese and Dutch in the Malay Peninsula and Java-Sumatra islands, where rubber and spice

Rakkapura is a hidden archaeological treasure and more

The historians refer our Rakkhapura as the 'lost kingdom'. It is also a hidden treasure of the archaeologists, as revealed by the following piece of news recently dispatched by Narajara News. I know, I have walked above the city many times. In 1966, when I went underground to join Bo Gri Kra Hla Aung's revolutionary party, his agent Aung Tha Hla (not real name), came and picked me up in front of Maha Mrat Muni Buddha Image (Replica). As we walked out of the temple complex and crossed the open field towards the revolutionary headquarter, Ranchaung, he said, "Shwe Lu Maung, we are walking in the land of Dhannyawadi now". Existence of Dhannyawadi City is a well-known fact to the local people there. In order to appreciate ancient Rakkhapura one must not only read the Sir Arthur P. Phyare's *History of Burma* (London: Trübner & Co., 1883), but also visit the Rakhine State inside Myanmar as well as the Rakhaing land which is in the southeastern Bangladesh. I have here hypothesized that Rakkhapura was part of the greater Brahmaputtra Civilization that existed in parallel with Indus Civilization of western India, Ganges Civilization of north central India and Deccan (derived from *dakshina,* Sanskrit meaning south) Civilization of south India some 5000 years ago. I am pretty sure the word Dhannyawadi means *the land of rice.* Today there is a subdivision known as Dhanmondi, which means *rice field,* in Dhaka, Bangladesh. With the rise of an ethnic group, with a distinct dialect, in the name of Rohingya, it is also an Eden of the anthropologists and linguists.

Date: Thu, 20 May 2004 01:45:57 +0600
Narinjara News

The city walls of ancient Arakanese City: Dainyawaddy unearthed

Akyab, May 20: A SPDC sponsored archeological dig unearthed both outer and inner walls of the Dainya Waddy city in Arakan state, in west Burma.

The remains of Dainyawadday lay 300 yards south of Mahamuni Buddhist Temple in Kyawk Taw Township. According to the Arakanese chronicle, the ancient city existed between 3,325 BC and 326 AD. The archeologists only dug 3 feet into the ground to reveal about 200 yards of the east-west double wall of the ancient city.

According to a monk who has visited the site, the east-west city wall could be about 3 miles long, but the dig has not finished yet. Even though the Burmese Archeological Department is doing the dig as part of a program, it is not a systematic archeological survey. Local residents are asked to do the digging, and this could lead to the ancient artifacts been destroyed.

A Similar program of archeological excavation in Arakan was conducted on the site of Way Tha Lee City (Vasali existed between 327-818 AD), between 1979 and 1984. From this dig many artifacts including gold and silver coins, city walls, and foundations of a monastery, a 3,500 square feet building, and some stone inscriptions were found. #

For further information, please contact Narinjara:
Phone: 880 189 255 018 (Mobile)
E-mail: narinjar@aitlbd.net

plantations were very big business of the time. The medieval Rakhaings conducted the piracy in collaboration with the Portuguese. Please note that the time frame is the same as the African slave trade in the American continent. It was patronized by the Rakhaing kings as a tactical operation to check the advancement of Mogol Empire. It was a wrong tactic, which greatly annoyed the Mogol Empire, resulting in its annexation of Chittagong province of the Arakan Empire during the Shah Shuja's crisis in 1666 CE.

On the other hand, a place known as Maghbazar (Magh Bazar) is a millenium old settlement of the Maghis inside Bangladesh. It now is a central district of Greater Dhaka, about 7 km (5 miles) away from old Dhaka. It is a very old settlement, believed to be a trade transit river port between Maghadha and its southeastern territories and overseas trade. It is totally improbable that this Maghbazar would mean 'pirate market place'. This leads to the second meaning of Magh.

Second, it is the synonym of the peoples of Maghadha, which is now known as Bihar[1] in India. The kingdom of Maghadha flourished from 6th century BCE to 12th century CE, spanning through Maurya, Gupta, and Pala dynasties, covering a period of 1,800 years. Its pre-Maurya king, Bimbisara (r. 543-491 BCE), who patronized Buddha and his Sangha, was the first Buddhist king in the history. Emperor Asoka the Great (b.304?, r.269-232 BCE), the third king of Maurya Dynasty, is the best known Maghadha ruler. His empire expanded to Persian border in the west. He became a Buddhist and sent Buddhist missions all over the world, and Buddhist historical records show that it reached as far as Egypt. Asoka Pillars are also found in Afghanistan. Today, India's national insignia is Asoka Lions. These historical facts remind me of the biblical wise men from the east, known as the Maghis who came to see baby Jesus. Could they also have their origin in Maghadha?

How far to the south and southeast Maghadha Empire extended is not well recorded. it is reasonable to believe that Bengal and Rakkhapura would also be under the influence of Maghadha Empire, if not part of it. In my childhood my parents took and showed me the ruins of the palaces and even an Asoka Water Reservoir which was said to be made by the Emperor Asoka the Great (b.304?, r.269-232 BCE) of Magadha. Relationship of my Rakkhapura Kingdom and Emperor Asoka is not known except for an interesting fact that, even today, the Bengalis call us Magh or Maghi, meaning the peoples of Magadha. According to the Buddhist chronicles, Emperor Asoka built 48,000 water wells, 48,000 water reservoirs, and 48,000 pagodas, across his vast empire. There is also a place that the local people claim to have existed an Asoka Pa-hto. A pagoda that have an entrance into its interior chamber is called a Pa-hto. I also know of another still existing pagoda, which our local historians claimed to have built by Emperor Asoka. I am not identifying it here with fear that the Myanmarese authorities might destroy it[2]. Most of the ancient Rakkhapura historical heritage have been destroyed by the ruling Myanmarese.

6.6.2. The Kala. The word 'Kala' is a term equivalent to 'nigger' in America. The Rakhaing/Myanmarese word 'Kala' is means 'foreigner'. It is a noun and written as 'Kula', but pronounced 'Kala'. Its counter part adjective form is 'Kulâ', which means 'international'. For example, the United Nations is called *Kulâ Thamagâ*. The Rakhaings and the Myanmarese call

---

Notes.
1. Bihar is the derivative of Vihar or Vihara, Buddhist Monastic University.
2. I am ready to tell their location if an international body is willing to guarantee security of Asoka's historical sites in Arakan.

everyone to the west of their land 'Kala'. Some of common names are Khaw-taw Kala for black Indian or Bengali, Punjabi Kala for the Punjabi, Kala Pru or White Kala for the white European. The worst form of a Kala is a Khaw-taw Kala or Black Indian/Bengali. Here comes in skin color discrimination. The Rohingyas are either Kala, if their skin color is not black, or Khaw-taw Kala when the skin color is black. This skin color discrimination is ironical because the Rakhaing's skin color shade also varies from pitch black, bright yellow to snow white, as a product of the Indo-Aryan, the Dravidian, and the Mongolian races, as I described earlier. The worst part is that the Rohingyas are discriminated as the illegal immigrants. Therefore in its secondary meaning a Kala means an illegal immigrant.

This alienation angers the Rohingyas who proudly present themselves as the descendants of those Muslims, who were the founding partners of Mrauk-U Dynasty in 1430 CE and Arakan Empire from 1430 to 1784. When I analyze the rise of the Arakan Empire I have no doubt that the Bengali Muslims greatly contributed to the Rakhaing imperial glory. The wealth of the Arakan Empire was earned through the Chittagong, which was (and still is) the major international port city in the South and Southeast Asia. Her army was manned by Muslims. Her king was served by the Bengali Muslim ministers. In return, the Rakhaing Buddhist kings adorned Muslim titles and minted gold coins bearing the Muslim faith, *Kalima*. On the other hand, the Rakhaings are upset by the Bengali chauvinistic discrimination against them as the primitive tribal people (e.g. Alamgir M. Serajuddin, a professor of history, Chittagong University, in his article, Muslim Influence In Arakan and the Muslim Names of the Arakanese Kings, published in the journal of Asiatic Society Bangladesh (Hum.), Vol. XXXI (I), June 1986)[1]. In anguish with crushed ego, the Rakhaings charge them as the infiltrators who settled in their land when their land was part of India during the British rule from 1826 to 1948. They also accuse them of being illegal immigrants from East Pakistan and Bangladesh into newly independent Burma. Accordingly, General Ne Win's military socialist regime drove out more than 200,000 Rohingyas into Bangladesh in 1978. Moulvi Nur Ahmad documented this exodus in his small book *History of Arakan (Burma)*, that was published by the Department of Dawah, World Muslim Congress, Karachi, 1978. Later, in 1991 again, some 250,000 Rohingyas were pushed out of Myanmarese Rakhine State into Bangladesh, accused as the illegal immigrants. In both occasions, Bangladesh sought international intervention presenting the case at the United Nations. The United Nations High Commission for Refugees (UNHCR) investigated the matters in cooperation with the Myanmarese authorities and established that most of the Rohingyas are truly the citizens of Myanmar. Accordingly, under the world pressure the Myanmarese government accepted their repatriation. In a recent news from Kaladan Press, the UNHCR and Bangladesh authorities plan forcefully repatriation of some remaining 20,000 Rohingyas who refuse to return Myanmar in fear of prosecution, forced labor, and utter discrimination. Therefore, it has been proven that the Rohingyas are the legal citizens of Myanmar by the UNHCR, a well-respected international body under the United Nations.

This business of the Magh and the Kala surely is a historical time bomb, which is ticking amidst the political chaos of Bangladesh and Burma to explode into a full-fledged Muslim-Buddhist war in near future.

Notes.

1. A section of the Chittagonians are regretful that they are ruled by the foreigners throughout the history. They also consider the Dhakayas (Dhaka people) foreigners. They prefer to call themselves Chittagonians, but not Bengalis.

6.7. The Rise of Rohingya Nationalism. *"To every action there is an equal and opposite reaction."* The fore-mentioned Newton's *Third Law of Motion* is a household word these days. One does not need to go to school to know it. Launching of the Rohingya nationalism is the Burmese Muslim's struggle to escape from the modern slavery as *the Kala*. The Rohingyas came to its first official record in 1958 when the Mujahids gave up their armed insurrection in exchange for Rohingya nationalism in 1958. The Muslim separatist's armed-insurrection rose soon after the independence with the intent of annexing Muslim-dominant areas such as Maungdaw and Buthidaung Townships with the erstwhile Pakistan. Please do not count on my words for this statement. Please read Prime Minister U Nu's autobiography *U Nu, Satruday's Son* (New Haven: Yale University Press, 1975). Credit goes to U Nu for the peaceful settlement of the conflict, and General Ne Win for his implementation of the peace agreement in 1958.

The Muslim separatists called themselves 'the Mujahids'. It was a time of chaos. It was a time of civil war. The Mujahids were just a part of more than a dozen armed insurrections that counted the communists, the Rakhaings, the Karennis, and the Karens as well. This Mujahid separatist rebellion is a legend that never dies. It officially abandoned armed struggle upon the Rangoon government's recognition of its ethnic identity, the Rohingya, in 1958. General Ne Win was the head of government as the prime minister in the so-called caretaker government, in 1958-1960. It was Brig. General Aung Gyi, Vice-Chief of Staff of the Burmese Armed Forces, who accepted the surrender of the Mujahids in exchange of the Rohingya identity, as a national race of the Union of Burma. The 1962 military coup and establishment of a Revolutionary government erased all traces of pre-1962 Union of Burma. The Socialist Republic of Union of Burma was established under the 1974 Military Socialist Constitution. With the infamous King Dragon operation more than 200,000 Rohingyas were driven out of Burma into Bangladesh in 1978, with the accusation that they were the illegal Bengali immigrants. Under the pressure of the international community they were repatriated in 1979 and 1980, but Burma Citizenship Act of 1982 erased off their citizenship.

The 1978 Muslim exodus into Bangladesh brought Muslim's armed struggle into life again and a number of Rohingya armed organizations emerged. However, Rohingya majority did not favor violence and the armed struggle was barely simmering with less than hundred men, in contrast to the forty thousand armed personnel boasted by the combined forces of the Mao Thai, the Shan, the Wa, the Karen, or the Kachin, and the Karenni Armies. Nevertheless, they used the mass communication media very effectively and gained international recognition. As a matter of fact, the post-1962 Rohingya's armed rebellion does not gain any support from the general Muslim populace in Burma and Arakan, and never poses a threat to the junta or law and order situation.

In the 1990 election, the Rohingyas showed their major force in the name of the National Democratic Party for Human Rights (NDPHR), contested in 17 of 26 constituencies in Arakan, and won all four seats in Buthidaung and Maungdaw townships, where they were majority. They were in a position to make alliance with the National League for Democracy (NLD), which won nine seats, and form a coalition government in the Rakhine State had the election results were honored by the military junta. I do not think that the Arakan League for Democracy (ALD), which won eleven seats, would have a chance to form the state government. The victory of the National Democratic Party for Human Rights angered the military junta and some 250,000 Rohingyas were forced out into Bangladesh in 1991. On the coming pages, I present a chart and three tables, featuring the Rohingya politics in revolution and democratic movements.

Evolution of the Rohingya's armed insurrection and democratic movement

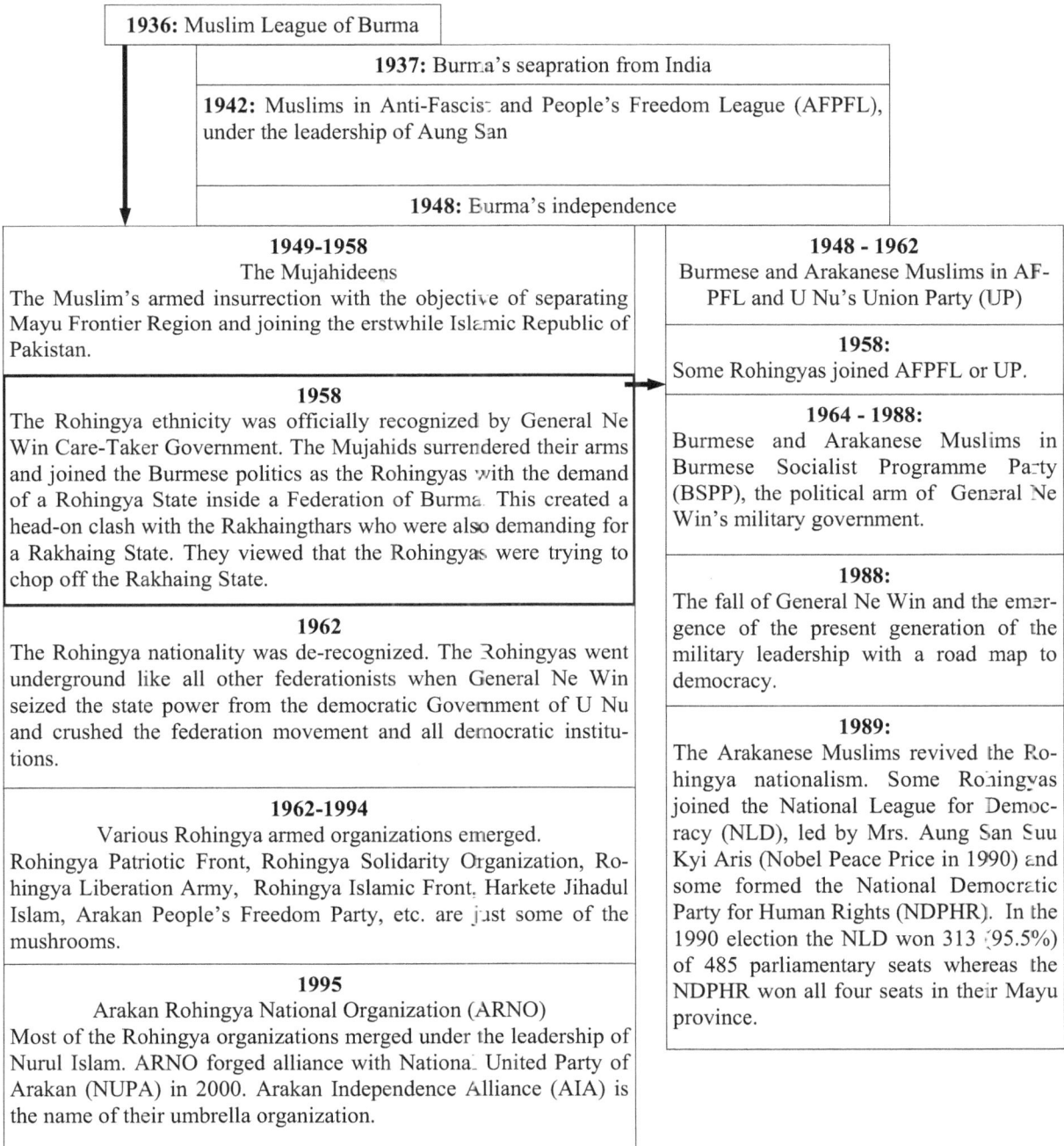

1936: Muslim League of Burma

1937: Burma's seapration from India

1942: Muslims in Anti-Fascist and People's Freedom League (AFPFL), under the leadership of Aung San

1948: Burma's independence

1949-1958
The Mujahideens
The Muslim's armed insurrection with the objective of separating Mayu Frontier Region and joining the erstwhile Islamic Republic of Pakistan.

1958
The Rohingya ethnicity was officially recognized by General Ne Win Care-Taker Government. The Mujahids surrendered their arms and joined the Burmese politics as the Rohingyas with the demand of a Rohingya State inside a Federation of Burma. This created a head-on clash with the Rakhaingthars who were also demanding for a Rakhaing State. They viewed that the Rohingyas were trying to chop off the Rakhaing State.

1962
The Rohingya nationality was de-recognized. The Rohingyas went underground like all other federationists when General Ne Win seized the state power from the democratic Government of U Nu and crushed the federation movement and all democratic institutions.

1962-1994
Various Rohingya armed organizations emerged.
Rohingya Patriotic Front, Rohingya Solidarity Organization, Rohingya Liberation Army, Rohingya Islamic Front, Harkete Jihadul Islam, Arakan People's Freedom Party, etc. are just some of the mushrooms.

1995
Arakan Rohingya National Organization (ARNO)
Most of the Rohingya organizations merged under the leadership of Nurul Islam. ARNO forged alliance with National United Party of Arakan (NUPA) in 2000. Arakan Independence Alliance (AIA) is the name of their umbrella organization.

1948 - 1962
Burmese and Arakanese Muslims in AFPFL and U Nu's Union Party (UP)

1958:
Some Rohingyas joined AFPFL or UP.

1964 - 1988:
Burmese and Arakanese Muslims in Burmese Socialist Programme Party (BSPP), the political arm of General Ne Win's military government.

1988:
The fall of General Ne Win and the emergence of the present generation of the military leadership with a road map to democracy.

1989:
The Arakanese Muslims revived the Rohingya nationalism. Some Rohingyas joined the National League for Democracy (NLD), led by Mrs. Aung San Suu Kyi Aris (Nobel Peace Price in 1990) and some formed the National Democratic Party for Human Rights (NDPHR). In the 1990 election the NLD won 313 (95.5%) of 485 parliamentary seats whereas the NDPHR won all four seats in their Mayu province.

Table 6.1. The voting pattern in the Myanmar Election-1990, in the Arakan State. A Statewide figure of 73.04% voters turnout indicates the enthusiasm of the people for democracy.

Sl. No.	Constituency	Eligible voters	Votes cast	Valid votes	Voters turnout %	No. of Candidates
Con1	Saitetwey 1	49,899	36,441	30,332	73.03	8
Con2	Saitetwey 2	54,617	35,995	29,640	65.90	10
Con3	Munbra 1	40,237	27,084	22,286	67.31	7
Con4	Munbra 2	37,764	25,233	20,431	66.82	6
Con5	Pauktaw 1	31,257	20,294	15,356	64.93	4
Con6	Pauktaw 2	29,819	15,376	10,857	51.56	6
Con7	Kyautaw 1	48,809	35,172	27,620	72.06	7
Con8	Kyautaw 2	49,307	36,575	28,500	74.18	5
Con9	Maungdaw 1	87,174	72,633	64,019	83.32	7
Con10	Maungdaw 2	84,166	68,440	58,230	81.32	7
Con11	Buthidaung 1	58,449	46,065	41,668	78.81	7
Con12	Buthidaung 2	55,095	46,037	40,143	83.56	8
Con13	Ponnakyaun	54,968	44,396	37,331	80.77	6
Con14	Rethedaung 1	35,108	25,118	19,626	71.54	5
Con15	Rethedaung 2	33,843	23,629	18,918	69.82	6
Con16	Mrauk-U 1	43,550	33,173	27,900	76.17	5
Con17	Mrauk-U 2	44,524	32,026	27,200	71.93	6
Con18	Kyaukpru 1	38,660	26,831	21,834	69.40	5
Con19	Kyaukpru 2	39,697	27,439	20,958	69.12	4
Con20	Thandwe	67,679	53,398	46,402	78.90	6
Con21	Ann	46,770	26,081	19,945	55.76	4
Con22	Man Aung	42,170	32,996	27,161	78.25	6
Con23	Gwa	36,589	27,363	22,461	74.78	4
Con24	Rambre	59,883	42,095	35,656	70.30	5
Con25	Mrepon	45,361	31,221	25,031	68.83	4
Con26	Taungup	63,319	42,904	35,740	67.76	4
	Total	1,278,714	934,015	775,245	73.04	152

Calculation of the Rohingya Muslim population in the light of the data given in the 1990 election results published by the Myanmar Election Commission in June-July, 1990

(Please see the Tables 6.1, 6.2, and 6.3 for the figures used here. The 1990 election results were not honored by the military junta and there has been no election since 1990.)

The combined votes for the ND-PHR and SYLMPD represent the Rohingyas' votes, totaling 176,025 (i.e. ND-PHR 128,119 + SYLMPD 47,906) out of the Statewide sum total of 745,079, making it 23.625% of the total votes. According to the data posted at the United Nations population website http://esa.un.org/unpp/index.asp?panel=2, there were 22,908,000 persons within the age 18-100 years in the total population of 40,753,000 in Myanmar during the election year 1990. This means the eligible voters (i.e. age 18-100) constituted 56.21% of the total population. If we back-calculate using the national voters percentage 56.21% and the Rakhine state total eligible voters 1,278,714 (Table 6.2), we get a population of 2,274,887 in the Rakhine State in 1990. Now, as I mentioned earlier the Rohingya voters made up 23.625% of the total valid voters. Therefore, with good confidence, I can calculate that there would be 537,442 Rohingya population versus 1,737,445 non-Muslims in the Rakhine State in 1990. Again, in Maungdaw and Buthidaung, there are 284,884 total eligible Rohingya voters, giving a figure of 506,884 for the total Rohingya population in the given areas. In the 1953 Census Release No.3 of the Burmese government, a Muslim population of 45% in Maungdaw and 60% in Buthidaung were classified as the aliens. The Muslims, regardless of the status of their citizenship or alienage, are not allowed to move from village to village or township to township. Therefore, assuming that the population growth is the same for both the citizens and the aliens, I can comfortably conclude that there still is the same percentage of aliens in these two townships. In turn, I can calculate to get a figure of 47.75% citizens and 52.25% aliens in the area considered. This means there will be a total Muslim population of 1,061,537 (i.e. 1.1 millions approximately), consisting of 506,884 citizens and 554,653 aliens in the Maungdaw and Buthidaung townships. Furthermore, with reasonable reliability, I can conclude that there were approximately 1.5 million Muslims versus 1.7 million non-Muslims, at a ratio of 8.8 Muslims for every 10 Buddhists, in the Rakhine State in 1990. This means there were a total of 3.2 million people in the Rakhine State. In 2005, the population in Burma is around 50 millions, about 10 million increase from the 1990 figure, with an increase by a factor of 1.25. When I apply this increment factor to the 1990 Rakhine State population 3.2 millions, I get a figure of 4.0 millions, consisting of 1.87 million Rohingya Muslims and 2.13 million non-Rohingyas. The Kamen, the Mro and other small ethnic groups (Table 6.2) make up about 0.17 million. Therefore, it is reasonable to conclude that the Rohingya Muslims constitute 46.75% of the Rakhine State population, and 3.74% of the total Myanmar population in 2005. The Rakhaings form 1.96 million, which is 49% of the Rakhine State and 3.9% of Myanmar populations.

Table 6.2. The political parties that competed in the Rakhine State of 1990 national election. The Rohingyas are in the National Democratic Party for Human Rights (NDPHR), Student and Youth League for Mayu Province Development (SYLMPD), and National League for Democracy (NLD).

Sl. No.	Political Parties Competed	Seats Won	State-wise result		
			Total Votes won	% of Sum Total**	
P1	National League for Democracy (NLD)	9	225,552	30.25	
P2	National Unity Party (NUP)		100,151	13.43	
P3	Arakanese Nationalities League for Democracy (ANLD)		*	*	
P4	Arakanese People's Democractic Front (APDF)		27,620	3.7	
P5	Arakanese Natives Unity League (ANUL-Ratanya)		4,752	0.34	
P6	Arakan League for Democracy (ALD)	11	158,503	21.26	
P7	Kamen National Democracy League (KNDL)	1	10,180	1.37	
P8	National Democratic Party for Human Rights (NDPHR)	4	128,119	17.18	
P9	Arakanese League for National Development (ALND)		1,136	0.15	
P10	Native Nationalities Party for New Society (NNPNS)		717	0.1	
P11	Mro aka Kamee League for National Unity (MKLNU)	1	21,521	2.89	
P12	Chin League for Democracy (CLD)		2,889	0.39	
P13	Party for Democracy and Peace (PDP)		5,662	0.76	
P14	Peasants Unity Party (PUP)		3,304	0.44	
P15	Student and Youth League for Mayu Province Development (SYLMPD)		47,906	6.42	
P16	United Nationalities Party (UNP)		2,177	0.29	
P17	Natives Unity Party (NUP)		4,498	0.6	
P18	National Party		392	0 05	
P19	Youth Unity Party (YUP)		*		
P20	Democracy Party		*		
P21	Independents		*		
	Total number of people Representatives elected	26			
	**Sum total (total votes attributed to the parties)		745,079		

* No data given in the Election Commission publication I had in my hand. As per my calculation the total valid votes sum up to 775,245. Please see Table 3. However, the total valid votes attributed to the parties count only 745,079. There is a discrepancy of 10,166 votes. These votes probably belong to the smaller parties and independents that are marked with '*' in the table.

NDPHR (in exile). Arif Hussain *alias* Hla Aung is the President of the National Democratic Party for Human Rights (in exile) that was formed in 2003. He was one of the founding members of NDPHR in 1988/1989 and the Secretary-2 of Arakan State party Unit. He was also the Affiliated Candidate for U Tin Maung, elected member from the Buthidaung Constituency 2, in the 1990 election. In the photo, along with Bikhu Ashin U Kumara (a refugee and NLD supporter) and Mr. Farid, Chairman of Info-Birmanie, a NGO working for the interest of democracy in Burma, Mr. Arif is seen speaking in the 2005 Birthday celebration of Nobel Laureate Mrs. Aung San Suu Kyi Aris, in France. NDPHR (in exile) has its members in (1) France, (2) Holland, (3) England, (4) Germany, (5) Switzerland, (6) Denmark, (7) Norway, (8) Malaysia, (9) Saudi Arabia, (10) Bangladesh, and (11) UAE.

Table 6.3. The popular votes netted by the political parties in the 1990 Myanmar Election, in the Rakhine State. Bold letters indicate the winning votes. The indexes of the parties and constituencies are given.

	P1	P2	P4	P5	P6	P7	P8	P9	P10	P12
Con1	2,547	2,891	4,916	303	8,166	**9,821**				
Con2	2,712	3,661	5,560	382	**8,819**	359	7,122		70	
Con3	965	3,800	699		**12,301**		3,292	1,136		
Con4		2,871	1,522		**11,899**					2,889
Con5	1,855	2,744	1,541		**9,216**					
Con6	2,995	1,823	1,133		**3,528**					

	P1	P2	P5	P6	P8	P10	P11	P13	P14	P15	P16
Con7			1,306	**12,937**	4,781	647		4,037	3,304		
Con8	4,893	5,252	1,489				**15,801**				
Con9	672	3,046		3,508	**32,620**					12,309	2,177
Con10	2,221	3,746		2,210	**24,881**					24,203	
Con11	2,049	3,933		3,717	**30,997**						
Con12		3,387		4,235	**20,045**					11,394	

	P1	P2	P4	P5	P6	P8	P11	P19
Con13	7,509	9,303	3,389		**14,251**		2,634	
Con14	**7,310**	3,829			6,063			1,960
Con15	5,300	3,774			**7,987**			
Con16	2,639	4,539		314	**17,322**		3,086	
Con17	2,415	4,574			**14,861**	4,381		
Con18	**14,848**	2,903	3,041					

	P1	P2	P4	P5	P6	P13	P17	P18
Con19	**16,289**	2,100	2,177					
Con20	**36,789**	8,196						392
Con21	**13,379**	3,026	2,121		1,419			
Con22	**17,781**	5,786			2,430	387		
Con23	**15,931**	4,800				1,238		
Con24	**28,322**		1,521		962		4,498	
Con25	8,700	4,610		958	**10,763**			
Con26	**27,431**	5,557			1,909			

Index of the Constituencies	
Con1	Saitetwey 1
Con2	Saitetwey 2
Con3	Munbra 1
Con4	Munbra 2
Con5	Pauktaw 1
Con6	Pauktaw 2
Con7	Kyautaw 1
Con8	Kyautaw 2
Con9	Maungdaw 1
Con10	Maungdaw 2
Con11	Buthidaung 1
Con12	Buthidaung 2
Con13	Ponnakyaun
Con14	Rethedaung 1
Con15	Rethedaung 2
Con16	Mrauk-U 1
Con17	Mrauk-U 2
Con18	Kyaukpru 1
Con19	Kyaukpru 2
Con20	Thandwe
Con21	Ann
Con22	Man Aung
Con23	Gwa
Con24	Rambre
Con25	Mrepon
Con26	Taungup

Index of the Political Parties	
P1	National League for Democracy (NLD)
P2	National Unity Party (NUP)
P3	Arakanese Nationalities League for Democracy (ANLD)
P4	Arakanese People's Democractic Front (APDF)
P5	Arakanese Natives Unity League (ANUL-Ratanya)
P6	Arakan League for Democracy (ALD)
P7	Kamen National Democracy League (KNDL)
P8	National Democratic Party for Human Rights (NDPHR)
P9	Arakanese League for National Development (ALND)
P10	Native Nationalities Party for New Society (NNPNS)
P11	Mro aka Kamee League for National Unity (MKLNU)
P12	Chin League for Democracy (CLD)
P13	Party for Democracy and Peace (PDP)
P14	Peasants Unity Party (PUP)
P15	Student and Youth League for Mayu Province Development (SYLMPD)
P16	United Nationalities Party (UNP)
P17	Natives Unity Party (NUP)
P18	National Party
P19	Youth Unity Party (YUP)
P20	Democracy Party
P21	Independents

The Rohingya's demand for rightful citizenship, on equal footing with any other people in Myanmar, is legitimate under the 1947 constitution of the Union of Burma, and the world sympathetically renders its support. Similarly, their demand for due recognition of their ethnic identity, 'Rohingya', is legitimate as per 1958 agreement between them and the Myanmar government and they are recognized by the United Nations and all its member nations, except Myanmar. The more oppressed by the Myanmarese and the Rakhaings the stronger the Rohingya's politics becomes in such a formidable manner that they are now seen as a threat to the Myanmarese culture by the ruling Myanmar military junta as well as by the Rakhaing political forces.

6.8. Oppression and Segregation. The Rohingyas are the most oppressed people of Myanmar and Arakan. Their struggle is for the liberation from the oppressed life. However, with the rise of the Rohingya nationalism, the history of the Mujahids, the recent renaissance of Pan-Islam and Islamic fundamentalism they are charged as the Islamic fundamentalists. The charge is an offshoot of the world prejudice against the Muslims. In this matter the United Kingdom has a vigorous research program and I would like the readers to consult the writings of scholars like Professor Lord Bhikhu Parekh (http://imm-live.wmin.ac.uk/sshl/page-148-smhp=1 and http://jmm.aaa.net.au/articles/1690.html), others like Abdelwahab El-Affendi, Ehsan Massod, Merryl Wyn Davies, and M. Iqbal Asaria who write articles in the journal *New Internationalist* (http://www.newint.org/issue345/democracy.htm). It is my strong belief that the Muslims of Burma are liberal and if the Burmese people treat them equal and give opportunity to adapt with the Burmese cultural mainstream there would be no Rohingya rebellion or separate political party. Here I will present some examples of my experience with the Rohingya Muslims.

6.8.1. Mohamad. Although the Muslims and the Buddhists lived a totally segregated life from each other I had Muslim friends since I was a small boy of 8-12 years old. Two of my neighbors at Munbra (Minbya) were Muslims in the period of the years 1953-1957. The judge of the civil court (*tarama tarathugri*), the township officer, and the postmaster were the Muslims. When I was at the People's Private School at Sittwe (Akyab) during the period from 1957 to 1960 I had four Muslim students as classmates. I remember them well because they, with due permission of the school, always left the class early for their compulsory *Jumma* prayers on Fridays. The parents of one of them operated a bicycle repair shop where I used to fix my bicycle free except for the parts. The name of his shop is *Mainstreet Sathii Prun Hsaing.* We used to tell him that he spelled *Sathii* wrong because we write *sebii* not *sathii* in Burmese literature since *sathii* is the Rakhaing colloquial and not used in literature. He used to argue with us saying, "What is wrong? We call *sathii*, not *sebii*. We do not speak *Bama* dialect." His name was Mohamad. It was in 1958. Now I would like to admit that he was right. He left the school in 1959 because his parents could not afford the tuition fees at the private school. He was just one of thousands of students whom the poverty took away from school. The principal of the school was Aung Hla Zan (1927-2001) who, with the ALD ticket, won the People's Representative seat of the Mrohaung constituency-1 in the 1990 election, defeating my cousin, Col. Kaung Hla Pru, the National United Party (pro-junta) candidate and a former cabinet minister in the last days of General Ne Win's rule.

6.8.2. Dr. Yunos and Nurul Islam. I would like to make clear that I am giving an account of Dr. Yunos and Nurul Islam simply because I see them as the victims of discrimination and alienation under the Myanmar ultranationalism. Since 1978 I watched their moves with much worry that they might happen to be pushed into the realm of Islamic extremists. Today, most observers classify Dr. Yunos as a religious fundamentalists and Nurul Islam as a moderate.

After matriculation in 1960 I left Sittwe[1], never to return. I got admitted at the Rangoon University as my father was stationed at Syriam, near Rangoon in 1960. In those days, Rangoon University had five campuses across the Greater Rangoon Municipality, housing a total of twelve thousand students. As a freshman science student I was at Yankin College, about five miles east of the main campus. There were a one thousand five hundred freshmen at Yankin College and Yankin Hall hosted five hundred thirty four male students from various parts of Burma. It was really exciting to meet every ethnic group of Burma, speaking in their own dialect and accent. Yankin Hall was constituted with 36 bamboo-walled, wooden floored, tin-roofed cottages, each of which houses up to 18 students, with a very large dinning-cum-assembly hall. It was a breeding ground of future military, civilian, political, and rebel leaders. Presently disgraced and imprisoned General Khin Nyunt was a Yankin College graduate, two-years senior to me.

In that breeding ground of future leaders I became a friend of a student named Yunos, who became Dr. Yunos, the President of Rohingya Solidarity Organization, and made a sensation by publishing a two-paged advertisement for the establishment of an independent People's Republic of Arakandesh in a Bangladesh newspaper in 1990. I learned that he paid Tk250,000.00 for the advertisement. The Rangoon government was mad at him and the Rakhaing people came to hate him as an arch enemy of the Rakhaing Land. He was charged as an Islamic fundamentalist and eventually he was forced to flee Bangladesh. Whenever the people blame him, I happen to defend him saying, "It was not his fault, but it was the fault of the Burmese society itself." I shall present the reasons behind my answer.

At Yankin Hall I was at the Cottage 9 and Yunos was at Cottage 34. He had to pass the Cottage 9 whenever he went to the dinning hall for breakfast, lunch and dinner. He always greeted me as he passed my cottage and time to time we chatted for a few minutes. One evening, on his way to the dinning hall he greeted me as usual and the following conversation took place.

I: "Ako Yunos, why didn't you come to the meeting?"

Yunos: "What meeting?"

I: "The Rakhaing Student Association meeting, of course."

Yunos: "Ako Shwe Lu Maung, we were not invited."

I: "Ako, everyone from the Rakhaingpray can come. There is no special invitation, but the time and date of the meeting was announced by the posters. You must have seen the posters everywhere."

Yunos: "We were not welcomed there, Ako Shwe Lu Maung."

With these sad words he left me. It made me very uncomfortable. In next few days I met the seniors and the Rakhaing Student Association officers asking them about Yunos. The common answers I got were: "The Muslims have their own organization," and "Ours is a

Notes.
1. At Sittwe, I witnessed that the Rakhaing youths treated the Muslims with contempt. It was quite common seeing the Rakhaing youths took bananas, beetle leaves, cigarettes, etc. from the Muslim's shops and went away without paying money. It was a sad sight to see that the Muslims' shops were protected with the iron netting, with a small window to deliver the goods and to receive the payments. In other words, it was like the gangster's menace at the small business. I was equally sad when I saw the Bangladeshi Rakhaings were also treated with contempt at some parts of Bangladesh. This kind of belligerence generates communal riots.

Rakhaing association; *the Kala* have their own association." Later I learned that they had the University Rohingya Student Association and also the University Muslim Student Association. I view it as a segregation. It was my view that all students who came from the Rakhaing State must be organized into the University Rakhaing Student Association because it represent the province that is known as the Rakhaing State. Even if the Rohingyas of the Rakhaing State has their own ethnic or religious association, I view that it was wrong not to take effort to bring them into the main stream of the Rakhaing State social and cultural life. Of the three districts, namely Sittwe Kyaukpyu and Sandway, I noticed that the Muslim students from the Kyauk Pyu and Sandway Districts were in the University Rakhaing Student Association; only the Muslim students from Sittwe District were absent. It, therefore, was mainly a segregation of the ethnic Rakhaing and the Rohingyas. It was this ethnic segregation that pushed Yunos to the camp of rebellion. Yunos was a good student and a bona fide citizen of Burma. As a result he got admitted to the medical school. Just like in the United States of America, only the citizens are allowed to get admitted in the professional schools like the medical, engineering, education etc. The military takeover in 1962 ignited the ethnic rebellions across the nation. Every ethnic groups of Burma, such as the Rakhaing, the Chin, the Kachin, the Shan, the Palaung, the Wa, the Mon, and the Rohingya etc., rebelled against the Rangoon government. The rebellion of the Karenni and the Karen were there since 1948. Especially, the Rohingyas were sad and angry since the government did not recognize them as an ethnic group of Burma anymore.

After graduation we drifted in our own directions. I went and joined the Arakan National United Organization (ANUO) led by Bogri Kra Hla Aung, a WWII veteran and Dr. Yunos went to his Rohingya groups. I abandoned the guerrilla camp in 1967 as I determined that it was not an effective way to change the society. Time has proven that I was right.

The 1978 King Dragon Operation flushed out all the rebels from the Rakhaing State into Bangladesh, along with 200,000 Muslim refugees. While the Rakhaing rebels, such as the Arakan Independence Organization (AIO), Arakan National Liberation Party (ANLP), and Arakan Communist Party (ACP) etc. barely survived, the Rohingyas organizations especially the Arakan Rohingya Islamic Front (ARIF) led by Nurul Islam, another Rangoon University graduate, and the Rohingya Solidarity Organization (RSO) led by Dr. Yunos, emerged strong. Their strength came from the sympathy of the Islamic Umma on the event of the 200,000 Muslim refugees. The Islamic organizations generously supported them for their education and political activities. When the Rohingyas were stripped off the Burmese citizenship under the Burma Citizenship Law (1982) the international Islamic support became stronger. They again gained a new wave of sympathy in 1992 when the Burmese junta freshly drove out 250,000 Muslims into Bangladesh. However, the support was mainly educational and political. Neither the ARIF nor RSO grew in military force. Their combined armed wing never exceeded more than one hundred fighters, a miniscule number when compared to the 180,000 fighting force of Burmese government in pre-1988 condition. Today, Burma's armed forces with a strength of 500,000 men is the largest in the Southeast Asia. For their survival, the Rohingyas factions merged as the Arakan Rohingya National Organization (ARNO) under the leadership of Nurul Islam and Dr. Yunos was isolated. After the Muslim terrorist attack of September 11, 2001, the aid flows to the Rohingya organizations came to a stop. Today, apart from their website it is hard to say they exist. Dr. Yunos is now in a Middle Eastern country whereas Nurul Islam seeking refuge in an European country.

6.8.3. Mahmud Shah and Mohd. Mohiuddin When my father was transferred to Kyaukpyu in 1962 I also moved to the Kyaukpyu College. It was a wonderful place. There were only 76 students from all Arakan. We had seven Muslim students and we got a very good opportunity to know each other. Among those who were very close to me I would like to list (1) Ako Khin Maung Yin (now a retired Captain of Burma army who lost both legs by a land mine at the Kachin front), (2) Ako Phone Kyaw (now a doctor), (3) Ako Than Aung (now a doctor), (4) Ako Kyaw Win (now a High Court Justice), (5) Ako Mahmud Shah, and (6) Ako Kyaw Hla (Mustafa Kamal). The last two were the Muslim students. You may notice that I cannot attach any profession to them.

Mahmud Shah disappeared in the 1963. I remember him as a handsome and friendly bodybuilder who loves speaking English. The College Principal, U Kyaw Khin, used to praise him for having the most handsome body in the college. In 1980s, I learned that he, depressed in anguish from discrimination and alienation, drifted away to East Pakistan, then to the Middle East working with the Palestinian Liberation Organization. Later, he became an international Mujahid fighting against the Soviet occupation in Afghanistan. After 1987, I did not get any news of him and I assume that he might have been killed during the Afghanistan liberation war.

A similar story can be attributed to another Muslim student named Maung Sein *alias* Mohd. Muhiuddin. He was compelled to leave the Sittwe College before graduation. Kyaukpyu College was closed in 1968 and reopened it in Sittwe with the new name, Sittwe College. It was a move of General Ne Win to win the hearts of the hardliner Rakhaings. The Sittwe Rakhaings objected opening of the college in Kyaukpyu with the argument that the college should be at the Rakhine State Capital, Sittwe, since its establishment in 1956. U Nu opened it at Kyaukpyu as a favor for U Ba Saw, a WWII hero and a minister in his cabinet. The Sittwe Rakhaing students boycotted Kyaukpyu College, and went to Yankin or Htidan Colleges at Rangoon, though all these colleges are under the Rangoon University. U Nu's reasoning was that Kyaukpyu was at the center of the Rakhine State, easy to reach from every corner of the State, and the law and order situation was better there. At that time, the civil war was still raging at the Sittwe District and riots between the military servicemen and the local youths were very common at Sittwe. One factor that U Nu or U Ba Saw did not mention was that the Rakhaings of Sittwe District discriminate the people from Kyaukpyu and Sandway districts, as well as the Arakanese Muslims. The discrimination was the major factor of U Nu's rejection of Sittwe as the college town. I now agree that he was right. At the Kyaukpyu College there was no discrimination, but at the Sittwe College there is discrimination; the Rakhaing-Kala (i.e. Buddhist-Muslim) riots are common. The racial discrimination faced by the Muslims of the Rakhine State is very comparable to that of the African Americans in the United States in 1950s and 1960s. After the military takeover, General Ne Win gave more favors to the Sittwe Rakhaings to strengthen his power grip. He terminated the recognition of the Rohingyas nationality. His action encouraged the Rakhaings to discriminate the Muslims as the Kalas (i.e. niggers). The constitution of United States of America, which is the supreme law of the nation, gave protection to her African American citizens. With the strength of the constitutional rights the African Americans fought against the discrimination. The echo of Dr. Martin Luther King Jr.'s "I have a dream" and George Wallace's "Segregation forever" were heard across the world. But, in Burma, the people known as the Rohingyas are constitutionally discriminated on account

Mohd. Mohiuddin

of their origin and religion. What will a person do when the nation disowns him or her on the ground of his or her origin and religion?

It was this discrimination that kicked out Maung Sein, a young college student of mathematics major, drifting across the world, in the same manner like Mahmud Shah. In search of freedom and liberation from the ruthless discrimination, he left the study and entered into the cold world with a ray of hope in 1974. He was arrested by the Bangladesh authorities and put into the Chittagong jail.

When free, he ended up in Malaysia where some 7,000 to 10,000 Rohingyas had taken refuge. He founded an organization in the name of the Organization of the Displaced Rohingya Muslims (ODRM) and operated a primary school and rendered community services to the Rohingyas in Malaysia. In 1997, he established the contact with me when I was serving as the Diplomatic Representative of the Arakan League for Democracy (ALD-in exile) and Personal Emissary of U Tha Noe, MP-elect. I extended my recognition of the Rohingya nationality in my capacity of the Diplomatic Representative the ALD (in exile) and Personal Emissary of U Tha Noe, MP-elect., and invited him to join the ALD (in exile). He was very happy and under his leadership and with the coordination of a Rakhaing leader U San Tun Maung, more than one thousand people of Arakan of all ethnic groups became the members of the ALD (Malaysia-in exile). When the ALD terminated my service in anger

ORGANISATION OF DISPLACED ROHINGYA MUSLIMS

OD-ALD-04-98

July 15, 1998

Dr.Shwelu Maung alias Dr.Shahnawaz Khan,
Diplomatic representative of ALD(in Exile)
P.O. 7475, COLUMBIA,
MO 65205 - 7475, U.S.A.

Dear brother Shwelu Maung, May Allah bless you to fulfil your dream !

With thanks I acknowledge the receipt of your letter dated 3rd July '98 on July 12, 1998 and to say frankly I was overwhelmed with joy to see the big envelope sent by you first,but,l found myself really shocked to read,the martyrdom of six leaders of Arakan Army (AA) and the arrest of 73 Freedom Fighters at the hands of Indian Army on Feb.11, 1998.

Ko Saw Tun and Khine Raza, from among the six, are known to me when I was in the borde 'area with APFP comarades. It is a great loss for the entire people of Arakan. This is the second biggest loss after the FALL of ALP.

So, I am willing to co-operate within my capacity for the movement of Arakan national independence with you provided you have adopted a formula of Rakhaing-Rohingya Reconcialition to forge a political unity of all Arakanese people without regarding chauvinistic racial supremacy.

I am not a religious fundamentalist nor an ultra-racist but a person who believes in democracy, human rights and peaceful coexistence

Yours faithfully,
Maung Sein alias Mohd.Mohiuddin

Chairman
ODRM Kuala Lumpur
Malaysia

Note. I deface his signature in order to prevent any possible ID theft. Mr. Mohd. Mohiuddin is facing personality assassination by the military junta's fifth columnist at the time writing this report on April 27, 2005. SLM(SK)

of my recognition of the Rohingyas as the natives of Arakan, they formed the Arakan Democratic Forces (ADF) and honored me as their Patron and Chief Executive Officer. When he was relocated at the United States of America U San Tun Maung succeeded him as the Coordinator of the Arakan Democratic Forces and submitted their demand for "Decolonization of Burma" to the United Nations. The activities of the ADF can be found at my website www.shwelumaung.org. I present here some of his letters that show his mature politics.

6.8.4. Ako Kyaw Hla. A top leader of the Arakan Liberation Party (ALP) rejected Ako Kyaw Hla saying, "Rakhaingpray liberation is not a Kala's business." The result was that Ako Kyaw Hla founded the Muslim Liberation Organization of Burma (MLOB) and became its Chairman and In-Charge of the Foreign Affairs Committee, Democratic Alliance of Burma (DAB).

He is a lawyer by profession and a college friend of mine at Kyaukpyu College in early 1960s. The stories of my Kyaukpyu College friends are remarkable. Ako Mahmud Shah got killed in Afghanistan as a Mujahid, fighting against the Soviet occupation. Ako Khin Maung Yin became a captain in Burma army and lost both legs by a landmine at the Kachin front. Ako Phone Kyaw and Ako Than Aung became doctors. Ako Kyaw Win became a High Court Judge. Ako Kyaw Hla and I became the rebels. We used to be together at the College gymnasium in the evenings. If the Union of Burma was as fair as Kyaukpyu College I believe we will be able to meet each other, at least once in a while, at the Kyuakpyu College Alumni re-union. Full

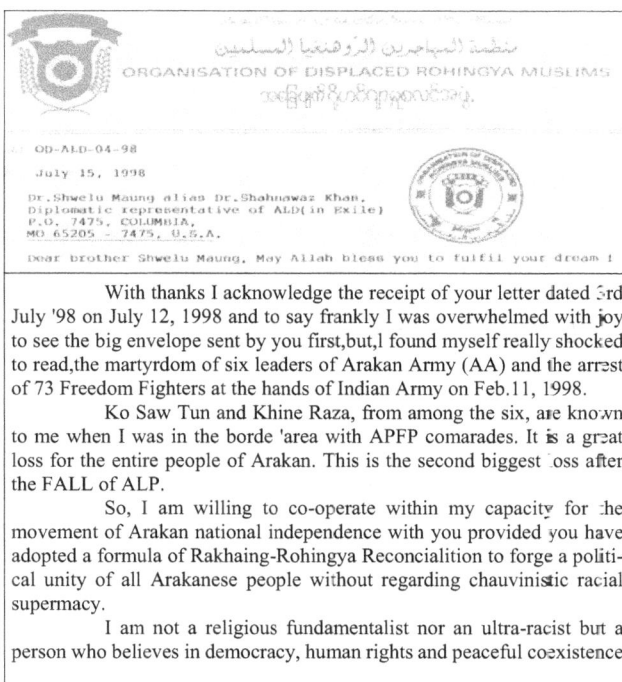

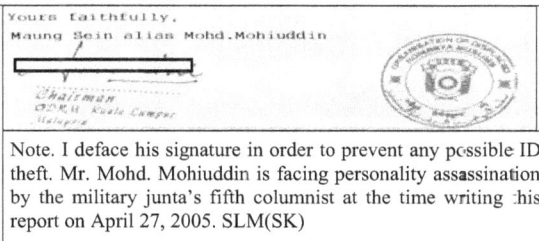

credit must be given to Principal U Kyaw Khin, a Kyaukpyu Rakhaing, who was also a Lecturer in English and taught us Emily Brontë's *Wuthering Heights.* With his excellent British English it was simply wonderful; I will never forget Heathcliff and Catherine. He retired as the Registrar from the Rangoon Institute of Medicine in mid 1980s.

In late 1977, along with few other dragon-opponents, who were also my friends, Ako Kyaw Hla daringly plotted a coup d'état. It was exposed by one of their followers. He managed to escape into Karen-controlled liberated areas while the others got arrested. He identifies himself as a Rakhaing Muslim in local politics, and embraces the philosophy of Burmese or Myanmar Muslim in a broader national politics. In 2003, he published a

The Arakan Democratic Forces submitting their demand for "Decolonization of Burma" at the office of the UN Resident Representative (UNDP) at Kuala Lampur in 2001. Please see the details at http://www.shwelumaung.org/ADFdemands.

MADRASAH AL-KHAIRIAH
AL-ISLAMIAH
(For Neplees, Rohingya Muslim Refugee Children)

No. 62, Jalan Bunga Melor 16, Taman Seraya Ampang, 56100 Kuala Lumpur
Tel : 03 - 49638192

Ref No.: MKI-ALD-01-331/98
Date 14th June 1998

Dear Dr. Shahnawaz Khan, Assalamu Alaikum wr.wbr

With due respect, I would like to inform you that there are eight thousand Rohingyas from Arakan in Malaysia comprising many families (men,women and children) who entered in Malaysia afterwards 1978 KING DRAGON OPERATION and 1992 PYITHAYA OPERATION launched by Myanmar security forces, however, they were not officially recognised refugees although most of them registered their names and statements in the UNHCR(Kuala Lumpur) and holding UNHCR letter of Refugee concern overhere.

Due to lack of birth certificate and language problem as well as undecided status of their parents the children are not allowed to take admission in the Govt. and private schools for learning even the basic religious teaching and primary education.

It is also not allowed to form any political Organisation of Rohingyas overhere and open school without legal stay and Govt.'s permission.

Therefore,the Rohingya children overhere are spoiling and illiterate leading to a destructive future.

In view of this, I have undertaken a project on self-help basis with the co-operation of Muslim Youth Movement of Malaysia(ABIM) and the World Assembly of Muslim Youth(WAMY).

Note. I deface his signature in order to prevent any possible ID theft. Mr. Mohd. Mohiuddin is facing personality assassination by the military junta's fifth columnists and extremists at the time of writing this report on April 27, 2005. SLM(SK)

book, *Burma and Muslims,* in Burmese. He kindly presented me one copy. It is a laudable scholarly effort depicting the most neglected views and stand of the Burmese Muslims who are loyal to Burma (Myanmar) since the heydays of Myanmar Empires, enduring and struggling together with all other compatriots in the rainy days of British colonialism, and again enduring and struggling against the tyrannical military rule in independent Myanmar, up to today. The main objective of his party, MLOB, is to live and serve the country a responsible citizen with due religious right. He places his allegiance to the nation first. He does not demand special rights for Muslims, but simply says that all brutal inhuman laws must be abolished and the Muslims must be guaranteed equal rights with all other citizens. As a son of Rakhaingpray he believes that the Rakhaing people deserve to have their state with their own legislature and state government within a Federation of Myanmar. He does not identify himself as a Rohingya. In his

ဦးကျော်လှ

 بِسْمِ اللّٰهِ الرَّحْمٰنِ الرَّحِيْمِ

စာ-ဆရာ-သုတ-ရှိ-ဖြေ-ရသ-တည်း-ဆိ
ဖွ့်-ၮၖၖ-ရာဗ-တို့ (၃၉-၀-၂ ၁၉၃၉)

To,

Dear Dr. Shahnawng Khan Ph.D

With best compliments from

[signature redacted]

16/7/2003
(Kyaw Hla)

မြန်မာနိုင်ငံနှင့်မွတ်စလင်(မ်)များ
Burma and Muslims

ရခိုင်ပြည်၊ မြောက်ဦးမြို့ရှိ ဆင်္ဂေ...၊ စစ်တွေမြို့၌ ကြီးပြင်း ကျောင်းနေခဲ့သည်။

U Kyaw Hla (b. December 15, 1939). A native of Mrauk-U, ancient capital of Arakan Empire. He grew up and went to school in Sittwe. His mother was a descendant of a traditional farming clan whereas the father belonged to a clan of government civil servants. He worked as a private high school teacher, and later, as a principal of government middle school. He graduated with a Bachelor of Arts degree from Rangoon Arts and Science University in 1968 and passed Higher Grade Pleader examination Part-I in 1970. Thenceforth he became active in democracy movement. The blackout on his signature to prevent possible ID theft. (Information given here is from his autobiographical sketch in Burmese).

---

political concept, all are the Burmese Muslims, and must learn local state language as well as national language, and live as a part and parcel of local, state and national community. He put emphasis on the loyalty of the Muslims to the nation and state since days of the Rakhaing and Myanmar kings. Accordingly, he highlights that the Muslims are the honorable citizens and they should be treated as such. What he says genuinely represents what he truly is. I knew him since 1962. He is a truly democratic and liberated person, and he is not alone. Hundreds of democratic Muslims support him and follow him.

Another prominent democratic and liberated person is U Maung Tin aka Md. Yacoob, who was the General Secretary of Arakanese Muslim Association. U Maung Tin, now settled in Canada through the arrangement of UNHCR, was truly a civil rights activist and got arrested several times by the Myanmarese military government and kept confined in isolation in a small cell which is similar to what we see in the movie *The Bridge Over River Kwai*. He is well known as a nephew of the Rakhaing Muslim leader Sultan Mahmud, who served as a cabinet minister in the days of Prime Minister U Nu, and was expelled from the country by General Ne Win 1978. The Kingdom of Saudi Arabia granted him political asylum, but he went back to Burma and died at Rangoon, according to his nephew Maung Tin. His followers are still living in Saudi Arabia.

However liberal they may be, both of Kyaw Hla and Maung Tin are rejected as *the Kalas* (i.e. the despised foreigners, or the *niggers*) by both the Rakhaing and the Myanmar. It must be a very painful experience for them; imagine yourself being disowned by your own compatriots just because of your religion and ancestral origin being different from them. In 1977-78, when U Kyaw Hla first reached Myanmar-Thai border, he ventured to join Arakan Liberation Party (ALP), at Wunkha which toady is a major component of Arakan National Council that I cited earlier. The top ALP leader of at Wunkha outright rejected him saying, "Arakan liberation is not a Kala's business". Today the Rakhaing leader is the key founding member of the Arakan National Council (ANC), which has adopted an ultranationalist doctrine in line with the neo-Nazism as I described earlier.

Later, with the support of the exiled Arakanese Muslims, he and U Maung Tin formed Arakan Liberation Organization (ALO) at the Myanmar-Bangladesh border in late 1980s. I was at Dhaka at that time, was informed in advance of the establishment. My university pal and comrade, U Kyaw Hlaing, the Chairman of Arakan Independence Organization (AIO), now diseased, helped them with logistic support. Two months later, a Rohingya armed organization attacked and destroyed their camp and arrested their members who were set free after extracting under duress a promise that they would support only the Rohingya. It was then that U Maung Tin resettled in Canada and U Kyaw Hla went back to Myanmar-Thai border and founded his broader organization, MLOB, in late 1980s.

6.9. Rebellion and Democracy. When the magnifying lens is focussed at Arakan, we can easily see a divided nation with a segregated society flourishing lavishly. The segregated society is now advancing dangerously toward neo-Nazi culture under the patronage of Myanmar ultranationalism. Unfortunately, not only the violent rebellions but also peaceful democratic movements are crushed with equal tyranny by the ruling military junta. The well-rooted Rakhaing Neo-Nazism in the so-called democratic camp, as I mentioned in the previous section, indicates that the military government alone is not to be blamed, but the society as a whole must bear the responsibility of religious segregation and ethnic cleansing. Accordingly, I view that people like Br. Mahmud Shah, U Maung Sein, Dr. Yunos, Br. Nurul Islam, U Kyaw Hla, and U Maung Tin are mere victims of the unltranationalistic Myanmarese society.

Nurul Islam's party, the Arakan Rohingya National Organization (ARNO), has established Arakan Independence Alliance (AIA) with Dr. Khin Maung's National United Party of Arakan (NUPA)[1] *with the goal of restoration of right to self-determination.* Nurul Islam's and his ARNO's reasons behind their armed rebellion can be best understood from his writings, some excerpts of which are given here.

FACTS ABOUT THE ROHINGYA MUSLIMS OF ARAKAN

By Nurul Islam
President
Arakan Rohingya National Organisation (ARNO)

Arakan, formerly called Rohang, lies on the north–western part of Burma with 360 miles coastal belt from the Bay of Bengal. It borders 167 miles with Bangladesh both by land and sea. Rohingyas have been living in Arakan from time immemorial. They are a people with distinct culture and civilization of their own. They trace their ancestry to Arabs, Moors, Pathans, Moghuls, Bengalis and some Indo-Mongoloid people. Early Muslim settlements in Arakan date back to 7th century AD.

Burma is a home to numerous ethnic groups and about 60% of the area is inhabited by nearly 140 ethnic races and Rohingya is one of them. Burma has a population of about 50 million of which nearly 8 millions are Muslims. Of the Muslim population about 3.5 millions (both at home and at the places of refuge) are Rohingyas of Arakan. The Rohingyas are a majority community in Arakan.

Due to large scale persecution through ethnic cleansing and genocidal action against

---

Note.
1. As of June 10, 2005, the Narinjara News indicates that NUPA will be having a new leadership that probably will terminate the Alliance and de-recognize the Rohingya nationality.

them, about 1.5 million Rohingyas are forced to leave their hearth and home since Burmese independence in 1948. This unfortunate uprooted people are mostly found in Bangladesh, Pakistan and Saudi Arabia; also in UAE, Thailand and Malaysia. Present distribution of the Rohingya population is given below:

Inside Burma: 2 million*
Bangladesh: 600,000 *
Pakistan: 350,000*
Saudi Arabia 400,000*
Others (U.A.E., Thailand, Malaysia.) : 100,000*

* Approximation

1. Occupation: The Rohingyas are living on agriculture. Arakan state's agricultural output is mainly contributed by Rohingyas. Small percentage of them are engaged in fishing and trade & business. Besides there are Rohingya artisans, blacksmiths and carpenters. Due to discrimination against them, the Rohingyas have become landless and homeless. Their farm lands are being grabbed by the new Buddhist settlers being invited from within and outside the country. Over and above, high taxation on agricultural produce, continued forced labour and confiscation of farm lands and various restrictions on farming, conspire them to abandon their lands, live below poverty line or face starvation. At present, the number of Rohingya traders and businessmen sharply declined. They are not allowed to do trade and business freely. Sometimes, they require to share their business with the Buddhists giving them lion shares without investment. The military regime has prohibited the Rohingyas of their right to freedom of movement within the country, *and* within the same locality seriously affecting the socio-cultural, economic, educational activities and daily life of the Rohingyas. The regime has stopped recruitment of Rohingyas even in civil services since 1970s. No Rohingyas are allowed to enter into defense services.

2. Religion, Culture and Civilization of Rohingyas: Rohingyas are staunch followers of Islam. Most of the elderly Rohingya grow beards and the women wear hijab. All Rohingya houses are surrounded by high bamboo walls. There are mosques and Madrassahs (religious schools) in every quarter and village. The men pray in congregation, where as the female pray at home. There is still in existence of a social bond in every village called "Samaj". All social welfare activities like Adhahi meat distribution, helping the poor, widows, orphans and needy, marriage and funereal functions are done collectively by the Samaj. The Ulema play a very prominent role particularly in matters relating to personal laws, like family affairs of the Rohingyas. Unfortunately, today the cultural problem becomes one of the most important problems of the Rohingyas in Burma. The Muslims have to encounter strong pressure of the Buddhist culture. Particularly the Rohingyas have to confront ideological assault from all directions. The Rohingyas are considered practicing the foreign way of life having no origin in Burma. According to the ruling military the Rohingyas are to adopt and entertain no ideas but those of Burman race and culture and Buddhism. The Muslims or Rohingyas are told to discard Islamic names and adopt Burman names. Everywhere Muslims' or Islamic are razed to the ground. Hundreds of mosques have been demolished. Construction of new mosques or repairs to the old ones are prohibited. Pagodas, monasteries and Buddhist temples have been erected in every nook and cranny of the Rohingya homeland. Muslim students have been brainwashed in schools where anti-Islamic materials are being taught to them. Islam and Islamic culture are always projected or presented in humiliating, derogatory, degrading and distorted forms.

3. Education of Rohingya: Before 1962 military take over Rohingya Muslims did not lag behind their Buddhist sister community. Due to poverty, serious discrimination and continued persecution against them, the number of Rohingya students have declined much. To get admission in colleges and universities for higher studies is a problematic matter for the Rohingyas. Severe restrictions have been imposed on their pursuing professional courses for citizenship question. There are a number of voluntary religious schools educating a good percentage of Rohingya students. However, because of various restrictions, lack of funds and facilities these institutions are unable to modernize the teaching methods thus failing to produce efficient students or manpower for the society. Most of the Rohingyas living in exile have little means to educate their children.

4. Political status of Rohingya: Prior to 1962 the Rohingya community has been recognized as an indigenous ethnic nationality of Burma. They have their representatives in Burmese parliament and some of them have bean appointed as ministers, parliamentary secretaries and in high government positions. After the military take over they have been systematically deprived of their political rights. With the promulgation of the most controversial and discriminatory citizenship law of 1982 they are declared as "non-national" or "foreign residents". Very much contradictory to their declaration, the military could not disallow the Rohingyas to participate in multi-party elections held in 1990, the result of which was not implemented by the military junta. Today the Rohingyas are living in sub-human condition with uncertain future. They are declared a people fit to be exterminated.

5. Junta's policy towards the Muslims of Burma: the ruling military junta practices two pronged de-Islamisation policy in Burma: -- physical extermination through genocide and ethnic cleansing of Rohingya Muslims of Arakan and cultural assimilation of Muslims living in other parts of Burma -- Their main objective is to turn strategic Muslim Arakan into a Burmanised Buddhist region by reducing the Muslims into insignificant or manageable minorities.

6. Crimes committed against Rohingyas and present situation: Arbitrary arrests, torture, summary execution, custodial killings are rampant.The Rohingyas are engaged in forced unpaid slave labor days in, days out. Confiscation of farm lands, uprooting of Muslim settlements, eviction of inmates, establishment of new Buddhist settlements on evacuated Muslim land. Demolishing of mosques, religious schools and erection of pagodas, Buddhist temples with a view to changing the landscape of Arakan. Rape and dishonouring of women, forced marriage of Muslim women by Buddhists, banning hijab wearing and forced use of contraceptives and imposition of restriction on marriage of Rohingya couples. Restriction on movement, even from one village to another within the same locality, on socio-cultural and religious activities, trade and business. Revocation of citizenship depriving the Rohingya of citizenship rights including the right to seek higher and professional education. Unbearable taxation on all agricultural produces and even on domestic livestocks like cattle, goats, fowls etc. Uprooting of villages and eviction of inmates creating internal refugees or making them to wander from place to place while causing refugee exoduses off and on in to the neighbouring countries.

7. Refugee exodus: As a result of physical extermination, ethnic cleansing operations, large scale persecution and uprooting of villages and eviction of inmates, there were unprecedented refugee influxes into Bangladesh once in 1978 and the other in 1991-1992 with constant trickle of refugee exodus all along.. About 1.5 million Rohingyas have so far been evicted from Arakan since the year of Burmese independence in 1948.

End of the article.

Except for the strong-worded statements, the Rohingya armed rebellion can be considered as a nuisance, but not a threat to Burma. From their tropical border bases, the rebels, with their 100-men band, had made a few raids at the military and police outposts as deep as 20-miles inside the Rakhine State of Burma. It was just a tickle to the 500,000 soldiers of the Myanmar Armed Forces. As a matter of fact, the people inside Burma hardly knows its existence. The actual political threat comes from the democratic movement of the Rohingyas inside the legal framework of the Burmese racial tyranny.

The Rohingyas are good farmers, fishermen, businessmen, government servants and students. Above all they are highly religious. Inside the given oppressive laws of Burma, they struggle with great endurance and strength rejecting violence. Great majority of the Rohingyas rallied around the democratic forces and emerged in two major political parties, the National Democratic Party for Human Rights (NDPHR) and Student and Youth League for Mayu Province Development (SYLMPD) in 1989 and vigorously competed in the 1990 national election. The election results of the Rakhine State are summarized in the Tables 6.1, 6.2, and 6.3 in the upcoming pages. On the basis of the statistics given in the tables, I have calculated the Rohingya Muslim population in comparison with that of the Rakhaing Buddhist. The calculation is given in the next page, along with the Table 6.1. From the calculation it can be seen that the Rohingya Muslims constitute 46.75% of the Rakhine State or 3.74% of Myanmar populations whereas the Rakhaings form 49% of the Rakhine State or 3.9% of Myanmar populations. Therefore, the Rohingya Muslims are not a minority in the Rakhaing State, but are in par with the ruling Rakhaing race. If the equal opportunity is given to them the Rakhaing Buddhists can hardly remain as the ruling class. This Muslim's parity with the Rakhaing Buddhists has great bearing on the Myanmar Buddhist society. Therefore, the 1982 Citizenship Law of Burma was introduced, making more than 50% of the Rohingyas Muslims aliens. That is also why the Rakhaings support the discriminatory citizenship law and their political party, Arakan League for Democracy (in exile), adopted *the Bhumi Rakkhita Putra Principle* to maintain the Rakhaing's status quo as the ruling race in the Rakhine State. In 1989, the Rohingyas approached[1] Dr. Saw Mra Aung and ALD's leadership with the bargaining chip that if the ALD accepted them as the Rohingyas they would join the ALD and support Dr. Saw Mra Aung. Only when Dr. Saw Mra Aung and ALD's leadership rejected them they formed their own party, NDPHR. Dr. Saw Mra Aung, the President of ALD, is a British-trained physician and won the 1990 election in the Mrauk U Constituency 2. He is seen as a deputy to Mrs. Aung San Suu Kyi

Please visit http://www.aldexile.org

Arakan League For Democracy (ALD-Exile)

Notes.
1. U Maung Sein (Mohd. Mohiuddin) who was the founding President of the Organization of the Displaced Rohingya Muslims (ODRM), Coordinator of the Arakan Democratic Forces (ADF) and presently the President of the National Democratic Party for Human Rights (NDPHR, in USA), told me this fact in 1998. Later U Kyaw Soe Aung (Mohammad Islam), who was the founding Jt. Secretary General of ODRM and Deputy Coordinator of ADF, independently confirmed it in 2005, with a note that he was in Arakan at time of the Rohingyas' approach to Dr. Saw Mra Aung and ALD and personally witnessed the event. U Kyaw Soe Aung is presently the General Secretary of the National Democratic Party for Human Rights (NDPHR, in USA).

The attempt to maintain its status quo of the Bama ruling race in all Burma and the Rakhaing ruling race in the Rakhine State is the prime culprit of the Myanmar ultranationalism and Rakhaing neo-Nazism. There is no question that it is very hard to bring the Muslims into the mainstream of the national culture in non-Muslim nations. The United Kingdom has experienced this difficulty since her Empire[1] colonized her in 20th century. We should not overlook that Great Britain colonized her Empire from 17th to 19th century and her Empire in turn colonized her in 20th century. As a matter of fact the Empire's colonization of Great Britain is still going on even though the Great Britain has given her colonialism more than half-a-century ago.

Very factual report of Professor Lord Bhikhu Parekh, F.R.S., Centre for the Study of Democracy, University of Westmister, London, United Kingdom (Great Britain), deserves a study by the reader in this subject. He was chair of the Runnymede Commission on the Future of Multi-Ethnic Britain (1998-2000) and author of *Rethinking of Multiculturalism: Cultural Diversity and Political Theory*, and many other books (http//imm-live.wmin.ac.uk/sshl/page-148-smhp=1). I am quoting some part of his article, which is relevant with the context of my presentation here. In July, 2003, Lord Parekh wrote in his article *Muslims in Britain* (http://www.prospect-magazine.co.uk/start.asp?P_Article=11979) and I downloaded it from http://jmm.aaa.net.au/articles/1690.htm. The excerpt begins below.

"British Muslims do not have a problem with democracy. Some of them do have a problem with multiculturalism........According to the census of 2001, Britain has around 1.6m Muslims in a population of just under 58.8m-just under 3 per cent of its population. Around three quarters of British Muslims come from the Indian subcontinent, mainly from rural areas of Pakistan and Bangladesh. This is important because some of their difficulties in settlement arise not from their religion but their unfamiliarity with the western way of life. They began coming in the early 1960s and by the early 1990s the migration was largely complete. ....

....

There have been four Muslim riots so far, compared to about eight race-related riots by Afro-Caribbeans. One of them concerned Salman Rushdie's The Satanic Verses; others police insensitivity and racist marches. ...

....

Citizenship. After some theological debate about Muslim obligations to a non-Muslim state, Muslims have widely accepted that they owe loyalty to the British state. However, there is some ambiguity about what to do when the claims of the state clash with those of the umma (the global Muslim community). Muslims strongly opposed both Gulf wars-and in the case of the latest one demonstrated peacefully in their thousands alongside non-Muslims. A tiny number of young Muslims fought with the Taleban in Afghanistan. They were condemned by most of their fellow Muslims, who insisted that loyalty to Britain came first. The imam of Finsbury Park mosque, who preached hatred of the west and support for Muslim terrorists, was long tolerated. But

---

Notes.

1. In 1974, when I was a graduate student in the United Kingdom, I remember reading a comic strip that showed the Red Coats landing all over the world with a caption, "17th century: Great Britain colonized the Empire." The lower panel of the comic strip showed the Indians, the Sikhs, and the Africans landing in Great Britain with a caption, "20th century: The Empire colonized Great Britain."

when the mosque was suspected of becoming a terrorist cell, it was raided and the weapons were confiscated by the police with broad Muslim support...

....

Although Muslims do not have much of a problem living in a democracy, they do have some difficulty coping with one that is multicultural. Far more than the followers of any other religion, Muslims are convinced of the absolute superiority of Islam. The Koran is believed to be the literal, direct and unmediated word of God. It claims to represent the final and definitive revelation of God, superseding all other religions, including Judaism and Christianity-which are at best early versions of Islam. Hinduism is dismissed as idolatrous, and not really a religion at all. The military success of early Islam gave it a triumphalist side, confirming its absolute superiority in the eyes of its adherents.

This spirit of Islamic superiority is reflected in many of its beliefs and practices. The constant invocation of its past glory and the desperate desire to revive it is one example. Muslims are supposed to have a positive duty to convert the followers of other religions, but they are not themselves free to give up their religion in favour of another. Most Muslims are anxious that others should learn about their religion and appreciate its insights, but they have themselves little interest in other religions. Muslim men may marry non-Muslim women, but they do not allow others to marry "their" women, and expect those marrying within Islam to convert to it. Some of this can be attributed to the current Muslim feeling of siege or fear of loss of identity. But even in the self-confident Ottoman empire where Jews and Christians enjoyed considerable tolerance, they were treated as second-class citizens. And while they were free to convert to Islam, they were strictly forbidden to convert Muslims or to covert their women.

Thanks to this history, the Muslim attitude to multicultural society is often one-sided. They welcome it for the freedom it gives them to retain their religious identity and familiarise others with their beliefs, practices and history. However some Muslims also resent it because it puts them on the same level with other religions and cultures, and exposes their children to other religions and secular cultures.

British Islam is no doubt becoming more open to a genuine inter-religious and intercultural dialogue. But it still has a long way to go before it can enthusiastically participate in the creative tensions and controversies of a multicultural society in a spirit of humility and open-mindedness. Over time western Muslims should come to feel fully at home in multicultural societies. As this happens, it will most certainly have a profound impact on the rest of the Muslim world, and may even help to trigger a movement for multicultural democracies there." The excerpt ends here.

The British Muslim population of 1.6 millions in a nation of 58 millions in Great Britain is quite comparable with the Rohingya Muslim population of 1.87 millions in the Myanmarese nation of 50 millions. The Muslim settlement in Great Britain is recent, but the Muslim settlement, in Arakan (i.e. the Rakhine State) and Maynmar is some 600 years old. The Muslim titles of the Rakhaing Buddhist Kings for more than two hundred years from 1430 CE to 1666 CE strongly testify the presence of Muslims and their influence in the Myanmarese Rakhine State since the15th century. The name of the capital of the Third Myanmar Empire (1753 CE -1885 CE), *Amarapura*, itself was of Bengali origin. The major difference is that Great Britain is the cradle of the parliamentary democracy whereas Myanmar has hardly seen democracy. Magna Carta, the basis of British democracy was signed in 1215 CE, 790 years ago. The first parliament known as the Simon[1] de Monfort's parliament that represented commoners as well as barons was held in 1265. Myanmar is still in the very initial stage of laying her roadmap to democracy in 2005.

We can clearly see that Myanmarese have been facing the problem in absorbing the Muslims into the mainstream of the national life, which is being democratically tackled by Great Britain, the European countries and the United States of America these days. The observations made in the British Muslim community by Professor Lord Bhikhu Parekh in Great Britain are not isolated Muslim characteristics confined to Great Britain, but are visible all over the European countries and the United State. These characteristics had been very handy in the West's war against communism and its Godfather, *the evil empire*[2]. The Muslims were looked upon as a sort of heroes after the international Mujahids[3] dethroned the USSR in Afghanistan, leading to the disintegration of *the evil empire*. The Afghanistan Mujahids even helped a British Secret Agent in his crusade against the evil empire's warlords. You can see the heroic Mujahids helping Commander James Bond (007) in *The Living Daylights* (released in 1987, starring Timothy Dalton), which earned $191.2 millions across the world (http://www.universalexports.net/Movies/daylights-cast.shtml). In that period, the West translated the Arabic *Mujahid* into *freedom fighter* in English.

Indeed the Muslims across the world became villains after the Muslim terrorists exploded World Trade Center of New York City on the 11th of September 2001 using a Boeing 747 as the flying bomb. Instantly, and understandably, the West's definition of the term Mujahid became *terrorist*. Even in the City of Columbia, Missouri, USA, which I have made my hometown, these Muslim characteristics manifest creating concerns among the citi-

The minaret of Columbia Islamic Center decorates the skyline of the sleepy university town, challenging the Missourian traditional values.

zens. The sleepy city of this university town became a kind of the national focus when it was revealed that one of the top Iraqi dictator Sadam Hossain's cabinet minister, Dr Huda Salih Mahdi Ammash, earned her doctoral degree in microbiology from the University of Missouri at Columbia (UMC), in 1983. A professor at the University of Baghdad, she was believed to be the main scientist in the production of Iraq's biological weapons. The rumors said that the Federal Bureau of Investigation (FBI) scrutinized all Muslim members of the UMC faculty, staff, and students. They also monitored the Islamic Center of Columbia for any irregularities. The world news were filled with public outrage over the Muslims. With my own ears, I have heard the hysteria of a WWIII raging between the Muslims and non-Muslims. While the governments and the responsible citizens tackle to quench the hysteria and anti-Muslim sentiments the rise of

Notes.
1. Simon de Montefort (1200?-1265) was an English statesman and soldier, who was married to the youngest sister of Henry III, king of England, and played a leading role in the early development of constitutional monarchy in Britain. (Source: Microsoft Encyclopedia Encarta 1997 CD), and online BBC NEWS UK Westminster Hall Cradle of Parliament.htm, Thursday, 4 April, 2002.
2. The US 40th President, Ronald Reagan (1911-2004), a former Hollywood movie star, gave the theatrical name, *Evil Empire,* to the USSR.
3. My college friend, Mahmud Shah, was one of those heroes. See the section 6.8.3 in this chapter.

Pan-Islam across the world cannot be ignored. I have vividly illustrated the case of Bangladesh. Similarly, Islamization of Malaysia and Pakistan is a subject of the international concern. The outbreak of Muslim rebellion in the southern Thailand rocked the crown of the Southeast Asian nations.

Under the above mentioned international atmosphere of predicament against the Muslims, the Rakhaing nationalists under the banner of the Arakan National Congress (ANC) adopted the *Bhumi Rakkhita Putra Principle*, a policy of neo-Nazism with the intention of containing the Muslim's influence in Arakan. The *Bhumi Rakkhita Putra Principle* has four major political implications.

(1) Its policy that *the Rakhaings ought to be given priority and preference* creates two classes of citizenship and advocates a doctrine of neo-apartheid in the line of religio-racial segregation.

(2) Its support of the Citizenship Law of Burma-1982 puts the Rakhaing Nationalists in the same boat of the Bama militarists who rule the country under the doctrine of Myanmar ultranationalism.

(3) Its designation of the Muslims of Arakan as *the Arakan Bengalis* provokes patriotism of the 140 Bengali Muslims of Bangladesh.

(4) Overall discrimination and oppression of the Arakanese Muslims provokes the Muslim Brotherhood of the Islamic Umma, which is constituted by the 1.4 billion Muslims across the world.

As a result, *the Bhumi Rakkhita Putra Principle* has invited international Muslim intervention in the Arakan and Myanmar affairs. The rise of Pan-Islam in Bangladesh has made the situation volatile. The definition of Arakan itself is double-edged. As I described earlier the Arakan Empire flourished from 1430 CE to 1666 CE and the present Chittagong District and Hill Tracts of Bangladesh were under its control. The Rakhaing King Razagri *alias* Salim Shah (r. 1593-1612 CE) seized Pegu and became the Emperor of Pegu. His son Mun Kha Moung *alias* Hossain Shah (r.1612-1622 CE) even seized Dhaka for a short time in 1615 CE. Under these traditions Arakan is not merely the present Rakhine State of Myanmar, but it also includes Chittagong Districts and Hill Tracts of Bangladesh, and parts of India's Tripura and Manipura. On this historical ground, the Chittagonians can claim that Arakan belongs to them. Again the definition of the term Rohingya is not clear. If we define Rohingyas as the Muslim descendants of Arakan Empire, then, we have some 40 million Rohingyas inside Bangladesh, mainly in the Chittagong Districts adjacent to Burma. They are popularly known as the Chittagonians and many of them do not like to be called Bengalis. This is one reason why Bangladesh President Ziaur Rahman adopted Bangladeshi nationalism deviating from the traditional Bengali nationalism. In terms of ethnology, the Chittagonians are of multinational origin since Chittagong was established by the sailors, traders, missionaries, and mercenaries from time immemorial. By nature, they do not cherish loyalty to a particular nationalism or sovereignty. With such political fluidity that the Chittagonians served the Rakhaing kings of Arakan Empire that dominated Bengal and Burma for more than two centuries. Today, the same political fluidity manifests among many Chittagonians creating a concern in Dhaka. On the top of that, the Chittagonians are ardent followers of Qu'ranic teachings and they tend to be fundamentalists. The history has witnessed that Chittagong and Chittagonians have played key roles in political changes. In 1971, General Ziaur Rahman declared independence of Bangladesh from Chittagong. The assassination of Bangladesh's Father of Nation, Bangabandhu Sheikh Mujibur Rahman, his family members and top Awami League leaders was masterminded by a Chittagonian military officer.

President Ziaur Rahman was killed in Chittagong in 1987. Chittagong is the stronghold of Muslim League and Jamat-e-Islami. It is believed that the gold coins of Arakan Empire were minted in Chittagong and a good number of them can be seen at the Chittagong Museum today. Even, Raza Kumar, the son of Pagan King Kyansittha (r.1057 CE - 1085 CE) with his wife Sambul, a Mrama woman, who introduced Myanmar language into Burma, is believed to be Mainamati-educated. The capital *Amarapura* of the Third Myanmar Empire is a Bengali name meaning *our village,* which is believed to a settlement of the Bengali weavers who accompanied King Kyansittha's favorite Queen Apeyratana, a princess of Pattikara (Mainamatai)[1].

Strategic Alliance. Under such complicated historical background and today's political sophistication that the Rohingya's struggle for equal political rights in Arakan and Burma encounters *the strategic alliance* of Myanmar ultranationalism and Rakhaing neo-Nazism. The Rakhaing's opposition to the Myanmarese military rule is nothing more than a tactical discord with their commander-in-chief, *the Bama.* Religious and racial discrimination against the Rohingyas has provoked the patriotism of the Bengalis, especially of the Chittagonians, as well as the consciousness of the Islamic Umma. The big question now is:- Will the Arakan affairs ignite a Muslim-Buddhist War between Bangladesh and Burma?

In the past the Burmese king's claim of Chittagong and Dhaka had led to the First Anglo-Burman War in 1824, as evidenced in the history quoted below.

"Lord Amherst[1] became the Governor-General of India in August 1823. During his tenure the most important event which took place was the First Anglo-Burmese War.

Causes for the Declaration of the War

The Burmese had already seized Tenasserim from Siam in 1766, subjugated the kingdom of Arakan in 1784, and also conquered Manipur, near the Surma valley, in 1813. This advance of the Burmese towards the eastern frontier of the Company's dominion made an Anglo-Burmese conflict inevitable. The British were engaged in other parts of India and so they first tried to avoid the direct conflict with the Burmese by sending envoys to Burma - Captain Symes in 1795 and in 1802, Captain Cox in 1797 and Captain Canning in 1803, 1809, 1811 - but it was unsuccessful. Then when the British were fighting with the Pindaris, the King of Ava sent a letter to Lord Hastings demanding the surrender of Chittagong, Dacca, Cassimbazar and Murshidabad. This letter was sent by the Hastings to the Burmese Government stating it as a forged one.

Arakan Gas

Courtesy: Arakanpost, Narinjara News

Soon in 1821-1822, the Burmese conquered Assam and in September 1823 the Shahpuri island near Chittagong which was belonging to the Company. The Burmese were then making preparations for an attack on the territories in Bengal. All these events frustrated the British and so finally on February 24, 1824 Lord Amherst declared war on Burma."

(Source as of January 20, 2003: http://www.itihaas.com/modern/british14.html).

Today's Arakan of Burma is not a political backwater anymore. Asian Highway that joins New Delhi, Dhaka, Rangoon, Bangkok, Kaula Lumpur, and Singapore will be completed

---

Note.

1. According to Dr. Htin Aung, King Kyansittha was the son of an India Princess and a Burmese noble. Please see his book, *A History of Burma*, Columbia University Press, 1967, page 40. I incline to believe that she must be a Princess of Pattikera. This could be the reason why Kyansittha had sentimental attachment with Pattikera. His favorite queen, Apeyratana, was a Padikkhara Princess; their daughter, Shwe Ei Thi, married to a Pattikera Prince, and their son, Alaungsithu (i.e. grandson of Kyansittha), also made a Pattikera Princess his Queen, see page 283 in this book.

when the construction of the bridge over the River Naff is finished in near future. The Myanmarese oppression of the Arakanese Rohingya Muslims has drawn international focus. Arakan Gas has created an international consortium comprising of the Koreans (Daewoo International Corp and Korea Gas Corp), the Indians (the government-owned Oil and Natural Gas Commission Videsh Ltd. and Gas authority of India Ltd.), the Myanmarese (government-owned Myanmar Oil and Gas Enterprise). Bangladesh has been pulled into the consortium as the Arakan Gas will be transported to energy-hungry India through a Trans-Arakan-Bangladesh pipeline. Bangladesh will earn US$ 250 millions a year from the pipeline while Myanmar expects to earn up to three billions a years after giving out the dividends to the Koreans and the Indians. The Arakan gas field is guarded by 50,000 Myanmarese infantry soldiers who are supported by upgraded navy and airforce, as will be described in next chapter. Trans-Arakan-Bangladesh gas line raises a concern when we recall the crises that surrounded Suez and Panama Canals, which were built and operated by the international consortium. The British, the French, and Israeli waged the Suez War against Egypt when Egypt nationalized Suez Canal in 1956. The war came to an end when the Soviet Union and the United States compelled the Europeans to withdraw. Later in 1967, the British-French-Israeli alliance revenged Egypt and the Arabs with the 6-Day War when Israel occupied the Gaza Strip, the Sinai Peninsula, and the West Bank of Jordan River. Even day in 2005, the 6-Day War between the Israelis and Arabs has not ended yet. Similarly, the US control of Panama Canal for one hundred years resulted in American imperialism over Panama, which in turn led to political chaos in that central American nation, only to end in 1999 when the US handed over the canal control to the government of Panama. In the light of these histories can we negate a possible Indian-Myanmar joint occupation of Bangladesh for the sake of the security of the Trans-Arakan-Bangladesh gas line? Besides, the Chinese are going to drill oil at Man Aung (Cheduba) in Arakan. The presence of the Chinese military buildup in Myanmar is already a serious concern in the region. The Chinese interest in Arakan Oil could complicate the situation of Arakan gas.

It appears that the classic Muslim-Buddhist war in Arakan is being compounded by modern economic and technological globalization. Where will it lead to and how will it end? Could there be an Arakan Gas War featuring a conflict of Muslims versus non-Muslims?

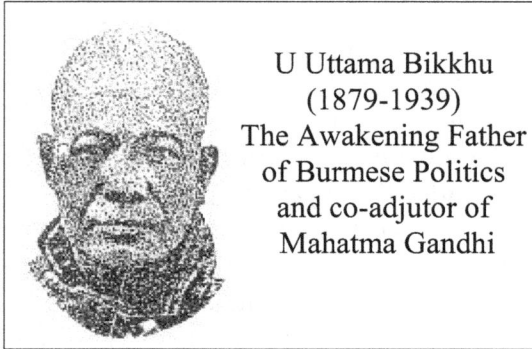

Chapter-7. The Myanmarese Fear

U Uttama Bikkhu
(1879-1939)
The Awakening Father of Burmese Politics and co-adjutor of Mahatma Gandhi

Islamic prophecy says, "Golden age of Islam will arise from Arakan and Afghanistan." How true will this prophecy be? I may not live long enough to know the answer, but I do know what is going on in Arakan today.

The Myanmarese fear of the Muslims and their religion, Islam, originated in the misfortune of the Rakhaing people. Their national kingdom Rakkhapura lost her western territory to the Mogul Empire in 1666 and finally independence to the Myanmar colonialist in 1784. It came under the British rule in 1826 and lasted till 1948. Inside that vast British Empire which ruled half the world, Rakkhapura was just a piece of broken arrow, very insignificant and useless. She had already lost her original name and by then was known as Arakan, her Persian name. Most historians believe that Arakan is the English name for the Rakhaingpray. As a matter of fact it is the Persian name. Rakkhapura entered into the world map as Arakan in the days of King Mun Saw Mwan in 1430, as I described in the preceding chapters. He was multilingual with good proficiency in Bengali, Hindi, and Persian, on the top of his mother tongue Rakhaing. Among his advisors were a good number of highly educated Muslims and his royal international language was Persian. Being influenced by the Muslim Mogul Empire, the Persian language was adopted by the Rakhaing as well as the Bama kings of those days. It was the fashion of the time. Because of this, Rakkhapura was known as Arakan.

Deeply lost in the world of colonialism, the Arakanese did not know if they should fight for sovereign independence or stay inside India or Burma. In fear of the Muslims and the Hindus they opted to join hands with the Buddhist Bama (Myanmar) on the basis of common religion. *It was a religious decision*. The Bama (Myanmar) is seen as a lesser threat by the Arakanase. Only a small faction, for example U Seinda party, opted for sovereign independence to no avail. U Uttama Bikkhu was the only one who favored remaining part of India. Subsequently a vast majority of the Arakanese youths and intellectuals joined Anti-Fascist and People Freedom League (AFPFL) at its birth in 1943, signaling their acceptance of the Burman leadership.

The Rakhaing people's post-WWII decision to take independence together with Myanmar people was a religious decision based upon their fear of the Muslims and Hindus who were their populous western neighbors. Bikkhu U Uttama who favored to stay inside India was driven out of his native town SaiteTwey (Akyab). U Uttama awakened the people of British Burma when he commanded, "Craddock, go home", in 1920, at a time when the Burmese humbly addressed to a Britisher as "Great Master" *(Thakin-gyi)*. Sir Reginald Henry Craddock was the Lieutenant Governor of Burma from 1918-1922. For his brave words that woke up Burma, U Uttama was honored as *the Awakening Father* of Burmese politics by her people including General Aung San, U Nu, and General Ne Win. He was also a coadjutor of Mahatma Gandhi. Under the 1935 Government Act of Burma, the British Masters planned to separate Burma from India. Burma was an administrative unit of the British India since 1885. At that time, U Uttama advocated the Burmese to stay inside India opposing the separation. This greatly angered the Rakhaing Buddhists who charged him as a pro-Kala (pro-Indians). A Buddhist monk survives on the charity of the Buddhist lay-people. The people of Saite Twey boycotted U Uttama and did not supply him any food or other essential commodities. It was an act of excommunication.

Therefore, the monk left Saite Twey for Rangoon where he was looked after by his Burman disciples. It is a shame to SaiteTwey people. This demonstrates the hate and fear of the Rakhaing people to the Indians and pro-Indians, whom they call *Kala* and *Kala Yaukpha* (i.e. Kala brother-in-law), respectively. They even starved a Buddhist monk, who was an international figure in politics and academia. He taught Pali at Tokyo University. This is a very peculiar situation since Gautama Buddha, whom they worship, is none other than a *Kala* himself.

Other Buddhist Bikkhu named U Seinda wanted to establish an independent sovereign Rakhaingpray. He did not cooperate with General Aung San and rebelled against Rangoon government upon the Burmese independence in 1948. He did not get any due support from his Rakhaing people and eventually surrendered to the Burmese Government.

Not only the Rakhaings but also the Myanmarese are afraid of the Muslims. They are not afraid of the other ethnic rebels such as the Kachin, the Karen, the Shan, the Karenni, the Mon, the Chin or the Rakhaing, because these minorities are genuine minorities who exist only inside Myanmar. Internationally, they do not exist. In contrast, the Muslims are minorities inside Myanmar, but they are the majority in the world boasting 1.4 billion faithfuls, exactly double of the world Buddhist population. Most of the Muslim countries are rich whereas most of the Buddhist countries are poor, except for Japan. The Myanmarese also believe that the Muslims are militant with the philosophy of *jihad* around the world, always ready to form an international Jihad whenever and wherever Muslim's interest is threatened. The international Mujahideens in Afghanistan struggle against the Soviet occupation in early 1980s and today international Muslim urban guerrillas in Iraq against the US occupation set the examples. In the previous chapter I have mentioned about Mahmud Shah who died as an international Mujahid fighting against the Soviet occupation in Afghanistan. Similarly, I am aware of that some Rohingyas of young generation are active in the international arena of Muslim guerrillas. As such, the international Muslim brotherhood will not hesitate to return the Rohingya's courtesy if the need arises. Islamic Umma has been insulted by the Myanmarese quite frequently and Muslims have good reasons for a Jihad against Myanmar. The Myanmarese and Yangon government are fully aware of the situation and they are very much concerned.

Recently Muslims have developed Islamic nuclear bomb. The Islamic Republic of Pakistan with her first test of explosion on 28 May 1998 , Pakistan became the 7th nuclear power on this planet. Pakistani scientist, Dr. Abdul Qadeer Khan, who is known as *Father of Islamic bomb*, is a hero in the Islamic world. A young scientist named Dr. Muhammad Arshad, who was a Chief Scientific Officer at Pakistan Atomic Energy Commission (PAEC), pushed the button of trigger with a cry of "Allahukbar," according to the nuclear weapon archives at http://nuclearweaponarchive.org/Pakistan/PakTests.html. It was Pakistan's response to India's nuclear bomb, which is dubbed as the Hindu Bomb. The Pakistan bomb is known as the Islamic bomb, contrasting it from Hindu bomb of India, Jewish bomb of Israel, Christian of US-Europe, and Communist bomb of China and Russia. There is no Buddhist nuclear bomb yet. North Korea is a communist, not a Buddhist country. India joined the international nuclear club with her first nuclear test on May 18, 1974. The nuclear race in Asia was initiated by the 1962 Sino-India war and a series of Indo-Pakistan wars from 1947 to 1971. The question is:- Does Myanmar plan to join the nuclear club? Upgrading and expansion of the Myanmar Armed Forces in last 15 years have raised the concern. While the neighbors and the world is concern with Myanmar's activities, Myanmar is also concerned with the rising Muslim population in Bangladesh and Islamic militancy around the world. Similarly, she is also concern of the United States' aggressive international policy. In 1990, just a few days before the Gulf War commenced, a US diplomat at Bangkok said that they will take care of Burma after the Gulf War. I was at Bangkok at that time and read the news in *Bangkok Post* and *Nation* newspapers. In 1992, the visit to Bangladesh of Saudi Prince Khalid Ibn Sultan Ibn Abdul Aziz, who was the Commander-in-Chief of the 1990-91 Gulf War Allied Forces, made a vortex. During his visit, he toured the Bangladesh-Myanmar border area and was deeply touched by the plight of the Rohingya Muslim refugees from Myanmar. Emotionally disturbed, he happened to suggest a Gulf War style treatment to Burma and resettle 250,000 Burmese Muslims in their native land. Bangladesh media reported it on April 14, 1992. His suggestion raised the eyebrows across the region. The Myanmarese and Yangon government have not forgotten the vortex yet. At present Prince Khalid Ibn Sultan Ibn Abdul Aziz is the Assistant Minister of Defense and Aviation and Inspector General for Military Affairs of the Kingdom of Saudi Arabia. You will be able to understand his emotion if you visit the border areas and the Rohingya refugee camps. I am sure you will also be very, *very* disturbed; they have been inflicted with inhumanly suffering. With utmost sympathy, Saudi Arabia has been hosting the Rohingya refugees since 1978. During my Haj in 1985, I visited a number of Rohingya villages near Medina in Saudi Arabia. The same situation of the Rohingya exists not only in Bangladesh but also in Thailand and Malaysia. Recently, in November 2004, Malaysia decided to grant some 10,000 Rohingya Muslims legal refugee status and giving out work permits. We are grateful to the Malaysians and their government for this act of kindness. I am also glad that I have advocated for the Rohingya's cause in my capacity of the Patron and Chief Executive Officer of Arakan Democratic Forces (ADF) in 2001. The ADF Coordinators U San Tun Maung, U Khaing Re Myint (Al-Haj Sheikh Ahmed), and other ADF members must also be very proud of their struggle and sacrifice to achieve this end. My web site http://www.shwelumung.org serves as a window to their struggle. Please also visit the web pages at

1. http://www.shwelumaung.org/Appeals%20to%20Malaysia%20Prime%20Minister/,
2. http://www.shwelumaung.org/PRD3/,
3. http://www.shwelumaung.org/PleaseRelease/stm6/p6/, and
4. http://www.shwelumaung.org/PleaseRelease/stm6/p7/.

You will be able to see their desire for freedom. The Myanmarese and Yangon government are well aware of their wrongdoing and are afraid of retaliation. With such fear the Myanmarese and the military junta have been exhibiting hysteria in many ways. I shall examine these concerns in some more details.

7.1. Manifestation of Fear. The Myanmarese express their fear in various ways, some of them might amuse the readers. The ways they expressed are illustrated in the coming pages. In last 15 years, they have expanded and upgraded their armed forces. In this process it is possible that they also thought of arming themselves with the nuclear power. At the moment Myanmar does not have a research nuclear reactor yet. But, her ambition has surfaced in recent years with a contract with Russia to build a research reactor and her reported approach to North Korea for the nuclear technology. A piece of BBC news reported that a US Senate advisor accused Myanmar of attempting to obtain nuclear technology from North Korea. Please see the web clip from BBC news next page. I also present a table of the existing nuclear powers with their stockpiles of arsenals so that you can see a good picture of the nuclear race in the region as well as in the world. Some analysts have already dubbed this era as the Era of Second Nuclear Race.

It will be wrong for the citizens of the world to ignore the Second Nuclear Race.

BBC Online News: Thursday, 12 February, 2004, 08:51 GMT
Burma denies N Korea ties

Burma has rejected a suggestion by a senior US congressional adviser that it might be seeking nuclear technology from North Korea. Keith Luse warned that the US should pay special attention to what he called a growing relationship between the two. He was part of a US delegation that visited North Korea's Yongbyon nuclear plant in January.

In a statement, the Burmese government said it did not require nor want to develop weapons of mass destruction.

Mr. Luse, who works for Senator Richard Lugar, the chairman of the US Senate's Foreign Relations Committee, did not give any details about alleged contact between Burma and North Korea.

Note. Please allow me to boggle your mind. We know that the US nuclear bomb, which was dropped on Hiroshima on August, 06, 1945 was about 20,000 tons of TNT. It destroyed an area of 1.5 square kilometers and killed 70,000 people instantly. A similar bomb was dropped on Nagasaki on August 09, 1945, destroying a smaller area and killing some 40,000 instantly. In the aftermath, some 340,000 died from burns and radiation. If we take the Hiroshima destruction as the example it will need about 162,643 megatons of TNT to destroy entire world land area, which is 148,940,000 square kilometers (please refer back to Chapter 1, page 22). It means we will need 162,643 one-megaton nuclear bombs. Now, we have only 33,437 bombs equaling to 10,293.084 megatons of TNT. But, please do not relax. It is the nuclear fallout and nuclear winter, the aftermath of the nuclear war, which will make us extinct like the dinosaurs. Scientists believe the giant dinosaurs went extinct due to the environmental changes as a result of an asteroid collision with earth, at the Yucatán Peninsula of Mexico some 65 million years ago.

The table given below is based upon the data provided by Wm. Robert Johnston at http://www.johnstonsarchive.net/nuclear/nucstock-i.html. Please visit his web site for more details. I included Burma (Myanmar) for a comprehensive comparison.

Country	Number of Nuclear bombs	Total Megaton TNT equivalent	As of the year
Burma (Myanmar)	nil	nil	2005
China	541	568.6	2003
French	480	72	2003
Korea	10	0.40	2003
India	60	1.5	2003
Israel	208	20.4	2003
Pakistan	40	0.9	2003
Russia (USSR)	21,400	7310	2003
South Africa	6	0.084	1990
United Kingdom	192	19.2	2003
USA	10,500	2300	2003
Total	33437	10293.084	2003

Earlier, C. S. Kuppuswamy, a scholar at the South Asia Analysis Group in India, reported that two Pakistani nuclear Scientists, Suleiman Asad and Mohammed Ali Mukhtar, moved to Myanmar in November 2001 and he believes it assumes greater significance as Myanmar has recently acquired a nuclear reactor from Russia. (Source: http://www.saag.org/papers5/paper401.html, SAAG paper no. 401, January 29, 2002).

I am of opinion that the Myanmarese do have a mind or a fascination on nuclear power and weapon. While I was working as a junior faculty at the universities of Myanmar - both at Mandalay University (Magwe College), and at Rangoon University, we now and then discussed about the development of nuclear power among the faculty members. And the junior faculty members were most eager about it. It is the way to solve the energy problem as well as to deter the big neighbors, India and China. My colleagues and friends, who are the physicists, insist that nuclear technology is not a big deal, but the cost is. For your information, the Myanmar universities are under the Ministry of Education, and as such the university faculty and staff are the government employees. They simply carry out the duty assigned to them under the government policy. The entry level junior faculty, known as the demonstrators and tutors are selected and appointed by the Public Service Commission (PSC) through laborious examinations and screening process. It is an honor with prestige to get selected and appointed by the PSC; I proudly remember my service there. It was long time back in 1960s and 1970s. My friends and colleagues are now retired. Nevertheless, I always believe that the new and young generation in the universities of Myanmar will be thinking in the same way we used to do in our time.

Nuclear power is not the only source the Myanmar people can think of. The *occult power* is also in their hand, readily available, and cost effective. The following piece of news reveals that the Myanmarese put the occult power into practice whenever they think the need arises. Below, please read the news dispatched by Narinjara News, which is manned by Khaing Mrat Kyaw and his team, who are the 1988 veteran pro-democracy activists.

The Myanmarese are worried that Maungdaw might become another Normandy.

Date: Tue, 02 Sep 2003 10:20:42 -0700
To: narinjara@yahoo.com
From: "narinjara" <narinjar@aitlbd.net>
Subject: Buddhist rites to prevent foreign invasion!

Narinjara News
Buddhist rites to prevent foreign invasion!

Maungdaw, 2nd September 03: Burma's ruling junta, State Peace and Development Council, began to conduct a Buddhist religious ceremony at the border town of Maungdaw on the Naaf River in the western part of the country on 27th August 03. Sources said that the ceremony began at 0441 hours local time and ended at 5:45 pm (1745 hrs).

U Pandithara, the abbot of Alodawbreh Monastery, and fifteen other monks initiated the ceremony. For the first thirty five minutes they chanted the Upakathindhi Sutta while nine other groups of lay people continued to chant the same sutta.

The ceremony was conducted in a stage built so as to face Bangladesh in the garden in front of the Mroma Market. The cost of the building of the stage and the entire ceremony was collected from the townspeople by force.

For the ceremony each of the quarters of the township had to bear the cost of nine sets of ritualistic offerings of mostly fruits. According to a Buddhist monk attending the function, the ceremony will be continued to be held at nine hours a day, nine times a month and nine months in a year. The monk said that the number nine so used shows that the entire ceremony is a practice of magic aimed at lengthening the rule of the junta.

In the township the people have been forced to take civil defence training, what the junta termed as preparation for defending the country from foreign invasion, that has greatly hampered the agricultural and other works for their own sustenance.

The ceremony has been conducted throughout Burma since that day, the first day of the Burmese month of Tawthaling. The ceremony was attended by six hundred people including Brigadier General Maung Oo, the chairman of the Rakhine State Peace and Development Council.

The junta believes that the sutta helped the ancient Burmese kings to prevent the war with China on many occasions. #

It is unfair from my part to get amused with the recitation of Buddhist rites to prevent the foreign invasion. It simply is an expression of religious culture. In Bangladesh, I have also seen the Muslims do the same in their Islamic prayers to attain the same results and goal. I have heard world religious leaders praying for world peace, at the head of the mass assemblies. Adoption of this practice by the Myanmar military junta is a psychological warfare. Today, the Rohingya Muslims' presence is felt in the Myanmarese nerves as the Rohingya Muslims stand tall and strong internationally with the united backing of some 1.4 billion Muslims across the world (i.e. about 23.333% of total 6 billion *Homo sapiens*). The Myanmarese have never faced such a formidable enemy in their history since the time of their creation by the Brahma. The Rohingya.com makes the Myanmarese panic. Please see the web clip given here.

Please note the Rohingya's demands that are posted in their web site, especially the one that says *Rohingya autonomous state a must in the future constitution of Burma*. The reconvened National Convention to draft a new constitution at Yangon, Myanmar is going on at time of writing this book, in May 2004. What will they do if there is no Rohingya autonomy? Surely, there are many things they can.

277

I have earlier mentioned that the Myanmar government was very much concerned about the Burmese communists because the communists are a world class ideologue, and the communist giant China is just next door in the north. In a parallelism, the Muslims constitute a greater world class of ideologue, and an Islamic nation shares Myanmar's western border. I have discussed the Islamic theology and ideology before. This is the reason the Myanmar military and the Myanmarese are worried. As a matter of fact they live in constant fear and nightmare.

The political pressure exerted by the Rohingya Muslims of Arakan is considered as a real danger by all Myanmarese. The Rohingyas, by themselves, are not a military threat. On the other hand, if 1.4 billion Muslims stand up by them Myanmar will be in a helpless condition. The potential power of the Rohingyas is vividly expressed in their web site rohingya.com.

Historical Fear. The Myanmarese fear is based not only on the present circumstance but also in the historical trail. Please see the historical advancement of the Muslims with the practice of Islamic Expansionism in the given word diagram next page. The diagram has been given in the page 67, Chapter 2, but is again reproduced here for easy reference. The dates are presented in the diagram are in AD (After Delivery of Jesus), which is now widely referred as the Common Era (CE or C.E.). The Islamic calendar dates in Hijra (H) are given as presented in the *Great Dates in Islamic History*[1]. The information given in *The Comprehensive History of Bihar*[2], and our Rakhaing historical chronicles are also consulted as counter references for the Muslim advancement into Bihar, Bengal and Rakkhapura.

It will be seen in the map that Nalanda, the capital of the Buddhist world, fell into the hands of Muslims in 1192 CE, the northern Bengal, i.e. Paharpur, in 1193 CE, southern Bengal, i.e. Mainamati, in 1203 CE, and Arakan in 1660 CE. Please see the pictures of these fallen Buddhists centers in the coming pages. If the British did not occupy India, it is probable that Burma will now be in the hands of the Muslims. These historical evidence of Islamic Expansionism, in addition to the persistent assertion of the Muslims over the main land Arakan (i.e. Myanmarese Rakhine State), has driven the people of Burma into a realm of hysteria. As a result, they are rallying around the Myanmarism and getting ready to encounter the Islamic Expansionism in befitting manner. The fear is multiple as illustrated in the coming pages. Please assume yourself as a jury in criminal trial, and consider these illustrations as 'the exhibits of the case' to come to your own verdict.

Notes.
1. *Great Dates in Islamic History*, General Editor Robert Mantran, Facts On File (publisher), 1996, page xii.
2. *The Comprehensive History of Bihar*, Volumes I & II, edited by Dr. Bindeshwari Prasad Sinha, published by the Kashi Prasad Jayaswal Research Institute, Patna, 1974, Copyright Government of Bihar.

Myanmarese Fear-1
The Ghost of Islamic Empire

The following diagram from Chapter 2, page 67, is reproduced here again for your easy reference. The dates presented in the diagram are in AD (After Delivery of Jesus), which is now widely referred as the Common Era (CE or C.E.). The Islamic calendar, Hijra (H), begins in 622 CE. Here, I would like to emphasize that the southeast expansion of the Islamic Empire stopped at the Kingdom of Rakkhapura. As described earlier, when the British decolonized the region the Kingdom of Rakkhapura was left divided into three parts - 10% inside India, 15% inside Bangladesh (former East Pakistan), and 75% in side Burma. The Rakkhapurean land inside Burma is now known as the Rakhine State in Myanmar. The advancement of the British Empire into India terminated the Mogul Islamic Empire. If the British did not come into India it was probable that Burma would have become part of the Islamic Empire. This is the historical ghost that keeps haunting the Myanmarese in their nightmare.

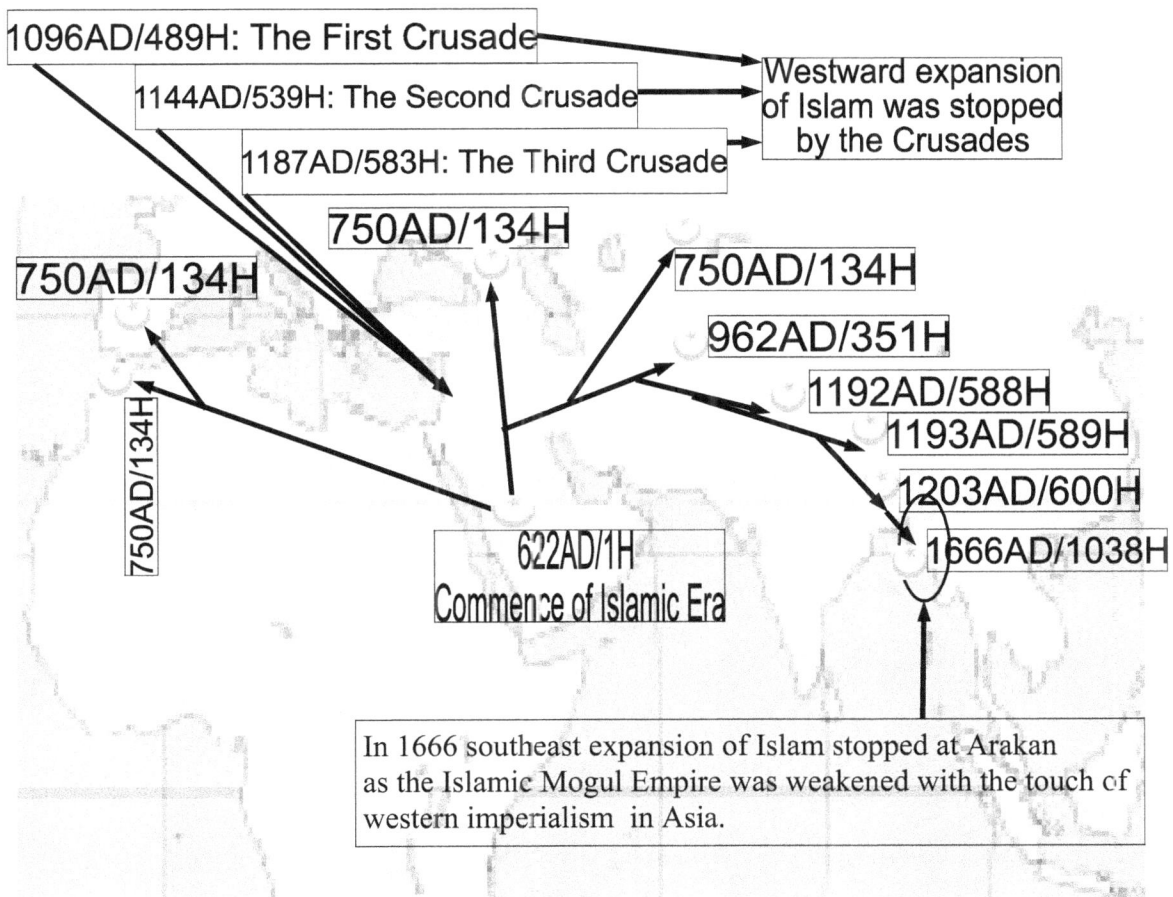

1096AD/489H: The First Crusade

1144AD/539H: The Second Crusade

1187AD/583H: The Third Crusade

Westward expansion
of Islam was stopped
by the Crusades

750AD/134H

750AD/134H

750AD/134H

962AD/351H

1192AD/588H

1193AD/589H

1203AD/600H

1666AD/1038H

750AD/134H

622AD/1H
Commence of Islamic Era

In 1666 southeast expansion of Islam stopped at Arakan
as the Islamic Mogul Empire was weakened with the touch of
western imperialism in Asia.

A world map showing the advancement
of Islamic Expansionism into present Myanmar

Please see next page to learn about the Islamic Era, months and days.

For your easy reference the following is a table of the Islamic dates and calendar as presented in the *Great Dates in Islamic History*, General Editor Robert Mantran, Facts On File, 1996, page xii.

The Islamic Calendar

The Islamic calendar dates from the Hijra (Hegira) in 622 CE It is based on the lunar year and so is shorter than the Western or Gregorian calendar, which is based on the solar year Islamic festivals are therefore celebrated at different times of the Western year

1 MUHARRAM (30 days)	**NEW YEAR'S DAY** I MUHARRAM celebrates the Hijra in 622 CE when Muhammad left Mecca to start the first Muslim community at Medina
2 SAFAR (29 days)	
3 RABI I (30 days)	**MAWLID AL-NABI** 12 RABI I celebrates the birthday of the Prophet
4 RABI II (29 days)	
5 JUMADA I (30 days)	
6 JUMADA II (29 days)	
7 RAJAB (30 days)	**LAILAT AL-MI'RAJ** 27 RAJAB the night Muhammad ascended to heaven
8 SHABAN (29 days)	**RAMADAN** The month of fasting Muslims go without food or drink from dawn to sunset each day
9 RAMADAN (30 days)	**LAILAT AL- QADR** 27 RAMADAN the Night of Power commemorates the revelation of the Qur'an to Muhammad
10 SHAWWAL (29 days)	**'ID AL-FITR** (also: al- id al saghrir; Turkish: küçük bayram, seker bayrami) I SHAWWAL the festival of breaking the fast, end of Ramadan
11 DHU'L-QA'DA (30 days)	**HAJJ** 8–13 DHU'L-HIJJA the annual pilgrimage to Mecca
12 DHU'L-HIJJA (29 days, in leap year 30 days)	**'ID AL-ADHA** (also: al id al kabir; Turkish: büyük bayram) 10 DHU'L-HIJJA the feast of sacrifice

The only reliable way of converting Islamic (Hijri) dates (H) to dates in the Christian era (CE) is by consulting conversion tables An approximation can be obtained by applying the following formula:

Islamic dates to CE:
$$CE = (H \cdot {}^{32}/33) + 622$$
CE to Islamic dates:
$$H = (CE - 622) \cdot {}^{32}/33$$

* On March 1, 1917, **Turkey** introduced the Gregorian calendar
* In 1925, **Iran** reintroduced the Persian sun year, which is adjusted to the Gregorian calendar, but begins with the Hijra The conversion of these "hijra sun years" (*hijri shamsi*, H Sh) is easy: HSh + 621 (for dates between March 21 and December 31), and HSh + 622 (for dates between January 1 and March 20)

The days of the week are named by ordinal numbers, except for Friday and Saturday:

yawm al-ahad (the first day) = Sunday
yawm al-ithnayn (the second day) = Monday
yawm al-thulatha' (the third day) = Tuesday
yawm al-arbi'a' (the fourth day) = Wednesday
yawm al-khamis (the fifth day) = Thursday
yawm al-jum'a (the day of congregation) = Friday
yawm al-sabt (the day of rest) = Saturday

Myanmarese Fear-2
Will Nalanda's fate visit Myanmar Buddhist institutions?

Nalanda Excavations, Archaeological Survey of India. (Source: *The Comprehensive History of Bihar*, editor Dr. Bindeshwari Prasad Sinha, The Kashi Prasad Jayaswal Research Institute, Patna, Vol. 1, Plate 46, 1974, copyright Government of Bihar.

Nalanda[1] was the epicenter of the three world religions namely, Brahmanism, Jainism and Buddhism from 5th century BCE to 12th century CE spanning a period of 1,700 years. In the vicinity of Nalanda, Buddha met and converted Maha Kassapa who became head of Buddhist community after Buddha Parinibbana. Arahat Sariputta and Moggalana were also known to be born in the area of Nalanda. Nalanda Vihara was the main monastery of Buddha during his 45 years of mission. It is not wrong to say it was *the* capital of the Buddhist world. He delivered many of his discourses there and converted many people including well known Upali who was a disciple of Jain Guru Niganta Nataputta. (Please read Upalisutta, Majjhima Nikaya, which can be found in any standard book of Buddhism). From 5th to 12th CE, under the patronage of Gupta and Chandra dynasties Nalanda university was the biggest university in the world housing more than 1 million copies of books and manuscripts covering all religions, and all subjects in Sanskrit and Pali. A Chinese scholar named Hiuen Tsiang, a student of Nalanda in 7th century recorded that there were 1510 teachers and 8500 students in his days. In 1234, the Tibetan pilgrim Dharmasvamin left an a gripping account of the monastery's destruction by the Muslims. Myanmar sources say Nalanda burns for 30 days and 30 nights. The Myanmarese are afraid that the fate of Nalanda might visit their Buddhist institutions. Please visit http://www.myanmar.com/pagoda/pagoda.html to see the Myanmar Buddhist institutions.

Notes.
1. The information given in this section are collected from (1) *The Comprehensive History of Bihar*, editor Dr. Bindeshwari Prasad Sinha, The Kashi Prasad Jayaswal Research Institute, Patna, Vols. 1&2 , 1974, copyright Government of Bihar, (2) Buddhist traditions of Myanmar, and (3) http://www.buddhanet.net/e-learning/pilgrim/pg_19.htm, A Pilgrims Guide to Buddhist India: Nalanda, as of April 15, 2003.

Myanmarese Fear-3
The Ruins of Paharpur

With the advancement of the Muslims to the southeast the Buddhist civilizations came to an end, one after another. The Ruins of Paharpur and Mainamati stand as the ageless witness of the Muslim invasion in its wilderness. Mahayana Buddhist University known as Somapura Mahavira was situated at Pahapur, Northern Bangladesh. The United Nations Education, Science and Cultural Organization has inscribed Paharpur as a world heritage. Today Paharpur is just a piece of mound. It survived some 500 years from 7th to 12th century till the Muslims Islamized Bengal. UNESCO's patronization possibly, but not probably, will help prevent further destruction. Mainamati, though, was still a cattle grazing ground when I visited last in 1987, and it has not changed its status yet. Please see next page.

The Ruins of Paharpur Buddhist Vihara, Northern	Source: http://whc.unesco.org/sites/322.htm
	Inscribed :1985 **Criteria:** C (i) (ii) (vi) **Justification for Inscription:** Report of the 9th Session of the Committee **Brief description:** Evidence of the rise of Mahayana Buddhism in Bengal from the 7th century onwards, Somapura Mahavira, or the Great Monastery, was a renowned intellectual centre until the 12th century. Its layout perfectly adapted to its religious function, this monastery-city represents a unique artistic achievement. With its simple, harmonious lines and its profusion of carved decoration, it influenced Buddhist architecture as far away as Cambodia.

Myanmarese Fear-4
The Ruins of Mainamati

Mainamati today is nothing more than a cattle grazing ground. Whenever the needs arise the local people go and dig two or three bricks from there to make stepping stones in the muddy footpath or a fire place in the kitchen. It gives some honor and credibility to the scholars who study its historical significance. Bangli Muslims simple try to earn a few tourist dollars from it. For the Buddhists it is a site to mourn and to grieve. Fully understanding such *ends*, Buddha - the Enlightened One - in his last words said, "Impermanent are compound things; strive with earnestness"[1].

Mainamati is believed to be part of Pattikera kingdom. It was very probable that Prince Raza Kumar who wrote Myasedi Stone Inscription (1084 CE) in four languages namely Pyu, Mon, Pali, and Myanmar, was educated in Mainamati. Since it was the first time the Myanmar script appeared in writing, it was very likely that Prince Raza Kumar introduced it to the country. He was the only son of the powerful Myanmar Pagan King Kyansittha with his Mrama[2] wife Sambul or Thanbulla. According to the Myanmar chronicles Pattikera King established alliance with Myanmar King Alaungsithu (1085-1160) by wedding his daughter to the latter. With the charges of sorcery, Alaungsithu's son King Narathu killed the Pattikera Princess. Pattikera king sent four commandos who killed Myanmar King, Narathu, right on his throne and then they all committed suicide immediately. The Myanmarese historians dubbed their king as 'Kala-kya-min' meaning the 'king-dethroned-by-kala'. By now I believe the reader will be familiar with the meaning of Myanmar word 'kala'. Yes, it means the foreigners.

My question is-: Was Pattikera-Myanmar alliance[3] an attempt of Bengal king to form a Buddhist front in response to the rise of the Muslims in the northwest India?

Excavations at Mainamati: An Exploratory Study/Abu Imam[4]. Dhaka, The International Centre for Study of Bengal Art, 2000, 189 p., ISBN 984-31-1144-3. [Studies in Bengal Art Series: No. 2]

Contents: Preface. 1. Introduction. 2. Salban Vihara. 3. Kutila Mura. 4. Itakhola Mura. 5. Rupban Mura. 6. Ananda Vihara. 7. Charpatra Mura. 8. Bhoja Vihara, Mainamati Ranir Bunglow & Mainamati Mound 1A. 9. Other sites. 10. Retrospection. Appendix: 'Recent archaeological discoveries along the Mainamati and Lalmai ranges, Tippera District, East Bengal', Reproduced, from Dr. Bhandarkar et al. (ed.) B.C. *Law Volume, Part II*, The Bhandarkar oriental Research Institute, Poona, 1946/T.N. Ramachandran. Bibliography. Index. No. 20744.

Notes.
1. Please read *Maha-Parinibbana-sutta* in any Buddhist cannon book or in *Buddhism, A Religion of Infinite Compassion* by Clarence H. Hamilton, New York Liberal Arts Press, 1952, p45.
2. Please note the affinity of Mrama, Mranmar and Myanmar.
3. King Kyansittha's most favorite queen, Abeyratana, was also a Pattikera princess. Alaungsithu was their grandson. Please also see the foot noate on page 270.
4. You might like to read this book on Mainamati. It is available at https://www.vedamsbooks.com. It can also be ordered from Vedams eBooks(P) Ltd., Vardhaman Charve Plaza IV, Building #9, KP Block, Pitampura, New Delhi 110 088, India, Fax: 91-11-25745114 or 91-11-27255613, e-mail: vedams@vedamsbooks.com.

Myanmarese Fear-5
Will Shwedagon Pagoda face the fate of Paharpur and Mainamati?

The Myanmarese fear that one day the Muslims might change their sacred pagoda Shwedagon into an archaeological mound, just like Paharpur and Mainamati. There is some substance in it. In addition to the ruins of Nalanda, Paharpur, and Mainamati that are mentioned here, there also exists Borobudur meditating in the ruins of Java Island of Indonesia. In recent days the reader will be aware of the dispute of Ayodhya Hindu Temple and Babri Mosque in Uttar Pradesh of India. It is an open secret in Burma that in the days of British colonial rule the Muslims tried to build a Mosque near Shwedagon pagoda, to level in its size and glamour. In the beginning, the British Authorities were in favor of it, but later declined in the face of a strong protest from the Buddhists. The Mosque was then allowed to build in the vicinity of Sulé pagoda at Rangoon downtown. Similarly, Akyab Mosque was planned to build next to the most revered Buddhist shrine, Phragri, in Akyab (Sittwe or Saite Twey). The City Square now known as Wunkaba Gwun was the proposed site of the Akyab Mosque. Again, due to the strong opposition put up by the Buddhists it was moved to the present place, south of the city. Under these circumstances that the Myanmarese remain shrouded with fear of Islamic activities.

Shwedagon

According to the legend, the original stupa on this site would have been built during the Buddha's lifetime in the sixth century B.C. Such an irrational idea only adds to the magic this holy place holds for believers.

Magic or not, the Shwedagon complex is impressive and beautiful. The main stupa, that rises 98 meters above its base, is surrounded by a forest of some 60 small ones and by an equal number of shrines, pavilions and temples on a 5.6 hectare (14 acre), marble paved platform.

Acknowledgement: The above Photo with caption is by Mr. Bernard Cloutier (2000), produced here with his kind permission. Many thanks to Bernard. Please visit his web site at http://berclo.net/page00/00en-myanmar-7.html. He has many wonderful photos.

Myanmarese Fear-6
Will Maha Mrat Muni Rakhaing Buddha face the fate of Afghanistan Bumiyan Buddha?

I may not need to write many words about Afghanistan Bumiyan Buddha. I believe every human being knows that 1,500-year-old Buddha was blown up by the Islamic Taleban regime of Afghanistan, in 2001. The first year of the 21st century is filled with extreme Islamic activities across the world. The 11th of September, 2001 was just like a micro-Hiroshima in New York City of the United States when the twain towers of the World Trade Center were blown up by the airplane bomb. The world will never be the same again. The fear of Islamic extremism will permeate throughout this century. Myanmarese are also frightened with the thought that their prime booty Maha Mrat Muni Rakhaing Buddha could be next Bumiyan Buddha. In the eyes of the Muslims and in the theology of Islam, Buddha images are nothing but man-made idols.

Maha Mrat Muni Rakhaing Buddha was made with Buddha's permission in His own

The UNESCO should inscribe Maha Mrat Muni Rakhaing Buddha, or the Prisoner of Mandalay, as a world heritage.

presence according to the Rakkhapura chronicles. Most historians believed that it was made in the 2nd century CE. Thus Rakhaing Buddha is older than Bumiyan Buddha, and probably is *the first Buddha image* made in the world. It was robbed away by the Bama king Maung Wyne from Rakkhapura Rakhaingpray in 1784 CE. During that brutal and savage invasion-cum-robbery the Bama Nation killed 250,000 or a quarter of our total population. Another 100,000 were chained and driven to Mandalay. The most painful event was that they had to carry Maha Mrat Muni Rakhaing Buddha, the greatest booty of the Bama. Since then Rakhaing Buddha has been kept as the Prisoner of Mandalay. It will be 221 years on the 31st of December, 2005. Arakan Democratic Forces (ADF) has demanded to free the Maha Mrat Muni Rakhaing Buddha and return it to its original temple in Rakhaingpray. Please visit http://www.shwelumaung.org/PrisonerofMandalay/.

Bumiyan Buddha, general view as presented by the UNESCO, just before it was dynamited to dust by the Taliban.
Source:-
http://portal.unesco.org/en/ev.php@URL_ID=1259&URL_DO=DO_TOPIC&URL_SECTION=-459.html.

RECLAIMING AFGHANISTAN'S PAST

NEWS

Buddhas May Stretch Out, If Not Rise Again

A UNESCO team finds that at least the larger of the destroyed Buddhas could be salvaged, although the smaller one is mostly powder

Even the science fundamentalist American Association For the Advancement of Science (AAAS) was intrigued with the destruction that it printed the news in its journal *Science* Vol. 298, 8 November 2002, with a cover-page story, pages 1123-1286.

Myanmarese Fear-7
The fear of re-defining freedom

Today, Islamic cultural renaissance can be seen all over the world. The culture of Islamic address, especially that of the Muslim women's head scarves, has become a world-wide issue. The free societies in Germany, France, Netherlands, United Kingdom, United States, and Canada are now engaged in the debates of dress codes and religious freedom in public schools, offices, and armed forces. The same issues are in debate in Burma. Daw Suu was presented as a free and bold leader by her exiled followers in the front cover page of their *'Pan Sagar'* magazine (Forum Publication, Number (16), August September 1996). The fear is:- Will the day come when Daw Suu has to hide inside a burqas when she goes around campaigning for democracy? This is a symbolic question of the dangers that the Myanmarese society ponders. In deed Burmese women's social freedom, in contrast to political freedom, is well respected across the world.

Burqas originally was a desert dress to protect the whole body from scorching sun heat of the desert. This desert dress becomes religious garment in the religions such as Christianity and Islam that were born in the desert culture. In Christianity, only the nuns wear burqas, and it is accepted as appropriate. It is a suitable outfit for the nuns. In contrasts, in Islam there is no female clergy, to whom the burqas can be confined. The Islamic dress code is derived from two Quranic verses, namely 24:31 Al-Nour (The Light) and 33:59 Al-Ahzab (The Confederates). The interpretations of this Quranic revelations still remain controversial and debated in fury, even after 1300 years. Such heated debates will always infuse fear in Myanmar which is neighboring an Islamic country with a population of 140 millions.

Quran 33:59 Al-Ahzab (The Confederates)
O Prophet! Tell thy wives and daughters, and the believing women, that they should cast their outer garments over their persons (when abroad): that is most convenient, that they should be known (as such) and not molested. And Allah is Oft- Forgiving, Most Merciful. Translation by Yusuf Ali, http://www.islamicity.com.

Daw Suu was presented as a free and bold leader by her exiled followers in the front cover page of their *'Pan Sagar'* magazine (Forum Publication, Number (16), August September 1996). But, Imagine Daw Suu in burqas?

Quran 24:31 Al-Nour (The Light)
And say to the believing women that they should lower their gaze and guard their modesty; that they should not display their beauty and ornaments except what (must ordinarily) appear thereof; that they should draw their veils over their bosoms and not display their beauty except to their husbands, their fathers, their husband's fathers, their sons, their husbands' sons, their brothers or their brothers' sons, or their sisters' sons, or their women, or the slaves whom their right hands possess, or male servants free of physical needs, or small children who have no sense of the shame of sex; and that they should not strike their feet in order to draw attention to their hidden ornaments. And O ye Believers! turn ye all together towards Allah, that ye may attain Bliss. Translation by Yusuf Ali, http://www.islamicity.com.

The Myanmarese Fear is:-
Will the Myanmar society get Islamized and the Myanmar girls have to go out in burqas like this Rohingya Muslim girl shown in the rohingya.com?

World News

Aung San Suu Kyi: Symbol of Burma's Free Soul

Shwe Lu Maung

Mrs. Aung San Suu Kyi Aris was awarded Noble Peace Price in 1991.

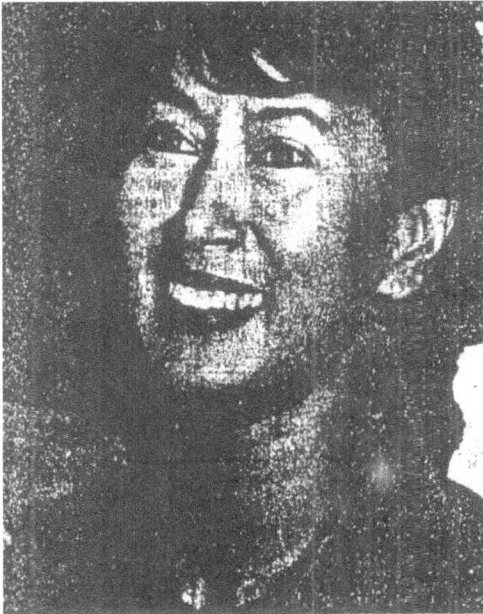

In early 1989 while Aung San Suu Kyi was happily and boldly campaigning for her National League for Democracy (NLD), looking forward to the day of election on 27 May 1990, she confidently said, "I believe I must now call myself a politician." Thus, she entered politics following in the foot steps of her father, General Aung San. On 20 July 1990 her father's army which is now ruling the country under the name of the State Law and Order Restoration Council (SLORC) put her under house arrest.

Illustrated Weekly, Friday 15 May 1992, Dhaka, Bangladesh
(You can read this article at my website http://www.shwelumaung.org/BurmaFreeSoul/page2.html).

When I wrote the article 'Aung San Suu Kyi' for the Illustrated Weekly, (Friday 15 May 1992), Dhaka, Bangladesh, the editor added 'Symbol of Burma's Free Soul' as the subtitle. I was a contributing reporter of the magazine at that time. Today, the Myanmarese are afraid that their 'free soul' might have to hide behind a burcas in coming days if the Islamic expansionism takes roots in Myanmar. Fear is illustrated in the previous page. In such fear, the Myanmarese are cooperating with the military junta, prolonging her detention. I ended the above-mentioned article of 1992 as follow.

"On 19 June this year *(i.e. 1992)* she will be celebrating her 47th birthday all by herself. How many birthdays she has thus to celebrate alone is what naturally causes deep concern around the world."

As I conclude this book in 2005, she observed her 60th birthday alone.

Myanmarese Fear-8
The fear of being cornered

Today the Myanmarese feel that they are being surrounded and cornered by the Muslims. It is in the same way they felt being surrounded by the communists in 1950s and 1960s. Please see the Islamic activities map below and compare it with the communist power map in page 200. This 'fear of Muslim' is the current psychopathology of the world. The Americans feel that they are being attacked by the Muslims and they have to destroy every Muslim nation. Accordingly they invaded Afghanistan and Iraq, and also voice preemptive strikes at Libya, Syria, and Sudan. This is the foreign policy that won President George W. Bush the 2004 election for his

Islamic Activities Map. A sketch map showing the Islamic activities in Burma and Thailand, in relation to their neighboring Islamic countries. Please compare this with the Communist powers map in Chapter 5.2, page 199.

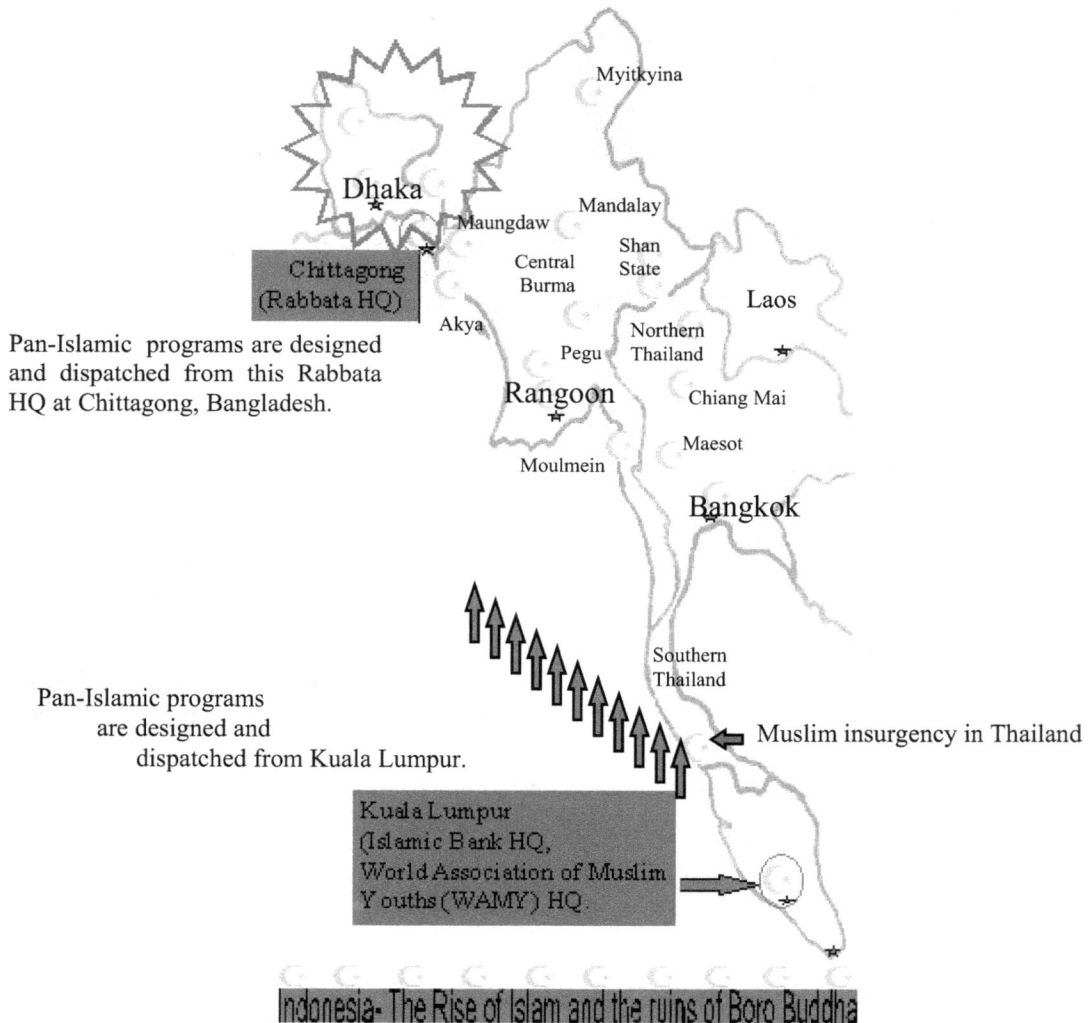

Myitkyina

Dhaka

Mandalay

Maungdaw

Shan State

Chittagong (Rabbata HQ)

Central Burma

Akya

Laos

Northern Thailand

Pegu

Pan-Islamic programs are designed and dispatched from this Rabbata HQ at Chittagong, Bangladesh.

Rangoon

Chiang Mai

Maesot

Moulmein

Bangkok

Pan-Islamic programs are designed and dispatched from Kuala Lumpur.

Southern Thailand

Muslim insurgency in Thailand

Kuala Lumpur (Islamic Bank HQ, World Association of Muslim Youths (WAMY) HQ.

Indonesia- The Rise of Islam and the ruins of Boro Buddha

Islamic star and crescent moon symbols indicates major Islamic centers in the given country.

second term. The American Muslims are being alienated in many US cities and people look at them as the terrorists. Similar news are coming out from United Kingdom, Netherlands, France, Germany, Spain, and Italy. The reactions of the Europeans and Americans are equally matched by the Muslims with increased militancy around the world. Recently Thailand encounters Muslim insurgency in her Muslim dominated southern region. Malaysia has voiced that Thailand should give her Muslims autonomy. Existence of Muslim separation struggle in Burma since 1950 is a well known fact across the world. In the light of these political realities it is natural that the Myanmarese feel being surrounded and cornered.

The news clips given below will give the reader a clear picture of the Islamic activities that raise the Myanmarese goose pimples.

Source as of April 19, 2003
http://www.washtimes.com/upi-breaking/20021220-023332-3744r.htm

Kashmir women 'slain over Islamic dress'

By Harbaksh Nanda
UNITED PRESS INTERNATIONAL

NEW DELHI, Dec. 20 (UPI) -- Suspected Islamic rebels killed three young women in India's Kashmir region for not wearing burqas, the head-to-toe veiled dress worn by Muslim women.

---

http://news.bbc.co.uk/2/hi/asia-pacific/2116032.stm

Monday, 8 July, 2002, 12:53 GMT 13:53 UK
Malaysian state passes Islamic law

A state government in Malaysia has approved a bill to bring in Islamic criminal laws, including death by stoning for adultery and cutting off hands and feet for theft.

The bill on hudud law - the Islamic penal code - was proposed by the government of Terengganu, a rural state in the north-east run by Islamic party PAS.

Last Updated: Monday, 2 June, 2003, 23:52 GMT 00:52 UK
✉ E-mail this to a friend   🖨 Printable version

Pakistan province cheers Sharia

By Paul Anderson
BBC correspondent in Pakistan

There were cheers and shouts of "Allah is Great" in Peshawar's elegant assembly building when the bill introducing Sharia, or Islamic law, went into the statute books.

BBC NEWS UK EDITION

Last Updated: Sunday, 16 May, 2004, 16:23 GMT 17:23 UK
✉ E-mail this to a friend   🖨 Printable version

Blasts rock Thai Buddhist temples

Bombs have exploded at three Buddhist temples in Thailand's troubled mainly-Muslim south.

A bystander was slightly wounded outside one temple, Reuters reports.

BBC NEWS
Last Updated: Thursday, 29 April, 2004, 07:06 GMT 08:06 UK

Analysis: Thailand's Muslim divide
By Tony Cheng
BBC, Bangkok

Over 100 years ago the kings of Siam absorbed the Islamic kingdom of Pattani into their territory. Many people see this as the start of the region's Muslim insurgency. Others point to much more modern reasons for the problems in the south.

BBC NEWS
Last Updated: Friday, 30 April, 2004, 01:50 GMT 02:50 UK
Who was behind the Thai attacks?
By Kate McGeown
BBC News Online
Wednesday's militant attacks on a series of police outposts have left many in southern Thailand reeling.
Mystery surrounds the identity of the attackers - and the reason for what many see as little more than a suicide mission. Prime Minister Thaksin Shinawatra has blamed the violence on local gangs involved in smuggling and drug trafficking. But there is an increasing fear that Islamic separatists were behind the attacks - helped by international militant organisations.

7.3. Myanmarese Reaction in Response to Their Fear

Articles like the following in the Journal of Institute of Peace and Conflict Studies (IPCS) elevates Myanmarese blood pressure. Are the Indians making the Myanmarese frightened? Not necessarily. The Myanmarese intelligence services and political analysts are world class. The very fact that the Yangon junta has stayed in power for long 43 years from 1962 to 2005 itself will testify that they are damn good in political analysis. As a matter of fact, they are not only the oldest but also strongest military government in the world. Even Pakistan military government suffered short interludes when the civilians, like Zulfiqar Ali Bhutto, Banazir Bhutto and their Pakistan Peoples' Party (PPP) ruled them. What is that they are afraid of actually? They are not concerned or worried that India, China, Bangladesh, Thailand or United States will embark at their borders and invade them. It is not politically or militarily feasible to invade Myanmar by any of these countries. Strategically speaking all these countries, counter balancing each other, serve as the guardians of Myanmar. This is the main reason why the Myanmar military junta has been able to remain in power and easily quench the internal challenges. Nonetheless, the Myanmarese surely are afraid of the irregular armies of the Islamic militants. Weathered and hardened in their professionalism, the Myanmarese Armed Forces

---

Harkat-ul-Jihad-al-Islami Bangladesh (HuJI-BD) PG Rajamohan
Research Scholar, Jawaharlal Nehru University

Origin: The *Harkat-ul-Jehad-al-Islami Bangladesh* (HuJI-BD) was established by drawing inspiration from Osama bin Laden and with the assistance of bin Laden's *International Islamic Front* (IIF) in 1992. Earlier, *Harkat-ul-Jehad-al-Islami* (HuJI) and *Harkat-ul-Mujahideen* (HuM) were under the single banner of *Harkat-ul-Ansar* (HuA). The US State Department placed HuA in the world terrorist organizations list soon after the group kidnapped few American and European tourists in Jammu and Kashmir through its *Al-Faran* operation in 1995. The HuA, therefore, forked as HuM and HuJI and continued its subversive activities in Pakistan and Kashmir. In Bangladesh, however, the HuA just renamed itself as HuJI-Bangladesh and started functioning under HuJI-Pakistan.

Leaders: HUJI-BD is headed by Showkat Osman *alias* Sheikh Farid while Imtiaz Quddus is the General Secretary.

Objectives: The primary objective of HuJI-BD is to establish the Islamic *Hukumat* (Islamic rule) in Bangladesh.

Strength: It is estimated that HuJI-BD might have 15,000-20,000 cadres, majority of whom *madaris* (religious scholastics) educated in *madrassas* (religious seminaries); ...... The new recruits receive their training in camps based in Bangladesh and, sometimes abroad, like Afghanistan and/or Pakistan.

Harkat recruits not only its own nationals; a significant source for its membership is the huge refugee population from Myanmar. The stateless *Rohingya* Muslims, who fled their native place from Myanmar over the years, have enthusiastically joined the HuJI due to religious persecution. In the 1990s, the *Harkat-ul-Ansar* (HuA) had set up training camps in Bangladesh for training local recruits as well as those from India, Arakan, and the Abu Sayyaf group in southern Philippines. It is reported that *Harkat's* recruits were present in Jammu and Kashmir, Afghanistan and Chechnya.

Internal Network: The most important alliance of the HuJI-BD inside Bangladesh are the Islamic fundamentalist political parties like *Jamaat-e-Islami, Islami Oikya Jote, Kilafat-e-Majilis, Islami Shasantantra Andolan* and *Islami Chattra Shibir*. Among these, the *Jamaat-e-Islami* and *Islami Oikya Jote* are partners of the ruling Bangladesh

---

You can read full article at:-
http://www.ipcs.org/ipcs/databaseIndex2.jsp?database=1004&country2=Harkat-ul-Jihad-al-Islami%20Bangladesh%20(HuJI-BD)

understand that irregular armies are the most difficult to beat, especially the Islamic irregular armies. It is highly probable that Bangladesh could fall into the grip of the irregular Islamic armies or Islamic Communes if the present trends of Islamic sociology, culture, economy and politic continue there for next ten to twenty years. Myanmarese are calculating that in near future they will have to confront the Islamic irregular armies that could be as much well organized as the Mongolian Golden and White Hordes of Genghis Khan's grand children. It was the Great Khan's grand children who embraced Islam and used the Muslim forces to establish the Khanates and Mogul Islamic Empire from 12th to 16th centuries.

Burdened with these fears and blinded by tinted ego of the First, the Second, and the Third Myanmar Empires, the Myanmarese have given up their struggle of democracy and joined hands with the military junta that calls itself the Armed Forces Government (AFG). As I mentioned earlier all armed rebel forces have either made peace or surrendered to the AFG. Today, the Myanmarese, a nation of 45 millions, stand out with a 450,000-strong† Armed Forces in contrast to a less than 125,500-strong armed forces of Bangladesh that houses 140 million citizens. If we include the people militia the Myanmarese fighting force will exceed 500,000 mark. In the coming pages I will show how the Myanmar Armed Forces stand today.

The analyses of the military strength of Myanmar and her surrounding neighbors, Thailand, China, India, and Bangladesh, are presented below. The analyses are based upon the conservative estimates† given by *The Military Balance 2003-2004*, the International Institute of Strategic Studies (IISS), London. Please consult the IISS publications for the details.

The military strength of Bangladesh, Myanmar and their neighbors as stand in early 2004. (Source: *The Military Balance 2003-2004*, the International Institute of Strategic Studies (IISS), London).		India	Bangladesh	Myanmar†	China	Thailand
	Military Total*	1,325,000	125,500	381,000	2,250,000	314,200
	Army	1,100,000	110,000	350,000	1,700,000	190,000
	Navy	55,000	9,000	16,000	250,000	79,200
	Air Force	170,000	6,500	15,000	400,000	45,000
	SMF**	0	0	0	100,000	0
	Paramilitary	1,089,700	63,200	107,000	1,500,000	113,000
	Reserve	535,000	0	0	600,000	200,000

* Paramilitary not included. **Strategic Missile Forces (SMF).

Proportional Strength of 5 countries of interest in relative to Myanmar strength, which is defined as 1. For example Bangladesh strength is only 30% of Myanmar's whereas China's is about 5 times more. This data is derived from the above table.

India	3.478
Bangladesh	0.329
Myanmar	1
China	5.906
Thailand	0.825

Visualization of Bangladesh and Myanmar Armed Forces in a graphic pie

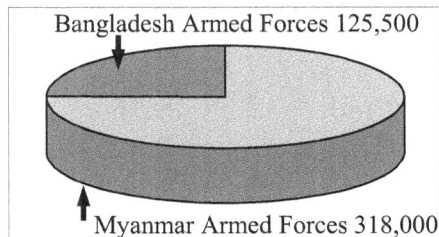

Bangladesh Armed Forces 125,500

Myanmar Armed Forces 318,000

† In 2004, the Rakhaing observers estimated that Myanmar military total strength was around 450,000, due to aggressive and forceful recruitment in the Rakhine State including 12-year old boys. The Rakhaing sources told me that only old men and women were left in their land Roughly 30% of the Myanmar Armed Forces is constituted by the ethnic Rakhaings. Most of them are compelled by absolute poverty while some are also motivated with the propaganda *'in defence against the Kala invasion'*, though the Rakhaing soldiers are never stationed in their own Rakhaing land.

The following map shows today's stand and positioning of the Myanmar Armed Forces in the western Myanmar Rakhine State that borders Bangladesh. The Myanmar Armed Forces are headed by a Senior General (5-star), who is assisted by a Vice Senior General (5-star), three Generals (4-star), nine Lt. Generals (3-star), one Air Force Admiral and one Naval Admiral. The country is divided into nine military commands; each command zone is kept under the command of a Major General or Lieutenant General. The Rakhine State is under the Western Command.

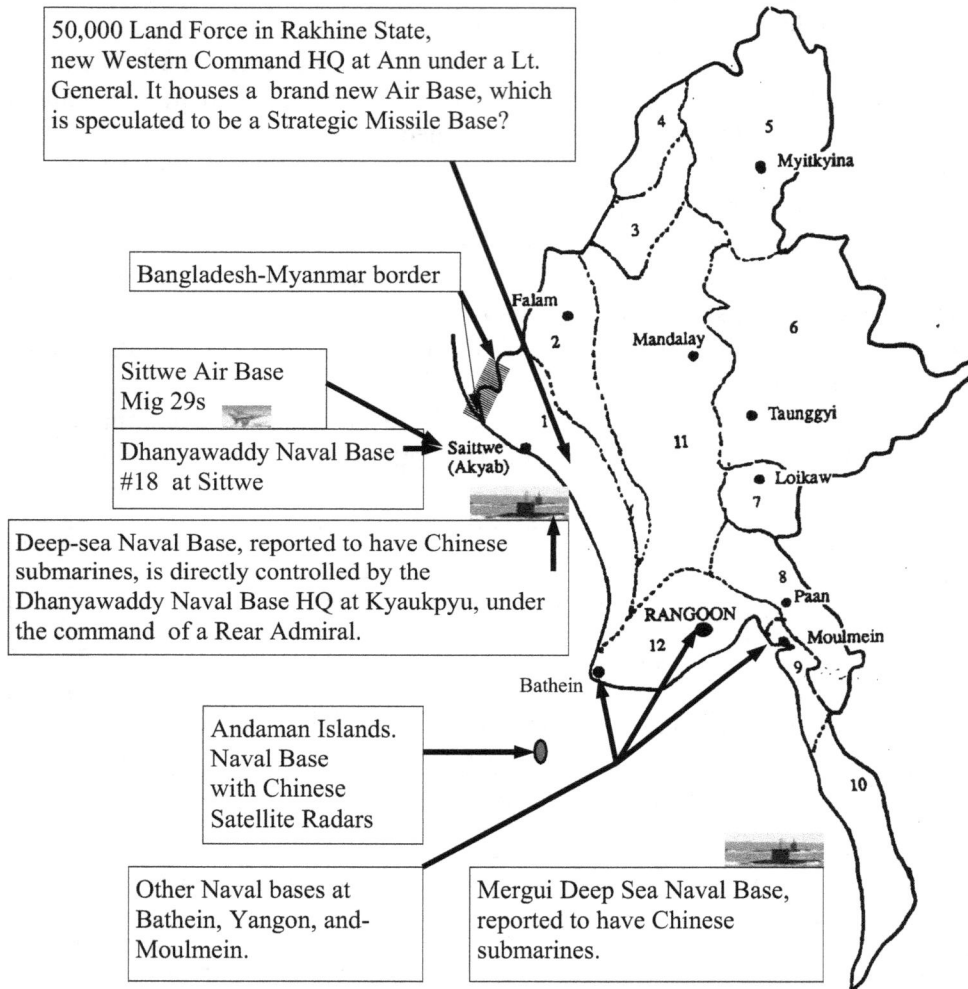

50,000 Land Force in Rakhine State, new Western Command HQ at Ann under a Lt. General. It houses a brand new Air Base, which is speculated to be a Strategic Missile Base?

Bangladesh-Myanmar border

Sittwe Air Base Mig 29s

Dhanyawaddy Naval Base #18 at Sittwe

Deep-sea Naval Base, reported to have Chinese submarines, is directly controlled by the Dhanyawaddy Naval Base HQ at Kyaukpyu, under the command of a Rear Admiral.

Andaman Islands. Naval Base with Chinese Satellite Radars

Other Naval bases at Bathein, Yangon, and Moulmein.

Mergui Deep Sea Naval Base, reported to have Chinese submarines.

The Western Command headquarter is at Ann, which also controls Ann-Ngaphéy serpentine highway over the Rakhaing Roma Mountains. This highway is part of the Asian Highway that links New Delhi to Singapore. The observers speculate that Ann Military Base could be a strategic missile base with the Chinese help. The Chinese involvement can be seen in four places, namely Ann Air base, Kyaukpyu and Mergui Deep-sea Naval bases and Satellite Reconnaissance Stations at the Adamans Islands. Ann Military Base was constructed and built solely by the military personnel, not even a single civilian coolie was employed. In general, the civilians are drafted as hard laborers. Chinese supervised the construction of the deep-sea naval base at Rambree Island to house the submarines. But, I believe a missile base could be detected by the spy satellite. No such report is out yet.

Sighting of the submarines have been reported by the local fishermen. It is believed that these must be the Chinese submarines.

China has the following submarines.

1. Ballistic Missile Submarines
2. Nuclear Powered Attack Submarines
3. Diesel-Electric Submarines

Please search the world wide web for the Chinese submarines. This piece of information is taken from an article by Andrew Toppan at http://www.hazegray.org/worldnav/china/submar.htm#ssbn. It is possible that Myanmar has older version of 'Ming' or 'Romeo' class patrol submarines with diesel-electric powered engines. Andrew Toppan's specifications are given below.

'Ming' Class. Andrew Toppan determines that this submarine class is technologically obsolete but are still *"useful as patrol and coastal defense assets"*.
Displacement: 2,113 tons submerged
Dimensions: 76 x 7.6 x 5.1 meters/249.3 x 25 x 16.7 feet
Propulsion: Diesel-electric, 2 diesels, 2 shafts, 3,500 shp, 18 knots
Crew: 55
Sonar: Herkulese active/passive, Feniks passive
Armament: 8 21-inch torpedo tubes (6 bow, 2 stern; 16 torpedoes or 28 mines)

'Romeo' Class. Andrew Toppan classifies this submarine class, built between 1960-1984, as obsolete.
Displacement: 1,712 tons full load
Dimensions: 76.6 x 6.7 x 4.95 meters/251.3 x 22 x 16.2 feet
Propulsion: Diesel-electric, 2 diesels, 2 shafts, 2,700 shp, 13 knots
Crew: 51
Sonar: Tamir-5L active, Feniks passive
Armament: 8 21-inch torpedo tubes (6 bow, 2 stern; 14 torpedoes or 28 mines)

It can be argued that strengthening of the military resources in Myanmar Rakhine State is to provide effective security to the newly discovered offshore gas field. This surely is a logical reasoning. On the other hand, in the contemporary world history there has been a number of wars over the gas and oil resources. The experts have estimated that the Rakhaing gas field could generate a revenue up to 3 billion dollars a year (Supratim Mukherjee, Arakanpost, March, 2004, pp12-13). Officially there lives some three million people in Myanmar Rakhine State. This gives a $1,000.00 annual income per head by the gas revenue. As Myanmar's per capita income is less than $200 this is something that could add one more good reason to kill and die for. Please see the gas field next page; Arakanpost presented it as its cover story in 2004 March issue.

A scholar named C.S. Kuppuswamy, in his article *Myanmar-China Cooperation; its implications for India* (paper no. 596. 03. 02. 2003, SAAG, http://www.saag.org/papers6/paper596.html), highlights India's concern over the extension of Myanmar naval facilities on Great Coco Island, Indian Ocean. According to him "....The strategic location of Myanmar as

ARAKANPOST
Monthly Journal

Issue - 3
March, 2004

Arakan gas field constitutes
one more good reason to kill and die for.

an entry point to the Indian Ocean and the ostracization of this nation by the West since the military take over in 1988 has been taken full advantage of by China to make it virtually *a China satellite in the Indian Ocean*". Please note 03. 02. 2003 is February 03, 2003; it is the Euro-Asian style of the date, dd/mm/yyyy, in contrast to the US style mm/dd/yyyy.

Similarly, Lt Cdr Atul Bharadwaj, *Defence Analyst,* reported Myanmar acquirement of MIG-29s, in 2002. I have added more information that are collected from a number of websites. It is clear that Myanmar is arming herself from feet to teeth.

Myanmar and MiG-29s

Article No: 751
Date: 21 May 2002

Lt Cdr Atul Bharadwaj
Defence Analyst

Myanmar's Armed Forces known as *Tatmadaw* became the proud owners of one of the most sophisticated fighter aircraft when they purchased eight Russian MiG-29 'Fulcrum' fighters and two MiG-29 UB trainers in July 2001. Since *Tatmadaw* assumed power in 1988, the acquisition of advanced fighter jets was a prime requirement in their wish list. (Institute of Peace & Conflict Studies, Article no. 751, (May 21, 2002), at http://www.ipcs.org/ipcs/issueIndex.jsp?mod=b&status=article&issue=1013).

Mig29

http://www.hotel.wineasy.se/ipms/stuff_eng_detail_mig29.htm

Photos by Stephan Voellings
Text by Martin Waligorski

Please visit the above website to see the photo. Search for Mig 29. Many websites are there. An excerpt of the text is given here.

Of a size comparable to the F/A 18 Hornet, the design reflected a change in the Russian tactics in the air. The Mig bureau created an aircraft capable of independent action rather than relying on ground control and guidance. The Mig 29 has a high level of manoeuvrability. The coherent pulse Doppler radar (which can track up to 10 targets simultaneously) combined with a laser range finder and infra-red search and track (IRST) device linked to the Helmet Mounted Sight (HMS) make it an excellent dogfighter. Two engines provide for high degree of survivability in combat.

The website, http://www.airforce-technology.com/projects/mig29/index.html#mig292, says India, Bangladesh, and Myanmar have 70, 8, and 10 MIG-29s respectively. It can "carry two R-27R1 BVR missiles and four R-73E WVR missiles; radar upgrades allow it to carry the new R-77 BVR missile". Its maximum speed is 2,400 km/hour at altitude and 1,500 km/hour near the ground and the service ceiling is 18,000 m

The Fear and The Surrender

In 1989, I proposed to the Democratic Alliance of Burma, which was a consortium of 23 rebel groups as follow.

1. Form a Provisional Government of Federation of Burma. We don't like the word Burma; so let us call it Thuwanna Bhumi. Let us form a Federation of Thuwanna Bhumi.

2. Seize Moulmein and cut off Tanessarim.

3. Attack from all sides. See the map next page. We have 23,000 battle-hardened guerrillas. In three years with a guerrilla warfare we can overthrow the military junta.

But the rebels made peace or surrendered to the military junta. It was the rise of Myanmarism in defense against Islamic Expansionism that killed the cause of rebellion. Credit goes to the present military junta.

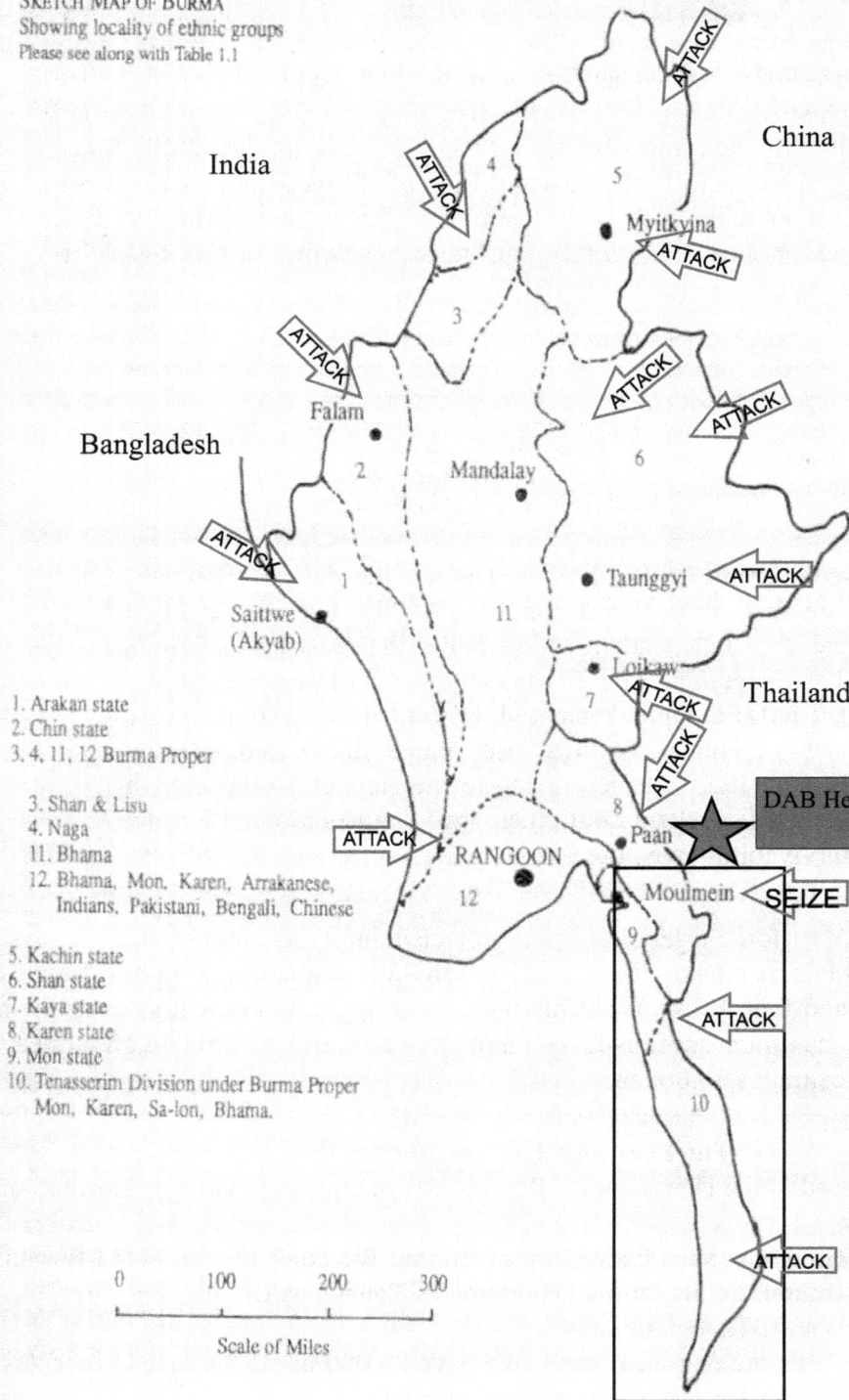

Map 1.1
SKETCH MAP OF BURMA
Showing locality of ethnic groups
Please see along with Table 1.1

India

China

Myitkyina

Falam

Bangladesh

Mandalay

Saittwe (Akyab)

Taunggyi

Loikaw

Thailand

1. Arakan state
2. Chin state
3, 4, 11, 12 Burma Proper

3. Shan & Lisu
4. Naga
11. Bhama
12. Bhama, Mon, Karen, Arrakanese, Indians, Pakistani, Bengali, Chinese

5. Kachin state
6. Shan state
7. Kaya state
8. Karen state
9. Mon state
10. Tenasserim Division under Burma Proper
Mon, Karen, Sa-lon, Bhama.

RANGOON

Paan

DAB Headquarter

Moulmein

SEIZE

0   100   200   300
Scale of Miles

This map shows the stands of the Federationist Rebels in 1989, under the umbrella of Democratic Alliance of Burma (DAB). I was there as *one* of 120 members of the legislative Central Committee. "Seize Moulmein, cut off Tanessarim, and attack from all fronts", I propose in 1989, but they all made peace with the junta. I am the loser! Minorities may demand and fight for equal status and equal rights, but they fail to keep up with the struggle.

The offensive fronts I proposed are indicated by the ATTACK arrows. We had 23,000 well-armed guerrillas comprising of more than 10 ethnic groups encircling Myanmar from all sides. But, they all surrendered. Why? Because their fear of Islamic Expansionism drowned their desire for freedom.

296

National United Party of Arakan (NUPA). The faction rebelled against the party when it formed Arakan Independence Alliance with Arakan Rohingya National Organization (ARNO). In the mind of the mutineers the Rohingyas simply are the illegal immigrants who occupy their Rakhaing land with the backing of Islamic Expansionism. Arakan Army was the only rebel armed force with a ragged navy as shown below. I do not know the marines who are posed in this picture. Are they still with NUPA? I do not have any information. A company of AA is detained by the Indian government at Port Blair, Adamans Islands. Please visit http://www.shwelumaung.org/ and follow the link to Port Blair. Recently Myanmar government has announced that Arakan Army's representatives are participating in the National Convention for drafting a new constitution, which began at Yangon (Rangoon) on the 17th May, 2004.

Arakan Army Marine (Courtesy: National United Party of Arakan)

The above is a photo of the ragged naval marines of Arakan Army(AA), the military wing of National United Party of Arakan(NUPA). A faction of AA surrenders to Myanmar military government and takes part in the National Convention to draft a new constitution. The objective of NUPA and AA is to re-establish Arakan sovereignty that was lost to Myanmar in 1784. When NUPA made alliance with the Rohingya Mulsims they rebelled and surrendered. By doing so, they abandon their goal of sovereign freedom, but embraced Myanmar colonialism.

The combat vessel 'Arakan Marine', shown above, is a locally manufactured ragged war machine, diesel powered with a speed of more than 20 knots per hour. It serves as a marine armored carrier with a capacity to carry up to 30 marines. In this photo it is seen armed with machineguns and shoulder-held rocket launchers. In history, the Arakanese made their fame as the able marine soldiers in the Bay of Bengal.

The Final Scenario

The final scenario will come as early as 2015, or if late, in 2025. In the year 2015, Bangladesh will have a population of 183.16 millions with a population density of 1272 whereas in 2025 the respective figures will be 210.82 millions and 1464. Myanmar will still remain comfortable in terms of total population, 55.26 and 60.24 millions, as well as population density, 82 and 89, respectively in these years. The reader may please refer back to the chapter one for the figures.

These years will be the time Bangladesh population will overflow into the low density areas in the neighboring countries. It will be compounded by wide-spread absolute poverty. Lost of habitable and agricultural land due to flood, erosion, and green house effect will compel Bangladeshi people to look for new land and new pastures. It will be then that the Muslim-Buddhist war in Arakan will enter into its final showdown. The Muslim's claim of Arakan as their Islamic kingdom Rohang will be enforced by the Bangladeshi Muslims in their desperate struggle for existence. Present Bangladesh Chittagong Division, which consists of Chittagong, Feni, Naokhali, Bandraban, and Cox Bazar, was inside the Arakan Empire for two hundred years, from 1460 to 1666. Now there lives some 40 million Bangladeshi who can easily claim to be the Rohingyas. It is not wrong to call Chittagong Division as Bangladesh Arakan while the Rakhine State is Myanmar Arakan.

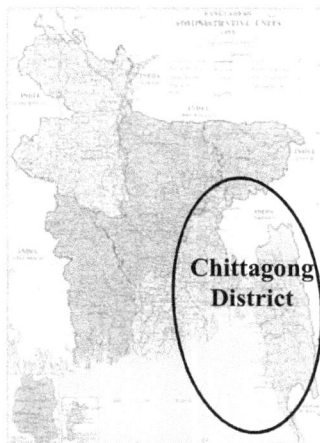

Chittagong District was part of Arakan Empire.
Base map from:-http://www.bangladesh.gov.bd/bdmaps/bdadmin.jpg

One more disturbing point is that many Chittagonians resent that Dhaka people (Dhakaya) are living a good life at the expense of them. This resentment is based on the economic factor that Chittagong generates more national revenue than Dhaka. They also have a different dialect, which is a brew of Arabic, Urdu, and Bengali. This is also the Myanmar Rohingya language. In ethnic content, there are more Arabian and Persian descendants as it originally is a port city promoted by the Arabian and Persian traders since pre-Islamic time. Even, today Chittagonians are recognized as the good business persons. Since late 1970, there even exists a small group of Chittagonian separatist movement that also patronizes a stronger Islamic fundamentalism. The group also considers that Arakan belongs to them.

Inside Myanmar Arakan, the Myanmarese tyrannical oppression imposed upon the Muslims, combined with alienation of their ethnicity and denial of their citizenship has already laid a fertile ground for sprouting of an Islamic revolution.

All these factors that are today simply ignored as merely disturbing nuisance will come to the forefront and play a major role in the days of apocalypse in 2015-2025. As reported in the previous pages the Myanmarese and Myanmar Government are aware of this grave concern and they are getting ready for the showdown, methodically and professionally. In Bangladesh side, it would be an upheaval in a manner of Islamic Commune (*cf.* Paris Commune) that will penetrate into Arakan.

Chaos will set in Arakan and Chittagong District. The Myanmarese and Bangladeshi governments will be obliged to send their armies to protect their citizens and interest. The outcome will be the clash of the two countries and a full-scale Muslim-Buddhist war. It will be a war of brutal ethnic cleansing with heartfelt hatred.   Bangladesh-Myanmar Friendship Highway will turn into a Muslim-Buddhist War Highway.

India will not be able to sleep in peace. She had been compelled to intervene in the East Pakistan revolution that gave birth to Bangladesh in 1971. What will India do in the case of upcoming Muslim-Buddhist war between Bangladesh and Myanmar? Although the career Indian diplomat, whom I mentioned in the Preface, was diplomatic enough not to answer this question, it is obvious that India will not watch the war with folded arms. Her northeastern territories such as Tripura, Mizoram, and Assam will be trembled with the exodus and influx of the Bangladeshi Muslims, Hindus and Buddhists. Her national security will be severely compromised.

On the other hand, China will not hesitate to protect her interest in Myanmar and the Bay of Bengal that she has been so dearly investing since 1988. Will India allow China to gain the control of the bay of Bengal? What about the Islamic interest of Pakistan?

It is highly probable that China and Pakistan will be drawn into the war once India stretches her arms. It will then be called *the Asian War*. Kashmir and Punjab will boil with blood along the Pakistan-India border. With a grin of fate, Myanmarese Irrawady river may witness the battles of the Indian and the Chinese armies along her banks in their combat over the control of the Bay of Bengal and the Indian Ocean. Alternatively, they might happen to shake hands at Naaf River in their joint effort to quench the Bangladeshi Islamic Commune that spills into Myanmar.

Whatsoever way the history may plough, it will leave no Buddhists inside Bangladesh and no Muslims inside Myanmar.

Nevertheless, we will still hear the claim that Islam is a religion of peace, and Buddhism is a religion of infinite compassion. Human civilization will go on in the core of this irony.

Summary and Prospects

Now is the time to summarize my report on Muslim-Buddhist War Over Myanmar. At the same time, we shall also determine its impregnated prospects.

It manifests with the following features and characteristics.

1. Overall, it is a complex case of social, cultural, racial, economical, political and religious issues.

2. It has universal significance.

3. It has roots in the historical conflict of two great religions, Islam and Buddhism.

4. It is a hate-war of racial religions, and is being generated at the grassroots level.

5. It is complicated by the overgrowth of Muslim population in Bangladesh.

6. The recent rise of global Pan-Islam and Mujahids makes it volatile.

7. Revival of Myanmar imperial racism adds more fuel to it.

8. Strengthening of Islamic fundamentalism in Bangladesh and her policy *"look east"* create new strategy in the warfront.

9. Failure of both Bangladesh and Myanmar to establish a nation state, in which sovereignty emanates from citizens, has escalated the potential of a full-scale war.

10. The Asian nuclear age makes it extremely dangerous.

11. International effort is urgently needed to abort the full-scale war as well as eliminate its existing causes.

With this prospective summary I will lead the reader to the epilogue in next page.

Epilogue

If Socrates were a man of our time he could have been detained without any formal charges, and tortured to death, being suspected as a communist, a reactionary, or a terrorist, under a variety of national security acts. A journey of 2,500 years has not made us better humans than those Athenians. As a man of science, Charles Darwin would be disappointed to know that many schools and universities across the world do not teach the evolutionary principles that he so methodically outlined in his book *Origin of Species*. To billions, he is just another atheist. Inspired by John Lennon, one may be able to imagine 'there is no heaven, no hell below us, no religion', or 'all the people living life in peace', but one will simply be discredited as a counter-culturist. Everyone has a dream that he or she would like to realize. Carl Sandburg made it worthwhile saying, "Nothing happens unless first a dream". It may be beautiful, but in reality it may just be another Shakespearean *midsummer night dream*.

Although we hold that 'all men are created equal', as inscribed in the US Declaration of Independence, there always exists a privileged class of human. This has led to hatred, conflicts, and wars. In Gettysburg, 1863, when "we here highly resolve these dead shall not have died in vain — that this nation, under God, shall have a new birth of freedom — and that government of the people, by the people, for the people, shall not perish from the earth" Abraham Lincoln laid down the principle of a universal reason to kill and to die for.

For an ordinary person, the bitter reality of Niccolo Machiavelli's *The Prince* is very hard to bear. Helpless in the deep sea of anguish, I may just join Rabindranath Tagore in his silent prayer.

Where the mind is without fear
and the head is held high
Where knowledge is free
Where the world is not broken into fragments
by narrow domestic walls
Where words emanate from the depth of truth
Where tireless striving stretches its arms
towards perfection
Where the clear stream of reason hasn't lost its
way into the dreary sand of dead habit
Where the mind is led forward by thee into
ever widening thought and action
Into that heaven of freedom, *o Sire*, let my
country awake.

SLM(SK)
A Social Darwinist
August 03, 2005

Name Index-cum-Glossary

1 Abbas — A son of Hazarat Ali and Ummul Banin bint Hizam. P218

2 Abdul Muttalib — Grandfather of Prophet Muhammad. P74, 213

3 Abdullah — Father of Prophet Muhammad. P74, 213

4 Abdullah — A son of Hazarat Ali and Ummul Banin bint Hizam. P218

5 Abu Bakr — The First Caliph of the Isalmic Ummar. P213, 220, 223

6 Abu Bakr — A son of Hazarat Ali and Layla bint Masud. P218

7 Abu Talib — Father of Hazarat Ali. Also spelled as Abi Talib. P74, 213

8 Afghani, Jamaluddin — An Islamist who is considered as the father of modern Pan-Islam. P73,

9 AFPFL — Anti-Fascist People's Freedom League that wrested Burma's independence. P143, 144, 146, 195, 251, 272

10 Ahmad, Moulvi Nur — A Rohingya leader of Burma. P213, 225, 249,

11 Ahmed, Dr. Iajuddin — A professor of Soil Science at Dhaka University, who became president of Bangladesh. P92

12 Ahmed, Khandakar Mushtaq — A leader of Bangladesh. P91

13 Ahmed, Sheikh, Al-Haj — A former Muslim guerrilla of Arakan Liberation Party (ALP) and later a Co-ordinator of Arakan Democratic Forces. He was in the Company of ALP President Khaing Moe Lunn when they made the long march from the Tahi-Burma border to Arakan, across the Shan Plateau and Kachin Hills in 1976-77. His Rakhaing name is Khaing Re Myint. Also known as Commander Khaing Re Myint. P274

14 Ahmed, Tajuddin — A Prime Minister of Bangladesh who was killed in the jail by the military officers in 1975. P91

15 Akyab — English name for Burmese Sittwe or Arakanese Saite Twey, present capital of the Rakhine State of Myanmar. It is derived from a Pagoda named Ahkyaib-daw, which is a most ancient spiritual center of the Rakkhapura people. P174, 186, 247, 255, 272, 284

16 Alaungphaya — A Burmese (Myanmarese) King(CE), who founded the Third Myanmar Empire(CE). His orginal name is Aungzeya. The ttile Alaungphaya means the 'Embryo of Buddha'. P129-131, 134, 143, 173

17 Alaungsithu, King — A famous king. P270 (Footnote), 283

18 Ali Khan — The Muslim title of king Mun Khari. Also see Mun Khari. P138, 140, 209, 212, 244

19 Ali Shah — The Muslim title of Tha Tsa Ta. P209, 212

20 Ali, Mansur — A Prime Minister of Bangladesh who was killed in the jail by the military officers in 1975. P91

21 Amama bint Abil Aas — The sixth wife of Hazarat Ali. P218

22 Ameer — see Emeer.

23 Amherst, Jeffery, Lord — Uncle of Earl Amherst of Arakan. He is well known in the British wars of North America. P141(footnote).

24 Amherst, Willaim Pitt, Lord — Earl of Arakan, and Governor-General of British India (1823-1828 CE). He later was appointed as the Governor of Canada. P141, 270

25 Amherst, William, Lt. Geneal — Father of Earl Amherst of Arakan, P141(Footnote).

26 Amir — see Emeer.

27 Amphipithecus mogaungensis — A species of extinct primate primates. Its fossilzed bones were found in Pondaung Formation, north western Burma. P160, 161

28 Anawrahta — A Burmese (Myanmarese) King (r.1044-1077CE), who founded the First Myanmar Empire(1058-1297CE). Indian and Thai historians refer him as Anuruddha. P129-131,134-136, 139, 143, 169, 170

29 Anglo-Burman War — There are three Anglo-Burman wars. P140, 141-143, 174, 232, 244, 270

30 Anuruddha — Burmese version of Sri Aniruddhadeva. Aslo see Anawrahta. P134, 139

31 Apeyratana, Queen — The most favorite queen of the Pagan King Kyansittha. She is referred as Apeyadana in Burmese chronicles. P270, 283.

32 Arahan — A Mon monk who converted King Anawrahta into Buddhism and introduced the religion in the Central Burma. P134

33 Arahat — A Bikkhu who has attained nibban. P134, 281

34 Aris, Mrs. — See Suu, Daw.

35 Arshad, Mohammad — A Bangladeshi historian. P223

36 Arshad, Mohammad, Dr. — A Pakistani nuclear scientist. P273

37 Asad, Suleiman — A Pakistni cuclear sceintist. P276

38 Asma bint Umyas — The fourth wife of Hazarat Ali. P218

39 Asoka the Great — The most famous Emperor (r. 269-232 BCE) of ancient India. P139, 170, 248

40 Assam — A State of the Indian Federation in the northeastern frontier. Once it was an independent kingdom. P139

41 Attlee, Clement Richard — British Labour Prime Minister, 1945-1951, who gave Burma independence. P143, 144, 151

42 Aung Gyi — A Brigadier General and a famous veteran of Burma Independence War. P143, 157, 186-188, 190, 202, 253

43 Aung San — Bogyoke or a Major General, founding father of the modern Myanmar Armed Forces, Prime Minister of British Burma. P121, 129, 130, 143, 144, 146, 148-150, 152, 154, 157, 166, 186, 192, 204, 232, 251, 272, 273, 204

44 Aung Zan Wai — An Arakanese who was an AFPFL leader and Cabinet Minister in Aung San's Cabinet, 1944. P143, 146, 157

45 Aungzeya, U — Headman of Shwebo village, Upper Burma. He became a king in the name of Alaungphaya. Also see Alaungphaya. P131, 173

46 Ava — An ancient capital of Myanmar on the east bank of Irrawady river, west of Mandalay. P130, 173, 211, 244, 270

47 Aye Kyaw, Dr. — A professor of history. P232, 233, 235, 238

48 Ayutthaya — The capital of Thai Siamese kingdom. P139, 140, 165, 183, 198,

49 Azad, Dr. Humayan — A Dhaka University Professor of Bengali, famous writer and liberal thinker. He was killed by the extremists in 2004. P92, 93-95, 120

50 Azam, Professor Golam — A revered leader of Jamaat-e-Islami. P111, 122, 124

51 Ba Saw, U — A famous Rakhaing politician during Burma's Independence struggle. He was one the few secret agents who parachuted down with the help of the Allied Forces into Burma to organize the revolution against the Japanese occupation in 1944. Served as a member of Parliament and Cabinet Minister in the independent Burma. P258

52 Bagan — A new name given to Pagan by the Myanmar military junta in 1988. Please see Pagan.

53 Bahinia pondaungensis — A species of extinct primate primates. Its fossilzed bones were found in Pondaung Formation, north western Burma. P160, 161, 162, 163

54 Bangladesh — Formerly East Pakistan, became sovereign nation after in 1971 through a liberation war

55 Basawphru — A king (1459-1482 CE) of Rakkhapura. P209

56 Bayinnaung — A Burmese (Myanmarese) King, who founded the Second Myanmar Empire(CE). P129, 139, 140, 143, 165, 198

57 Bayintnaung — A variant spelling of Bayinnaung. Please see Bayinnaung.

58 BCE — Before Common Era. It is a global version of Before Christ, B.C. It is also defined as the Before Christian Era and written as B.C.E.

59 Begum, Dr. Anawara — A professor of zoology in Dhaka University. Wife of Presdient Dr. Iajuddin Ahmed. P92

60 Bharadwaj, Atul, Lt. Cdr. — A personnel of Indian armed froces. P294

61 Bhashani, Maulana Abdul Hamid Khan — A great leader of India and Bangladesh. P81, 114, 116, 118

62 Bhutto, Banazir — Daughter of Zulfiqar Ali Bhutto. She led the PPP after her father's death, overthrew the military government and became the first woman Prime Minister of Pakistan in the Muslim World, in 1989. She became the prime minister for second time in 1993. She is now in exile in Dubai, United Arab Emirates. P290

63 Bhutto, Zulfiqar Ali — A Prime Minister of Pakistan and founding leader of liberal Pakistan Peoples' Party (PPP). A fierce opponent of the Pakistan military government. He was found guilty of murder by the military ruler General Zia-ul-Haq and was hung in 1979. P290

64 Bibi Fatima Binte Asad — Mother of Hazarat Ali. P213

65 Bikkhu — A person who has gone forth to homeless life, abandoning the homestead. A Buddhist monk. P134, 163, 169, 272, 273, 242,

66 Bimbisara, King — A king (r. 543-491 BCE) of ancient India in the days of Buddha. P248

67 Bo Mya, General — A famous General of Karen Army and a revolutionary leader. P199.

68 Bodhisatta — A living being who strives to become a Buddha. P164

69 Brahma — The Creator and the ancestors of the Myanmars. P162, 163, 166, 277

70 Buddha Slave — An untouchable slave assigned to look after the pagodas in feudal Burma. Also see Phya Kyaun. P134

71 Buddha, Lord — The Enlightened One, a great sage who originated the religion of enlightenment, Buddhism. P18, 134, 163, 164, 167, 168, 172, 237, 244, 245, 247, 248, 273, 281, 283, 284, 285

72 Buddhism — A religion founded upon the philosophy , teachings, and practices of Lord Buddha.

73 Burma — A country in Southeast Asia, bordered by Thailand, Laos, China, India , and Bangladesh. It is the English version of the Bama who are the majority racial group in the country. Also written as Myanmar, Myanma, and Mranmar.

116	Ilyas Shah Sultan	The Muslim title of Gadzabadi. P209
117	Imam	A spiritual leader of Muslim community. P213
118	Iqbal, Muhammad	Muhammad Iqbal (1877–1938), the first person to advocate a separate Muslim State with the Indian Federation. P77
119	Isalm, Mohammad	A Rohingya democracy activist. P265(Footnote)
120	Islam, Nurul	A Rangoon University graduate who became the President of Arakan Rohingya National Organization. P251, 255, 256, 257, 262
121	Islam, Syed Nazrul	A Vice President of Bangladesh who was killed in the jail by the military officers in 1975. P91
122	Jafar	A son of Hazarat Ali and Ummul Banin bint Hizam. P218
123	Jalal Uddin, Sultan	A king of Bengal. P173
124	Jawaharlal Nehru	A very famous Prime Minister of India. P195
125	Jayapala	A famous king of Pala dynasty. See Pala dynasty. P139
126	Kaisánís	An Arabian tribe who were the followers of Imam Muhammad ibn Hanafiya. P221, 222
127	Kalima Shah	The Muslim title of Basawphru. P209, 212
128	Kamruzzaman	A Cabinet Minister of Bangladesh who was killed in the jail by the military officers in 1975. P91
129	kappa	The duration of the earth from its formation to dissolution. P163, 164
130	Kassapa, Maha	An Arahat who was elected as the head of the Sangha at the death (Parinibbana) of Buddha. P281
131	Khaing Aung Kyaw	A Rakhaing writer and democracy activist. P182
132	Khaing Mrat Kyaw	A Rakhaing democracy activist and editor of Narinjara News. P276
133	Khaing Re Myint	See Ahmed, Sheikh, Al-Haj.
134	Khan III, Aga	Aga Khan III (1877-1957), founder of Muslim league in 1906. Aga Khans are the descendants of Prophet Mohammad, through his daughter Fatima and Ali. P77
135	Khan, Abdul Qadeer, Dr.	A Pakistani nuclear scientist.P273
136	Kharijites	Mutineers against Hazarat Ali. Also known as Kharijis. Hazarat Ali was killed by the Kharijites. P218, 219
137	Khawla bint Jafar bin Qais al-Hanafiya	The seventh wife of Hazarat Ali. P218, 219
138	Khin Maung Yin, Capt.	A college friend of mine, who beacme a captain in Burma Army and lost both legs on a landmine at the Kachin Front. P258, 259
139	Khin Nyunt, General	A general and prime minister, from August 2003 to October 2004, of Myanmar. P130, 131, 158, 160, 176, 184, 196, 203, 256
140	Khomeini, Ayatollah (Ruhollah)	Iranian Islamic revolutionary leader. P125
141	Khrit	An anceint capital and dynasty of Rakkhapura Kingdom. P139
142	Khun Sa, General	A famous as well as notorious General of Mong Tai Army. P199
143	King Thibaw	The last Burmese king who was dethroned by the British East India Company in 1885. Literally Thibaw means 'abundance of death' in Rakhaing language. P130, 142
144	Kissinger, Dr Henry	A fromer US Secretary of State. P122, 123, 124
145	Ko Cho	A friend of mine and communist cadre. His original name is Ko Myint Thu. P202
146	Konbaung	An ancient capital and dynasty of Burma. P130, 132, 133, 140
147	Koran	Koran is the also spelled Qur'an according to the online Oxford Advanced Learner's Dictionary, http://www1.oup.co.uk/elt/oald/bin/oald2.pl. Merrium-Webster Online Dictionary (http://www.m-w.com/cgi-bin/dictionary?book=Dictionary&va=Koran,) mentions that it is derived from Arabic qur'An. It is Muslim's Holy Book. Also see Qur'an.
148	Kra Hla Aung, Bo Gri	Guerrilla Commander-in-Chief of the Arakanese guerrillas who, in alliance with the Allied Forces, fought against the Japanese in 1944 Allied re-occupation of Burma. A Rakhaing national leader. P143, 157, 203, 204, 247, 257
149	Kra Zan, Daw	An Arakanesewoman who was an AFPFL leader. P143
150	Kubali Khan	The Emperor of China and Conqueror of Pagan. P170, 194, 195
151	Kuppuswamy, C. S.	A scholar at the South Aisa Analysis Group in India. P276, 293
152	Kyansittha, King	A Burmese (Myanmarese) King, who strengthened the First Myanmar Empire (1058-1297CE). P129, 130, 134, 270, 283
153	Kyaw Hla, U	A friend of mine, who is the founding Chairman of Muslim Liberation Organization of Burma. His Muslim name is Mustafa Kamal. P289-262
154	Kyaw Khin, U	A Rakhaing academic who was the principal of Kyaukpyu College and later Registrar of Rangoon Institute of Medicine No.1. P258, 260

238 Myanmarese A term introduced by the Southeast Asian journalists referring to the people of Myanmar. I have used this term generously throughout the book, in both noun and adjective forms.

239 Myanmarpithecus yarshensis A species of extinct primate primates. Its fossilzed bones were found in Pondaung Formation, north western Burma. P160, 161, 162

240 Myawadi A famous border city at the Thai-Burma border. P132

241 Myawadi Magazine A monthly Burmese magazine published by the Burmese Armed Forces. P132

242 Myinsaing An ancient capital of Burma. P130

243 Nanda The last king of the Second Myanmar Empire. P 139

244 Narameit Hla, King A king of Rakkhapura, who is also known as Mun Saw Mwan or Solomon. See Mun Saw Mwan.

245 Narapati A king of Ava, a Myanmar kingdom. P238

246 Narathu, King A Myanmar Pagan King who killed the Pattikera Princess. P283

247 Nareikmeithla A variant spelling and pronunciation of Narameit Hla *alias* of Mun Saw Mwan. P208

248 Naresuan A warrior Thai king who wrested her independence from the Second Myanmar Empire. P139, 140 (painting)

249 Ne Win, General A General who seized the state power in 1962 and established the Socialist Republic of the Union of Burma. P103, 121, 122, 129, 132, 157, 158, 166, 167, 169, 171, 176, 185-188, 190, 192, 195, 196, 198, 202, 204, 226, 233, 236, 249, 250, 251(Chart), 255, 258, 261, 272

250 Nee Lay Maung A friend of mine and a Army Officer. He was wounded in 1968 at Kachin Front. P203

251 Nibban Pali for the State of Enlightenment. The end of all sufferings. P18, 134

252 Niganta Nataputta A very famous Jain Guru who was contemporary with Buddha. P281

253 Nivirna Sanskrit for the State of Enlightenment (Nibban). The end of all sufferings. P18, 164

254 Nizami, Maulana Motiur Rahman Present chief of Jamaat-e-Islami. P112, 124

255 Nu, U The parliamentary prime minister of Burma who gained independence of Burma from the Great Britain. P13, 134, 143, 144, 146, 149, 152, 154, 155, 156, 157, 167, 169, 188, 191(webclip), 192, 195, 204, 226, 250, 251(Chart), 258, 261, 272

256 Nu-Attlee Treaty The treaty that established an independent country known as the Union of Burma. It was signed by U Nu and Lord Attlee, who were the prime ministers of Burma and Great Britain respectively. P143, 144, 151

257 Nur Ahmad, Moulvi A Rohingya Muslim leader of Arakan. P213, 225, 249

258 Nyo Tun An Arakanese who was an AFPFL leader and Cabinet Minister in U Nu's Cabinet, 1944. P143, 157

259 Oo Khin Maung, U A member of Arakan Communist Party politbureau and a friend of mine. P189, 204

260 Pagan An ancient kingdom in the Central Burma. It is also known as Pugan or Paukan or Paukarama. The most ancient name is Paukkarama, which means the Fort of Rama. Could it be that *Prince Rama of Ramayana* founded it? The present military government calls it Bagan. P130, 131, 133, 168, 170, 173, 246, 270, 283

261 Pa-hto A pagoda that has an entrance into its interior chamber. P139, 248

262 Pala dynasty A powerful rulers of Pala Empire in ancient India. P139, 246

263 Panglong Agreement The most important agreement that generated the Union Treaty of the Myanmarese people. P143-146, 152, 155, 157, 192

264 Parami Pali for Perfections, total in ten, that are needed to become a Buddha. Its Sanskrit version is Parami. See P164

265 páramitá Sanskrit for Perfections, total in ten, that are needed to become a Buddha. Its Pali version is Parami. P164

266 Parin An anceint capital and dynasty of Rakkhapura. P139

267 Parinibbana Pali. Buddha passing away to Nibban. Its Sanskrit version is Parinirvana. P281

268 Pattikera A Bengal kingdom that established alliance with Myanmarese Pagan Kingdom. P270(Footnote), 283

269 Pattikera Princess There were three Pattikera princesses in Pagan history. P270(Footnote), 283

270 Pegu The capital of the Second Myanmar Empire, 43 km north of Rangoon. P137, 139, 187, 202, 204, 209(Footnote), 269, 288(Map),

271 Phone Kyaw, Dr. A college friend of mine who became adoctor. P258, 259

272 Phwa May, Daw My sister, the eldest among four siblings of us. P201

273 Phya Kyaun Burmese for 'salve of Buddha'. They are untouchable. P134

274 Pike Thay Lay A king of ancient Pagan, Burma. Son of Yin Min Pike. P170

275 Pinnya Thiha, U An Arakanese Buddhist monk who was an AFPFL leader. P143

276 Pinya An ancient capital of Burma. P130

277 Pitakts, Three Three Pitakts are the three canonical volumes of Lord Buddha's teachings and practices. P134

362	Thein Phay, U	A Rakhaing communist and president of Democratic Party of Arakan. P206
363	Thera	Pali. A venerable elder Buddhist monk, eg. Venerable Maha*thera* Anuruddha. P134
364	Theravada	A major sect of the Buddhists, which prospers in Sri Lanka, Burma, and Thailand. *Thera* means 'venerable elder', and *vada* means 'doctrine'. P131
365	Thiri Thu Dhamma Raza	A king (1622-1638 CE) of Rakkhapura. P209
366	Thirty Comrades	Founding fathers of the Burma Independence Army lead by General Aung San. P166, 188, 204
367	Thura	A military honor of bravery. There are three bravery honors in the Myanmar Army - Thura, Thiha Thura, Aungsan Thuriya, in the ascending of order of greatness. For example General Thura Shwe Mann. P176, 184
368	Thuwanna Bhumi	Pali. A golden land. A country that is great in wealth and happiness. Also see Thaton.
369	Thuwanna Bhumi	Pali. A golden land. A country that is great in wealth and happiness. Also see Thaton. A very ancient kingdom of Mon-Khmer people. Present city of Tha-Hton is identified as her capital. Please see Tha-Hton and Thaton.
370	Tibeto-Burmans	An anthropological classification of the Mongolian tribes who inhabit in the region of Tibet and Burma. P237
371	Tin U (Lanky), Colonel	A Colonel and Chief of the Burmese Military Intelligence Service (MIS). P196, 198
372	Tin U, General	A popular General in Myanmar. Also spelled as Tin Oo. P196, 204
373	Tito, Marshal Josip Broz	A very famous leader of Yugoslavia. P103, 157
374	Tsiang, Hiuen	A 7th century Chinese scholar who studied at the Nalanda University. P281
375	U	The respectable title prefixed to the name of a Burmese gentleman, eg. U Nu. P157
376	Ubaidullah	A son of Hazarat Ali and Layla bint Masud. P218
377	Ullah, A.H. Jaffor	A political analyst. P92
378	Umar	The son of Hazarat Ali and Umm Habiba bint Rabia. P218
379	Umar, Caliph	The Second Caliph of the Islamic Ummar. P213, 248, 220, 223
380	Umm Habiba bint Rabia	The fifth wife of Hazarat Ali. P218
381	Umm Sa'id bint Urwa bin Masud	The eighth wife of Hazarat Ali. P218
382	Umm-e-Kulsoom	A son of Hazarat Ali and Hazarat Fatima. P218
383	Ummul Banin bint Hizam	The second wife of Hazarat Ali. P218
384	Ummul Hasan	The son of Hazarat Ali and Umm Sa'id bint Urwa bin Masud. P218
385	Union of Burma	The first republic of Burma, 1948-1962. General Ne Win abolished it in 1962. P143, 144, 152, 228, 234, 244, 250, 255, 259
386	Upali	A disciple of Jain Guru Niganta Nataputta. Later he became Buddha's disciple. P281
387	Upraza	Burmese word for the crown prince. P139, 140(painting)
388	Uthman	A son of Hazarat Ali and Ummul Banin bint Hizam. P218
389	Uthman, Caliph	The Third Caliph of the Islamic Ummar. Also known as Osman. P213, 220, 223, 225
390	Vijya of Bengal	A Begali prince who is believed to have founded Sri Landa and introduced Buddhism probably in the second century BCE. P167
391	Wali Khan	A General of Bengal Sultanate in the 15th century CE. P209
392	Yahya	A son of Hazarat Ali and Asma bint Umyas. P218
393	Yangon	Post-1988 version of Rangoon, e.g. P273
394	Yin Min Pike	A king of ancient Pagan, Burma. Son of Hti Min Yin. P170
395	Yodhaya	Burmese name for Ayutthaya and Thailand. P139
396	Yunos, Mohd., Dr.	A college friend of mine who abandoned the medical practice and became a rebel and President of the Rohingya Solidarity organizarion. P239, 255-257, 262
397	Zabuk Shah	The Muslim title of Mun Ba Gri who is also known as Mun Bun. P209
398	Zainab	A son of Hazarat Ali and Hazarat Fatima. P218
399	Zaw Myint Htut	A Rohingya democracy activist. P234
400	Zia, Khaleda	President Ziaur Rahman's widow who became leader of BNP and Prime Minister of Bangladesh. Popularly known as Begum Khaleda. P90, 92, 107, 111, 112, 124, 125

Book and Journal Reference Index

1 Azad, Humayan, *Pak Sar Jamin Sad Bad* (The Sacred Blessed Land), Dhaka, 2004. p92
2 Ahmad, Nur, Moulvi, *History of Arakan (Burma)*, Department of Dawah, World Muslim Congress, Karachi, 1978. p225
3 *Arakanpost*, Issue-3, March, 2004. p294
4 *Arakanpost*, Issue 1, December 2003. p131
5 Arakanpost, Issue-5, July, 2004. p232
6 *Arakanpost*, issue-6, November 2004. p168
7 Arakanpost, Issue-6, November-2004. P158(Footnote)
8 Arshad, Mohammad, *An Advanced History of Islam*, Ideal Publications, Dacca, 1967. p223
9 Bakshi, S.R., *Gandhi and Khilafat*, Gitanjali Publishing House, New Delhi, 1985. p73
10 Brockett, Adrian, *The History of al-Tabari, Vol. XVI, The Community Divided: The Caliphate of Ali I*, State University of New York Press, 1997. P212
12 Charles Darwin, *Origin of Species,* the Harvard University Classics, PF Collier & Son, New York, 1909. p12, 14, 18, 301
13 *CIA World Fact Book 2002.* CIA Publications. p194
11 Daniken, Erich von, *Chariots of the Gods,* Putnam & Bantan Books, 1968. P163
14 Dawood, N.J., *The Koran,* Penguin Books, 1974. p66
15 *Dhannyawadi Razawuntheit* (New Edition of Dhannyawadi History). p140
16 Donaldson, Dwight M., *The Shi'ite Religion, a history of Islam in Persia and Irak*, Luzac & Company, London, 1933. P212, 221, 223
17 *General Saw Maung's addresses and discussions*, the Ministry of Information (Government of Myanmar), Department of Newspapers and Journalism, 1989. p130
18 Hamilton, Clarence H., *Buddhism, A Religion of Infinite Compassion*, New York Liberal Arts Press, 1952. P283
19 Hitchins, Christopher, *The Trial of Henry Kissinger*, Verso Press, 2001. p122
20 *Illustrated Weekly*, Friday 15 May 1992, Dhaka, Bangladesh. p287
21 Imam, Abu, Excavations at Mainamati: An Exploratory Study, International Centre for Study of Bengal Art, Dhaka, 2000. P283
22 Khaing Aung Kyaw (Sittwe), *Uncontrollable Tears From The Jail*, Human Rights Violations in Arakan State, Series 2. P182
23 Kyaw Hla, *Burma and Muslims*, Muslim Liberation Organization of Burma, 2003. P260, 261
24 Lenin, V.I., *State and Revolution*, 1918. P201
25 *Licence to Rape*, a report by the Shan Human Rights Foundation (SHRF) & the Shan Women's Action Network (SWAN), May 2002. P176-178

26 Machiavelli, Niccolo, *the Prince*, 16th century. P169-172
27 Madelung, Wilfred, *The succession to Muhammad, A study of the early Caliphate*, Cambridge University Press, 1997. P212
28 Mantran, Robert, General Editor, *Great Dates in Islamic History*, Facts On File, 1996. P278, 280
29 *Mao Ze Dong's Selected Works.* p201
30 Marx, Karl, *Capital*, 1867. P201
31 Maung Maung, *Burma's Constitution*, Martinus Nijhoff, The Hague, 1961. p150,
33 *Microsoft Encarta 97 Encyclopedia.* P22, 222
32 *Microsoft Encarta 97 World Atlas CD.* P10, 126, 136, 137, 138, 222, 224, 243
34 Myanmar Election Commission, *The 1990 Election Results*, 1990. P252-254
35 *Myawadi* Magazine, Myawadi Press, Yangon, September 1995. p132
36 *New Internationalist.* P72, 255
37 Nu, U., *Satruday's Son*, New Haven, Yale University Press, 1975. P250
38 *On the Origin and Evolution of European Fascism*, monograph, Claremont Mckenna College. P232
39 Parekh, Bhikhu, *Rethinking of Multiculturalism: Cultural Diversity and Political Theory.* Harvard University Press, 2002. P266
40 Phyare, Sir Arthur P., *History of Burma*, London: Trübner & Co., 1883. p136, 137, 138, 208, 247
41 *Qu'ran.* P69, 71, 111, 286
42 Rakhaing Thu Mrat, *Lauka-thara-pyo, 14th century.* P169
43 *Science* Vol. 298, 8 November 2002. P285
44 *Science*, volume 286 of 15 October 1999. p160
45 Serajuddin, Alamgir M., *Muslim influence in Arakan and the Muslim names of Arakanese kings*, Journal of Asiatic Society of Bangladesh (humanity) Vol. XXXI (1). P209, 246, 249
46 Shahrastani, *Milal wa nihal*, Vol. 1, p. 232; Nawbakhti, Firaq al-shi'a, Najaf edition. P221
47 Shakespeare, William, *midsummer night dream.* P301
48 Shwe Lu Maung, *Burma: Nationalism and Ideology*, the University Press Ltd., Dhaka, Bangladesh, 1989. p9, 12, 64, 117, 132, 143, 152, 158, 164, 166, 167, 169, 185-190, 195, 199, 202, 226
49 Sinha, Bindeshwari Prasad, editor, *The Comprehensive History of Bihar*, Volumes I & II, Kashi Prasad Jayaswal Research Institute, Patna, 1974. P278, 281

50 Tagore: Rabindranath Tagore's poems such as *Gardeners, Crescent Moon, Gitanjali.* P80. The poem quoted at Epilogue, page 301, is from *Gitanjili.*

51 *The Bohra Chronicle,* February 1998. P215

52 *The Correlation of Man and His Environment,* published by the Burmese Socialist Programme Party, Rangoon, 1964. p169

53 *The Last Days of Thakin Than Tun,* 1967. p204

54 *The Manifesto of Communist Party,* 1848. P201

55 *The Military Balance 2003-2004,* the International Institute of Strategic Studies (IISS), London. p291

56 Varma, C.B., *The Illustrated Jataka & Other Stories of the Buddha.* p164

57 Yegar, Moshe. *The Muslims of Burma,* Wiesbaden, O Harrassowitz, 1972

Website Reference Index
Websites and web pages consulted in this book are indexed here. The web addresses are also mentioned in the text. Please connect to the domain address if the connection to the sub-directory does not work.

36. http://www.jei.org/Archive/JEIR97/9711f.html#comparative, p59
37. http://www.fao.org/sd/eidirect/eire0047.htm, p60
38. http://www.ffwc.net, p61
39. http://www.terradaily.com/2004/040803094924.dwe5xh8u.html, p61
40. http://www.bangladeshobserveronline.com/new/2004/08/09/front.htm#head2, p61
41. http://www.reliefweb.int/w/rwb.nsf, p62
42. http://www.cia.gov/cia/publications/factbook/geos/bg.html, p62
43. http://yosemite.epa.gov/OAR/globalwarming.nsf/content/ImpactsCoastalZones.html, p62/63
44. http://www.un.org/News/ossg/sg/index.shtml, p63
45. http://www.ben-center.org/flood_essay.htm, p63
46. http://news.bbc.co.uk/2/hi/science/nature/4171591.stm, p63
47. http://www.globalissues.org/EnvIssues/GlobalWarming/globaldimming.asp, p63
48. http://www.mnforsustain.org/erickson_d_pond_lily_parable.htm, p65
49. htttp://www.ecofuture.org/pop/facts/exponential70.html, p65
50. http://www.susps.org/why/lily.html, p65

Chapter 2
1. http://www.islamicity.com/mosque/arabicscript/1/1.htm, p66 (Footnote)
2. http://www.unn.ac.uk/societies/islamic/jargon/keycon1.htm#JIHAD, p68
3. www.unn.ac.uk/societies/islamic/jargon/jihad1.htm, p68
4. http://www.islamworld.netjiad.html, 69
5. http://www.natcath.com/NCR_Online/archives/100501/100501g.htm, p71
6. http://imm-live.wmin.ac.uk/sshl/page-148-smhp=1, p72
7. http://jmm.aaa.net.au/articles/1690.htm, p72
8. http://www.newint.org/issue345/democracy.htm, p72
9. http://groups.msn.com/Pashtanaloyepashtana.msnw?action=ShowPhoto&PhotoID=50, p73
10. http://cyberistan.org/islamic/muhammad.html, p74
11. http://www.islamicsupremecouncil.com/tabarruk/tabarrukat.htm, p76
12. http://www.pakistani.org/pakistan/constitution/preamble.html, p77
13. http://www.pakistani.org/pakistan/constitution/part1.html, p77
14. http://www.pakistan.gov.pk, p77
15. http://www.infopak.gov.pk/Quaid/quaid_index.htm p79
16. http://www.virtualbangladesh.com/biography/mujib.html, p83
17. http://www.ferdous.org/ohongkar.htm, p83
18. http://www.bangladeshgov.org/pmo/cevents/cevent_5.htm, p83
19. http://www.dhaka-bd.com/categories/History_Culture.htm, p84
20. http://www.bangladeshgov.org/pmo/21february/shahid_minar.htm, p86
21. http://www.bangla2000.com/News/Resources/Snapshots/Bangabandhu/default.asp, p89
22. http://www.bangla2000.com, p89
23. http://www.joybangla.net/, p89
24. http://www.bangladeshgov.org/pmo/introduction/bang_in1.htm#4, p89
25. http://www.polymernotes.org/biographies/BGD_bio_rahman.htm, p90

Chapter 3.
1. http://www.univdhaka.edu/president_of_bangladesh.htm, p92
2. http://www.bangladeshgov.org/, p92
3. http://news.bbc.co.uk/1/hi/world/south_asia/country_profiles/1160896.stm, p93
4. http://www.drishtipat.org/nuke/modules.php?name=News&file=article&sid=103&mode=thread&order=0&thold=0, p94
5. http://www.thedailystar.net/2004/03/02/d4030201022.htm, p94
6. http://news.bbc.co.uk/1/hi/world/south_asia/3561184.stm, p94
7. http://www.lainsignia.org/2004/marzo/der_018.htm, p94
8. http://www.mukto-mona.com/Articles/humayun_azad/humayun_azad_dhormanubhuti.htm, p94

20. http://www.myanmar.gov.mm/religious/buddha2002/feb/feb.html, p168
21. http://www.geocities.com/Athens/Bridge/1256/monhistory1.htm, p 173
22. http://www.albany.edu/~gb661, p173
23. http://hrw.org/doc/?t=asia_pub&c=burma, p175, 183
24. http://msxml.excite.com/info.xcite/search/web/, p175
25. http://www.cnn.com/2001/WORLD/asiapcf/southeast/11/15/myanmar.ilo/, p176
26. http://www.commondreams.org/headlines02/0717-06.htm, p176
27. http://www.shanland.org/HR/HR_Frame.htm, p176, 177, 178
28. http://www.myanmar.com/today/SHRF.html, p176, 178, 179, 180
29. http://www.shanland.org/HR/Publication/LtoR/license_to_rape.htm, p176, 177
30. http://hrw.org/doc/?t=asia_pub&c=burma, p183

Chapter 5
1. http://shwelumaung.org/publications/series4.pdf, p189
2. http://www.myanmar.com/Union/interference.html, p191
3. http://www.myanmar.com/Union/union.html, p191
4. http://www.odci.gov/cia/publications/factbook/geos/bm.html, 194
5. http://www.un.org/Overview/unmember.html, p194
6. http://www.shwelumaung.org/OutlawMG/page2.html, p197
7. http://users.erols.com/mwhite28/, p197
8. http://www.un.org/popin/, p197
9. http://www.mizzima.com/Solidarity/07-mar04-06.htm, p206
10. http://www.myanmar-information.net/bcp/bcp.htm, p206
11. http://www.rohingyatimes.i-p.com/history/history_maa.html, p210
12. http://www.amaana.org/contents/contents.htm, p213
13. http://www.darulfalah.org/article/caliphs.shtml. p213
14. http://www.amaana.org/ali/hazratali.htm, p213
15. http://www.sunnah.org/publication/khulafa_rashideen/caliph4.htm, p213
16. http://www.al-islam.org/masoom/sayings/sayings.html, p214
17. http://www.mubai.cc/sayings.htm, p214
18. http://www.al-islam.org/nahjul/letters/letter12.htm#letter12, p214
19. http://www.al-islam.org/nahjul/letters/letter19.htm#letter19, p214
20. http://www.dawoodi-bohras.com/chronicle/mar98/index.htm, p215
21. http://www.geocities.com/Tokyo/Spa/7220/imam-ali.html#a17, p215, 216
22. http://www.karbala-najaf.org/abuturab/social.html, p217
23. http://www.amaana.org/ismaali.html, 217
24. http://www.al-islam.org/nahjul/letters/letter53.htm#letter53, p217
25. http://amaana.org/ismaali.html, p217
26. http://www.14masumeen.com/html/21ramazan, p218
27. http://www.rafed.net/towns/english/najaf.html, p218
28. http://www.islamknowledge.faithweb.com/ali_ibn_abi_talib.htm, p218
29. http://www.ismaili.net/Source/hist/full.txt, p218
30. http://www.sicm.org.uk/suduk/Suduk41.html, p219
31. http://www.al-islam.org/kaaba14/6.htm, p219
32. http://ismaili.net/histoire/history03/history343.html, p219
33. http://www.allaahuakbar.net/scholars/al-madkhalee/so_who_are_ahl_hadith.htm, p219
34. http://www.masmn.org/Hadith/Sahih_Bukhari/057.htm, p220
35. http://www.meforum.org/article/490, p220
36. http://www.tzemachdovid.org/Facts/claim.shtml, p220
37. http://www.karbala-najaf.org/shiaism/235-258.htm, p224
38. http://www.themuslimhistory.info/INenglish/ImamNeal/Chap11.htm, p220
39. http://www.al-islam.org/mahdi/nontl/Chap-2.htm#n1, p221

40. http://www.bartleby.com/65/ir/IranIraq.html, p222
41. http://www.jana.org/ashura/ashura.html, p224
42. http://www.shianews.com/low/middle_east/news_id/0001001.php, p224
43. http://www.victorynewsmagazine.com/ImamHassanMadePeaceWhyDidImamHussainFight.htm, p225

Chapter 6

1. http://www.rohingya.com, p226, 252
2. http://www.burma.no/publikasjoner/juni2003_bcn.htm, p226
3. http://www.thebigview.com/greeks/heraclitus.html, p227
4. http://www.ibiblio.org/obl/docs/Citizenship%20Law.htm, p229
5. http://www.un.org/aboutun/charter/index.html, p230
6. http://www.webcom.com/hrin/parker/selfdet.html, p230
7. http://www.unhchr.ch/tbs/doc.nsf/(Symbol)/f3c99406d528f37fc12563ed004960b4?Opendocument), p230
8. http://www.webcom.com/hrin/parker/selfdet.html, p230
9. http://www.un.org/Overview/rights.html, p231
10. http://gould.claremontmckenna.edu/publications/monograph/pdf/Moss.pdf, p232(Footnote)
11. http://rakhapura.com, p234, 239
12. http://www.arakan.homestead.com/files/Articles/Report.htm, p235
13. http://rohingya.com, p251
14. http://esa.un.org/unpp/index.asp?panel=2, p252
15. http://imm-live.wmin.ac.uk/sshl/page-148-smhp=1, p255, 263
16. http://jmm.aaa.net.au/articles/1690.htm, p255, 266
17. http://www.newint.org/issue345/democracy.htm, p255
18. http://www.shwelumaung.org/ADFdemands, 257
19. http://www.aldexile.org, p265
20. http://www.prospect-magazine.co.uk/start.asp?P_Article=11979, p266
21. http://www.universalexports.net/Movies/daylights-cast.shtml, p268
22. http://www.itihaas.com/modern/british14.html, p270

Chapter 7

1. http://nuclearweaponarchive.org/Pakistan/PakTests.html, p273
2. http://www.shwelumaung.org. p274, 297
3. http://www.shwelumaung.org/Appeals%20to%20Malaysia%20Prime%20Minister/, p274
4. http://www.shwelumaung.org/PRD3/, p274
5. http://www.shwelumaung.org/PleaseRelease/stm6/p6/, p274
6. http://www.shwelumaung.org/PleaseRelease/stm6/p7, p274
7. http://www.johnstonsarchive.net/nuclear/nucstock-i.html, p275
8. http://www.saag.org/papers5/paper401.html, p276
9. http://rohingya.com, p277
10. http://www.myanmar.com/pagoda/pagoda.html, p281
11. http://www.buddhanet.net/e-learning/pilgrim/pg_19.htm, p281(Footnote)
12. http://whc.unesco.org/sites/322.htm, p282
13. https://www.vedamsbooks.com, p283(Footnote)
14. http://berclo.net/page00/00en-myanmar-7.html, 284
15. http://www.shwelumaung.org/PrisonerofMandalay, p285
16. http://portal.unesco.org/en/ev.php@URL_ID=1259&URL_DO=DO_TOPIC&URL_SECTION=-459.html, p285
17. http://www.islamicity.com, p286
18. http://www.shwelumaung.org/BurmaFreeSoul/page2.html, p287
19. http://www.washtimes.com/upi-breaking/20021220-023337-3744r.htm, p289
20. http://news.bbc.co.uk/2/hi/asia-pacific/2116032.stm, p289
21. http://www.ipcs.org/ipcs/databaseIndex2.jsp?database=1004&country2=Harkat-ul-Jihad-al-Islami%20Bangladesh%20(HuJI-BD), p290

22. http://www.hazegray.org/worldnav/china/submar.htm#ssbn, 293
23. http://www.saag.org/papers6/paper596.html, p293
24. http://www.ipcs.org/ipcs/issueIndex.jsp?mod=b&status=article&issue=1013, p295
25. http://www.hotel.wineasy.se/ipms/stuff_eng_detail_mig29.htm, p295
26. http://www.airforce-technology.com/projects/mig29/index.html#mig292, p295
27. http://www.bangladesh.gov.bd/bdmaps/bdadmin.jpg, p298

www.ingramcontent.com/pod-product-compliance
Lightning Source LLC
Chambersburg PA
CBHW080230270326
41926CB00020B/4195